Sound Mapping

the New Testament

Sound Mapping

the New Testament

Margaret Ellen Lee

and

Bernard Brandon Scott

POLEBRIDGE PRESS
Salem, Oregon

For information address Polebridge Press, Willamette University, 900 State Street, Salem, OR 97301.

Cover and interior design by Robaire Ream

Library of Congress Cataloging-in-Publication Data

Lee, Margaret Ellen, 1954-
Sound mapping the New Testament / Margaret Ellen Lee and Bernard Brandon Scott.
p. cm.
Includes bibliographical references and index.
ISBN 978-1-59815-015-5
1. Bible. N.T.--Criticism, interpretation, etc. 2. Voice in literature.
I. Scott, Bernard Brandon, 1941- II. Title.
BS2361.3.L44 2009
225.4'8--dc22

2009045312

For **Daryl Schmidt**

1944–2006

"It was always about the collegiality."

Contents

Introduction

Why Sound?

In the Greco-Roman world writing was heard, not read silently. The implications of this observation have been dawning on New Testament scholars for the past generation, especially since Werner Kelber's *The Oral and Written Gospel* (1983). Modern New Testament scholarship is a child of the printing press, centered around silent reading. The assumptions of print have shaped scholarship in unintended and unrecognized ways. While aware that modern composition does not correspond with the situation in the ancient world, scholars have struggled to deal methodologically with the implications of this change.

Once it became clear that oral composition proceeds differently than literary authorship and is governed by different dynamics,[1] scholars began to frame the issue in terms of orality and literacy. The result was much creative work that recaptures some of oral performance's dynamics among illiterate audiences, the kind Jesus himself most likely addressed.[2] But enthusiasm for these insights and what they might illuminate in New Testament study has tempted scholars to leap over the onset of literacy in the ancient world and thus to construe "orality" simply as speech, and "literacy" as the production of manuscripts according to modern notions of authorship. Failure to appreciate the processes of literary composition in the memorial culture that produced the New Testament has thrown methodology off track.[3] Those who have focused on the importance in the first century BCE of rhetoric (Robbins 1996), performance (Rhoads 2005, URL: http://www.biblicalperformancecriticism.org/), and the memorial arts (Shiner 2003) have alerted scholars to this deficiency; but their work has not provided an analytical approach that addresses the spoken character of New Testament compositions—that is, their sounded quality. Our work seeks to fill this methodological gap.

Since we today lack native fluency in hearing and speaking Koine Greek, our hearing is always secondary to our silent reading of a printed Greek text.[4] To analyze a composition's sounds, we need a reliable model that does not depend on facility in listening to a dead language. We find a basis for such analysis in Greek grammar itself together with extant written reflections on Greek grammar and literary composition from the ancient world. Because Greek grammar analyzed spoken sound and sound's effects, we find support for sound analysis in the very structure of the Hellenistic Greek language and in the analysis by its own practitioners of the sounded quality of literary compositions. By paying attention to their clues, we can develop a sensitivity to a composition's sounds and their effects.

Our analytical approach proposes to map in graphic form a composition's sounds and then to analyze those sound effects according to the listening conventions in place when the compositions were created. So we begin with the composition itself[5] and plot its sounds—its cola, periods, rhymes and other sound effects. This exposes a composition's structure, a structure meant not to be seen but heard. Perhaps a modern example will help. When we read silently, the printed text provides us with an astonishing array of typographic clues—word division, punctuation, capitalization, paragraph and chapter divisions. These cue the silent reader's perception of a composition's structure even before we begin to apprehend its meaning. Ancient manuscripts have almost no chirographic equivalences for these typographic clues.[6] An ancient listener who heard a manuscript read out loud had to hear the structure rather than see it. Sound mapping proposes to illustrate those structures that are implemented through sound. Our work shows that a composition's sound structure frequently differs substantially from structures construed by the New Testament editors who added chapter and verse numbers and by modern editors who even later have supplied section titles and paragraph marks, usually driven primarily by abstract theological concepts.

Once a sound map is developed, it must be analyzed. Maps are not self-explanatory, but require interpretation. Just as in statistical analysis that plots data points on a graph and draws a regression line, data thus graphically displayed must be interpreted. And in the same way that many collections of statistics can illustrate various aspects of any phenomenon, many sound maps can be developed to analyze a composition's various features. Our analysis is guided by analytical tools provided by native speakers and hearers of Hellenistic Greek in their written reflections on language.

Sound mapping and analysis is a foundational method—not higher criticism, but lower criticism. It falls between text criticism and other methods of interpretation.[7] While higher methods operate more at the semantic level of meaning, sound mapping and analysis operates in sound units. It contends with semantics, but also recognizes the independent contributions to meaning made by sound itself in cultures that relied on public performance for literary publication. Sound mapping and analysis does not aim to replace other traditional analytical methods, but offers new data that other methods must incorporate and explain. The disclosing of a composition's structure and sound effects indicates what needs interpretation. Thus a sound map together with sound analysis operates in a positive fashion to indicate what a composition has selected for hearers to attend to; and employed negatively, the technique can rule out some of the things it does NOT mean.

To develop this analytical approach, the book is divided into two sections: Theory and Examples. Part 1, "A Theory of Sound Analysis," lays out programmatically the theoretical foundation for understanding sound mapping and analysis. We begin with the material basis of writing and communication in the Greco-Roman world. Chapter 1, "The Technology of Writing in the Greco-Roman World," explores how writing technology determines both *what* can be communicated and *how* it can be communicated. The next two chapters pursue the question of how communication was conceived by Greco-Roman authors. Chapter 2, "The Woven Composition," investigates the memorial character of literary composition and the role of literature in a memorial culture. As the title suggests, weaving provided the primary metaphor for literary composition in antiquity. Chapter 3, "The Grammar of Sound," explores the prevailing science of sound in the Greco-Roman world, Greek grammar.[8] From these first three chapters, it becomes clear that repetition plays a critical role in sound's ability to communicate. Chapter 4, "Repetition: Sound's Structuring Device," redefines repetition in terms appropriate to oral performance and surveys the ways that repetition organizes compositions and guides meaning-making. Finally, Chapter 5, "Developing Sound Maps," explains step by step how to develop a sound map.

Part 2, "Illustrations from the New Testament," selects six examples from the New Testament to exemplify various aspects of sound mapping and sound analysis. In actuality, any Greek composition could have been selected, or for that matter any number of compositions. These six examples were selected for a variety of reasons, some of which turned out to be irrelevant or misguided after we developed and analyzed their sound maps. We selected these New Testament[9] compositions because (1) they represent styles and genres found in the New Testament and (2) each composition posed an interpretative problem that commentators have not yet solved. Thus if we could illuminate an unsolved issue in New Testament scholarship, it would demonstrate the value of sound mapping and sound analysis. The reasons for the selection are made clear in each chapter.

Because sound's dynamics are powerful and plentiful, printed maps can hardly do them justice. In developing our sound maps we strained to capture each composition's unique governing dynamics, especially at the level of structure. Our sound maps eliminate chapter and verse numbers and supply new references based on cola and periods, since these comprised the atomic literary units in Hellenistic Greek. We have not rigidly imposed a single numbering scheme or method of text display on our examples, but instead have allowed each composition to dictate appropriate display methods. While our graphic conventions vary, our attention to a composition's organic architecture remains consistent.

Sound mapping requires reading in Greek, yet a number of our readers have requested English translations to make the Greek text more accessible, especially for use in class with students beginning the study of Greek. To accommodate this use, we have provided English translations from the Scholars Version, adapted where necessary. We have tried to do this in a way that does not make the text cluttered or confusing. Because the SV translation renders dynamic equivalents and employs colloquial English, the translation sometimes does not correspond colon by colon to the Greek text, or is misleading in other ways when compared with the Greek. In such cases we have modified the SV to achieve a closer correspondence, although we have been conservative in this regard. Modified passages are noted with the abbreviation *Lit.* Such modifications also facilitate cross-referencing between the Greek and English versions by colon number, since we do not use conventional versification. We hope the translations will promote a fuller understanding of the sound analysis and its uses, even though the translated passages cannot exhibit the sounds and structures evident in Greek.

Each chapter has its own list of Works Consulted, since at times the references have little overlap. Similarly, Part 1 and Part 2 pursue somewhat different strategies, and thus require different protocols for footnoting. In footnoting Part 1, we have tried to be comprehensive. Ancient authors are quoted in the accepted form for classical citations.[10] In Part 2, the example chapters, we have sought to be not so much comprehensive as illustrative. Since sound mapping and sound analysis are foundational, we have not argued with others' conclusions, but instead have illustrated how sound mapping re-orients interpretative questions.

In a joint work of this nature, we are both responsible for the final product. At times we find it difficult to remember who wrote what, but lines of responsibility are clear. An initial paper exploring sound mapping was a joint effort that was presented to the Society of Biblical Literature Matthew Seminar (Scott and Dean 1993) and subsequently published in a collection of essays from that seminar (Scott and Dean 1995).[11] In the introduction to that volume, Bauer and Powell remarked: "Still, of all the papers in this volume, theirs is the most adventuresome, offering what they call 'a first step.' It is a promising experiment with a new approach that appears to have enormous potential for future study" (Bauer and Powell 1996, p. 21). In retrospect, we were just feeling our way, hardly taking a first step. Scott had the first intuitions and Lee subsequently took those insights and developed them in her dissertation (Lee 2005), which has formed the basis for chapters 2, 3, 4, and 5 in Part 1 and Chapter 10 in Part 2. She has extensively reworked these chapters for this volume. Scott is responsible for Chapter 1 in Part 1. All the other chapters are so jointly co-written that we no longer know who did what. All the example chapters have been extensively reworked by both of us.

If the argument of this book is correct, we have inaugurated a method to help scholars of the Greco-Roman world analyze the sound that animated ancient compositions.[12] We have accomplished this amid lively dialogue with many who have intuited the importance of sound and oral performance for New Testament criticism. These include Werner Kelber, who has long encouraged this project and mentored Margaret Lee in the Regional Scholar program of the Society of Biblical Literature (SBL), and Thomas Boomershine, Joanna Dewey, Vernon Robbins, Arthur Dewey, and the Bible in Ancient and Modern Media Section of the SBL. We are also extremely grateful to Phillips Theological Seminary and Tulsa Community College, who granted sabbatical leaves to support this project. Tom Hall has provided an expert proof-reader's eye.

Vernon Robbins once urged, "When I hear you explain this, I know you're on track; but when I try to do it myself, I don't know where to start." We hope this book answers his implicit challenge and encourages other New Testament scholars to carry these insights forward in ways we have yet to imagine.

ENDNOTES

1. Foley (1988) has sharply focused these differences, building on the work of Lord (1960) and others.
2. Dewey (1989) and Horsley and Draper (2006) are good examples.

3. See below Chapter 2, "Manuscripts, Orality and Literacy."
4. This is why our book does not advance a theory of the pronunciation of Hellenistic Greek, and why we have not attempted a sound recording of the language. We cannot know for certain how Hellenistic Greek was pronounced in any particular time or place in the Greco-Roman world, but we know that its spelling was phonetic and letters were pronounced consistently, whatever the pronunciation scheme. See chapter 2, p. 81, for further comments on the pronunciation of Hellenistic Greek.
5. We take the composition to be the text printed in Nestle-Aland[26]. We realize this is a constructed text, but it represents the best we have available at this time.
6. As is well known, Greek manuscripts employ *scriptio continua.* Early Latin manuscripts do have word divisions, but under the influence of Greek, writers began to employ *scriptio continua.*
7. Nonetheless, the strategy has a contribution to make to textual criticism. Sometimes the analysis of the sound indicates another explanation for a textual variant.
8. This chapter draws on an early exploration of the grammar of sound, one first published under Margaret Lee's former surname, Dean (1996).
9. We could also have selected compositions outside of the New Testament. They would have worked just as well. There is nothing about this method that is specific to the New Testament, just as Koine Greek is not specific to the New Testament.
10. Abbreviations from *The Oxford Classical Dictionary*. English translations are from the Loeb Classical Library editions, unless otherwise noted.
11. This paper was published both times under Margaret Lee's former surname, Dean.
12. We want to emphasize that we do not consider sound mapping and analysis as a full-fledged methodology but rather a pragmatic basis for critical methods.

WORKS CONSULTED

Bauer, David R., and Mark Allan Powell. 1996. Introduction. In *Treasures New and Old: Recent Contributions to Matthean Studies*, edited by D. R. Bauer and M. A. Powell. Atlanta, GA: Scholars.

Dean, Margaret E. 1996. The Grammar of Sound in Greek Texts: Toward a Method of Mapping the Echoes of Speech in Writing. *ABR* 44:53–70.

Dewey, Joanna. 1989. Oral Methods of Structuring Narrative in Mark. *Int* 43:32–44.

Foley, John Miles. 1988. *The Theory of Oral Composition: History and Methodology, Folkloristics*. Bloomington: Indiana University Press.

Horsley, Richard A., Jonathan A. Draper, and John Miles Foley, eds. 2006. *Performing the Gospel*. Minneapolis: Fortress.

Lee, Margaret E. 2005. A Method for Sound Analysis in Hellenistic Greek: The Sermon on the Mount as a Test Case. D.Theol., Melbourne College of Divinity, Melbourne.

Lord, Albert B. 1960. *The Singer of Tales, Harvard Studies in Comparative Literature, 24*. Cambridge: Harvard University Press.

Rhoads, David. 2005. Performance Criticism: An Emerging Methodology on Biblical Studies. In *Society of Biblical Literature Annual Meeting*. Philadelphia, PA.

Robbins, Vernon K. 1996. *Exploring the Texture of Texts: A Guide to Socio-Rhetorical Interpretation*. Valley Forge, PA: Trinity.

Scott, Bernard Brandon, and Margaret E. Dean. 1993. A Sound Map of the Sermon on the Mount. In *SBLSP*, edited by J. Eugene H. Lovering. Atlanta: Scholars.

———. 1995. A Sound Map of the Sermon on the Mount. In *Treasures Old and New: Recent Contributions to Matthean Studies*, edited by D. Bauer and M. A. Powell. Atlanta: Scholars Press.

Shiner, Whitney Taylor. 2003. Proclaiming the Gospel: First Century Performance of Mark. Harrisburg, PA: Trinity.

Part 1

A Theory of Sound Analysis

Chapter 1

The Technology of Writing in the Greco-Roman World

INTRODUCTION

To understand how Greco-Roman society made use of writing, we must first understand how written materials were produced, for the material and physical aspects of writing laid the foundation for communication. Indeed, as a technological process, writing is inconceivable without technology.[1] And since the implications of technology for interpretation are frequently neglected or taken for granted, interpretation can suffer. Tools are not neutral. Haas (1996, p. 21) warns, "Technology is implicated in every literate act, and to ignore this implication is to remain confused about the essential relationship of writing to technology, and about our relationship—as writers, as teachers, as scholars—to both of them".[2] The tools and methods used to write constrain both writing and thinking. An interpreter must avoid either technological determinism or its opposite, instrumentalism.[3]

Because we remain in the dark about many issues, our conclusions must be tentative (Small 1997, p. 144); (Kenney 1982, p. 4); but as we begin to outline the writing process, it will become clearer how the technology of writing shaped and constrained communication in the Greco-Roman world. We are tempted to fill the gaps in our evidence and understanding by using what seems common sense, and since the technology of writing often is transparent to a writer, we tend to assume that our practices are universal and obvious. But this is not necessarily so. Frequently in what follows issues will arise that violate our common sense understanding of writing.

INSCRIPTIONS: A MODEL OF INTERACTING WITH WRITING

Discussions of writing materials in the ancient world normally do not consider inscriptions, probably because our eye unconsciously remains on the codex, book, paper, and the printing press.[4] We assume that our own situation is the universal model. Yet in the ancient world, the most common forms of writing with which most people interacted were inscriptions and engravings on coins. The Greco-Roman world was a literate society in the sense that, although most people were illiterate, everyone had to interact with writing.[5]

Who was literate in the ancient world? Harris's study of *Ancient Literacy* (1989) is well known. His general conclusion has stood strong scrutiny:

> There was without doubt a vast diffusion of reading and writing ability in the Greek and Roman worlds, and the preconditions and the positive causes of this development can be traced. But there was no mass literacy, and even the level which I have called craftsman's literacy was achieved only in a certain limited milieu. The classical world, even at its most advanced, was so lacking in the characteristics which produce extensive literacy that we must suppose that the majority of people were always illiterate. In most places most of the time, there was no incentive for those who controlled the allocations of resources to aim for mass literacy (p. 13).[6]

The safest conclusion is that in major urban areas not more than fifteen percent of the population was capable of reading and/or writing.[7] But the modern, western distinction between literacy and illiteracy should not be imposed on the situation. The ancient world attached no stigma to illiteracy, and the inability to read did not necessarily disadvantage the illiterate financially. "The stance of Greek and Roman governments toward illiteracy was one of casual indifference" (Hanson 1991, p. 162). Furthermore all social classes worked out ways to interact with writing and so the lines are fluid and at times inconsistent. Some folks' reading and writing ability extended only to writing their names, of which they were proud.[8] Not only the upper classes wrote, although they were much more likely to be educated because they had time to send their children to school.[9] As Small (1997)[10] reminds us, most of our evidence comes from elites (see also Harris 1989, chapters 1 and 2). Yet slaves were often trained for the tasks of reading, taking dictation, and copying.[11] And even fewer women than men could read and write, though a famous image from Pompeii shows a young woman with stylus and wax tablet.[12] Ironically "One might almost say that there was a direct correlation between the social standing that guaranteed literacy and the means to avoid writing" (Bagnall 1995, p. 25).[13] Elites had others to read to them and do their writing (see Pliny the Elder below). But even those in the lowest social classes could use the services of a village scribe to write letters, bills, or deeds for them—even if they could not read what the scribe had written for them.[14]

Inscriptions, either on stone or bronze,[15] were ubiquitous, especially in cities. Like other forms of written Greek, they consisted of engraved lines of capital letters, with no division into words and no punctuation, although there sometimes appear word divisions with dots, but with no systematic approach.[16]

The most common sorts of inscriptions were epitaphs and epigrams, especially connected with funerary monuments. Dedications are the second most common form, and are found in temples, the agora, and other public spaces. Then follow decrees and royal/imperial letters and documents (Pleket 1996, p. 542). The range of inscriptions is quite diverse.

The earliest form of an inscription is the funerary memorial. The function of these monuments is "a public memorial of honour" (Thomas 1994, p. 40), and this honor aspect of inscriptions remains dominant. As Thomas concludes about later inscriptions, "So while these documents would also function to preserve or convey information, their public and visible nature is enlisted in a sense quite close to that of the memorial." It is not so much the content of the writing that is important, but as Bowman and Woolf (1994, p. 8) argue, "What the text says may, in any case, not be the whole, or even the primary, point if most people could either not see the writing or could not read it anyway. Monumental texts may exercise power through their location in space and the way they look."[17]

Because most inscriptions have survived apart from their contexts, there is a tendency to consider only what the inscription says, without recognizing its visual impact *in situ*.[18] In this regard, the discoveries at Pompeii offer an important corrective, because the inscription and context are often preserved together. Franklin (1991), in a discussion of Pompeian inscriptions and graffiti, gives a good example of how these monuments function *in situ*:

> Indeed, for all the major varieties of inscriptions, the most important reading was visual, not literate. Whether lapidary or parietal, the type of inscription was immediately clear to any passer-by from visual clues. For example, first one noted that it was an honorary inscription, for it was on an honorary gate and identified an impressive statue; secondly, a capable reader noted the name of the honoree, which could be read rapidly without stopping; finally the interested (normally an educated preserver of or striver for social status) could pause to decipher the detailed and abbreviated *cursus*. General cognition was not dependent upon reading ability (p. 86).[19]

Inscriptions are public, visual signs of honor and authority. "The use of inscriptions for power and display stands out dramatically: the name of the man who financed the erection or restoration of a building would be displayed prominently" (Thomas, 1994, p. 164).[20] Their content is secondary. This remains true in both the Greek and Roman contexts. The following two examples help illustrate the function of inscriptions.

Suetonius, in his description of Vespasian's restoration of Rome following the great fire at the end of Nero's reign, describes the emperor's effort to restore "the three thousand bronze tablets which were destroyed with the temple, making a thorough search for copies: priceless and most ancient records of the empire (*instrumentum imperii*), containing the decrees of the senate and the acts of the commons almost from the foundation of the city, regarding alliances, treaties, and special privileges granted to individuals" (Suet. *Vesp.*, 2, 8.5). While bronze tablets may seem to us an odd way to store an empire's archives,[21] this "archive" was not meant primarily to be consulted, although it could be, but its very existence is what is important. These are not so much documents but memorials. The material, bronze; the place, Capitoline Hill; and the age of the inscriptions all attested to their authoritative character. That is why they are "*instrumentum imperii*." When Julius Caesar removed a tablet from the Capitoline Hill, Cicero argued that he had cancelled several grants of Roman citizenship. As Thomas (1994, p. 165) maintains, "the removal of a bronze tablet seems to have been tantamount to a repeal of its written contents."

Towards the end of his reign, Augustus left with the Vestal Virgins three scrolls, one of which was "an account of what he had accomplished (*indicem rerum a se gestarum*), which he desired to have cut upon bronze tablets and set up at the entrance of the Mausoleum" (Suet. *Aug.* 1, 101.5). These bronze tablets were then reproduced in stone and set up in various places around the empire. A nearly complete copy in Latin and Greek has survived from the temple of Augustus and Rome at Ancyra in modern day Turkey. From these stone copies *Res Gestae* has been reconstructed (Brunt and Moore 1967). This example illustrates the complex interaction between memory, writing, and honor. Augustus' Mausoleum is his monument to his honor, to what will ensure his memory. *Res Gestae* posted at the entrance to the monument ties writing to inscription to monument. Reading it would have been difficult, but one visually sees the record and knows that it honors Augustus. Copying *Res Gestae* in stone in both Greek and Latin and displaying it in various Temples of Rome and Augustus render it a sacred text.

Inscriptions, one of the most common forms of writing in the ancient world, remind us that writing is a way of exercising authority[22] and that regardless of how many or how few people were literate, everyone in this society had to interact with writing and adjust to it. As Bowman (1994, p. 112) argues, even the portion of the population that was illiterate "lived according to rules and conventions established on the presumption that written communication was a normal and widespread form of regulating and ordering (in the broadest possible sense) its life."

While inscriptions help us understand the social context of writing, manuscripts give evidence of writing in contexts more familiar to us, i.e., literary works. Like inscriptions they functioned in their public environment, and just as inscriptions can be misinterpreted when separated from their monumental context, so manuscript writing is easily misinterpreted when separated from its context.

THE TECHNOLOGY OF MANUSCRIPT PRODUCTION

At a technical level writing involves a device for inscribing and something on which to inscribe.[23] The choices are, of course, interrelated and both affect writing.[24]

WRITING INSTRUMENTS

The choice of writing instruments was twofold: the metal (or sometimes ivory) stylus or the sharpened reed.[25] These two instruments account for the vast majority of manuscripts, although charcoal and chalk were occasionally used on wooden boards. The metal stylus was employed for writing on wax tablets. Often made of bronze, it was normally shorter than a modern pencil or pen. One end was sharp for the incision, while the other was flat for erasure. Writing on papyrus or parchment was done with a sharpened reed that became an ink pen.[26] The reed was normally prepared by the scribe, who would also prepare the ink. A knife was needed to sharpen the reed to a point and then split the sharpened end so as to hold and spread the ink. Ink requires both various substances and media for its manufacture, and inkwells or pots for the ink.[27] When writing with ink, a sponge was used for erasure.

WRITING SURFACES

Although the content of what one wrote was remarkably similar across the Empire (Bowman 1991, p. 130), writers wrote on whatever materials were readily available. In Egypt papyrus was most common, but in such far reaches of the empire as Britain and on the frontiers, wooden tablets made from local trees were employed.[28] Bagnall (1995, p. 10) points out that all the standard materials—ostraka, tablets, papyrus, parchment, etc.—were considered temporary by the ancients.[29] Furthermore, things were not always written in order to be read or consulted; sometimes the writing itself was of primary importance, as in the case of inscriptions.

OSTRAKA

Ostraka (broken pottery) were the cheapest writing surface and the most common. The found nature of this material would lead one to believe that it was used for unimportant things, but that was not always the case. The sheer number of ostraka that turn up in archaeological sites testifies to their widespread use. Cockle (1996, pp. 1082–3) lists tax receipts, orders, lists, notes, school exercises, letters, and religious texts; these are the same types of writing that are found on papyrus.[30] Ostraka were either incised, especially in Greece, or written on using pen and ink, as was typical in Egypt. A famous example involves their use for ballots used to expel (ostracize) citizens from Athens. Excavations there have turned up over ten thousand such ostraka, many with the same handwriting, indicating that they were either distributed by politicians to voters, or else voters who could not write got them pre-inscribed (Camp 2001, p. 56 with illustrations). Sometimes even an extended passage was written on ostraka. Diogenes Laertius reports that the philosopher Cleanthes was so poor he wrote on ostraka (Diog. Laet. 7.174).[31]

WAX TABLETS

The wax tablet is another relatively cheap[32] writing medium and was widely and continuously used until the widespread availability of paper in the 18th century. Roberts and Skeat (1987, p. 11) provide a good description of the wax tablet:

> It was commonly formed of two or more flat pieces of wood, held together either by a clasp or by cords passed through pierced holes; the central area of the tablet was usually hollowed slightly to receive a coating of wax, while a small raised surface was often in the centre to prevent the writing on the wax being damaged when the tablet was closed.

The tablets were normally made of wood, sometimes ivory, and tablets were bound together into diptych, triptych, etc. The largest number of bound tablets so far discovered is ten. The hollow tablet was covered with wax, normally dyed black (with pitch) or red, and the wax was inscribed with a metal stylus. The shape of the stylus and the character of the wax made for angular writing (Bischoff, p. 13).

The wax tablet is well attested in Greek. In the only passage in Homer that indicates the existence of writing, tablets are mentioned. The wife of King Proetus had fallen in love with Bellerophon but could not seduce him. So she deceived her husband by telling him that Bellerophon had tried to seduce her, so that the king would kill Bellerophon. He could not kill him,

> but he sent him away to Lykia, and handed him murderous symbols, which he inscribed in a folding tablet, enough to destroy life (*Iliad* 6.168–9).[33]

The Romans distinguished between *codex* or *tabula*—the two words are used interchangeably to refer to large tablets used for formal records—and *pugilaris*. The latter word, which means "something in the hand," refers to a small, hand-held wax tablet. The so-called Sappho from Pompeii shows a young woman holding a stylus in her right hand with the tip to her lips in a meditative pose. In her left hand she holds a *pugilaris* with four leaves.[34]

The wax tablet was very common in schools for taking dictation or notes and for making drafts, and it was widely used by government officials. While wax tablets appear to us as temporary, they were often used for official government[35] and business records. The wax tablet and the stylus were normal gear in the forum and other situations requiring writing. Suetonius notes that when Julius Caesar was attacked in the forum, "one of the Cascas stabbed him from one side just below the throat. Caesar caught Casca's arm and ran it through with his stylus" (Suet. *Iul.* 82. 2). This use of the stylus as a weapon is not unique. For the literate, then, the stylus and wax tablet were likely common, even daily implements.[36]

Because the vast majority of early New Testament manuscripts are on papyrus, we should not too easily dismiss the possibility that early drafts of New Testament writings were recorded on wax tablets. This is particularly the case since, as we shall see, writing often involved two people. For dictation, wax tablets were frequently used because of easy correction. Although they concern a student, Quintilian's remarks on this point are interesting:

> It is best to write on wax owing to the facility which it offers for erasure, . . . we must leave blank pages that we may be free to make additions when we will. For lack of space at times gives rise to a reluctance to make corrections, or, at any rate, is liable to cause confusion when new matter is inserted. . . . Space must also be left for jotting down the thoughts which occur to the writer out of due order, that is to say, which refer to subjects other than those in hand. For sometimes the most admirable thoughts break in upon us which cannot be inserted in what we are writing, but which, on the other hand, it is unsafe to put by, since they are at times forgotten, and at times cling to the memory so persistently as to divert us from some other line of thought. They are, therefore, best kept in store. (*Inst.* 10.3.31–33)

Pliny the Younger's description of his uncle's writing and research habits is well known, but again it accents the place of the wax tablet. Responding to Baebius Macer's request for all his uncle's works, Pliny describes his uncle's working habits. When he was resting, a book would be read to him "from whence he made extracts and observations, as indeed this was his constant method whatever book he read" (*Ep.* 3.5). This process of a book being read and his taking notes appears to be his normal process. Even while he was being rubbed down following his bath, "he was employed either in hearing some book read to him, or in dictating himself. In his journeys, as though released from all other cares, he found leisure for this sole pursuit. A shorthand writer, with book and tablets, constantly attended him in his chariot, who, in the winter, wore a particular sort of warm gloves, that the sharpness of the weather might not occasion any interruption to his studies." When in Rome, he was carried in a chair so that this process could continue. He even upbraided his nephew for walking and so wasting time! All of this reading and note taking produced a hundred and sixty scrolls of abstracts or excerpts, written in a small hand on both sides.[37] These were the foundation on which Pliny the Elder built his scholarship. While Pliny tells this story to indicate his uncle's prodigious work habits, it also points out that research and composition is a multi-person project. Someone reads aloud, while another person takes notes or dictation on wax tablets. As we will see, this process of two people involved together in writing continued until the fourteenth century.

PAPYRUS

The other two major options for writing material were papyrus and parchment.[38] Of the two, papyrus was more available and less expensive—although since a roll cost two or three days labor, it was not cheap (Bagnall 1995, p. 13). The reeds that constituted the raw material were grown in Egypt and then manufactured into scrolls.[39] Pliny the Elder has an elaborate description of the process of preparation, and a number of his comments are important for our discussion.

> Before we leave Egypt we shall also describe the nature of papyrus, since our civilization or at all events our records[40] depend very largely on the employment of paper [papyrus][41] (*HN* 13.21.68).
>
> . . .
>
> The process of making paper from papyrus is to split it with a needle into very thin strips made as broad as possible, the best quality being in the centre of the plant (13.23.74).
>
> . . .
>
> Paper of all kinds is 'woven'[42] on a board moistened with water from the Nile, muddy liquid supplying the effect of glue.[43] First an upright layer is smeared on to the table, using the full length of papyrus available after the trimmings have been cut off at both ends, and afterwards cross strips complete the lattice-work. The next step is to press it in presses, and the sheets are dried in the sun and then joined together . . . There are never more than twenty sheets to a roll (13.23.77).
>
> . . .
>
> Roughness is smoothed out with a piece of ivory or a shell, but this makes the lettering apt to fade as owing to the polish so given the paper does not take the ink so well, but has a shinier surface (13.25.81).
>
> . . .
>
> The common kind of paste for paper is made of fine flour of the best quality mixed with boiling water, with a very small sprinkle of vinegar. . . . Afterwards the paper is beaten thin with a mallet and run over with a layer of paste and then again has its creases removed by pressure and is flattened out with a mallet (13.26. 82–3).

Pliny's description indicates the amount of work and care necessary in the manufacture of papyrus rolls, and thus accounts for its expense. He also indicates the emperor's concern for and involvement in the production of papyrus, for the government was the largest user of this important product (Bagnall 1995, p. 13). The two finest grades of papyrus were named after Augustus and his wife Livia (13.23.74). Claudius (emperor 41–52 CE) set a new standard for the finest grade of papyrus:

> The reason was that the thin paper of the period of Augustus was not strong enough to stand the friction of the pen, and moreover as it let the writing show through there was a fear of a smudge being caused by what was written on the back, and the great transparency of the paper had an unattractive look in other respects. Consequently the foundation was made of leaves of second quality and woof or cross

> layer of the leaves of the first quality. Claudius also increased the width of the sheet, making it a foot across (13.24.79).

Pliny began his discussion by remarking how the *memoria* of humanity was dependent on papyrus. Throughout his discussion he is concerned both with the quality of the papyrus—because that affects the ease with which writing takes place—and with its permanence. He ends his remarks on a similar note.

> This process may enable records (*monimenta*)[44] to last a long time; at the house of the poet and most distinguished citizen Pomponius Secundus I have seen documents in the hand of Tiberius and Gaius Gracchus written nearly two hundred years ago; while as for autographs of Cicero, of his late Majesty Augustus, and of Virgil, we see them constantly (13.26. 83).

Pliny reminds us that papyrus is actually a quite durable product, although subject to rot. And because the edges of scrolls are vulnerable, reading stands were sometimes used to protect them.[45]

PARCHMENT

While papyrus rolls were much more available and common, parchment was still an important writing surface. Eventually it would overtake and almost replace papyrus in the west, especially with the rise of the codex.[46] The name parchment comes from Pergamum (περγαμηνή, *pergamena*),[47] where legend has it that parchment was invented. In his description of papyrus Pliny refers the reader to Varro for his version of the story: "when owing to the rivalry between King Ptolemy and King Eumenes about their libraries Ptolemy suppressed the export of paper, parchment was invented at Pergamum" (*HN* 13.21.70). While Pergamum did become a center of manufacture after shortages of papyrus arose in Egypt, we have no evidence that it was invented there. It had existed before King Eumenes.[48] Parchment was made from the skin of either sheep, goats, or sometimes calves. It is not tanned, as in leathermaking, but is soaked in a lime solution and the skin is then scraped.

Quintilian, in his discussion of wax tablets quoted above, had also discussed parchment as a substitute for those of weak eyesight, for whom it "may make it desirable to employ parchment (*membrana*)[49] by preference. The latter, however, although of assistance to the eye, delays the hand and interrupts the stream of thought owing to the frequency with which the pen has to be supplied with ink" (10.3.31). Interestingly, he considers the inkpot to slow down the writing process. But he discusses parchment in the context of wax tablets because his concern is with erasures. The carbon ink used at the time did not adhere well to parchment and was sufficiently easy to wash off that the sheet could be used again.

CODEX

Sometime in the first century, Romans began binding together parchment sheets into small notebooks in codex form. Once again, its use parallels that of the wax tablet, not the scroll; but as Roberts and Skeat (1987, p. 15) note, this transition is the definitive step in the march towards the codex.[50] Christianity's well-known preference for the codex began in the second century; as Gamble neatly summarizes the consensus, "early Christianity had an almost exclusive preference for the codex as the medium of its own writings and thus departed early and widely from the established bibliographic conventions of its environment" (Gamble 1995, p. 49, with references n. 33).

As noted above, Quintilian prescribed parchment in place of the wax tablet for those with poor eyesight. The Latin reads "*membrana,*" which means skins and, by extension, what we call parchment. Because of the context, it has been suggested that *membrana* here is a small parchment codex, a "notebook" (Gamble 1995,p. 50; Maehler 1996,p. 252; Roberts and Skeat 1987, p. 21). This should not be confused, however, with the later codex of the second century, which is larger in scale. Quintilian may be referring to a utilitarian notebook. Martial seems to be referring to the same thing in the following passage: "You, who want my little books to keep you company wherever you may be and desire their companionship on a long journey, buy these that parchment compresses in small pages (*quos artat brevibus membrane tabellis*). Give book-boxes to the great; one hand grasps *me*" (*Spect.* 1.2).[51]

Gamble (1995, p. 50) has suggested that 2 Timothy 4:13 refers to such notebook codices.[52] The author, supposedly Paul, is giving directions to Timothy to come to him and tells him: "When you come bring the cloak that I left with Carpus at Troas, also the books (τὰ βιβλία), and above all the parchments (τὰς μεμβράνας)" (NRSV). Μεμβράνα is a Latin loanword, which as we have seen means "skins/parchments." This passage also presents a textual problem: whereas Nestle-Aland[27] reads: τὰ βιβλία πάλιστα τὰς μεμβράνας, a number of manuscripts insert δε (D* *pc* lat; Ambrose) or καί (1175) between βιβλία πάλιστα, thus indicating that they are two items. Such a reading would support the meaning, "bring the scrolls and the notebooks." But the majority of the manuscripts have no conjunction, so that the phrase πάλιστα modifies τὰ βιβλία, and the meaning would thus be, "bring the scrolls, especially the parchment ones."[53] In favor of this translation is the fact that Hebrew scrolls were nearly always written on parchment, as the evidence from Qumran demonstrates. Gamble counters that if parchment scrolls had been meant, then διφθέραι would have been used. Since the dating of 2 Timothy is notoriously difficult (probably in the early second century), it may have been written after Christians had begun to adopt the codex form. If μεμβράνα here means notebook/codex, it is the earliest example of the use of this loanword in Greek.[54]

This survey of available writing materials indicates that the media employed are not easy to use. The physical limitations of ostraka, wax tablets, scrolls and other media favor short compositions as opposed to longer pieces. The more extended a piece of writing, the more difficult its organization because it must be kept in memory. There is no practical way to consult the whole of a work, to spread it out in front of one. The importance of this limitation will be reinforced as we examine the physical act of writing.

THE ACT OF WRITING

Burton Mack in *A Myth of Innocence* (1988) imagines that the Gospel of Mark "was composed at a desk in a scholar's study lined with texts and open to discourse with other intellectuals" (p. 323).[55] If any part of Mack's compositional understanding of the Gospel of Mark depends upon its author sitting at a desk (much less surrounded by a scroll-lined study), then that understanding must fall. The ancients did not write at a desk.[56] Once again common sense understanding leads us astray.[57]

We have ample evidence that when writing on a wax tablet, writers often stood (Parássaglou 1979, p. 7). Normally, however, one wrote while seated: Egyptian scribes squatted on the floor (Černý 1952, pp. 13–14); Greeks and Romans used a stool or chair.[58] Relatively few images show Greeks and Romans writing on (as opposed to reading from) a scroll,[59] while Egyptian scribes are often depicted in the act of writing. Skeat (1956, p. 184) suggests that this is due to the high status of Egyptian scribes and the low status of the actual act of writing itself among Greeks and Romans.[60]

According to Skeat, "Other representations show a different posture, in which one knee was raised in front of the writer to form a sloping support for the open section of the roll, which then rested on the knee[61] and the thigh" (p. 183). He quotes a colophon from a scroll of the *Iliad* copied in the first century CE to support this.

Ἐγὼ κορωνὶς εἰμὶ γραμμάτων φύλαξ
κάλαμος μ᾽ ἔγραψε, δεξία χεῖρ καὶ γονύ.

I am the coronis, the guardian of scribes.
The pen wrote me, the right hand and knee.[62]

A supply of wax tablets might be stacked on a bench, but the actual writing was done on one's lap, whether with a wax tablet,[63] a scroll, or whatever. The scroll was rolled out from right to left across the lap, the pen was held in the right hand, and the left hand controlled the scroll, rolling it up as it was written upon. Ovid describes this position. "My right hand holds the pen, a drawn blade the other holds, and the paper [*charta*] lies unrolled in my lap" (Ov. *Her.* 11.3–4). The ink pot for refreshing the reed pen was either on the ground, an inconvenient place for dipping the pen, or held by a slave.[64] Quintilian, as noted above in the discussion of wax tablets, singled out this need to refresh the pen as a major obstacle to writing with ink: The ink pot "delays the hand and interrupts the stream of thought owing to the frequency with which the pen has to be supplied with ink" (Quint. *Inst.* 10.3.31). Holding the scroll across the thighs[65] explains both the narrow width of the scrolls (about 12 inches) and the narrow width of the columns of writing, which match the width of a thigh.

This writing position is not comfortable. The technology of writing makes writing difficult and consulting laborious. "Writing on a papyrus roll placed on one's lap was indubitably a difficult task and, regardless of the expertise that many of the ancient scribes may have reached . . . must have placed serious limitations on what could be achieved" (Parássoglou 1979, p. 20). *Scriptio continua* makes consultation even more difficult. It "means that no external physical order is imposed on the text, with the result that its seamlessness makes it harder to divide mentally into logical segments" (Small, 1997, p. 187). With no desk or table on which to lay out scrolls or wax tablets, reading and consulting texts was very difficult.[66] Even library arrangements made consultation of the scrolls highly inconvenient: one found no tables,[67] no catalog of holdings, and scrolls were stored in jars and stacked in the same cupboards used to store other household goods (Richter 1966, pp. 79–81, pp. 115–16). While describing Augustus's library on the Palatine, Quinn (1982, p. 81) remarks that it "must have looked more like a modern wallpaper warehouse." This equally applies to all libraries. As Camp (2001, p. 203) notes of Hadrian's library in Athens, "Only a small portion of the building was actually given over to books" and much more to conversation space.

The position of writing, as Turner remarks (1987, p. 7), does not make it "easy to visualize satisfactory copying from an open roll placed on the ground beside the writer, even if he himself sits on the ground."[68] A major contention of Small's work is that retrieval was difficult. "It rarely occurred to them to use written words to find other written words. Instead they used one of the tools they already had: memory" (1997, p. 71).

READING IN A SOCIAL CONTEXT

Reading and writing need to be distinguished. "Writing prioritizes sound, as the spoken word must be transformed or deconstructed into representative sign(s)" (Fischer 2003, p. 11).[69] Since the reading of literary compositions in the Greco-Roman world was frequently an acoustic process, reading restored writing to sound and was a public performance. Ἀναγινώσκειν, "to read," literally means "to know again." And because authors wrote so others could listen,[70] reading was a more complex reality than a single person decoding the markings on a manuscript. Similarly in English, "to read" can mean "to be read to," and often it describes not a singular, but a group activity.

We must always ask who is reading? To whom are they (is he and sometimes she) reading? What are they reading? Where are they reading? And why are they reading? Reading is primarily a social activity[70], although as we shall see, the ancients could read to themselves.

Just as there is a range of writing skills, so also for reading skills. Some were trained, professional readers; others could barely stumble from syllable to syllable. Given the high level of illiteracy in the culture, reading was frequently done for the benefit of those who could not read. Occasions for reading varied widely; it could be entertainment at a dinner party, included in a conversation between friends, or a scholar's search for information. People read for a variety of reasons, not the least common of which was to enable an esthetic response to the sound of the language artfully employed.

"Reading is a corollary of writing, writing is not a corollary of reading" (Franklin 1991, p. 79). Cribiore describes the beginning steps of writing that precede instruction in fluent reading. "After introducing students to the letters of the alphabet and before teaching them formally to read through the syllabaries, teachers found it useful to make them practice their handwriting. For this purpose they made them copy, rather passively, sentences and verses from models" (Cribiore 1996, p. 143).[71] Plato compares learning to write to learning the laws: "just as teachers draw lines with the stylus for children who are learning to write and give them the tablet and make them write along the guide-lines, so the city draws the laws invented by good lawgivers in the old times and compels the young man to rule and be ruled according to them" (Pl. *Prt.* 326, c–e). Cribiore points to several factors for this delay in teaching reading. *Scriptio continua* presented formidable obstacles. "Grammatical and literary training were necessary to properly read aloud a text" (p. 148).[72] Even well educated people had to prepare to read aloud well.[73] Aulus Gellius tells a story about a foolish master who boasts that he alone can interpret (*enarrator*) the *Satires* of Marcus Varro. Gellius happens to have in his pocket "an ancient copy of the satire, of tested correctness and clearly written" which he hands to the master and dares him to read and interpret it. "[H]e took it with a most disturbed and worried expression . . . Ignorant schoolboys, if they had taken up that book, could not have read more laughably, so wretchedly did he pronounce the words and murder the thought" (*NA* 13. 31, 1–10). Gellius could not have made his challenge if he were not confident that reading sight unseen would be difficult.

The pace of writing and reading in the ancient world was slow. Debate has raged (and continues) about whether the ancients could read silently.[74] Extreme arguments have occurred on both sides and characterize even the latest contributions to the debate (Gavrilon 1997; Saenger 1997). Sanford (1967, p. 2) overstates the case: "There is no clear reference at all to silent reading by any Greek, named or unnamed, until the fourth century AD." This is clearly not the case. Knox, on the other hand argues too much from common sense: "common sense rebels against the idea that scholarly readers, for example, did not develop a technique of silent, faster reading" (Knox 1968, p. 421). For our purposes, this debate is somewhat beside the point. The evidence now makes it clear that some in classical antiquity could read silently, but that the normal process, especially with literary manuscripts, was to read aloud. Even Knox (1968, p. 421) admits that point. In a yet later essay he says, "it must not be forgotten that any book which had even the slightest claim to literary merit was written to be read aloud" (Knox 1985, p. 14).Thus literary manuscripts, like those of early Christians, were composed to be read aloud. That is the essential point.[75]

While clearly some ancients could read silently, actual reports of silent reading are very rare. Much more common are references to reading aloud.[76] For example, in all of extant Greek plays we find only two examples of people reading silently. In one case an oracle is read, in the other a letter. In both cases these are brief scenes, not extended readings (Lentz 1989, pp. 159–60). Despite the paucity of evidence, we should avoid being trapped by our evidence. Ancient authors were not concerned about our question. For the most part, reading is mentioned incidentally. On the other hand, we have many examples of characters reading aloud or being overheard. Consider, e.g., the famous example from St. Augustine's *Confessions*, where Augustine hears the voice of the young boy or girl reading aloud, "Take up and read." And yet, of course, later in the same passage Augustine notes that when he took the book of the Apostle [Paul], "I snatched it up, I opened it, and in silence I read that chapter which I had first cast my eyes upon" (*Conf.* 8.12). Gillard (1993, pp. 689–91) in a recent survey article adduced other evidence of people being able to read short letters or oracles and Gavrilon (1997) and Burnyeat (1997) have reviewed and reinforced this evidence. Thus it is beyond doubt that some people[77] could read silently, at least short works.

Carruthers in reviewing Augustine's astonishment at Ambrose's reading silently (*Conf.* 6.3),[78] notes that silence in this period does not have the same meaning as it does when we speak of silent reading.[79] Silent reading is connected with *meditatio* and *memoria*, i.e., private reading. Such reading aims to commit the reading to memory and to engage memory (Carruthers 1990, pp. 170–74, 186). It need not be "silent" i.e., without noise. She quotes the example of the Rule of St. Benedict that when reading silently monks should take care not to disturb other monks; clearly they were making some noise. Likewise in medieval libraries, silent reading produced less noise than that done in the monastic cell (Carruthers, 1990, pp. 170–2; p. 329, note 58).

True silent reading does not seem to have become standard until the medieval period. As Small notes, silent reading and punctuation arrived about the same time (1997, p. 22, dependent on Saenger 1982 and now see 1997). Punctuation, which is almost entirely missing in ancient manuscripts, facilitates silent reading. *Scriptio continua*, where the letters are run together with no separation, almost demands reading aloud so that word beginnings and endings can be sounded out and heard so as to delineate units. Saenger (1977, p. 2), on the basis of modern research into the physiology of reading,[80] argues that *scriptio continua* virtually demands reading aloud. "In general, graphic systems that eliminate or reduce the need for a cognitive process prior to lexical access facilitate the early adaptation of young readers to silent reading, while written languages that are more ambiguous necessitate the oral manipulation of phonetic components to construct words." In one study, a group of fifth graders was given a typed passage all in uppercase letters without spaces between the words. The students had no trouble reading the passage. They simply began reading it aloud (p. 5).[81] In another line of argument, Saenger points to studies of the Vai in Liberia. They employ a form of phonetic syllabary "without word separation, diacriticals, punctuation, or the presence of initial capital forms" (4), that is, it is remarkably similar to Greek and Latin writing. Oral recitation is important in teaching elementary reading and adults mumble "to sound out a text . . . when reading privately" (p. 5). Saenger's conclusion to this example is worth quoting.

> The reading habits of the Vai people, like those of the ancient Greeks and Romans, are phonosynthetic, and all three written languages employ similar modes of decoding polysyllabic words written in unseparated script. Thus, in historically unrelated circumstances, similar reading processes make use of the same human cerebral structures and mental capacities (which have remained biologically unchanged during the brief period of recorded civilization) to resolve analogous forms of graphic ambiguity (p. 5).[82]

Three principal reasons explain why the ancients normally read aloud: schooling, economics, and literacy. All three of these elements intertwine to produce reading aloud as the normal way of reading.

Greek education stressed recitation and memory. A student recited lessons and large sections of the poets were memorized. Grammar stressed sounds, and students learned all the sounds of the letters and possible syllable combinations as the way to learn to read.[83] Written exemplars guided a student in the basic mechanics of writing, forming letters, learning the syllables, and writing one's name. Fluency in writing came through dictation. Aristotle shows the dominance of speech in reading: "Generally speaking, that which is written should be easy to read or easy to utter, which is the same thing" (*Rh.* 3.5.6). Even in the philosophical schools, reading aloud was the normal practice, and one wrote so that it could be read aloud (Lentz, 1989, pp. 100–2). Not only did education assume reading aloud, but students were not taught to read silently. Anyone who observes modern reading instruction quickly recognizes that students do not naturally read silently, but must be taught to do so. Many students never fully master it, but continue to mumble their words and commonly employ silent subarticulation (Abramson and Goldinger 1997).

Economics discouraged silent, private reading. As Lentz (1989, p. 102) notes, "The simplest practical explanation for this absence [of silent reading] is the high cost of papyrus and the expense of having copies written upon it. Making multiple copies of discourses—for each member of a group, for example— would be prohibitively expensive." Furthermore it is clear that full literacy was not in the interest of the empire, which therefore failed to support education (Harris, 1989, pp. 5–7, p. 333).

Finally, only a small portion of the population at any time could read and write. Reading tended to be a phenomenon of the elites and reinforced the values of the elites. As Botha (1992, p. 202) has noticed, the ancient world offered few incentives for learning to read. So low was the literacy rate that publication in the ancient world consisted primarily of oral declamation (see below). The success of an author frequently depended on the fame of the declaimer (Hadas 1961, c1954, p. 60–4).

Schooling, economics, and literacy discouraged the development of widespread silent reading. For writing to communicate, it had to be read aloud.

COMPOSITION

With stylus and tablet or pen and scroll in hand, how does one go about composition? One of the most interesting descriptions of composition I know of comes from Pliny the Younger.

> [When I wake] my shutters stay closed, for in the stillness and darkness I feel myself surprisingly detached from any distractions and left to myself in freedom; my eyes do not determine the direction of my thinking, but, being unable to see anything, they are guided to visualize my thoughts. If I have anything on hand I work it out in my head, choosing and correcting the wording, and the amount I achieve depends on the ease or difficulty with which my thoughts can be marshaled and kept in my head. Then I call my secretary, the shutters are opened, and I dictate what I have put into shape; he goes out, is recalled, and again dismissed. Three or four hours after I first wake (but I don't keep to fixed times) I betake myself according to the weather either to the terrace or the covered arcade, work out the rest of my subject, and dictate it" (Plin. *Ep.* 9.36; See Small 1997, p. 181).[84]

Pliny makes clear that composition takes place in memory, as an act of memory. Much of this is due to the technology of writing. Manuscripts were not always available, and even if available, consulting them was difficult. This points to the fact that compositions existed more authentically in memory than in writing. Pliny is arranging in his memory the extracts that he has gathered on wax tablets (see practice of Pliny the Elder, above) or scrolls. These extracts are collected on tablet and scroll as a means to store them in memory. Quintilian makes this point in his description of the orator's memory:

> For our whole education depends upon memory, and we shall receive instruction all in vain if all we hear slips from us, while it is the power of memory alone that brings before us all the store of precedents, laws, rulings, sayings and facts which the orator must possess in abundance and which he must always ready for immediate use. Indeed it is not without good reason that memory has been called the treasure-house of eloquence. . . . since the mind is always looking ahead, it is continually in search of something which is more remote: on the other hand whatever it discovers, it deposits by some mysterious process in the safe-keeping of memory, which acts as a transmitting agent hands on to the delivery what it has received from the imagination. I do not conceive, however, that I need dwell upon the question of the precise function of memory, although many hold the view, that certain impressions are made upon the mind, analogous to those which a signet-ring makes on wax (*Inst.* 11.2.1–3).

The "mysterious process" to which Quintilian refers is what the ancients called the *ars memoria* (see below). These extracts become the basis for composition—their placement in ordered *loci* or τόποι makes composition possible. In making fun of the overdependence of some on extracts, the author of *Rhetorica ad Herennium* conjures up an imaginary dialogue in which someone says: "You are writing a treatise of your own . . . Beware of acting imprudently in seeking to extract from the labour of others praise for your own name." The author comments, "Indeed, if the ancient orators and poets should take the books of these rhetoricians and each remove from there what belongs to himself, the rhetoricians would have nothing left to claim as their own" (*Rhet. Her.* 4.3.5).

After completing a draft, whether on wax tablets or papyrus, how does revision take place? Here Quintilian's remarks quoted above bear remembering. He recommends leaving blank pages, whether tablets or spaces in the scrolls. This raises important issues about how technology sets limits to the act of writing. A group of stacked wax tablets or a scroll of 20 feet in length make it difficult to see or imagine the whole. It is much easier to insert, add, or edit smaller sections. Furthermore, as Pliny the Younger indicates, when composing in memory, one tends to work over smaller sections, rather than the whole piece. This limitation imposed by technology should be kept in mind when we envision the writing of gospels or editing of the Pauline letters.

Nor should we think of an author as a single individual. The lonely individual toiling away with pen and scroll is a modern convention, probably a creation of romanticism. After composing in memory, an author would dictate or work out drafts on wax tablets. Often the person taking dictation was a slave or freedman. Cicero's freedman, Tiro, is perhaps the best-known example of such a person. Even more, the one taking dictation is in some sense a participant in the writing. Gellius notes that he is surprised that neither Cicero nor Tiro caught a mistaken reference in one of Cicero's works. "I am not so much surprised that Marcus Tullius erred in that matter, as that it was not noticed later and corrected either by Cicero himself or by Tiro, his freedman, a most careful man, who gave attention to his patron's books" (Gel. *NA.* 15.6.1–2).

Then there would be discussions with friends.[85] Pliny the Younger in responding to his friend C. Plinius Celer about his writing method comments:

> In the first place, I revise my composition in private, next I read it to two or three friends, and then give it to others to annotate; if I doubt the justness of their corrections, I carefully weigh them again with a friend or two.

But now comes the real test. Pliny recites before a large audience and he admits that he has "author's nerves."

> Again nothing so much awakens the judgement as that reverence, and modest timidity, which one feels upon those occasions. For do but reflect and tell me whether you would not be infinitely less affected if you were to speak before a single person only, though ever so learned, than before a numerous assembly, even though it were composed of none but illiterate people? . . . The reason I imagine to be, that a certain large collective wisdom resides in a crowd, as such; and men whose individual judgment is defective are excellent judges when grouped together (Plin. *Ep.* 7.13).

Pliny is not here speaking of publication. He is still testing and improving his writing. Furthermore, he is testing his audience's response and even though he is upper class, he assumes there will be illiterate folks in his audience and trusts their response.

Finally a fair copy is produced, usually by a slave or scribe. It is quite conceivable that an ancient author never set down a single word in his or her composition, for others might well do the actual inscribing of the letters.

Afterwards publication takes place in two ways. The first and by far the most important was *recitatio*, the public performance.[86] Although writing was important in the ancient world, oral delivery was still the most pervasive means of communication, so a public performance was especially important in making a work known, much like advertising today. Quinn (1982, p. 154) summarizes a poet's possibilities during the age of Augustus as follows:

> The first is the traditional performance by the poet himself to a few friends; it is essentially a tentative reading to gauge reactions and elicit criticism. The second is a performance in some kind of contest in which more than one poet takes part. . . . The third is public non-dramatic performance by the poet himself. The fourth is professional performance in the theatre as some kind of spectacle.

Performance is publication. Often the process stopped here. Virgil did not finish his Aenid and on his deathbed left instructions—fortunately ignored—that it be destroyed. Horace remarks that one should not release a work for eight years: "then put your parchment in the closet and keep it back till the ninth year" (Hor. *Ars P.*388–9).

When a manuscript is turned over to the copyists, control is lost. The author would make copies for his friends, and others would obtain copies from these friends. Starr (1987, pp. 213, 216) notes that the circle of friendship accounts for the circulation of Roman literary works, both current writings and those from the past. When an author sends outs copies of his works to his friends, "that work can be said to have been *made public* or to have been *released*" (Starr, 1987, p. 215).[87] Cicero in a letter to Atticus complains "Come now, in the first place do you approve of publishing[88] without my instructions? . . . And another thing: do you think it was right to give the book to anyone before Brutus, to whom at your suggestion I address it? Balbus writes to me that he has copied 'On the Limits,' Book V, from your manuscript, a book in which I have made changes" (Cic. *Att.* 13.21a). He goes on to remind Atticus not to lend out copies in which Cicero's corrections have not been made. This letter vividly illustrates the problems of "publication."

Copies of works could also be made by the booksellers.[89] In large cities, such merchants would employ a staff of slaves or freedmen to make copies of various manuscripts available for sale. It is unclear just how widespread this was, but we ought not to imagine anything approaching modern availability of literature. The technology simply could not support it. Whatever profit came from selling books did not benefit the author, but the bookseller (Knox 1985, p. 20).[90] Unless one was an aristocrat and independently wealthy, as e.g., Pliny the Younger, financial advantage for an author came from a patron.

Martial complains of the unfairness of it: "How long shall I be a caller, earning a hundred coppers in a whole day, when Scorpus in a single hour carries off as winner fifteen heavy bags of gold hot from the mint?" (Mar. *Spect.* 10.74. 1–5).

Copyists were notoriously unreliable. Kenney (1982, p. 24) states, "the first task of a reader with a new book was to correct it." Strabo notes the problems surrounding the preservation and copying of Aristotle's library. Because of the loss of this library after Theophrastus's death, "they were unable to philosophize according to the principles of the system, and merely occupied themselves in elaborate discussions on common places." But then the library was recovered, restored, and recopied. In the process, many errors were introduced. Strabo continues, "Their successors however, from the time that these books were published, philosophized, and propounded the doctrine of Aristotle more successfully than their predecessors, but were under the necessity of advancing a great deal as probable only, on account of the multitude of errors contained in the copies." He concludes with a general comment about the unreliability of booksellers: "Some vendors of books, also, employed bad scribes and neglected to compare the copies with the original. This happens in the case of other books which are copied for sale both here [Rome] and at Alexandria" (13.1.54). Martial also complains about the copyists introducing mistakes:

> If some things in these pages, reader, strike you as too obscure or doubtful Latin, the error is not mine. The copyist did the damage in his hurry to tell out the number of verses for you (*Spect.* 2.8. 1–4).

When we consider the technology of writing, a number of inventions that would have facilitated writing seem obvious. The desk is a clear example. Another is the codex. It seems a small step from wax tablets to the codex, but that step was taken only slowly around the end of the first or the beginning of the second century CE. The unwieldy scroll remained the dominant form for literary manuscripts until fourth century.

THE TECHNOLOGY OF WRITING AND THE NEW TESTAMENT

The early Christian adoption of the codex as a replacement for the scroll is an important hermeneutical signal that begs explanation. Previous use of the codex having facilitated utilitarian writings (Gamble, 1995, pp. 49–50), abandonment of the scroll, normal for

Greek literary compositions, indicates a stance vis-à-vis that literature. How should we view this stance? Does it represent a rejection of the scroll's implications? Or does it imply a utilitarian use for Christian writings? This latter is especially likely in that surviving second century papyrus fragments do not indicate high scribal skill. This in turn raises important questions about how Christian writings were used before the rise of the great manuscripts of Constantine's era.

Since the technology of writing involves inherent constraints on the act of composition, this survey of the technology of writing raises important issues about how the physical composition of early Christian documents may have affected our understanding of them. Two brief and diverse examples will illustrate the importance of this issue. The synoptic problem raises important questions about the physical constraints of writing: is the proposed solution possible given the known conditions of writing? The second case, the rise of the Pauline corpus, allows us to consider the influence of the technology of writing over a larger time span.

SYNOPTIC PROBLEM

R.A. Derrenbacker, in *Ancient Compositional Practices and the Synoptic Problem* (2005), has written an important study that takes into account the technology of writing in the ancient world as it affects our attempts to unravel the synoptic problem. To my knowledge this is one of the first studies to take writing technology seriously, and Derrenbacker should be lauded for his efforts.

His focus, as his title indicates, is the synoptic problem, the literary relationships among the first three Gospels. His strategy—as well as the consequent value of his study—is that he judges various solutions to the synoptic problem on the basis of ancient writing practices. He considers two kinds of evidence—the technology of writing and the use of sources.[91] Because of the concerns of this study, we will attend primarily to Derrenbacker's consideration of the technology of writing materials.

After surveying the posture of the scribe and the absence of desks, Derrenbacker concludes, "all the main 'solutions' to the Synoptic Problem have proponents who are guilty of picturing the evangelists, not accurately as writers working without a writing desk, but as authors seated behind spacious (and sometimes elaborate) writing surfaces" (p. 38). He comments that while it is not difficult to imagine how Matthew and Luke wove together Mark and Q when they have the manuscripts in front of them on a desk, "Yet it becomes very difficult to imagine this conventional picture when Matthew and Luke are likely working without the benefit of a writing table or desk!" (p. 39). The evidence would suggest that "likely" is too tentative.

Derrenbecker is equally critical of the Griesbach or two-Gospel Source, i.e., that Matthew is prior, Mark abbreviates Matthew and Luke, and Luke uses Matthew. He criticizes the notion that Mark abbreviates or epitomizes Matthew and Luke, because the two Gospel theory would require Mark to abbreviate in a manner not attested in ancient sources (p. 157). The evidence indicates that epitomizers, such as Josephus, alternate between sources at the episodic level. But on the two gospel theory, Mark "'zigzags" within a single story" (p. 162 quoting Farmer and al. 1990, p. 222, n. 92). Derrenbacker asks, "How, then, does the Research Team [the multiple authors of the article] imagine Mark *physically* [emphasis added] working with his two written sources, often alternating between the two frequently *within* individual pericopes?" (p. 162). Likewise Derrenbacker attacks the two-gospel theory's understanding of Luke's use of Matthew. An example is "the Research Team's" analysis of Luke 4:14–16a.

> The Research Team asks the reader to imagine Luke moving from Matt 4,23a (καί) to Matt 4, 12b (εἰς τὴν Γαλιλαίαν) to Matt 9,26 back to 4,23b–24 then back to 4,13a, all in order to compose some two and half verses (35 words). Such a complicated procedure does not seem to be supported by what we do know about the compositional conventions of antiquity, *particularly the physical conditions* [emphasis added] under which writers worked" (p. 149–50. Derrenbacker is using McNicol, (1996, pp. 81–2).

Turning his attention to the two source theory (Mark is prior, Matthew and Luke use Mark and Q), Derrenbacker points out that on this theory, "Luke's method of working with Mark and Q is relatively simple and straight forward, consistent with the known practices of writers in the Greco-Roman world" (p. 215). Luke's use of Q is rather straight forward, alternating pericopes or episodes. Matthew's use of Mark is likewise straight forward. He basically follows Mark's outline. But Matthew's use of Q is much more problematic. Matthew reworks and reorders Q. And as we have seen, this type of composition poses physical problems.[92] Derrenbacker's proposed solution is interesting. "If Matthew's use of Q whose order is best reflected by Luke is to be taken seriously, one is compelled to imagine Matthew's Q in the form of a *codex*. Again, a codex would provide Matthew with the *random* access to Q, a feature not found in the scroll" (p. 253).[93] Derrenbacker has pursued a two-pronged approach throughout his study, adducing both the physical requirements of writing and the way the ancients used sources. Matthew's use of Q falters on the first of these two prongs.[94] Because Derrenbacher takes seriously the physical, material conditions of writing in the Greco-Roman world, he has to opt for the codex because of the need for random access—something that is extremely difficult when using scrolls.

In his description of "The Media and Materials of Writers in Antiquity," Derrenbacker had argued "there are two basic types of media in antiquity, to which I have already alluded: the scroll or 'book-roll' and the codex, which is the closest to our modern book medium" (p. 30). He makes the distinction that scrolls feature continuous or sequential access (p. 31), while a codex provides random access (p. 32). Here, of course, Derrenbacker has unnecessarily narrowed the options in the ancient world. His statement about the scroll and the codex as the two basic types of media is simply not true of the first century.[95] Furthermore the codex is a Roman invention, and no evidence of its use exists in Greek writing in the first century. While this is not an insurmountable obstacle to Derrenbacker's proposal, it presents a significant problem for one who takes seriously the importance of physical evidence. Another difficulty is that the codex initially suffered from the same problems as the tablet and scroll. As Small (1997, p. 155) has noted, until the invention of the stiff backing, and even more the use of desks, consulting a codex in the way imagined by Derrenbacker would be impossible.[96] It is telling that he refers to the codex as "closest to our modern book medium" (p. 30). It is not.

But other possibilities for dealing with this problem remain. Derrenbacker appears not to have considered whether Matthew might have used wax tablets. Though lacking evidence for this surmise, I suspect that Derrenbacker is blinded by a "paper prejudice," and does not consider wax tablets as a sufficiently permanent medium for Q. But Matthew's copy of Q could certainly have existed on wax tablets. Likewise, since composers of documents commonly gathered information by making extracts, it is quite possible that Matthew could have dictated extracts of Q onto a wax tablet as part of his compositional process. These extracts could then be manipulated in memory to compose sections of the gospel. (See chapter 11, "Manuscript and Memory, Q on Anxiety," below).

Such a method fully comports with our evidence about compositional practices in the Greco-Roman world. Finally, one should not let the name "Matthew" fix in our mind that this process was the result of a single individual's activity. Nor was it necessarily completed at a single time: we know that compositions tended to take form through a process of rewriting, a point Derrenbacker notes, but then does not develop.

PAULINE CORPUS

An examination of Derrenbacker's study of the synoptic problem indicates the importance of writing practices for conceiving various scenarios for the composition of the gospels. Likewise, a knowledge of the technology of writing can help us envision how the Pauline corpus came to be.

STAGE ONE: COMPOSITION OF PAUL'S LETTERS

Paul's letters can be divided into three groups, based on the way memory would most likely have functioned in their composition.

1. Common Letters

The classic example is Philemon, which falls within the common letter tradition analyzed by White in his *Light from Ancient Letters* (1986). As our analysis indicates (See Chapter 7, "Sound and Persuasion: Paul's Letter to Philemon") it was meant to be read in public before the ἐκκλησία (community). Such letters are short and deal with a single issue. Their demands on memory are not extensive. Philemon, like most common letters, could easily be composed in memory in one take, so to speak, and dictated to a scribe. Dictation is the more probable here because a striking feature of the papyrus common letters that White surveyed is the use of "boilerplate" and clichés. Such letters were probably not dictated, but their composition was entrusted to a village scribe who constructed the letter from a common stock of expressions. This too, of course, represents an index of conventional memory, but what is significant about the Pauline letters as a corpus is the almost total absence of these conventional clichés.

2. Letters Responding to Situations in a Local Community

The Corinthian correspondence is the exemplar of this type. Paul is responding to situations of which he has a firsthand knowledge and has received at least one letter from the Corinthian community. These letters chunk into topics. Much as Pliny describes, the author would have composed each section in his memory—and therefore seeking to discover an overall structure for the letter might be inappropriate.

3. Formal, Literary Letter

Finally, I would distinguish Romans as belonging technologically to a third type of letter. It has more in common with the literary letter. To compose Romans would have required imagining a diatribe, speech-in-character, as well as gathering extensive quotations from scripture. Again, on the evidence of ancient practice, one would assume that this was done from memory and excerpts, not by consulting manuscripts. The memorial effort required to write Romans implies formal memory training and higher skill in the memorial arts than any other Pauline letter.

When we consider the technology of writing and composition in memory we should expect to find letters broken into memory chunks. Thus we need to be alert to the possibility that breaks may not indicate an editor's hand, but chunks drawn intact from memorial τόποι. Small (1997, p. 186) observes that when composing in memory from several sources, "wholes are not dissected."

Clearly Paul used a scribe or secretary (Richards 1991). In both Galatians (6:11), 1 Corinthians (16:21), and Philemon (19) Paul adds a postscript, clearly indicating that another hand has inscribed the letter.[97] Romans represents a somewhat different situation in that the secretary, Tertius, inserts his own greeting into the letter (Roms 16:22). The name Tertius frequently appears in slave and freedman lists, once again raising the social status question implied in the act of writing. Tertius has occasioned some debate. Roller (1933), for example,[98] argued that Tertius was the author or had a major hand in the letter's composition. Cranfield (1975–79, pp. 2–3) has defended apostolic authorship with what appears to be an apologetic concern. Richards (1995, pp. 170–2) suggests that since Tertius is known in Rome and Rome is a center for tachygraphists, then Paul may have performed the letter to the Romans *viva voce* and subsequently entrusted Tertius to write a letter of recommendation for Phoebe, which became chapter 16. While the writing process in the ancient world was a collaborative effort, yet one side of that collaborative effort often remains hidden. Cicero's relation with his freedman Tiro is only one important example. Aulus Gellius describes Tiro as Cicero's *adiutor*, helper, assistant, co-worker (*NA* 13.91). Tertius might be a freedman or slave who is Paul's *adiutor*.

Paul's letters were sent with someone both to read aloud and interpret his letter, which is the same thing (see for example Timothy, 1 Cor 4:17; Phil 2:19; 1 Thess 3:2, 6). This reading of the letter to the community, which makes the apostle present in a form identified by Funk (1967) as the Apostolic Parousia, is related to *recitatio* of publication. The real letter is not the manuscript, but the letter's spoken sounds.

STAGE TWO: COLLECTING AND EDITING OF PAUL'S LETTERS

At some point the letters of Paul were collected, edited, and copied. These are three distinct though related tasks. First the letters must be collected. In the case of the Corinthian letters, obviously and famously the first letter to the Corinthians (1 Cor 5:9) was either omitted or missed. Once collected, the letters were edited. According to most reconstructions, the original order of the letters was not observed, but what is interesting is that the letters are, as the technology of writing and composition in memory would lead us to expect, chunked in rather complete units. In the process of editing, appropriate beginnings and endings may have been composed. Finally the letters would have been copied and recopied over and over again. In this process, notes made in the margins may have become incorporated into the main body of the manuscript, as for example, 1 Cor 14:33b–36. If copying is done from dictation, such incorporation is easy to imagine.

The process of collecting, editing, and copying the letters changes their status. Instead of representing correspondence with a particular church for particular situations, the edited letters are in effect stripped of their contexts.[99] To use Snyder's term, the users of this collection are becoming "text centered"(2000, p. 5). This process assumes that for the groups that use them, the letters or their author are an authority, like the founder of a school.

STAGE THREE: ADDITIONS TO PAULINE LETTERS

The process of collecting, editing, and copying not only creates a "text centered" community, but also provides the occasion for pseudepigraphic writing; accordingly stage two and three, while they can be distinguished formally, may well be coterminous. The technology of writing actually encourages this process. Many ancient scrolls and codices contain more than one type of writing or writings by more than one author. Therefore the process of copying facilitates incorporation of pseudepigrapha.[100] This same process happened with Homer, Plato, Aristotle, and other ancient authors. Goodspeed (1933, pp. 5–10, esp. p. 6) argued that Ephesians was written to head up the original collection of the Pauline letters. His argument goes beyond the evidence, but he is probably correct that the deutero-Pauline letters originated in the ongoing process of editing, collecting, copying, and reflecting on these letters—a process that resulted in forming a "text centered" group. This stage likely took place over a rather long period. The first collection occurs probably towards the end of the first century, with the Pastorals added to the Corpus several decades later.

STAGE FOUR: CANONIZATION

Canonization involves yet another step in the status of the collection. This question, like many suggested in this chapter is too complex to consider here in detail. But the trajectory we have been following suggests several things. 1) The Pauline collection stops growing, so that there are no more pseudepigraphic writings added to the collection and the corpus becomes fixed. Aland (see 1987, pp. 49–50 for a summary of the textual evidence) thinks this happens in the mid-second century. Most important pseudepigraphic additions predate Constantine. 2) The Pauline collection was combined with the Gospels collection probably in the third century. Unfortunately, we do not understand how the process of canonization actually came about (Gamble 1985, chapter 2; Gamble 2002).

From the point of view of the technology of writing, an important question remains: What was this collection's physical status? Was it real or virtual?[101] As Aland has pointed out, complete New Testaments do not occur until around the time of Constantine. Because they were simply too expensive for most churches to afford, lectionaries account for the greatest number of manuscripts. Many copies of the New Testament contain books not contained in the "official" New Testament canon, while other books are missing. Given what we know of the technology of writing, this is not surprising. Schmidt (2002, p. 476) wonders when Athanasius' list of books became a table of contents for a codex.[102] A related question is when books first get tables of contents. The answer to this latter question is easier: not until the early Middle Ages, when the list of books in the canon becomes the table of contents for a New Testament.

Since the technology of writing constrains and shapes composition, our understanding of the composition of early Christian writings—or any ancient composition—must comport with the material process of composition. The next four chapters will move beyond the material culture to consider literary compositional processes that depend on this material basis and writing technology.

ENDNOTES

1. Haas (1996, pp. x-xi). "Writing and technology are not distinct phenomena . . . Whether it is the stylus of the ancients, the pen and ink of the medieval scribe, a toddler's fat crayons, or a new Powerbook, technology makes writing possible. To go further, writing *is* technology, for without the crayon or the stylus or the Powerbook, writing is simply not writing."
2. Haas (1996) chapter 1, "The Technology Question," has a short and incisive discussion of this issue.
3. Chandler, Daniel (1995): "Technological or Media Determinism" **URL** http://www.aber.ac.uk/media/Documents/tecdet/tecdet.html

[*4/10/08*] has a very thorough discussion of this history and various theoretical stances to this issue.

4. Blanck (1992) is a good example.
5. Bowman (1991, p. 122) nicely states this paradox: "The interesting thing is not that there was no mass literacy in the ancient world, but that ancient society could be profoundly literate with a reading-and-writing population of, let us say, less (perhaps much less) of twenty percent, the precise figure being insignificant."
6. Two of the most important pre-conditions for mass literacy are missing in the Roman Empire: the invention of the printing press (Harris, 1989, p. 15) and mass, state-supported education (p. 16). Hezser (2001) deals with the situation in Palestine and estimates a literacy rate of 3%.
7. Harris' study has received a great deal of discussion, but his "basic point, that levels of literacy in Graeco-Roman antiquity were never high, has not been seriously challenged" (Humphrey 1991, p. 2). Bowman (1991, p. 119) says, "After reading Harris's book, few will feel that there is much to be said for arguing the opposite case." Or consider Kaster (1988, p. 35): "The overall impression, certainly, is one of massive illiteracy."

   New Testament scholars are beginning to take this evidence seriously. Botha (1992, p. 202) concurs: "The possibility of widespread literacy, and the probability of a literate culture cannot be very great with regard to Greco-Roman antiquity: as a society the major factors creating literacy were absent and many factors making it unlikely were fully present." New Testament scholars need to take this evidence to heart and skip such romantic pictures as that of Joseph teaching Jesus to read and write (Meier 1991, p. 276).
8. They are referred to as "slow writers" (βραδέως γράφων and βραδέως γράφουσα.) Those who know no letters are ἀγράμματοι (Cribiore 1996, p. 6); Harris, (1989, p. 5–6) deals with these terms and shows their ambiguity.
9. As Bagnall (1995, p. 15) points out, the group that could read and write was "drawn entirely from those groups that were able to afford both to pay for education . . . and to dispense with their children's labor while they were learning" (p. 15). Plato notes: "This is what people do, who are most able; and the most able are the wealthiest. Their sons begin school at the earliest age, and are freed from it at the latest" (*Prt.* 326c). What is meant by "school" is very fluid. Tutelage could take place in a rented room, at home,

or even outdoors. Depicting a school under a tree is a convention in pottery illustrations.

10. Small's *Wax Tablets of the Mind* is the best and most current treatment of the technology of writing in the ancient world.
11. Cornelius Nepos describes the slaves of Atticus, Cicero's good friend. "He had slaves that were excellent in point of efficiency . . . for there were among them servants who were highly educated, some excellent readers and great number of copyists" (Nep. *Att.* 13.3). It is interesting to notice the distinction between those who can read well and those who can copy well. (See Starr 1991, pp. 339–40).
12. For a discussion of this image see below, "*Wax Tablets*." While the image is stylized and not a realistic portrait, it does indicate that it is not unthinkable for a woman to write.
13. Business executives in the 1960's had secretaries who did their typing for them. Computers have to some extent changed this dynamic.
14. Hanson (1991, p. 164) lists three ways illiterates protected themselves when required to interact with literacy. 1) They used literate family members or relatives, 2) friends or business associates, and finally 3) professional scribes.
15. Bagnall (1995, p. 10) points out that the ancients viewed bronze and stone as "permanent" writing.
16. Early Roman writing did have word spaces, but during the first century BCE Romans switched to *scriptio continua* (See Johnson 2000).
17. Fischer (2003, p. 33) makes a similar point: inscriptions were "not to inform but to impress." Thomas (1994, p. 40) notes, "public inscriptions on stone seem to have an authority beyond their literal content."
18. Franklin (1991, p. 86) quotes with approval the remark W. Eck, "monument and inscription formed, for a Roman, a self-evident unity, to be sure; an inscription without an object to which it belonged was scarcely conceivable" (p. 132). Svenbro (1993, p. 232) demonstrates how an epigram inscription was originally interpreted and how, when the statue to which the epigram belonged was later discovered, the interpretation was altered. As *document* it was one thing, but as a *monument*, and ensemble, it is "obeying rules of its own."
19. Franklin gives several examples of both inscriptions and graffiti and indicates how those with a range of skills in reading from

highly literate, to craftsman literate, to illiterate, would have responded. It is a fine example of how people of all social classes and abilities interacted with writing.

20. Thomas (1994, p. 164) also notes that Augustus boasted in his inscription *Res Gestae* 20.1, "I restored the Capitol and the theatre of Pompey, both works at great expense without inscribing my own name on either" (Brunt and Moore 1967). Thomas comments: "a feat of considerable political restraint."
21. But as we shall see below, the Acts of the Senate were stored on wax tablets.
22. The position of Lévi-Strauss (Reprinted 1992, p. 301) is well known. "The only phenomenon with which writing has always been concomitant is the creation of cities and empires, that is, the integration of large numbers of individuals into a political system, and their grading into castes or classes. . . . My hypothesis, if correct, would oblige us to recognize the fact that the primary function of written communication is to facilitate slavery." For a nuanced series of studies on this topic, see Bowman (1994). Starr (1991, p. 338) notes the high number of slaves or freedmen who were *lectores*, copyists, note-takers, and clerks.
23. The University of Michigan Papyrus Collection (**URL** http://www.lib.umich.edu/pap/index.html) has extensive exhibits on writing and writing materials in the ancient world.
24. The interaction of writing material and alphabet needs to be underlined. Because it was written on wet clay tablets into which the stylus had to create a cut or incision, cuneiform has very sharp angles. Likewise, the cursive style was difficult on wax tablets and therefore saw little development until the wide availability of parchment (Saenger 1982, p. 386). Small (1997, p. 147) has a description of this.
25. Beck (1975, plate 7) has images of various styli. His display of "Tools of Learning" is very helpful. See Avrin (1991) pls. 127 and 130 for more samples.
26. The Egyptian scribe commonly used a soft brush.
27. See Avrin (1991) pl. 106 for images of various inkwells. Pl. 105 shows various tools used by a Sefardi's scribe from Jerusalem in the late nineteenth century. The number of tools reminds us how much skill and labor were involved in writing and copying a manuscript.
28. See **URL** http://vindolanda.csad.ox.ac.uk/ for a website dedicated to this important find.

29. As noted above, bronze and stone were for permanent writing.
30. Ostraka remained in use into the medieval period. Bagnall (1995, figure 8) shows a Coptic ostrakon from the Monastery of Epiphanius dated to the seventh century CE and bearing the words "concerning readmission of a person to communion."
31. As an example of an extended text, Cribiore (1996, p. 64) lists syllabary inscribed on ostraka.
32. Cheap is a relative term. Bowman (1994, p. 112) remarks that wax tablets were an import item in Britain so the soldiers at Violanda turned to wooden leaf tablets; while in Egypt, wax tablets are much rarer and here again an import item because of a lack of local wood supplies and the ready availability of papyrus (Cribiore, 1996, p. 65).
33. Trans. Lattimore (1951); γϱάψας ἐν πίνακι πτυκτῷ. See Kirk (1990, p. 181) for discussion of what kind of writing is probably mentioned.
34. Inv. 9084, (Caro 1996, p. 188). This is not a portrait of a real person, but is idealized since it shows no physiognomic traits. Also from Pompeii is an image of a husband and wife. While they are in a stylized pose, they are real people. He wears a toga and holds a scroll, an indication of his role as a magistrate. His wife holds a wax tablet in her right hand and in her left a stylus in the same pose as the Sappho portrait. Inv 9058, (Caro, 1996, p. 189).
35. The *Acta* of the Roman Senate were kept on wax tablets. At the funeral of Clodius (52 BCE) "the mob broke into the Senate House and piled up wooden furniture and *codices librariorum* to form a funeral pyre, which burned so fiercely that the Senate House itself was consumed" (Roberts and Skeat 1987, p. 13); Plin. *HN* 34.11.21; Cic. *Mil.* 5.13.
36. Beck (1975, plates 8–15) has numerous examples of the use of the wax tablets from school scenes. Avrin (1991, p. 141–44) has several good illustrations. His plate 128 from a Red-figure Greek kylix (5th century BCE) shows two women walking with one carrying wax tablets. The survival of wax tablets belies the common sense assumption of their fragility.
37. Roberts and Skeat (1987, p. 12) point out that consulting these abstracts on scrolls written on both sides would have been difficult, "and it is odd that, with the tablets at his side to point the way, Pliny did not anticipate the invention of the codex by substituting for the opisthograph roll a collection of folded sheets of papyrus." But they fail to observe that this would not have made

consultation much easier. A codex is not a modern book with its many typographic aids (see Small 1997, pp. 155–58).

38. Supply is always an issue for both papyrus and parchment. The further from the source, the more expensive the product. Thus the hoard of documents written on wooden leaf tablets from Vindolanda, on the very edge of the empire in Britain (see Bowman 1994). These small, extremely thin wooden tablets were found in the praetorium of the fort, which was later converted to a barracks. The tablets are from 90–120 CE and represent the same range of types that one would expect in a papyrus find. What matters, then, is not so much the type of writing material but the need to write. These wooden tablets are not made from waste material, but indicate careful manufacture (p. 112).
39. Lewis's two volumes (1974; 1989) are the definitive studies of papyrus.
40. *Memoria,* of which "the remembrance of past events" is the more accurate and felicitous translation of John Bostock and H.T. Riley, Perseus **URL** http://www.perseus.tufts.edu/cgi-bin//// ptext?lookup=Plin.+Nat.+13.21. Pliny also describes papyrus as "the material on which the immortality of human beings depends" (Plin. *HN* 13. 21. 70).
41. *Charta,* a leaf of papyrus is the primary meaning. Rachman in the LCL throughout translates *charta* as paper. Technically paper was not available in Europe until twelfth century (Valencia, Spain) and thirteenth century (Fabriano, Italy).
42. "Texitur" can mean to weave, but by extension it can also imply simply the formation of a web or tissue. This is its sense here, since technically papyrus is not woven because its strips are not interlaced. The strips are laid across, with the bottom strips in vertical alignment and the top or writing surface laid horizontally across the vertical strips. In Turner (1968), plates 1–3, show excellent examples.
43. Pliny is apparently mistaken here; so Lewis, (1974, pp. 50–51).
44. Variant of *monumentum,* "that which preserves the remembrance of any thing, a memorial, a monument;" often used of tombs and writings (Lewis and Short 1879).
45. Small (1997, p. 155–58) has a discussion of reading stands.
46. Roberts and Skeat (1987, p. 5) argue that there is no causal relationship between the eventual dominance of parchment and the rise of the codex.
47. These names did not come into use until the fourth century CE. In Greek, parchment is referred to as διφθέρα and in Latin *membrana,* "skin."

48. Roberts and Skeat (1987, p. 6) has a thorough discussion of issues with references, following Johnson (1970).
49. For more on this see below, the discussion on codex.
50. See also Gamble, p. 50. Even after the codex became dominant, the scroll continued to be used for literary texts, perhaps parallel to the continuing use of the wax tablet as the record of choice for the Acts of the Roman Senate. It indicates the conservative character of writing materials.
51. Quinn (1982,p. 82, n. 20) questions how successful this innovation was: "The fact, however, that the references to codex versions of standard authors in Martial are not supported from elsewhere leaves the impression these were not so much the Elzevirs or the Penguins of their day, as an isolated publishing venture, which did not catch on, despite Martial's publicity for it."
52. Derrenbacker (2005, pp. 32–36) has a good summary of the issues surrounding various theories on the rise of codex.
53. So BDAG, " μεμβράνα," (p. 629), although Danker acknowledges the possibility of the notebook/codex meaning. The textual evidence for 2 Timothy is slim. There are no papyri, but Sinaiticus, A, C are among the constant witnesses that support the lack of a conjunction.
54. Skeat (1979) originates this argument. He argues that μάλιστα has a particularizing function. Such an interpretation demands that the meaning of τὰ βιβλία has to shift from "scroll" to "codex." One must ignore the literal meaning of τὰ βιβλία ("scroll"), as Roberts and Skeat (1987, p. 22., n. 3) acknowledge. Because Skeat assumes that Paul is the author of 2 Timothy, he posits Christian use of the codex in the first century. This whole argument is tendentious.
55. See Derrenbacker (2005, p. 4, n. 11) for a partial list of other New Testament scholars who imagine gospel writers as sitting at a desk.
56. Skeat (1956, p. 183) remarks, "to forestall incredulity, I may perhaps recall that in the classical world, as in the Near East generally down to comparatively modern times, life is marked by a general absence of such conveniences as chairs and tables." (See esp. Small 1997, pp. 150–55; Turner 1987, p. 8; Metzger 1968). Tables were used by bankers, as the word for bank (τράπεζα) reminds us.
57. A famous example of this projection of common sense concerns the identification of the "scriptorium" at Qumran. Roland de Vaux identified it on the basis of three inkpots and what looked like a long, thin table and stools. De Vaux's monastic experience

may have led him to identify this object as a table and stools of a scriptorium. But the so-called table is much too flimsy, and to date no plausible explanation has been offered (Broshi 2000, pp. 831–2). Small (1997, p. 163) remarks about similar problem in the reconstruction of the Trajan's library.

58. Beck (1975, Plates 41–83) has a collection of images under the headings of "Literacy," "School Scenes," "Reading and Writing," and "Reading and Recitation." Avrin (1991) has some of the same images, plus a selection of Roman images. See esp. plate 141 of a Roman administrator with a tablet.
59. Parássouglou (1979, p. 16) notes, "it is quite exasperating to realize that we lack even a single representation of an ancient Greek or Roman professional scribe, a person, that is, whose task was the multiplication of literary texts."
60. As noted above, Bagnall (1995, p. 25) remarks, "One might almost say that there was a direct correlation between the social standing that guaranteed literacy and the means to avoid writing."
61. There is considerable evidence for the knee. Small (1997, p. 155) among others (Metzger 1968, p. 126. n. 2) quotes a fragment from Kallimachos, "the very first thing I put the writing tablet on my knees."
62. See Parássouglou (1979, p. 18–19) for the best discussion of this colophon; also Skeat (1956, p. 183–4) and Metzger (1968, p. 125).
63. Some images of wax tablets would seem to indicate standing. These tablets are all *pugilaris* and the writer may be thinking. See above, "*Wax Tablets*." Since these images are highly stylized, one should be careful about drawing conclusions.
64. Parássouglou (1979, p. 10–11, n. 18, plate 2) discusses an interesting funerary monument from the third century CE with a man in sitting position and a slave, perhaps a student, holding the inkpot.
65. Parássouglou (1979, p. 14–15) summarizes the evidence: "The artistic evidence, then, suggests that, when writing on papyrus rolls, the ancient Greeks and Romans assumed postures quite similar to those they adopted when writing on tablets. Unlike the ancient Egyptians, they did not normally sit on the ground; but like them, they did not use tables or writing desks. . . . the Greeks and Romans . . . used as a pen a stiff reed sharpened to a fine point, and there was the danger that its pressure, as a result of incautious movement, might puncture the papyrus. Consequently, a need for some support was felt by many, and the knee, or the thigh, was called upon to provide it."
66. One of the earliest examples of a table is a third century relief

from Ostia (see Turner 1987, pp. 189–90). Small (1997, p. 167), notes that "multiple tables for the literate are a recent innovation."

67. Richter (1966, p. 63) remarks about tables that "The chief use, therefore, of a table was during meals for the support of the dishes and the food; and as such a use was merely temporary, it was desirable that the tables should be light so that they could be removed without difficulty when not needed."
68. This difficulty is one major plank in Skeat's (1956) argument that both copying and correction of a manuscript most often was done by dictation.
69. He then adds "Reading, however prioritizes meaning." But as we shall see, this is really from the point of view of the printing press. Silent reading prioritizes meaning. Fischer goes on to add: "The faculty of reading has, in fact, very little to do with the skill of writing." Because of this distinction Fisher wrote a second volume, *A History of Writing* (2001).
70. Johnson (2000) in a programmatic essay has laid out an understanding of "the sociology of reading in classical antiquity."
71. Cribiore's chapter, "Learning to Write" (pp. 139–159) is especially important for its strong documentation. See below, chapter 3, Learning to Read and Write.
72. Cribiore (1996) also notes that in Egypt (her primary concern) and Rome, a student was learning Greek, while at home another language was primary.
73. Starr (1991, p. 343) notes that one of the most basic functions of a *lector* was to relieve the auditor of the "laborious task of deciphering the text. . . . For aristocratic readers, *lectores* provided the ultimate experience of literary texts: a polished rendition in which the auditor could focus on the literary work and not on the work of reading."
74. Johnson (2000, pp. 594–600) has an excellent summary of this debate. See also Benediktson (2006, p. 43, n. 1) for a recent bibliographic summary. Gavrilon (1997) does not appear in Benedikston's bibliography.
75. Modern authors compose for silent reading, even though sometimes their writing is read aloud, as in audio recordings of best selling books. Budiansky (2006), in an introductory note on the English language during the reign of Elizabeth I, notes: "The rise of the printing trade had . . . begun the evolution toward standardized spelling . . . Clearly most writers of English of this period still thought of words as *sounds* (emphasis added) rather than unique written forms: it was not at all unusual for educated

writers to spell the same word two different ways in the course of a single letter, or even to spell their own names differently on different occasions" (p. xv).

76. The evidence for reading aloud is so overwhelming that there has been in the literature an overstatement of the case. Josef Balogh(1926), the classic reference on this issue, was accused by Knox (1968, p. 421) of setting the "standard doctrine that silent reading (and writing) was, if not completely unknown in the ancient world, at least so rare that whenever it was observed, it aroused astonishment, even suspicion." Even accounting for Balogh's overstatement of evidence, his case was well made, as most subsequent commentators have acknowledged: the ancients normally read aloud. Even those critical of Balogh admit that "ancient texts were more often read aloud" (Gilliard, 1993, p. 691). Significant essays supporting Balogh: Stanford (1967); Hendrickson (1929); Clark (1930–31); Achtemeier (1990); (Saenger 1997); critical of Balogh: Knox (1968); Gavrilon (1997); Burnyeat (1997). Achtemeier's (1990) Society of Biblical Literature Presidential Address was important for New Testament studies, but it was uncritical and naïve in its acceptance of Balogh: (Gilliard 1993). Now Gavrilon (1997) has gone beyond Knox and argues that silent reading was common place. "These ancient reflections help us to see that the phenomenon of reading itself is fundamentally the same in modern and in ancient culture" (p. 69). Johnson (2000, p. 600) calls this conclusion into question. To read silently is not the same as to read as we do. Important aspects of Gavrilov's argument will be noted below, but his basic case goes too far because he ignores the abundant evidence for reading aloud—for example, Pliny the Elder's habit of having a slave read aloud to him so he could take extracts (See above, "*Wax Tablets*"). This is a clear example that the ancients did not think of silent, speed reading as necessary for research.
77. I note "*some* people" because of the sociology of reading. The more expert one's reading, the greater one's need to read large amounts of material, the more likely skill in silent reading would be present. This seems to be the proper conclusion to draw from Burnyeat's (1997, p. 74) quotation from Ptolemy. "That is . . . why *we keep quiet when engaged in the readings themselves* [sc. The reading required for research?] *if we are concentrating hard on the texts before us.* What talk is useful for, by contrast, is passing on the results of our inquiries to other people" (Ptolemy, Περὶ κριτηρίου καὶ ἡγεμονικοῦ, translation by Burnyeat, italics in text; Greek text also in his article). Nevertheless, Pliny the Elder was not

alone in doing research by having others read to him.

78. Carruthers (1990) and Gavrilon (1997, pp. 62–66) interpret this passage somewhat differently than the scholarly tradition. Both argue in Gavrilon's summary that "what puzzles Augustine is not Ambrose's method of reading in and of itself, but his resorting to that method *in the presence of his parishioners*" (63). I find this interpretation convincing. But even in this interpretation the clear expectation is that while in the presence of others reading is aloud. Gavrilon does not refer to Carruthers' similar interpretation.
79. Saenger (1997, p. 299, n. 42) makes the important distinction between "silent oral reading" and "true silent reading." He argues that "no classical author described rapid, silent reference consultation as it exists in the modern world" (9). Furthermore, he maintains that such true silent reading would be impossible because of the cognitive and neurological demands.
80. Saenger (1997) and Gavrilon (1997) clash and differ most significantly at this point. Neither, by the way, appears to know the other's work. Both rely on modern studies of reading. Gavrilon notes reading studies that indicate that reading aloud and reading to oneself always proceed together. He concludes, "if the ancients did not automatically start reading to themselves , or if starting from time to time to read to themselves, they failed to appreciate its advantages, or if, finally, they knew a way of artificially suppressing this capacity in themselves, then indeed they confront us with a highly peculiar anthropological phenomenon" (p. 61). Gavrilov plays down the problem of *scriptio continua*, which is central to Saenger, and it is unclear if modern reading studies deal with *scriptio continua*. More empirical studies are needed to resolve this issue. Johnson (2000, pp. 610–12) points out that the eye-voice span of 15–20 characters, often noted in the literature on reading, is the same as the standard width of literary scrolls. The ancients clearly taught reading aloud, but we have no evidence of their teaching reading silently, while silent reading is a part of the modern curriculum.
81. Saenger (1997, p. 3) also notes various studies indicating the existence of "discrete systems within the brain for aural understanding and the silent visual understanding of language."
82. Saenger's arguments are important to consider when scholars like Knox claim that ancient scholars had to read silently to do their work. Knox asserts this on the basis of common sense as print reader, but without any evidence. Gavrilov, on the other hand, makes his argument on the basis of modern reading theory. This

difference is important to note.

83. See chapter 3, The Grammar of Sound," below. See Cribiore (1996, pp. 40–42) for a discussion of syllabaries, a frequent find among school documents.
84. Quintilian (*Inst.* 10.6) has a long discussion of this same process, so the evidence from Pliny and Quintilian allow us to generalize about this process.
85. Cicero in writing to his friend Quintus remarks that he follows a similar procedure. He was composing a book on "The Ideal Constitution of the State" which he has set in a dialogue among men of ancient times. "But when these books were being read out to me at my Tusculan villa, in the hearing of Sallustius, it was suggested to me by him that these subjects would be discussed with far greater authority if the speaker on the Republic were myself" (Cic. *Q Fr.* 3.5.1). Cicero takes Sallustius' advice and makes the suggested change.
86. Starr (1991) deals with the Roman situation. *Lectores* in Rome were frequently slaves and read for their masters.
87. Starr (1987, p. 215, n. 18) argues, "The term 'publish' should not be used because it unavoidably bears a burden of modern implications." There were no Borders or Barnes and Noble in the ancient world. Starr (p. 216) lays out five ways in which an author could make a work available for copying. "First, . . . he could send a gift copy to a friend without placing any restrictions on its being copied. . . . Second, he could recite the work to friends and allow them to have copies made. . . . Third, he could deposit a copy in one of the great public libraries, where it was, so to speak, in the public domain. . . . Fourth, an author could allow or encourage his friends to make the book known. . . . Fifth, an author could deposit a copy with a bookdealer."
88. The verb used here is *edere,* to put out.
89. Kenney (1982, pp. 19–22) has a good discussion of this aspect of publication.
90. This situation persisted until the coming of copyright laws, beginning in England in 1662 with the Stationery Laws. William Shakespeare did not control the publishing of his plays, and the booksellers took the profit (Garber 2004, p. 9).
91. This is part one of his book. One chapter is devoted to "An Introduction to Writing, Books and Readers in the Greco-Roman World," and two chapters to the uses of sources, which we will not consider. Derrenbacker appears to have ignored Small's thorough and important study of the use of sources by ancient authors, although he knows her work. In my judgment his study

of the technology of writing is a very important and telling part of his critique of various solutions to the synoptic problem.

92. Since Matthew does not rearrange within pericopes, his use of Q does not run afoul of the problems besetting the Griesbach hypothesis.
93. Some have proposed that Mark was in a codex form to account for the so-called lost ending of Mark. See Taylor (1966, pp. 609–8).
94. While a codex form of Matthew would not solve the problems of the Griesbach hypothesis, it would make it more defensible. The Griesbach hypothesis more importantly falters because it imagines the use of sources in a way not attested in the ancients' employment of sources. Small's (1997, chapter 12) analysis of the subject corroborates Derenbacker's argument against the Greisbach hypothesis.
95. It may be that Derrenbacker is a victim of his own common sense. Because papyrus and codex account for the vast majority of evidence of extant New Testament manuscripts, it is common sense to focus on them. But they can by no means be represented as "the two basic types of media."
96. See also (Small 1997, p. 187), quoted above about the lack of an external physical order in *scriptio continua.*
97. There are examples of official letters written by a scribe but with a greeting added to the letter by official. See Bagnall (1995, p. 24). Cribiore (1998, pp. 4–5) concludes, "The habit of adding greetings in one's own hand was so widespread in the ancient world that it appears to have been a common epistolary courtesy." See also Parsons (1980–81, p. 4). So common is this practice that 2 Thess 3:17 and Col 4:18 (both pseudepigraphical) employ this added hand.
98. Richards (2004) ignores this important debate and does not refer to Roller. Cranfield (1975–79, p. 2–3) has the best discussion.
99. Gamble (1995, pp. 58–65), has an interesting and to my mind convincing argument that the gathering of the Pauline letters together towards the end of the first century accounts for the Christian adoption of the codex. In the process of shifting these letters from dealing with specific problems in specific churches, the collection adopts the pattern of letters addressed to seven churches (Romans, Corinthians, Galatians, Philippians, Thessalonians, Ephesians, Colossians). The number seven has a universal appeal. It should also be pointed out that Colossians and Ephesians are already moving in this universalist tradition.
100. Starr (1987, p. 219) remarks, "readers had no guarantee that a work was even *by* its putative author." Forgeries were common.

Quintilian in the introduction to his *Institutes* notes that he is desirous to bring out his book "because two books on the art of rhetoric are at present circulating under my name, although never published by me or composed for such a purpose" (*Inst.* 1.7). Both were written from notes students had taken of lectures.

101. Schröter (2006, pp. 120–22) argues that canonization does not "fix" the tradition, but acknowledges the continuity of tradition with the canon of faith. His arguments are suggestive in the matter of breaking up the canon's fixity.

102. "Our preliminary conclusion is thus that Athanasius' list became a kind of table of contents possibly by the eleventh century or at least the twelfth century, but apparently did not become at all widespread until the thirteenth . . . Even then, the Athanasian sequence had not become fixed" (Schmidt 2002, p. 478).

WORKS CONSULTED

Abramson, Marrianne B., and Stephen D. Goldinger. 1997. What the Reader's Eye Tells the Mind's Ear: Silent Reading Activates Inner Speech. *Perception & Psychophysics* 59:1059–1068.

Achtemeier, Paul J. 1990. Omne Verbum Sonat. *Journal of Biblical Literature* 109:3–27.

Aland, Kurt, and Barbara Aland. 1987. *The Text of the New Testament, An Introduction to the Critical Editions and to the Theory and Practice of Modern Textual Criticism*. Translated by E. F. Rhodes. Grand Rapids: Eerdmans.

Avrin, L. 1991. *Scribes, Script and Books. The Book Arts from Antiquity to the Renaissance*. Chicago.

Bagnall, Roger S. 1995. *Reading Papyri, Writing Ancient History*. Edited by R. Stoneman, *Approaching the Ancient World*. London: Routledge.

Balogh, Josef. 1926. "Voces Paginarum": Beiträge zur Geschichte des lauten Lesens und Schriebens. *Philologus* 82.

Beck, Frederick A. G. 1975. *Album of Greek Education: The Greeks at School and Play*. Sydney: Cheiron Press.

Benediktson, D. Thomas. 2006. The First Silent Reader of Latin Literature. *Classical World* 100:43–44.

Blanck, Horst. 1992. *Das Buch in der Antike*, Beck's Archaeologische Bibliothek. München: C. H. Beck Verlag.

Botha, P. J. J. 1992. Greco-Roman Literacy as Setting for New Testament Writings. *Neotestamentica* 26:195–215.

Bowman, Alan K. 1991. Literacy in the Roman Empire: Mass and Mode. In *Literacy in the Roman World*, edited by J. H. Humphrey.

Ann Arbor: Journal of Roman Archaeology.

———. 1994. The Roman Imperial Army: Letters and Literacy on the Northern Frontier. In *Literacy and Power in the Ancient World*, edited by A. K. Bowman and G. Woolf. Cambridge.

Bowman, Alan K., and Greg Woolf, eds. 1994. *Literacy and Power in the Ancient World*. Cambridge: University Press.

Broshi, Magen. 2000. Scriptorium. In *Encyclopedia of the Dead Sea* Scrolls, edited by L. H. Schiffman and J. C. VanderKam. Oxford: Oxford University Press.

Brunt, P. A., and J. M. Moore, eds. 1967. *Res Gestae Divi Augusti*. Oxford: Oxford University Press.

Budiansky, Stephen. 2006. *Her Majesty's Spymaster*. New York: Penguin.

Burnyeat, M.F. 1997. Postscript on Silent Reading. *Classical Quarterly* 47:74–76.

Camp, John M. 2001. *The Archaeology of Athens*. New Haven: Yale University Press.

Caro, Stefano de. 1996. *National Archaeological Museum of Naples*. Translated by M. Weir and F. Poole. Naples: Electa Napoli.

Carruthers, Mary J. 1990. *The Book of Memory, Cambridge Studies in Medieval Literature*. Cambridge and NY: Cambridge University Press.

Černý, Jaroslav. 1952. *Paper and Books in Ancient Egypt*. London.

Clark, W.P. 1930–31. Ancient Reading. *Classical Journal* 26:698–700.

Cockle, Water E. H. 1996. Ostraca. In *Oxford Classical Dictionary*, edited by H. S. and A. Spawforth. Oxford: Oxford University Press.

Cranfield, C.E.B. 1975–79. *The Letter of Paul to the Romans. Commentary on the Epistle to the Romans*. 2 vols. Edinburgh: T&T Clark.

Cribiore, Raffaella. 1996. *Writing, Teachers, and Students in Graeco-Roman Egypt*, American Studies in Papyrology. Atlanta: Scholars Press.

Derrenbacker, R. A. 2005. *Ancient Compositional Practices and the Synoptic Problem*. Leuven: University Press.

Farmer, William R., and et. al. 1990. Narrative outline of the Markan Composition According to the Two Gospel Hypothesis. In *SBL 1990 Seminar Papers*, edited by D. J. Lull. Atlanta: Scholars Press.

Fischer, Steven Roger. 2001. *A History of Writing*. Edited by J. Black, Globalities. London: Reaktion Books.

———. 2003. *A History of Reading*. Edited by J. Black, Globalities. London: Reaktion Books.

Franklin, James L, Jr. 1991. Literacy and the Parietal Inscriptions of Pompeii. In *Literacy in the Roman World*, edited by J. H. Humphrey. Ann Arbor.

Funk, Robert W. 1967. The Apostolic *Parousia*: Form and Significance. In *Christian History and Interpretation: Studies Presented to John Knox*, edited by W. R. Farmer, C. F. D. Moule and R. R. Niebuhr. Cambridge: University Press.

Gamble, Harry Y. 1985. *The New Testament Canon, Its Making and Meaning, Guides to Biblical Scholarship*. Philadelphia: Fortress Press.

———. 1995. *Books and Readers in the Early Church: A History of Early Christian Texts*. New Haven: Yale University Press.

———. 2002. The New Testament Canon: Recent Research and the Status Quaestionis. In *The Canon Debate*, edited by L. M. McDonald and J. A. Sanders. Peabody: Hendrickson.

Garber, Marjorie. 2004. *Shakespeare After All*. New York: Anchor Books.

Gavrilon, A.K. 1997. Reading Techniques in Classical Antiquity. *Classical Quarterly* 47:56–73.

Gilliard, Frank D. 1993. More Silent Reading in Antiquity: *Non Omne Verbum Sonabat*. *Journal of Biblical Literature* 112:689–96.

Goodspeed, Edgar J. 1933. *The Meaning of Ephesians*. Chicago: University of Chicago.

Haas, Christina. 1996. *Writing Technology: Studies in the Materiality of Literature*. Mahwah, NJ.

Hadas, Moses. 1961, c1954. *Ancilla to Classical Reading*. New York: Columbia University Press.

Hanson, Ann Ellis. 1991. Ancient Illiteracy. In *Literacy in the Roman World*, edited by J. Humphrey. Ann Arbor, MI.

Harris, William V. 1989. *Ancient Literacy*. Cambridge: Harvard University Press.

Hendrickson, G.L. 1929. Ancient Reading. *Classical Journal* 25:192–96.

Hezser, Catherine. 2001. *Jewish Literacy in Roman Palestine, Texte und Studien Zum Antken Judentum 81*. Tübingen: J.C.B. Mohr [Paul Siebeck].

Humphrey, J., ed. 1991. *Literacy in the Roman World, Journal of Roman Archaeology, supplement 3*. Ann Arbor, MI.

Johnson, Richard R. 1970. Ancient and Medieval Accounts of the 'Invention' of Parchment. *California Studies in Classical Antiquity* 3:115–22.

Johnson, William A. 2000. Toward a Sociology of Reading in Classical Antiquity. *American Journal of Philology* 121 (4):593–626.

Kaster, Robert A. 1988. *The Guardians of Language: The Grammarian and Society in Late Antiquity*. Berkeley: University of California.

Kenney, E. J. 1982. Books and Readers in the Roman World, II Latin Literature. In *Cambridge History of Classical Literature*, edited by E. J. Kenney and W. V. Clausen. Cambridge: Cambridge University Press.

Kirk, G. S. 1990. *The Iliad: A Commentary, books 5–8*. Vol. 2. Cambridge: Cambridge University Press.

Knox, B.M.W. 1985. Books and Readers in the Greek World, 1 From the Beginnings to Alexandria. In *The Cambridge History of Classical Literature, I Greek Literature,* edited by P. E. Easterling and B. M. W. Knox. Cambridge: Cambridge University Press.

Knox, Bernard M. W. 1968. Silent Reading in Antiquity. *Greek, Roman, and Byzantine Studies* 9:421–35.

Lattimore, Richmond. 1951. *Iliad of Homer*. Translated by R. Lattimore. Chicago: University of Chicago Press.

Lentz, Tony. 1989. *Orality and Literacy in Hellenic Greece*. Carbondale, IL: Southern Illinois University Press.

Lévi-Strauss, Claude. Reprinted 1992. *Tristes Tropiques*. Translated by J. Weightman and D. Weightman. New York: Penguin.

Lewis, Charlton, T., and Charles Short, eds. 1879. *A Latin Dictionary*. Oxford: Clarendon Press.

Lewis, Naphtali. 1974. *Papyrus in Classical Antiquity*. Oxford: Clarendon.

———. 1989. *Papyrus in Classical Antiquity: A Supplement*. Vol. 23, *Papyrologica Bruxellensia*. Brussels: Foundation Egyptologique Reine Elisabeth.

Mack, Burton L. 1988. *A Myth of Innocence, Mark and Christian Origins*. Philadelphia: Fortress Press.

Maehler, Herwig. 1996. Books, Greek and Latin. In *The Oxford Classical Dictionary*, edited by S. Hornblower and A. Spawforth. Oxford: Oxford University Press.

McNicol, A.J., D.L. Dungan, and D.B. Peabody, eds. 1996. *Beyond the Q Impasse: Luke's Use of Matthew. A Demonstration by the Research Team of the International Institute for Gospel Studies*. Valley Forge, PA: Trinity Press International.

Meier, John P. 1991. *A Marginal Jew: Rethinking the Historical Jesus, The Anchor Bible Reference Library*. Garden City: Doubleday.

Metzger, Bruce M. 1968. *Historical and Literary Studies. Pagan, Jewish, and Christian*. Grand Rapids: Eerdmans.

Parássaglou, G. M. 1979. ΔΕΞΙΑ ΧΕΙΡ ΚΑΙ ΓΟΝΥ: Some Thoughts on the Postures of the Ancient Greeks and Romans When Writing on Papyrus Rolls. *Sprittura e Civiltà* 3:5–22.

Parsons, Peter J. 1980–81. Background: The Papyrus Letter. *Didactica Classica Gandensia* 20–21:3–19.

Pleket, Henre Willy. 1996. Epigraphy, Greek. In *Oxford Classical Dictionary*, edited by S. Hornblower and A. Spawforth. Oxford: Oxford University Press.

Quinn, Kenneth. 1982. The Poet and His Audience in the Augustan Age. *Aufstieg und Niedergang der römischen Welt II* 30.1:75–180.

Richards, E. Randolph. 1991. *The Secretary in the Letters of Paul*. Edited by M. Hengel and O. Hofius, *Wissenschaftliche Untersuchungen zum Neuen Testament*. Tübingen: J.C.B. Mohr (Paul Siebeck).

———. 2004. *Paul and First-Century Letter Writing:Secretaries, Composition, and Collection*. Downers Grove, Ill: InterVarsity Press.

Richter, G.M.A. 1966. *The Furniture of the Greeks, Etruscans and Romans*. 2nd ed. London.

Roberts, C.H., and T.C. Skeat. 1987. *The Birth of the Codex*. London: Oxford University Press.

Roller, Otto. 1933. *Das Formular der paulinischen Briefe; ein Beitrag sur Lehre von antiken Briefe, Beiträge zur wissenschaft vom Alten und Neuen Testament*. Stuttgart: W. Kohlhammer.

Saenger, Paul. 1982. Silent Reading: Its Impact on Late Medieval Script and Society. *Viator* 13:367–414.

———. 1997. *Space Between Words: The Origins of Silent Reading, Figurae, Reading Medieval Culture*. Stanford: Stanford University Press.

Schmidt, Daryl. 2002. The Greek New Testament as a Codex. In *The Canon Debate*, edited by L. M. McDonald and J. A. Sanders. Peabody: Hendrickson.

Schröter, Jens. 2006. Jesus and the Canon: The Early Jesus Traditions in the Context of the Origins of the New Testament Canon. In *Performing the Gospel: Orality, Memory, and Mark*, edited by R. A. Horsley, J. A. Draper and J. M. Foley. Minneapolis: Fortress Press.

Skeat, T.C. 1956. The Use of Dictation in Ancient Book-Production. *Proceedings of the British Academy* 41:179–208.

———. 1979. Especially the Parchments: A Note on 2 Timothy IV.14. *Journal of Theological Studies* 30:172–77.

Small, Jocelen Penny. 1997. *Wax Tablets of the Mind. Cognitive Studies of Memory and Literacy in Classical Anitiquity*. London and New York: Routledge.

Snyder, Gregory H. 2000. *Teachers and Texts in the Ancient World, Religion in the First Christian Centuries*. London and New York: Routledge.

Stanford, W. B. 1967. *The Sound of Greek; Studies in the Greek Theory and Practice of Euphony*. Berkeley, CA.

Starr, Raymond J. 1987. The Circulation of Literary Texts in the Roman World. *Classical Quarterly* 37:213–23.

———. 1991. Reading Aloud: *Lectores* and Roman Reading. *Classical Journal* 86:337–343.

Svenbro, J. 1993. *Phrasikleia: An Anthropology of Reading in Ancient Greece*. Ithaca: Cornell University Press.

Taylor, Vincent. 1966. *The Gospel According to Mark*. 2nd ed. London: Macmillan.

Thomas, Rosalind. 1994. Literacy and the City-State in Archaic and Classical Greece. In *Literacy and Power in the Ancient World*, edited by A. K. Bowman and G. Woolf. Cambridge: Cambridge University Press.

Turner, E. G. 1968. *Greek Papyri. An Introduction*. Princeton, NJ: Princeton University Press.

Turner, Eric G. 1987. *Greek Manuscripts of the Ancient World*. 2nd, revised and enlarged by P. J. Parsons, Institute of Classical Studies. London: University of London.

White, John L. 1986. *Light from Ancient Letters*. Edited by R. W. Funk, *Foundations and Facets*. Philadelphia: Fortress Press.

Chapter 2

The Woven Composition

WHAT DO MANUSCRIPTS TELL US ABOUT COMPOSITION?

Artifacts from the Greco-Roman period show that writing was a laborious process that produced fairly inaccessible documents that were difficult to consult. Not only were papyrus rolls relatively expensive, but their length made them unwieldy and they were susceptible to rot, fraying, and tearing. Tablets were clumsy by virtue of their weight and leather thong bindings, and were small by comparison to rolls, so their content was more limited in scope. Consulting rolls or tablets presented additional challenges because they contained no apparatus to orient a reader. Writing was not divided into chapters, paragraphs, sentences, or words, nor were guidewords or titles provided to enable a reader to find his or her place. Worse yet, perhaps, papyrus rolls lacked page numbers because they had no pages, and even codices, which had pages, lacked pagination. Another difficulty was that since spacing for handwritten material is variable, multiple copies of the same manuscript made column or page breaks in different places, and page boundaries were not standardized. Therefore, since their elements could not be indexed with page numbers, most books lacked tables of contents, and when tables of contents did exist, they consisted of topical lists with no means of referencing the specific place in a manuscript where each topic appeared (Small 1997, pp. 11–19). When books on papyrus rolls carried titles, the titles typically appeared on external tags and at the ends of manuscripts rather than at their beginnings (Small 1997, p. 34). Clearly, anyone needing to look up a bit of information in handwritten manuscripts would need to know ahead of time where to look.[1]

The case for inaccessibility becomes even more convincing upon examination of how book collections were stored. Physical arrangements in libraries were less conducive to reading than to gathering, speaking, and conversing. Hadrian's library in Athens, for example, was arranged as a large peristyle court. It measured 90 by 125 meters and featured a central open-air courtyard with a shallow reflection pool. Reading and discussion likely took place there. The building complex contained a few small lecture and administrations rooms and one large room for the library's scrolls. Camp observes, "Only a small portion of the building was actually given over to books" (2001, p. 203).

Papyrus rolls were typically stored in clay or stone jars where they could neither be seen nor easily reached. Such jars seldom contained labels (Small 1997, p. 49), and collections of jars and manuscripts were often uncatalogued. Even in libraries that employed catalogues, for example the great library in Alexandria, the catalog consisted of papyrus rolls containing incomplete shelf lists arranged like the table of contents of a book, but with no spaces between words or any guides to a book's location. Finally, neither rolls nor tablets were arranged on desks or tables where they could be studied in a sustained way and collated with other manuscripts for comparison. Manuscripts were certainly consulted and read, although not with the frequency or for the purposes modern readers imagine. Readers were obliged to employ other methods of orientation to their written materials.

MANUSCRIPTS, ORALITY AND LITERACY

The difference between the role of literature in contemporary culture and the Greco-Roman world is vast and fundamental. This critical difference is obscured by our notions of orality and literacy, terms that are usually employed to distinguish those who can read and write fluently from those who cannot. Recently and in response to studies of contemporary oral cultures, scholars have developed a new appreciation of formal rhetoric in Greece and Rome. A growing scholarly awareness has acknowledged that reading aloud was typical in the ancient world. Many have emphasized the importance of speaking as a primary form of persuasion, the dynamics of auditory reception, and the importance of spoken performance in antiquity.

Recent discussions of the importance of speech in the ancient world have frequently and improperly applied the rubric of "orality" to such performance contexts, construing "orality" merely as speaking and listening. Use of "orality" in this sense fails to acknowledge the pervasive use of literature and documentary support for oral performance. Correlatively, people in the Greco-Roman world who exhibited familiarity with literature are too often thought to be "literate," when in fact many such scholars could not read or write. Their knowledge derived from remembered versions of oral performances. Frequently, such ancient scholars could compose literary works while lacking the technical skill to create manuscripts.

Western cultures from classical Greece through the Renaissance were literate cultures, but they depended on speech, auditory reception, and memory. In the Greco-Roman world, in which literacy rates never exceeded 10–15%, written materials were pervasive and effective, even among those who could not read them. For example, viewers of inscriptions were susceptible to imperial intent and illiterate merchants frequently retained written bills of sale. Similarly, much literature in the Greco-Roman world was composed by authors who lacked the scribal skill to write down their compositions. Many who could not read Greek or Latin script—and were therefore illiterate in the modern sense—were nevertheless thoroughly familiar with a wide range of literature and could quote Homer, Herodotus, Virgil and Cicero at length from memory. Many knew works of literature by hearing them read aloud without ever being able to decode the graphemes that stored these compositions on papyrus or in wax. Such reading and writing skills as individuals possessed might be only narrowly applied. "Writing" properly describes quite diverse activities: scraping letters in wax, signing one's name on an ostrakon, composing a literary work, and copying a manuscript by dictation or from an exemplar that had been inscribed by another. One might sign or even copy documents for pay, yet possess little ability to read what one wrote. Or perhaps one could read but could not write in a rapid or fluent hand.

Thus "orality" and "literacy" not only fail to specify precisely which skills are used in a society, they focus attention in the wrong place. As Carruthers has shown, the salient difference between modern and ancient culture lies not in the ability to use written materials, but rather in methods of information storage and retrieval (1990, p. 10). Whereas we rely primarily on documents, in antiquity information was stored primarily in memory. To use Carruthers' term, ours is not only a literate culture, but a documentary culture (1990, p. 8). Individuals transmit knowledge by capturing ideas in written form. We use documents to store and retrieve information. When we need to use the information that documents contain, we search those documents, either by reading or by visual or electronic scanning, and then collate relevant materials as resources to create new documents. Typically, we communicate our findings in documentary form. Whether communicating in writing or through speech, we refer to documents for support. The documented work is the authority for what we know. If we want to prove something, we look it up in authoritative sources. To advance new proposals, we furnish authoritative documentation for our theories. Not only do individuals search documentary resources and craft new documents privately, but documents that advance knowledge must be "original," meaning they do not duplicate other written documents or represent as one's own work that is contained in other documents. Knowledge, therefore, is something individuals possess; it is private and personal.

In the Greco-Roman world, knowledge was public and communal, the community's shared resource. Following Carruthers' nomenclature, the Greco-Roman world was not a documentary culture: even though it produced written documents, it was a memorial culture (1990, p. 9). Information was not stored primarily in documentary form but within a community's shared memory. Documents served as secondary references rather than as sources of information storage. They reminded people of what they had already committed to memory. Documents helped readers to store information in memory and retrieve it. When information recorded in a document was consulted, it was typically scanned in its remembered form, not in its documentary form. Carruthers explains that reading served primarily as a memorial process:

> [T]he idea that language, as a *sign* of something else, is always at a remove from reality is one of the cornerstones of ancient rhetoric. This idea gives to both books and language a subsidiary and derivative cultural role with respect to *memoria,* for they have no meaning except in relation to it. A work is not truly read until one has made it a part of oneself—that process constitutes a necessary stage of its "textualization." Merely running one's eyes over the written pages is not reading at all, for the writing must be transferred into memory from graphemes on parchment or papyrus or paper to images written in one's brain by emotion and sense. . . . "Memoria" refers not to how something is communicated, but to what happens once one has received it, to the interactive process of familiarizing—or textualizing—which occurs between oneself and others' words in memory (1990, pp. 10, 13).

Originality was not sought in antiquity because an original formulation could not have been comprehended or understood in the public arena. Pseudonymous attribution was common, accepted, and considered an honor. Writers attributed new formulations to acknowledged authorities who had earned the community's trust. Although documents helped to store and support what the community knew and valued, documents were not the repositories of authority. The community vested authority in those who articulated their shared values by applying them to each new social situation or occasion. Seen not as individual geniuses but as the community's voices, authors and not documents held authority. Their wisdom was stored in the treasure chests of memory.

MEMORY AS INFORMATION STORAGE AND RETRIEVAL

The ancient *ars memoriae* were designed to make accessible the creative work of a literate society. The tremendous amount of attention devoted to the arts of memory by Aristotle, Cicero, the author of *Rhetorica ad Herennium*[2], and Quintilian (35–100 CE) attest to their importance in classical education. The memory arts were employed to improve on the workings of natural memory.[3] *Rhetorica ad Herennium* explains this relationship.

> There are, then, two kinds of memory: one natural, and the other the product of art. The natural memory is that memory which is imbedded in our minds, born simultaneously with thought. The artificial memory is that memory which is strengthened by a kind of training and system of discipline. But just as in everything else the merit of natural excellence often rivals acquired learning, and art, in its turn, reinforces and develops the natural advantages, so does it happen in this instance. The natural memory, if a person is endowed with an exceptional one, is often like this artificial memory, and this artificial memory, in its turn, retains and develops the natural advantages by a method of discipline. This natural memory must be strengthened by discipline so as to become exceptional, and, on the other hand, this memory provided by discipline requires natural ability (3.16).

Training the memory was essential in literate society and was an important function of literacy. Indeed, the arts of memory remained fundamental to formal education in the West in a continuous tradition until the eighteenth century CE (Carruthers 1990, p. 11).[4] Their persistence indicates their utility and power.

The wax tablet and the storage chest furnish the dominant metaphors for memory in the ancient world. Although apparently unrelated, these images depict the mental processes for information storage and retrieval. Wax tablets represent the process by which sensory data are impressed upon the mind for storage. The treasure chest, with its orderly, internal compartments, represents the store of such images available for retrieval from memory.

Treatises on memory in antiquity from Plato and Aristotle through Cicero, *Rhetorica ad Herennium*, and Quintilian universally envision the recording of sensory experience on the mind as the impression a seal makes on wax. Plato proposes that our souls contain a block of wax (differing in type and quality according to the person), which

> . . . is the gift of Memory, the mother of the Muses, and that whenever we wish to remember anything we see or hear or think of in our own minds, we hold this wax under the perceptions and thoughts and imprint them upon it, just as we make impressions from seal rings; and whatever is imprinted we remember and know as long as its image lasts, but whatever is rubbed out or cannot be imprinted we forget and do not know (*Tht.* 191c–d).

The description of images stored in memory as likenesses made with signet rings also occurs in Aristotle:

> [T]he [sensory] stimulus produced [through normal experience] impresses a sort of likeness of the percept, just as when men seal with signet rings. Hence in some people, through disability or age, memory does not occur even under a strong stimulus, as though the stimulus or seal were applied to running water; while in others owing to detrition like that of old walls in buildings, or to the hardness of the receiving surface, the impression does not penetrate. For this reason the very young and the old have poor memories; they are in a state of flux, the young because of their growth, the old because of their decay. For a similar reason neither the very quick nor the very slow appear to have good memories; for the former are moister than they should be, and the latter harder; with the former the picture does not remain in the soul, with the latter it makes no impression (*Mem.* 450a).

Although as Yates (1966, p. 36) points out the metaphor functions differently for Plato and Aristotle in their theories of knowledge, it nevertheless expresses a common notion that a person is shaped and changed by experience, and that knowledge thus impressed upon the mind is subsequently available for recall. Quintilian (*Inst.* 11.2.4) reports the prevalence of the understanding of memory as wax: "[M]any hold the view that certain impressions are made upon the mind, analogous to those which a signet-ring makes on wax." Cicero employs the metaphor of the wax tablet:

> [P]ersons desiring to train this faculty [memory] must select localities (*locos*) and form mental images of the facts they wish to remember and store those images in the localities, with the result that the arrangement and the images of the facts will designate the facts themselves, and we shall employ the localities and images respectively as a wax writing tablet and the letters written on it (*De. or.* 2.86.354).

Rhetorica ad Herennium emphasizes the role of speaking in its wax tablet analogy:

> Those who know the letters of the alphabet can thereby write out what is dictated to them and read aloud what they have written. Likewise,

> those who have learned mnemonics can set in (places) (*loci*) what they have heard, and from these (places) deliver it by memory. For the (places) are very much like wax tablets or papyrus, the images like the letters, the arrangement and disposition of the images like the script, and the delivery is like the reading (3.17).[5]

This passage illustrates the aptness of the wax tablet as an image for information storage and its interconnectedness with reading, writing, and the sounded quality of speech. Two important features of this passage require emphasis. First, inscribing letters on wax tablets functions in antiquity as an obvious analog to storing sensory experience in the mind. Viewed from a modern perspective, it is noteworthy that ancient reflections on memory do not clearly distinguish the processes of writing on some material substance from imprints made on the wax tablets of the mind. Carruthers explains:

> [N]one of the texts I have encountered makes the slightest distinction in kind between writing on the memory and writing on some other surface. . . . All these early writers are agreed that writing on the memory is the only writing truly valuable for one's education, literary style, reasoning ability, moral judgment, and (later) salvation, for in memorizing one writes upon a surface one has always with one. And the corollary assumption is that what one writes on the memory can be at least as orderly and accessible to thought as what is written upon a surface such as wax or parchment (1990, p. 30).

Carruthers' observations suggest the second point of emphasis in the passage quoted above from *Rhetorica ad Herennium*. Information inscribed on the wax tablets of the mind is readily accessible by means of recollection through various "heuristic schemes," to borrow Carruthers' phrase (1990, pp. 20–21). Knowledge imprinted in memory was retrieved like valuable material brought out of a storage room, strongbox, treasure chest, or other storage container by means of a systematic internal organizational scheme, such as that found in a dovecote or beehive. Plato describes treasuring up (θησαυριζόμενος) reminders for later recall. He imagines the memorial storehouse as a dovecote with its pigeon holes, and recall as a seizing or hunt (ὑπολαμβάνω), as one would hunt birds (*Tht.* (197c–198a). For Aristotle, recollection "is a kind of pursuit" (ζήτησίς τις) (*Mem.* 453a). *Rhetorica ad Herennium* refers to the treasure-house (*thesaurum*) of ideas of which Memory is guardian (3.15.28). Cicero explains the utility of the architectural mnemonic with its divided spaces as an abode (*sede*) for stored visual images (*De or.* 2.357–58). Quintilian affirms the saying: "memory is the treasure-house (*thesaurus*) of eloquence" (*Inst.*

11.2.1). He draws an analogy between trained memory with its various stored impressions, and a beehive full of honey gathered from a variety of flowers (*Inst.* 1.10.7). Retrieval of material stored in a mental treasure chest (θησαύρος) was made possible through memory that had been trained to store information in an organized fashion and retrieve it completely and creatively on demand. Bolzoni summarizes the impact of metaphors for memory:

> Writing thus projects on the mind its model founded on space: the mind, and memory in particular, appears precisely as a space divided into places, where perceptible images are deposited that may be preserved or may vanish. This gives rise to metaphors destined for centuries of usage, describing memory as the wardrobe or treasure chest of our consciousness, the storehouse of our recollections (1991, p. 19).

The demand in a rhetorical culture for a system of storage and retrieval—one sufficiently complex to manage vast amounts of material and sufficiently sophisticated to enable random access and reliable recall for an oral performance—accounts for the importance of the memory schemes developed in antiquity. Carruthers isolates the crucial elements of mnemonic protocols:

> The fundamental principle is to "divide" the material to be remembered into pieces short enough to be recalled in single units and to key these into some sort of rigid, easily reconstructable order. This provides one with a "random-access" memory system, by means of which one can immediately and securely find a particular bit of information, rather than having to start from the beginning each time in order laboriously to reconstruct the whole system, or—worse—relying on simple chance to fish what one wants out from the murky pool of one's undifferentiated and disorganized memory (1990, p.7).

All the elements outlined above were recognized by teachers of Hellenistic and Roman rhetoric,[6] and each element's function was seen to play a critical role in successful remembering. One must separate information into manageable bits, associate each bit with a vivid and clear mnemonic tag, and store bits of information into distinct compartments made accessible by means of their ordered arrangement. The architectural mnemonic schemes articulated by Cicero, Quintilian, and the author of *Rhetorica ad Herennium* laid the foundation for the arts of memory in Western education precisely because they met these requirements so well (*Rhet. Her.* 3.15.29–34; Cic. *De Or.* 2.87.355–58; Quint. *Inst.* 11.2.17–22).[7] Architectural frames provided the empty, ordered compartments for information to be stored.

Information was divided into distinct units, each of which was represented to the memory in vivid images designed to evoke the sequential points of an argument or a list of persons or events. Images should be unusual, misplaced, comic, or grotesque to facilitate recall. Images representing the discrete bits of information to be stored were associated by means of homophony, pun, or pictorial representation. One with a well-trained memory situated images sequentially in dedicated spaces in the architectural framework and then recalled the images by moving through the arranged space in the imagination, viewing each space and its associated image in turn. This architectural framework provided a heuristic scheme that made possible the sequential recall of images in the order in which they were placed or in reverse order, beginning with any of the images so situated. Orderly sequence enabled accurate recall because, as Quintilian explains,

> [H]owever large the number of these [details to be recalled] which it is required to remember, all are linked to one another like dancers hand in hand, and there can be no mistake since they join what precedes to what follows, no trouble being required except the preliminary labor of committing the various points to memory (*Inst*. 11.2.20).

Architectural schemes made possible the creation of a memorial storehouse that enabled random access and recall for all material placed in its orderly framework.

As such schemes were built up over time with input from a variety of sources, the storehouse grew and became a precious repository of information available for rhetorical invention. Access and later creative use of information written on the wax tablets of the mind and stored in memory would not have been possible unless both the scheme of compartmentalization and the information stored were recognizable to a public audience in a rhetorical arena. Quintilian declares,

> [I]t is memory which has brought oratory to its present position of glory. For it provides the orator not merely with the order of his thoughts, but even of his words, nor is its power limited to stringing merely a few words together; its capacity for endurance is inexhaustible, and even in the longest pleadings the patience of the audience flags long before the memory of the speaker (*Inst* 11.2.7–8).

This is why training the memory comprised one of the five parts of rhetoric.[8] Rhetorical training emphasized fluency with common places (τόποι, *loci*), the locations in which information was stored for recall. In a rhetorical culture, these places or topics provided a shared grammar for public discourse. They were valued for their shared significance and common understanding within a community. Common places were common because they contained what the community agreed was needed for its social support. The memorial common places provided a meeting ground for author and audience to apply shared values to particular occasions and situations. They supplied a common, public meeting place for rhetor and audience. Like a seal in wax, reading made an impression. Its stamp shaped the person and formed character. The word character (χαρακτήρ) applied equally to an engraver's impression, the distinctive results of stamping ethical impressions on a person, and literary style. Works of verbal art created community, advanced its aims and reaffirmed its norms using shared bins (τόποι, *loci*) of knowledge.

READING AND WRITING SUPPORTED MEMORY

In the Greco-Roman world, reading and writing supported the primary memorial processes that made life possible in a rhetorical culture. Apprehending literary compositions by decoding a manuscript's graphemes, taking dictation, or attending an oral performance furnished information to be collected, organized, and preserved in memory's storehouse. Taking in a composition meant fully incorporating it in one's storehouse of knowledge in memory, and allowing oneself to be stamped and therefore changed by the process. This is why memory was understood to have an ethical function. It shaped the person and impressed upon each individual the demands of a society. Similarly, writing served primarily as a memorial process, supporting the memory with a medium for auxiliary storage. Writing in the sense of physically inscribing characters in wax supplied an image for the impressions made by sensory experience and also by literature on the wax tablets of the mind. Writing in our sense of composing a piece of literature involved launching some heuristic scheme to search memory's storehouse and bring out of its predetermined and distinct places (τόποι, *loci*) relevant material for creative invention and subsequent public declamation. For this reason, Seneca and others applied to reading the metaphor of a bee collecting pollen from a variety of flowers to be taken to the hive, and stored in a system of small cells, where it could be transformed into honey and its sweet taste enjoyed (Carruthers 1990, pp. 35–37 and sources cited there). Honey was a favorite Greek metaphor for pleasing (mellifluous) speech.

The literate cultures of antiquity as well as those of the European Middle Ages and Renaissance were primarily memorial cultures that met the demands of communication in public, rhetorical contexts. There endured a lively continuity of the memorial arts in Western education from the pre-Socratic philosophers through the late Renaissance, with late educational practices drawing directly on the architectural mnemonic schemes described by Cicero, *Rhetorica ad Herennium,* and Quintilian. Nevertheless, as the physical evidence shows, both the memorial arts and literature developed over time. Medieval manuscripts differ in important ways from such ancient documents as papyri of portions of the New Testament. Manuscript illumination and commentary, for example, illustrate how material collected from memory was graphically keyed and collated with related material in creative invention, resulting in a new literary composition. Similarly, the medieval embellishment of initial words with pictures in illuminated manuscripts served a mnemonic purpose. They summarized and presented visually a composition's gist to reinforce its vividness in memory.

In contrast to illuminated medieval manuscripts that also derived primarily from trained memory, the only compositional feature that was graphically recorded in Hellenistic manuscripts written in *scriptio continua* was sound. Sound furnished the means by which compositions were stored in memory and later retrieved. Sound alone –lacking any reinforcement from images or spacing—provided a composition's internal organization, without help from the graphic clues of an illuminated manuscript. Ancient listeners had to be able to divide, store, then retrieve from memory manageable bits of information apprehended through hearing. According to Kleist, "One may boldly say that all ancient composition, including the N.T., was primarily intended for the ear, rather than the eye" (1927, p. 18). Botha echoes this theme:

> Ancient communication, including reading and writing, was an oral, collective activity and not the private, silent experience that we consider it to be (such as reading books, magazines, watching TV and even listening to the radio and lectures). . . . Greco-Roman communication was connected to the physical presence of people and to living speech to an extent that is consistently underestimated today (1992, p. 207).

The compositions that comprise the New Testament, although preserved as manuscripts and then as printed documents, originated as speech. They were composed to be spoken, and for more than a millennium, speech served as their primary mode of their publication. "For most of written history, reading was speaking" (Fischer 2003, p.11). As Allison reminds us, ancient readers were in fact always listeners.[9] Achtemeier has commented about this culture of late Western antiquity:

> Such a predominantly oral environment presented a situation almost totally different from that within which we currently operate, even though they had written documents as do we. The apparent similarity has led modern scholars to overlook almost entirely how such an oral overlay would affect the way communication was carried on by means of written media (1990, p. 3).[10]

Foley has eloquently articulated the dynamic that lies at the root of the difference between reception by silent reading and oral performance. Although his studies focus on the dynamics of oral composition and not the literary processes that account for the composition of the New Testament, his observations about auditory reception remain relevant to an audience's meaning-making project. Compositions read silently convey information, whereas public, oral performances recreate the depicted events in community for performer and audience alike. Homer's prologue to the *Odyssey* (1.1–10) exemplifies the dynamic in a classic example.

> Homer acknowledges this collective environment by asking the Muse, located "somewhere" else (*hamothen*), to "speak also to us" (*eipe kai hēmin*)—not just to the poet himself, in other words, and not only to this group; the pronoun "us" and the adverb "also" bring the present audience and other poets and audiences integrally into the picture. Once again we have a portrayal of a rite of performance, a recurring and participatory experience shared by poet(s) and audience(s) as they re-create the events in question (2006, pp. 92–93).

Foley's "once again" alludes to the many examples that he adduces from cultures around the globe, across time, and in different languages. In any language, the "cooperative synergy of performance," Foley insists, is dynamic, participatory, public, and centered around speech as the medium for oral performance (2006, p. 93).

MANUSCRIPTS PRESERVE A LINEAR STREAM OF SOUND

Besides showing the technical impossibility that writing provided the primary medium for information storage in antiquity, physical evidence of writing in the Greco-Roman period also demonstrates that a manuscript's primary function was to capture and record a linear stream of sound. Manuscripts written in *scriptio continua* preserved only graphemes that captured the stream of syllables across a page (Cribiore 1996, p. 87). The Greek invention of a fully phonetic alphabet made possible a system of written marks that reduced speech to writing and preserved it for future vocalization.[11] The phonetic Greek alphabet graphically reproduced speech sounds in the same sequence with which they strike the ear.[12] As Fischer has shown, "the Greeks were the first in history to represent vocalic phonemes systematically and consistently" (2001, p. 124). The innovative improvement of the Greek alphabet on the Phoenician script from which it was derived is the addition of vowels, an invention that enabled a manuscript to capture spoken sounds and encode them in a linear sequence:

> By using consonants and vowels together in this way, they reproduced speech more faithfully than any system devised before or since. Thus the Greeks achieved the first "mapping" of a language's relevant sounds. . . . In this way, the Greeks "perfected" alphabetic writing, within given limitations (Fischer 2001, p. 124).

Saenger explains it this way:

> In the antique Mediterranean world, there existed a direct historical correlation between the achievement of unambiguous reproduction of the sounds of speech through the use of vowels and the adoption of *scriptura continua* (1991, p. 207).

The apparently (to us) retrograde phenomenon of *scriptio continua* in fact represented a momentous advance in antiquity, one made possible by the invention of a phonetic alphabet. Saenger writes,

> The uninterrupted writing of ancient *scriptio continua* was only possible in the context of a writing system that had a complete set of signs for the unambiguous transcription of pronounced speech. This occurred for the first time in Indo-European languages when the Greeks adapted the Phoenician alphabet and added symbols for vowels (1991, p. 206).

Both earlier and later than the invention of the phonetic Greek alphabet, alphabets in other languages employed word divisions. These became unnecessary in written Greek precisely because their phonetic alphabet facilitated reading aloud. Some early Greek inscriptions used interpuncts for word separation, but this practice was soon abandoned because it became unnecessary for reading comprehension. Nor can the differential development of *scriptio continua* properly be attributed to scribal ignorance of the writing conventions of different cultures. Saenger explains that bilingual documents in Latin, Greek, and Hebrew demonstrate that ancient scribes knew about different practices in other languages. In fact, Roman Latin followed their Semitic linguistic antecedents by maintaining spaces between words longer than Greek.

The use of *scriptio continua* remains connected with the phonetic Greek alphabet because of the ancient Greek practice of reading aloud.

> Precisely because those who read aloud relished the mellifluous sounds of pronounced text and were not interested in the swift intrusive consultation of books, the absence of interword space in Greek and Latin was not perceived to be an impediment to effective reading as it would be to the modern reader who strives to read swiftly (Saenger 1991, pp. 208–209).

Oralization made written compositions both comprehensible and cogent with the investment of a practical amount of time and effort; for word separation made a written document only moderately easier to decode, but vocalization made compositions eminently more memorable.[13]

> Oralization, which the ancients savored esthetically, provided mnemonic compensation through enhanced short-term recall for the difficulty in gaining access to the meaning of unseparated text. Long-term memory of frequently read-aloud texts also compensated for the inherent graphic and grammatical ambiguities of the languages of late antiquity (Saenger 1991, p. 209).

MANUSCRIPT AND COMPOSITION

The physical evidence of writing leads us to conclude that the manuscript, a literary work's written form, is not an adequate model for literary composition in the ancient world. Compositions were created through a complex, creative process in the mind of the author and stored primarily in this same mental place, with the assistance of writing. Papyrus rolls or other written materials may have supported the compositional process, but a composition was first written on the wax tablets of the mind and held in memory. In the literate culture of the Greco-Roman world, writing simply assisted memory in this process by supporting a composition's preservation through dictation, emendation, and copying. It provided an author and others something to read, making it possible to polish a work in progress and adapt it to particular situations. But the manuscript was not the composition. Written works captured only the sounds of literary compositions. The composition was a dynamic creation that lived in the public arena.

COMPOSITION AS συμπλοκή

The primary model for literary composition in the Greco-Roman world was woven fabric, an image that persists in our word "text," which comes from the Latin *texere*, to weave. The Latin usage remains consistent with the earlier Greek notion of composition as weaving (συμπλοκή), even though these terms are not morphologically related.[14] The absence of a morphological relationship between *texere* and συμπλοκή indicates the importance of the metaphorical association of weaving with verbal art. The pervasiveness of fabric production in antiquity enabled Greek and Latin independently to associate weaving and literary composition. The power and importance of woven fabric imagery is not obvious to a modern reader because we no longer experience the processes of textile production, activities that were not fully mechanized in the West until the industrial revolution. But up until that time, and therefore throughout antiquity, all fabrics—all clothing, all household fabrics, even the sails on ships—were hand woven from thread that had been spun by hand with a drop spindle. Along with food preparation, spinning and weaving were primary occupations of women and children throughout antiquity, even among the upper classes.[15] The emperor Augustus made a show of wearing homespun clothing made by his wife, daughter, and sister (Broudy 1979, p. 47).[16]

The weaving apparatus commonly used throughout the Mediterranean basin and Middle East was the large, vertical, warp-weighted loom.[17] Its use is widely attested in classical antiquity in vase paintings[18] and well established from archaeological evidence throughout the Middle East and in northern and eastern Europe from prehistoric times.[19] The warp-weighted loom stood upright at a slight incline, either leaning against a wall or free-standing in an A-frame configuration. Threads to be woven into cloth were attached at the top of the loom to the loom's crossbeam,[20] which was rotated to wind up the cloth as it was woven. Each warp thread was tied—either individually or, more often, in bundles—to a warp weight. Weights were fashioned from stone, lead, or pieces of pottery, with a hole drilled in each weight through which the warp threads were fastened.[21] The weights kept the warp threads under constant tension as the weaver worked at the loom, walking back and forth across its length. Looms, like language, produced a kind of music. Weaving made music with the tinkling warp weights as they clinked together like wind chimes while the warp was manipulated during weaving.[22]

Fabrics throughout the Roman empire were typically woven with wool.[23] As few as 10 warp threads per inch of weaving width (for heavy blankets or mats) or as many as 40 (for lighter and finer fabrics) could have been attached to the loom, depending upon the fiber available and the type of textile being woven.[24] With a thread count in this range, even a relatively narrow fabric three feet wide would require from 360—1,140 individual strands of wool yarn to be suspended from the crossbeam. Many textiles, such as those for use as robes, togas, and outer cloaks, would have been wider. Weaving required holding these warp threads straight and taut while interlacing them with an equal number of weft threads per inch running across the warp to create a balanced weave. The simplest possible interlacement is plain weave, in which the first weft thread passes over the first warp thread, under the second, over the third and so on across the entire width of the fabric. Once one weft thread was interlaced with the warp, the weaver pressed the thread into place against the header band. Each succeeding weft thread was pressed against the edge of the forming cloth, using a comb or smooth stick. In this manner, the cloth gradually grew in length from the top down, thread by thread. The intricate and laborious process of picking threads for each weft pass did not admit of error, since a mistake in the interlacement would compromise the cloth's integrity. Mechanical shedding using a shed stick and heddle rod sped the process and reduced errors but hand weaving on a warp-weighted loom remained slow and labor-intensive.

Effective management of so many fine, individual threads requires that the threads be kept under constant tension to prevent tangling and to organize them for weaving. The necessity of tension to organize the warp and weft is the common element in the various senses of συμπλοκή and accounts for the apparently strange collection of contexts in which the term συμπλοκή occurs. The term does not apply to simple juxtaposition or to mere additive processes, but only to combinations that involve close interlacement wherein the components combine under tension and are difficult to distinguish from each other. Συμπλοκή applies to combinations that create something new through effort or struggle, with various elements held under tension. All of its meanings entail some form of intertwining, complication, or combination (LSJ *s.v.* συμπλοκή). In addition to its applications to weaving and the verbal arts, the term is used to describe the struggle of wrestlers (Pl. *Lg*. 833a, Gal.15.126, 197), the close engagement of ships (Plb.1.27.12, 1.28.11), sexual intercourse (Pl. *Smp*. 191c, Arist. *HA* 540^{b}21, Corn. *ND* 24, Sor. 1.31), and the mixture of ingredients to make medicines (Sor. 1.50). These meanings all derive from the primary sense of συμπλοκή as weaving. The primary sense of the term as applied to the concrete processes of fabric production shapes its other usages.

Συμπλοκή describes the creation of Hellenistic Greek compositions on all levels of production, including the levels of grammar, syntax, and style. Plato uses συμπλοκή to describe the combination of letters to form words and of words to form statements. Teachers should instruct grammar students starting with letters the students already know. Then their task is to:

> . . . set them [the letters] beside the groups which they [the students] did not yet recognize and by comparing them to show that their nature is the same in both combinations (ταῖς συμπλοκαῖς) alike, and to continue until the letters about which their opinions are correct have been shown in juxtaposition with all those of which they are ignorant. Being shown in this way they become examples and bring it about that every letter is in all syllables always called by the same name . . . (Pl. *Plt.* 278b).

In a similar vein, Dionysius of Halicarnasus writes, "the varied effect of the syllables is produced by the interweaving of letters (τὰς τῶν γραμμάτων συμπλοκάς)" (*Comp.* 16). At the level of syntax, Plato refers to the techniques of weaving verbs and nouns together (συμπλέκων τὰ ῥήματα τοῦς ὀνόμασι) (*Soph.* 262d). Aristotle describes as συμπλοκή the combination of words to make statements (*Cat.* 1a 16) and the joining of subjects and predicates (*Top.* 112b–113a). Dionysius of Halicarnassus also refers to the combination of words as συμπλοκή:

> The most elegant writers of poetry or prose . . . both arrange their words by weaving them together with deliberate care (κατασκευά ζουσιν ὀνόματα συμπλέκοντες ἐπιτηδείως ἀλλήλους), and with elaborate artistic skill adapt the syllables and the letters to the emotions which they wish to portray (*Comp.* 15).

Dionysius applies συμπλοκή to the copula in grammar (*Dem.* 9) as well as to the interweaving of various rhetorical styles (*Rhet.* 8.8) and various rhythms (*Comp.* 18).

The compositional model articulated by Plato, Aristotle, Dionysius and others understands the construction of compositions as the interlacement of written signs with vocal sounds. The "nature" of letters to which Plato alludes and the "effects" of syllables that concern Dionysius are their sounds. Even Dionysius' use of συμπλοκή for a part of speech, as noted above, is based upon sound. He criticizes Demosthenes for using the turn of phrase, "καὶ τὸ οὐ μόνον ὑμᾶς ἀλλὰ καὶ τοὺς ἄλλους Ἕλληνας" (not only against you but against the rest of Greece), on the grounds that it makes his diction sound labored, since the statement would have been simpler if references to the two groups had been joined with a simple conjunction (*Dem.* 9). The manuscript, whose written letters encode vocal sounds, enables a reader to reconstitute the λόγος, the meaning or sense, of the interwoven nouns and verbs by pronouncing them. A composition was woven not when its words were strung together to create a written manuscript, but when its written signs were interlaced with a speaker's voice in oral performance, such as in the delivery of a public speech. The voice becomes the weft that interweaves the warp of a manuscript's written signs to form a woven verbal fabric. Thus compositions were understood as συμπλοκή, the creation of a rich fabric of beauty and meaning through the interlacement of written marks with the sound of the voice.[25] This image is fully consistent with surviving physical evidence for manuscripts, which enabled a composition's sounds to be reproduced, re-voiced, and the composition therefore recreated.

In addition to supplying a metaphor for composition, συμπλοκή and its related art of spinning provided powerful images for the organization and stabilization of society out of disparate social forces. Weaving depended upon spinning, since yarn must be spun from loose fibers before anything can be woven. Spinning employed simple tools: the fiber to be spun, a dowel or stick for a spindle shaft, and a spindle whorl to speed and stabilize the turning motion of the shaft. Greek mythology and literature is replete with images of spinning, by means of which fibers in a tangled mass are attenuated, aligned and twisted together by the whirling motion of the spindle to form a strong thread. The process of making long, strong threads by organizing short, fragile fibers from a disorganized mass and twisting them together seemed mysterious, even magical. Spinning is deified in images of Athena and Aphrodite, who are depicted as master spinners. The life span in the Greek imagination is truly something spun, as a living thread, by Κλωθώ (the Spinner), one of the Fates, until Ἄτροπος (*lit.*, No Turning) causes the spinning to stop, making the thread unravel and disintegrate as the twisting ceases. Thus death is conceived as the cessation of spinning the life thread.[26]

Woven fabric thus symbolized the often conflictual process of forming a social unit. Spinning creates uniform strands from a tangled mass of wool and weaving strictly organizes such strands running in opposing directions and held under tension. When accomplished with skill and artistry, the woven fabric performs a number of essential practical functions, exhibits beauty, and provides warmth and protection. By fully integrating disparate fibers into an integral web, the fabric becomes more than the sum of its parts. The woven fabric thus symbolized the Greek city-state and, by implication, the institution of civilized society (Scheid and Svenbro 1996, pp. 9–34). Just as spinning and weaving transform tangled wool into an integral fabric with an orderly pattern, political unity was construed as the interlacement of diverse and potentially conflicting social components that brought order by organizing everything into its proper place. These benefits were celebrated as advantages of social organization. Thus the climax of the Great Panathenaia entailed wheeling to the top of the Athenian acropolis the cult statue of Athena, wearing a newly woven πέπλος (robe) that symbolized the interlacement of the towns of Attica. For by the interweaving of disparate social constituents—which included conquered foreigners and therefore no doubt exhibited elements of tension—was created the strong, beautiful fabric that adorned the goddess and brought honor to the πόλις (city-state).

That the implications of συμπλοκή for both community and verbal art are intimately connected is precisely because of the sounded character of compositions. In oral performance, the recitation of a composition before a live audience drew the audience into the construction of the composition and created a new existential world. The act of συμπλοκή wove together both composition and community in the dynamic arena of oral performance. Carruthers explains this dynamic in her classic exploration of memory. She writes:

> It is in the institutionalizing of a story through *memoria* that textualizing occurs. Literary works become institutions as they weave a community together by providing it with a shared experience and a certain kind of language, the language of stories that can be experienced over and over again through time as occasion suggests (1990, p. 12).

The model of a composition as συμπλοκή thus coheres with an understanding of memorial culture that functions in a rhetorical environment and uses reading and writing as a support. The New Testament and all other Hellenistic Greek compositions have survived as artifacts of this lively, public context. If we are to appreciate the New Testament according to the ways in which documents were used in the Greco-Roman world, we must learn how their audiences used and understood manuscripts to construct and maintain their societies. Like the archaeological remains of an ancient city, ancient manuscripts comprise only a partial record of their dynamic performance arenas. As Foley has maintained, these written artifacts of oral performances are merely librettos; they preserve words, but the music is absent (1995, pp. 61–66). The voices of public performance linger in their written artifacts. The more fluency we develop in their medium, the more those voices remain available to us. Foley correctly prescribes that if we are to hear and comprehend those voices, "Performers and audiences need to play by the same rules"; we need to "know the code" (2002, pp. 18–20).

PROCESSING COMPOSITIONS IN TIME, NOT SPACE

Verbal art in antiquity took place in time, not space. Receivers of ancient poetry and prose were primarily listeners, not readers. Because speech provided the primary medium for communication, information was processed in aural, not visual form; it was delivered through sounds uttered in a linear stream, not by visible marks on a surface. The ability to process information in the rhetorical culture of the ancient world depended upon the ability to process sound in real time. While silent readers decode printed marks on a page, moving at a self-determined pace and re-reading at will, hearers must process speech in real time.[27] A spoken composition occurs one syllable at a time, with each syllable sounding only as the previous one is fading away. Once a composition is underway, its earlier moments cannot be retrieved, except through repeated spoken sounds that recall sounds uttered previously. Auditory reception relies on the activity of memory for the construction of meaning.

Having little or no access to scarce, expensive manuscripts and lacking the skill to decode a manuscript's written marks, ordinary people in the ancient world knew whatever they knew of Homer, Plato, and Aristotle "by heart"; they held in memory the stories and cadences remembered from repeated retellings. In the same way one enjoys music, ancient hearers had access to literary compositions one sound at a time. Like music, ancient literature became available to the general public through live performance, and sound provided its structure. Once a musical or spoken composition had been performed it was accessible only through reprisal of remembered portions.

The analogy of speech and music is not coincidental. Quintilian writes that, "the art of letters and that of music were once united," and cites anecdotes from Sophron, Aristophanes, Menander, and Cicero as evidence (*Inst.* 1.10.17–20). The approach to the alphabet as encoded sound coheres with the classical organization of academic disciplines that included the study of letters in musical education. The organization of these disciplines governed the old Athenian education that held sway until the intellectual revolution of the fifth century BCE. The study of letters and music were then separated in the formal academic curriculum (Marrou 1956, pp. 41–43, 69–72).

Music, like speech, consists of sounds that strike the ear one at a time in a linear stream but are retained in memory in groups and in meaningful form.[28] Although our auditory sense can perceive only one note or chord at a time, we comprehend musical compositions as unified wholes. A musical composition is heard as a whole rather than "as a series of events" (Lerdahl and Jackendoff 1983, p. 37). We recall intact entire melodies, sophisticated cadences, and subtle musical themes, even though we initially apprehend these complex structures one sound at a time in a linear stream. Similarly, verbal art in the rhetorical culture of the Greco-Roman world was remembered and recalled in terms of unified topics, vivid images, and complete, logical structures, even though these structures were apprehended by ear one syllable at a time. The unique dynamics of auditory reception enable us to apprehend structure through sound, and to store and recall these structures from memory.

The linear quality of auditory reception requires that a composition's organizational scheme unfold during oral performance, in the midst of the act of listening. Like music, a spoken composition must provide auditory clues at each step of the way to guide the listening process and to enable an audience to make meaning from a long sequence of sounds. Musical compositions are unified by means of such motifs as melodic theme, rhythmic pattern, or both. The famous four-note sequence from Beethoven's fifth symphony provides a familiar example of a motif: it consists of a simple rhythmic pattern of three quick notes followed by a fourth sustained note at a lower pitch. This brief, simple motif recurs countless times in various pitches and at different speeds throughout the symphony, sometimes as melody, sometimes as counterpoint. Yet this simple sequence both unites the symphony and provides great dramatic effect—nor would the symphony be improved by decreasing the frequency of its repetitions or varying it beyond recognition.[29] The initial statement of a thematic melody or rhythmic pattern can organize a composition's sounds by inviting an audience to listen for a recurring theme and to compare subsequent sounds to those of the thematic statement. In a similar way, speech must train the ear to listen for organizational clues.

With its emphasis on the construction of a composition during the process of reception, modern reception theory emphasizes reception's linear character. It regards a composition not as a static phenomenon, but as a dynamic creation of its audience. Reception theory holds that a composition encased between the covers of a book and left unread does not yet exist in any real sense. Rather, it comes to life when readers construct an artistic whole as they read word by word. The audience must experience each component of the composition sequentially and then imaginatively hold the elements together, filling in the composition's gaps and resolving its indeterminacies (Iser 1971).[30] In the dynamic process of reception, an audience creates a composition that amounts to much more than marks on a printed page.[31]

Audience-oriented criticism recognizes that written compositions prompt audience expectations, then confirm or frustrate those expectations in subsequent developments. Reception critics seek first to isolate the implied reader's response to each word in sequence and then reconstruct the reader's effort to build a consistent whole from the composition's separate words. The linear approach of modern audience-oriented criticism is in many ways appropriate for Hellenistic literature, in which authors crafted their compositions for public, oral performance with audience impact in mind. Kennedy notes that an implicit reception theory runs as a common thread through Greek reflections on literary composition, from Plato, Aristotle, and Isocrates through the rise of the formal study of rhetoric during the Roman period.[32]

Aristotle, for instance, emphasizes the rhetorical importance of an audience's disposition toward an orator (*Rh.* 2.1); and Demetrius's quotation of Theophrastus reads like a modern description of a reader's response to indeterminacy:

> You should not elaborate on everything in punctilious detail but should omit some points for the listener to infer and work out for himself. For when he infers what you have omitted, he is not just listening to you but he becomes your witness and reacts more favourably to you. For he is made aware of his own intelligence through you, who have given him the opportunity to be intelligent. To tell your listener every detail as though he were a fool seems to judge him one (*Eloc.* 222).

Modern reception theory, built on the practice of silent reading does not take adequate account of the spoken delivery and auditory reception of Hellenistic literature. Because publication takes place in live performance, an audience must process a composition as it is being performed, without the benefits of review and rereading that are available to a private, silent reader. This fundamental difference suggests that written artifacts of oral performances make meaning in different ways than modern works read silently. Written signs from antiquity signify meanings through strategies not employed in modern printed compositions intended for silent reading. The analytical methods this book proposes derive from understandings of literary composition as reflected in Hellenistic Greek grammar and literary criticism. These strategies are based on the methodological implications of the discussion above: that sound creates structure, sound trains the ear, and sound balances the importance of signifier and signified.

One obvious issue in any analysis of sound in Hellenistic Greek is its pronunciation scheme. Although Hellenistic Greek is a dead language, much can be known about its pronunciation through literary evidence and especially orthographic errors, puns, and descriptions of sounds in the natural world. The dating of the shift from a melodic accent to accentuation by stress is debated, but it certainly occurred after the fourth century BCE. In the first century BCE Dionysius of Halicarnassus provides detailed evidence of a melodic accent, to the point of measuring the tonal interval between an unaccented syllable and one with an acute accent (*Comp.* 19). Accentuation of New Testament material is uncertain (Davies 1996). Nevertheless, the primacy of speech remains.

> In the study of a "dead" language there is inevitably a main emphasis on the written word. But it is well to remember that writing is secondary to speech, and, however much it may deviate from it, has speech as its ultimate basis. . . . In ancient Greek, as in modern European languages, the correspondence is between symbols (letters) and phonological elements, and is much more regular than in some languages, such as English or French or Modern Greek . . . (Allen 1987, p. 8).

The analyses of sound set forth in this book are based on the understanding that however the sounds were pronounced, they were pronounced consistently.

Chapters 3–5 will develop a theoretical foundation for sound mapping. Chapter 3 explores the notions of γραμματική (grammar), λέχις (speech), and σύνθεσις (composition) for clues to the interpretation of compositions in the Greco-Roman world. Chapter 4 explains how sound in spoken literature builds structure that is received and comprehended in time, not space. It outlines the functions of repetition, sound's primary structuring device. Chapter 5 explains how to develop a sound map based on analytical strategies that comport with the linear, auditory mode of reception that prevailed in the Greco-Roman world.

We cannot, of course, resurrect the original performances of ancient literary compositions. Many aspects of such performances are lost to us: their ancient settings and the scenery surrounding their performances, the gestures and facial expressions of the performers, the precise pronunciation of a language now dead. But to the extent that written language encodes sound, essential aspects of ancient performances survive in the written artifacts of those performances. The printed versions of our sacred scriptures preserve a silent composition and an interpreted composition. This printed version contains only whispers from the past: echoes from the amphitheater, strains from the marketplace, murmurs from the household hearth. Like fossilized bones, our printed Bibles preserve only fragments of ancient, living things: real people speaking real words in a lively arena of public discourse. Printed versions of ancient compositions, while problematic, nevertheless transmit the sounds that once organized performances into meaningful parts, created thematic refrains, echoed familiar speech conventions, and spotlighted scenes for heightened attention. Sound mapping and analysis seek to restore the audible quality of speech to the συμπλοκή of ancient Greek compositions. With an appreciation of their character as sound comes fresh insight about their meaning.

ENDNOTES

1. This is true for the codex as well as for the papyrus roll. "With the exception of the possibility of placing bookmarks between the leaves of a codex, features that might have provided ease of reference were as rare in the codex as in the roll" (Gamble 1995, p. 56).
2. Although traditionally attributed to Cicero, dating and authorship are uncertain but a first century date seems reasonable, since the work seems to draw from the same source as Cicero's *De inventione*, written about this time. (Caplan and Winterbottom 1996, pp. 1314–15).
3. Quintilian (*Inst.* 10.2.6) attributes natural memory even to animals. Most classical commentators remark on the difference between the two kinds of memory and the need to develop the one on the foundation of the other. See, for example, Quint. *Inst.* 11.1.93 and Cic. *De or.* 2.88.360.
4. This important study provides a comprehensive and definitive study of the *ars memoriae*, originating in antiquity and persisting through the Middle Ages.
5. Harry Caplan's translation in the LCL has "backgrounds" for *loci*. The more literal translation, "places," is reflected above, since it more clearly indicates the memorial function being described.
6. They are also confirmed scientifically by the neuropsychology of memory (Carruthers 1990, pp. 46–79). See also Small (1997, pp.101–5) for an analysis of modern memory feats as reported by Luria, and neuropsychological evidence on mental imagery (pp. 105–9). The art of memory became established in formal rhetoric in the Hellenistic period and drew on mnemonic schemes in

Plato and Aristotle and attributed to Simonides as its inventor. See Yates (1966, p. 27 n. 2 and 28), for the broad attestation of Simonides as the inventor of mnemotechnics.

7. Cicero and Quintilian attribute the invention of the memorial arts to Simonides of Ceos (*De Or.* 2.86.351–54; *Inst.* 11.2.11–16).
8. The five are invention, arrangement, style, memory, and delivery (*inventionem, dispositionem, elocutionem, memoriam, pronuntiationem*). *Rhet. Her.* 1.2.3.
9. Allison elaborates, "Those who habitually listen to music over the radio can often identify a popular song after hearing just the smallest portion of it. There are in fact contests—I have heard them—which require people to name a musical piece after hearing only a slight excerpt from it, one lasting no more than a second or two, and consisting of no more than two or three notes or cords [*sic*]. The uninitiated will discern only noise. But to those with the requisite musical knowledge (gained, be it noted, not through arduous study but through effortless listening), the briefest extract can conjure up a world: a song, an album, a musical group. Was it maybe not similar with those Jews who first heard the Gospel of Matthew? Are we not sometimes forced to pick up a concordance in order to perceive connections which were once immediately grasped by trained ears with unconscious sureness?" (1993, p. 18).
10. Achtemeier (1990) demonstrates the importance of reading aloud in antiquity to the practice of New Testament criticism.
11. "The phonemicization implicit in the adaptation of the Semitic script to the consonants and vowels of Greek stands as a permanent linguistic achievement of western antiquity" (Robins 1957, p. 84).
12. Eric Havelock argues that this invention changed the Western mind. Capturing sounds in sequence and freezing them in time eventually made possible the sequential arrangement of ideas. The alphabetic preservation of sounds in sequence encouraged abstraction in Greek philosophy and made possible the eventual evolution of scientific method. The more the Greeks wrote, the more they needed to write because writing changed the way they thought. The onset of literacy in Greece triggered an escalating effect that accounts, in part, for the tremendous intellectual ferment that animated the Hellenistic world and placed the history of Western civilization in its debt. Havelock's classic exposition of this theory is *Preface to Plato,* in which he argues: "Direct evidence for mental phenomena can lie only in linguistic usage" (1963, p.

vii). He explores the methods by which written language made possible new developments in Greek philosophy in (1983, pp. 7–82).

13. "The ancient world did not possess the desire, characteristic of modern civilizations, to make reading easier and swifter because the advantages, which the modern world perceives as accruing from easier reading—the swift effective retrieval of information in reference consultation, the ability to read swiftly a great many difficult technical, logical, and scientific texts, and the greater diffusion of literacy throughout all social strata of the population—were never or seldom viewed as advantages by the ancients" (Saenger 1991, p. 208).
14. Although συμπλοκή is not retained in English, the Greek invocation of weaving as a metaphor for literary work persists in our reference to an established collection of works as a "canon." Canon transliterates κανών, a technical weaving term for a heddle rod, the mechanical shedding device on a warp-weighted loom. LJS *s.v.* κανών.
15. The archaeological record includes spindle whorls all over the ancient world made of precious materials such as ivory and bronze, and ancient depictions of spinners show them finely dressed in upper class clothing. Fabric production for trade and export was a lucrative occupation. Weave structure, fiber quality, and decorative embellishment indicate that textile production was not only a matter of duty and necessity but also of luxury and privilege (Barber 1991, pp. 41–68, 283–98). Homer's *Odyssey* attributes fabric production to queens and goddesses, depicting Penelope (2.94–110), Calypso (5.61–62), and Circe (10.221) as weavers, and Helen of Troy as a spinner (4.120). The myth of Philomela and Procne turns on the skill of Philomela, daughter of the King of Athens, as a tapestry weaver (Ov. *Met.* 6, 424–674; Apollod. *Bibl.* 3.14.8).
16. Admittedly, Augustus wore homespun not out of necessity but to protest luxurious indulgences by the wealthy and promote household industry. Nevertheless, the example indicates that members of the royal family were proficient weavers.
17. Use of the warp-weighted loom began to decline beginning in the first century CE as imperial expansion enabled Rome to outsource its weaving, especially silk weaving, to slaves and conquered peoples who had mastered these specialized technological skills. Distinctively Roman weaving in the late empire focused on tapestry weaving on a vertical, two-bar loom. Like the warp-weighted loom, the two-bar loom stood upright, employed mechanical

shedding, and functioned as a figure for literary composition. (Broudy 1979, pp. 47–48).

18. Marta Hoffmann summarizes the primary evidence of the warp-weighted loom from vase paintings in classical antiquity. The earliest vase painting evidence is preserved on an aryballos in Corinth from about 600 BCE. The best-known example is the fifth century Chiusi vase depicting Penelope and Telemachus in the foreground (1974, pp. 297–8). Clear photographs of fifth century BCE vase paintings depicting the looms of Circe and Penelope can be found in Broudy (1979, pp. 23–24).
19. Evidence from rock carvings in Italy dates from the fourteenth century BCE (Barber 1991, p. 91). Ideograms from Cretan Linear A script at the beginning of the Neolithic also preserve early evidence of the warp-weighted loom. Iron Age evidence from Hungary and on an Etruscan bronze pendant also predate Greek vase painting evidence (Barber 1991, pp. 91–92)).
20. To secure the threads on the crossbeam and hold them steady while weaving, the threads were first woven into a narrow band, with the threads from one long side of the band extended out in a considerable length along one long side of the band. The band was then stretched out lengthwise on the crossbeam, across the width of the loom's frame. The long, loose threads hung from the lower edge of the woven band and extended to the floor. These threads became the warp threads of the woven fabric. (Hoffmann 1974, pp. 151–83; Barber 1991, pp. 129–30).
21. Broudy (1979, pp. 24–28) presents an excellent schematic diagram of the warp-weighted loom, with clearly labeled parts and photographs of excavated loom weights.
22. This is the music that accompanies Calypso and Circe while they sang as they walked back and forth at their looms (*Od.* 5.61–62, 10.221–22).
23. Wool was the predominant fiber used for weaving in the Mediterranean and Middle East. In the imperial period, wool remained the primary fiber for household weaving, while cotton, silk, and linen weaving shifted progressively to conquered peoples as the empire expanded (Broudy 1979, p. 47). The situation was somewhat different in Egypt, where linen was the most frequently used fiber, and looms sometimes stretched out horizontally on the floor or the ground. Evidence also exists for the use of silk and hemp, but wool supplied the most commonly used fiber for the greatest variety of purposes (Barber 1991, pp. 145–62, 196–99; Hoskins 2004, pp. 26–27). And in that period, all other fibers were, like wool, spun and woven by hand.

24. This is a conservative estimate for wool. Much finer woolen fabrics were produced on warp-weighted looms, such as the Frisian textiles with 88–152 threads per inch from the Viking city of Birka in Sweden (Hoffmann 1974, pp. 229–30). Remnants from Egyptian tombs show that as early as the fourth millennium BCE linen fabrics were being produced with 200 threads per inch (Barber 1991, p. 148).
25. Scheid and Svenbro have shown the rich extent to which composers of classical Greek conceived of their linguistic art as weaving (Scheid and Svenbro 1996, pp. 111–130).
26. Iconography of the Fates frequently depicts Ἄτροπος with scissors, causing death by cutting the life thread. But the literal meaning of ἄτροπος requires no cutting to explain breaking a thread. The lack of twist, turning (ἄτροπος), causes a spun thread to unravel. I owe my gratitude to Lynn Tedder of the Tulsa Handweavers Guild and technical editor of *Handwoven* magazine for this observation.
27. "But readers can refer backward and forwards in the text" (Stubbs 1980, p. 13).
28. Both music and language are acoustic phenomena whose structures can be analyzed productively in terms of phonology, syntax, and semantics and whose behaviors can be assessed empirically (Sloboda 1985, pp. 11, 29). The analogy between music and language does not depend upon formal similarities between music theory and generative-transformational grammar, even though some such similarities have been observed (Lerdahl and Jackendoff 1983, p. 5–6). Rather, music and language have in common their "auditory-vocal medium," the natural ability of children to learn rules of music and language use through exposure to examples, the development of "culturally specific notational schemes," and the fact that "receptive skills" are developed before "productive skills" (Sloboda 1985, pp. 17–20).
29. I am indebted to Richard Dean, B.M., for this explanation of a musical motif's functions and the example drawn from Beethoven.
30. Iser (1978, pp. 165–69) shows that the process of filling in gaps of indeterminacy is basic to human interaction. He emphasizes the dynamic nature of this process (1974, pp. 226–27).
31. Reception theory does not imply that "a written work takes on meaning solely because of the reader" in the way Malina suggests in his treatment of "Contextualized-decontextualized Reading" (1991, pp. 20–21). Foley's use of Iser and modern reception theory

is to be preferred, for it proposes that ancient listeners filled in "gaps of indeterminacy" in a spoken composition from a socially constructed repertoire of traditional referents (1991, pp. 39–60).

32. Kennedy (1989, pp. 184–99) offers a fuller treatment of the implicit reception theory in ancient Greek literary criticism.

WORKS CONSULTED

Achtemeier, Paul J. 1990. *Omne Verbum Sonat. JBL* 109:3–27.

Allen, W. S. 1987. *Vox Graeca: A Guide to the Pronunciation of Classical Greek.* 3d ed. Cambridge: Cambridge University.

Allison, D. C. 1993. *The New Moses: A Matthean Typology*. Fortress: Minneapolis.

Barber, E.J.W. 1991. *Prehistoric Textiles: the Development of Cloth in the Neolithic and Bronze Ages, with Special Reference to the Aegean.* Princeton, NJ: Princeton.

Bolzoni, Lina. 1991. The Play of Images. The Art of Memory from Its Origins to the Seventeenth Century. In *The Enchanted Loom: Chapters in the History of Neuroscience,* edited by P. Corsi. New York: Oxford.

Botha, P. J. J. 1992. Greco-Roman Literacy as Setting for New Testament Writings. In *Neotestamentica,* edited by Nuwe-Testamentiese Werkgemeenskap van Suid-Afrika.

Broudy, Eric. 1979. *The Book of Looms: A History of the Handloom from Ancient Times to the Present.* Hanover: Brown University.

Camp, John M. 2001. *The Archaeology of Athens.* New Haven and London: Yale University Press.

Caplan, Henry, and Michael Winterbottom. 1996. *Rhetorica ad Herennium.* In *Oxford Classical Dictionary,* edited by S. Hornblower and A. Spawforth. Oxford: Oxford.

Carruthers, Mary J. 1990. *The Book of Memory, Cambridge Studies in Medieval Literature.* Cambridge and New York: Cambridge University Press.

Cribiore, Raffaella. 1996. *Writing, Teachers, and Students in Graeco-Roman Egypt.* Atlanta: Scholars.

Davies, Anna Morpurgo. 1996. Pronunciation, Greek. In *OCD,* edited by S. Hornblower and A. Spawforth. Oxford: Oxford University Press.

Fischer, Steven Roger. 2001. *A History of Writing.* Edited by J. Black, *Globalities.* London: Reaktion Books.

———. 2003. *A History of Reading.* Edited by J. Black, *Globalities.* London: Reaktion Books.

Foley, John Miles. 1991. *Immanent Art: From Structure to Meaning in Traditional Oral Epic.* Bloomington: Indiana University Press.

———. 1995. *The Singer of Tales in Performance*. Bloomington and Indianapolis: Indiana University Press.
———. 2002. *How to Read an Oral Poem*. Urbana: University of Illinois Press.
———. 2006. Memory and Oral Tradition. In *Performing the Gospel: Orality, Memory, and Mark,* edited by R. A. Horsley, J. A. Draper and J. M. Foley. Minneapolis: Fortress.
Gamble, Harry Y. 1995. *Books and Readers in the Early Church: A History of Early Christian Texts*. New Haven and London: Yale University Press.
Havelock, Eric A. 1963. *Preface to Plato*. Cambridge: Harvard University Press.
———. 1983. The Linguistic Task of the Presocratics. In *Language and Thought in Early Greek Philosophy,* edited by K. Robb. La Salle, IL: Hegler Institute.
Hoffmann, Marta. 1974. *The Warp-Weighted Loom: Studies in the History and Technology of an Ancient Implement*. Oslo: Robin and Russ Handweavers.
Hoskins, Nancy Arthur. 2004. *The Coptic Tapestry Albums and the Archaeologist of Antinoé, Albert Gayet*. Seattle: University of Washington.
Iser, Wolfgang. 1971. Indeterminacy and the Reader's Response in Prose Fiction. In *Aspects of Narrative,* edited by J. H. Miller. New York: Columbia University Press.
———. 1974. *The Implied Reader: Patterns of Communication in Prose Fiction from Bunyan to Beckett*. Baltimore: The Johns Hopkins University Press.
———. 1978. *The Act of Reading: A Theory of Aesthetic Response*. Baltimore: The Johns Hopkins University Press.
Kennedy, George A. 1989. The Evolution of a Theory of Artistic Prose. In *The Cambridge History of Literary Criticism,* edited by G. A. Kennedy. Cambridge: Cambridge University Press.
Kleist, James A. 1927. Colometry and the New Testament. *Classical Bulletin* 3:18–19.
Lerdahl, Fred, and Ray Jackendoff. 1983. *Generative Theory of Tonal Music*. Cambridge, MA: MIT.
Malina, Bruce J. 1991. Reading Theory Perspective: Reading Luke-Acts. In *The Social World of Luke-Acts: Models for Interpretation,* edited by J. H. Neyrey. Peabody, MA: Hendrickson.
Marrou, Henri-I. 1956. *A History of Education in Antiquity*. Translated by G. Lamb, *Wisconsin Studies in Classics*. Madison, WI: University of Wisconsin Press, [1982].

Robins, R. H. 1957. Dionysius Thrax and the Western Grammatical Tradition. *TPS*:67–106.

Saenger, Paul. 1991. The Separation of Words and the Physiology of Reading. In *Literacy and Orality*, edited by D. R. Olson and N. Torrance. Cambridge: Cambridge.

Scheid, John, and Jesper Svenbro. 1996. *The Craft of Zeus: Myths of Weaving and Fabric*. Edited by G. W. Bowersock, *Revealing Antiquity*. Cambridge: Harvard University Press.

Sloboda, John A. 1985. *Musical Mind: The Cognitive Psychology of Music*. Oxford: Clarendon.

Small, Jocelyn Penny. 1997. *Wax Tablets of the Mind: Cognitive Studies of Memory and Literacy in Classical Antiquity*. London and New York: Routledge.

Stubbs, Michael. 1980. *Language and Literacy: The Sociolinguistics of Reading and Writing, Routledge Education Books*. London: Routledge and Kegan Paul.

Yates, Francis. 1966. *The Art of Memory*. Chicago: University of Chicago Press.

Chapter 3

The Grammar of Sound

PROCESSING SOUND THROUGH WRITING AND READING

Writing and reading in the Greco-Roman world exhibited a shared dependence upon speech.[1] The human voice served as the primary mode of communication, and oral performance the primary means of literary publication.[2] Even in the midst of a rich literary tradition, writings were secondary to speech and served primarily to preserve and support it (Yates 1966). The literature of the ancients reflects the importance their cultures placed on articulate sound.[3] Aristotle describes written symbols as signs of their spoken, sounded counterparts. He describes letters and words first of all as sounds (φωνή) (*Poet.* 20) and plainly regards the spoken forms as primary. Speech symbolizes the affections of the soul, he writes, and written words (τὰ γραφόμενα) symbolize spoken ones (τὰ ἐν τῇ φονῇ) (*Int.* 1).

In a similar way, reading retained a link to speech as the essential tool for decoding written documents.[4] Sounds, not the written symbols used to encode them, communicated ideas in antiquity. In his important study of the sound of Greek, Stanford explains that readers had to pronounce words to understand them:

> Normally, it seems, an ancient Greek or Roman had to pronounce each syllable before he could understand a written word. The written letters informed his voice; then his voice informed his ear; and finally his ear, together with the muscular movements of his vocal organs, conveyed the message to his brain (1967, p.1).

Manuscripts implied spoken contexts and supported oral performances.[5] Fischer explains that in antiquity writing served as an "immortal witness," jogging a reader's memory and enabling the reader to verify facts and announce them aloud. He writes: "During its first three millennia, the 'immortal witness' was the spoken word incarnate" (2003, p. 14). Lentz describes the function of writing in Greek public life this way: "The spoken word is the direct tool of the living intelligence; the written word is a form of advertising" (1989, p. 109).

LEARNING TO READ AND WRITE

In the Greco-Roman world, information was shared primarily through public speaking because speech provided the most efficient access to the primary storehouse of knowledge, memory. Even written compositions were shared by means of speech, since documents and therefore reading skill were scarce. One learned a document's contents, digested them, and made them one's own by committing them to memory, either by reading the composition aloud or by hearing the composition read aloud by another. The Greek word for reading, ἀναγινώσκειν, means to know again, signaling the secondary role of documents in ancient memorial cultures. One usually searched one's memorial storehouse and only rarely consulted a manuscript. Knowledge was transmitted primarily through speech instead of silent, private reading. When a manuscript recorded the information to be transmitted, it was read or recited aloud.

In antiquity, educational systems aimed to teach how to encode speech with alphabetic signs, decode graphemes to reproduce speech, and store knowledge of all kinds in memory. Authorship entailed drawing on the resources of remembered knowledge to create new compositions. It did not depend on sustained or intensive consultation of documents, or even on the ability to read, since literature could be conveyed and stored in memory more directly and efficiently by listening to literature as it was read aloud. In the ancient world, few could write, and even fewer could compose literature according to our modern sense of authorship. All writers could make marks for alphabetic characters but the writing skill of some went no further than this. In the early stages of their education, scribes could write their names or copy a few lines from a written exemplar, but they were not necessarily able to read what they had inscribed. Highly proficient writers, a small percentage of the few who had acquired writing skill, could take dictation and read back what they had written. But even this degree of writing proficiency did not necessarily provide the ability to create a literary work, or even to compose a letter or business document.

Since reading and writing were distinct skills and neither was necessary for authorship in the sense of creative invention, it is not enough to say that one has "written" a text. Kloppenborg cautions, "Given what has been said about the constant interaction between oral performance and written scripts and the possibility of authors revising their own works, the notion of a single "text" lying behind all others is an abstraction" (2000, p. 110). To consider ancient literature in terms of its "texts" evades what we know about ancient writing technology and therefore obstructs appropriate reconstruction of a composition's social function. Adequate appreciation of ancient literature requires more precise definitions of reading and writing in order to reflect ancient practice. We must specify whether a scribe has copied marks on papyrus or some other surface (which the scribe might not be able to read or understand), whether an author has composed a work (which the author may not possess the skill to inscribe), or whether both processes are implied.

Writing skill was slowly acquired. Comparatively few of those who learned to write ever fully mastered the craft.[6] Some learned only to write their own name, still others to copy letters from an exemplar without fully comprehending their meaning. Students first learned the names of the letters by rote in alphabetic sequence and then learned the shapes of the upper case letters by tracing a teacher's model carved in wood or by copying a written model on a wax tablet (Cribiore 1996, pp. 122–25, 131). Plato explains that children learned written signs (γράμματα) from the elements of sounds (στοιχεῖα) (*Plt.* 277e–278b). Quintilian's condemnation of this practice implies its prevalence. He objects to "teaching small children the names and order of the letters before their shapes" because it "makes them slow to recognize the letters, since they do not pay attention to their actual shape, preferring to be guided by what they have already learned by rote" (*Inst.* 1.1.24–25). Students then learned to write their names—a very useful skill, judging from the amount of physical evidence that survives (Cribiore 1996, p. 147).[7] Next, they practiced copying short passages, again from a teacher's model. Primary emphasis at this stage of learning fell upon developing the mechanical skill to inscribe the alphabetic characters in wax, or, less often, to form them with a reed pen or paint them using a thin brush on papyrus. The scribe's goal was to develop a smooth, clear hand, or "good penmanship" (Cribiore 1996, p. 155).

It is unlikely that students understood the sense conveyed by their writing exercises. In the beginning stages of writing instruction, students typically could not read. Cribiore demonstrates from extensive paleographic evidence from Greco-Roman Egypt that syllabaries were employed by advanced writing students, not beginners. Virtually all extant syllabaries are written by "evolving" and "rapid" hands, and none by the "zero-grade" and "alphabetic" hands that produced copying exercises of short passages. This is consistent with the literary evidence in indicating that writing associated with vocalization—and therefore with making sense of written marks—was employed when taking dictation and when reading, but not when learning the alphabet. Learning to read came later, after basic writing instruction (Cribiore 1996, pp. 133, 145–46, 155). As more advanced hands progressed to the next step, writing syllabaries, they usually wrote from dictation (Cribiore 1996, 131–33).[8] Then students learned to produce word lists, with the words divided into syllables.[9] Next, scribes practiced copying declensions and verb paradigms, as well as progressively longer passages from written models. Eventually they could inscribe statements they had formulated themselves. Only then could they compose a text or engage in what we would call authorship.

Dionysius of Halicarnassus narrates this laborious process to justify the effort required of his prime exemplar, Demosthenes, to produce effective prose. Demosthenes painstakingly worked and reworked the organization and wording of his speeches, which then seemed to flow effortlessly. Just as extraordinary effort was required of the rhetor to construct an argument and frame it in a suitable literary style, acquiring scribal skill took place slowly and proceeded through predictable stages:

> When we learn grammar properly, we begin by learning by heart the names of the elements of sound, which we call letters. Then we learn how they are written and what they sound like. When we have discovered this, we learn how they combine to form syllables, and how these behave. Having mastered this, we learn about the parts of speech—I mean nouns, verbs and conjunctions and their properties, the shortening and lengthening of syllables and the high and low pitch of accents; genders, cases, numbers, moods and countless other related things. When we have acquired knowledge of all these things, we then begin to write and to read, slowly at first and syllable by syllable, because our skill is as yet undeveloped. But as time goes on and endows the mind, through constant practice, with a sound understanding, we proceed unfalteringly and with great ease, and read through any book we are given at sight, without thumbing through our text-books for all those rules (*Dem.* 52).[10]

Thus writing education first imparted the mechanical skill of forming letters and associating the written marks with letter names. The ability to write at this level, as limited as it seems to us, had various social and even commercial applications—for example, signing documents written by others and making copies of brief texts. Those who pursued the craft beyond this mechanical level learned to associate written marks with vocal sounds in order to take dictation. Aristotle considers it axiomatic that students write from dictation, not from silent copying of written texts: "Those who know, learn; for it is those who know the use of letters that learn what is dictated to them" (*On Soph. el.* 4.30). Metzger explains in his classic manual on textual criticism that errors entered the manuscript traditions not only because of "faulty eyesight," but also due to "faulty hearing," as scribes made copies by dictation and incorrectly transcribed from the exemplar different words that had similar sounds (1992, pp. 186, 190).

Once a student scribe had acquired the ability to associate combinations of letters with spoken syllables, he could capture in writing the component sounds of speech and could therefore begin to make sense of written marks. Practicing syllabaries from dictation and copying lists of words that were divided into syllables served the dual purpose of advancing the scribal hand and teaching the scribe to read (Cribiore 1996, p. 131). Both skills were necessary to reach the highest attainable level of writing proficiency.

Education in reading followed a slightly different sequence from that used to learn writing (Cribiore 1996, p.137). Initially, at least, writers lacked the ability to make sense of their own marks. Because writing necessarily entailed the acquisition of a mechanical skill, the techniques of the craft occupied its early stages. Some students mastered only these writing mechanics, and applied their scribal skill only in mechanical ways. Reading, which consisted in interpreting written marks as speech sounds, built upon this skill because it presumed the existence of a written text and entailed no mechanical processes of its own. In short, after writing had reduced speech to its phonetic elements, reading aloud from written texts reconstituted it.

Aristotle specified, "That which is written should be easy to read or easy to utter, which is the same thing" (*Rh.* 3.5.6). His prescription suggests reading's close association with sound. The author of *Rhetorica ad Herennium* writes: "Those who know the letters of the alphabet can thereby write out what is dictated to them and read aloud what they have written" (3.17.30). Writing entailed the ability to analyze and encode speech sounds, and it preceded reading, which reconstituted written symbols as speech. Sound, not sight, triggered meaning. A word read silently was difficult or impossible to comprehend because it was inaudible (Stanford 1967, p. 1). Perfect spelling was unnecessary, as long as written marks prompted a reader to utter the appropriate sound. If the proper word could be reconstructed from whatever letters were used, the word was thought to be adequately represented in writing (Pl. *Cra.* 432e–433b).

The connection between reading and speaking becomes evident when one confronts the difficulties of reading manuscripts written in *scriptio continua*. Cribiore's explanation illustrates the problem:

> Reading a text in *scriptio continua* required careful preparation. A reader was supposed to proceed from identification of the different elements—that is, letters, syllables, and words—to comprehension of the whole text. Lack of punctuation signs required him to examine the nature of each sentence and to recognize and identify words and linguistic markers. Grammatical and literary training were necessary to properly read aloud a text. Readers in antiquity who could not rely on word separation and punctuation had to interpret a text before reading it. Reading a text aloud with expression and appropriate pronunciation was not a simple matter. . . . Lack of word separation and punctuation were formidable hurdles, especially for beginners. One of the purposes of teachers' models was to present texts that offered reading assistance, particularly in the form of word separation. The precision and discipline of the syllabic method that was followed in teaching reading were the only guarantees of success. Reading was the accomplishment of the intermediate [writing] student who dedicated much time to penmanship in the process of learning (1996, pp. 148–49).

Declamation at sight from a manuscript simply was not possible. It required careful technical training and long years of practice. Only reading aloud enabled the efficient apprehension and full comprehension of a written text. Once heard and understood, the text generally was subsequently consulted from memory. The well-read person was one who listened effectively and who had learned to search the wax tablets of the mind rather than scrolls in a library.

γραμματική τέχνη: A SCIENCE OF SPEECH SOUNDS

Once students had mastered the mechanics of writing and could form syllables to represent sounds, the formal study of grammar could commence. As the Greek language changed during the Hellenistic period and as written materials proliferated in the Graeco-Roman world, systematic study of grammar developed over time. The canons of Greek grammar remained fluid well into the fifth century CE when the grammar attributed to Dionysius Thrax (c. 170—c. 90 BCE) was accepted as a standard. Dionysius Thrax studied under the Homeric scholar Aristarchus in an Alexandrian scholarly group under Ptolemaic patronage. His τέχνη γραμματική (*Science of Grammar*) is, "so far as we know, the first grammar of Greek to be written, and the first grammar of any language to be written in the western world" (Robins 1957, pp. 67– 68).[11] Thrax set forth a scheme of word classes that eventually became canonical, but his descriptions of the parts of speech were not agreed upon in his own time. According to Dionysius of Halicarnassus, not even the total number of letters is universally accepted in the first century BCE, and not all letters have the same power to affect the ear. He writes,

> It is not easy to say precisely what the number of these letters is, for the subject has caused our predecessors much perplexity. Some have thought that there are only thirteen "elements" of speech altogether and that the other letters are formed from these; while others have thought that there are more even than the twenty-four which we employ today. Now the discussion of these matters belongs more properly to grammar and prosody, or even, if you like, to philosophy (*Comp.* 14).

From its inception, however, grammar primarily served to analyze and preserve speech sounds.

Grammarians were concerned with the flow of language, the ability to capture and preserve it in writing and then reconstitute writing as speech. Initially, grammar was embedded in philosophy in ancient Greece. Robins observes: "The study of grammar started among the Pre-Socratics as part of the wider study of the nature of speech . . ." (1951, p. 6). Robins emphasizes the centrality of speech to Greek philosophical reflection on their language.

> Greek grammar, γραμματική, began by including what we are inclined to separate, if not from grammar, at least as a sub-group within it, phonetics and phonology—the study of speech sounds and their functions in language (1951, p. 13).

In Greek philosophical literature grammar is typically defined as a science of sound.[12] For Dionysius Thrax, the first element of grammar is the practice of reading (ἀνάγνωσις ἐντριβης), including delivery (ὑπόκρισις), prosodies (προσῳδία), and divisions in the composition (διαστολή) (1–2). Thrax's concern with reading reflects the earliest sense of γραμματική, which "dealt only with reading , writing, and the phonetic values of letters and their combination into syllables" (Robins 1957, p. 78).[13]

Through grammatical study students learned to associate the names of letters with their sounds, match written symbols with each letter, and finally record in writing the spoken word (Dion. Hal. *Dem.* 52). Plato writes: ". . . that which makes each of us a grammarian is the knowledge of the number and nature of sounds. . . . And it is this same knowledge which makes the musician (*Phlb.* 17b).[14] Quintilian writes that, "the art of letters and that of music were once united," and cites anecdotes from Sophron, Aristophanes, Menander, and Cicero as evidence (*Inst.* 1.10.17–20). The author of *De Musica* defines grammar as "an art adapted to the production of vocal utterances (τὰς φωνάς) and their preservation for recollection by means of letters" (Plut. *[De musica]* 1131d).[15] The approach to the alphabet as encoded sound coheres with the classical organization of academic disciplines that included the study of letters in musical education.[16]

Grammar derives its name from τὸ γϱάμμα (*LSJ s.v.* γϱάμμα), meaning a picture or the lines of a drawing and, eventually, the written alphabet. Plato's retelling of the Egyptian myth of the phonetic alphabet's origin with a "god or godlike man," Theuth, demonstrates the primary importance of sound.

> [Theuth] was the first to notice that the vowel sounds in that infinity were not one, but many, and again that there were other elements which were not vowels but did have a sonant quality, and that these also had a definite number; and he distinguished a third kind of letters which we now call mutes. Then he divided the mutes until he distinguished each individual one, and he treated the vowels and semi-vowels in the same way, until he knew the number of them and gave to each and all the name of letters. Perceiving, however, that none of us could learn any one of them alone by itself without learning them all, and considering that this was a common bond which made them in a way all one, he assigned to them all a single science and called it grammar (*Phlb.* 18b–c).

Grammar's fundamental concern, especially as expressed by Dionysius Thrax, was phonology, which was not sharply distinguished from phonetics. Theorists in the Hellenistic period developed extensive phonetic catalogs that describe the anatomy of vocal production, classify the elements of sound by their phonetic properties, and account for their impact on the ear (Dion. Thrax 7; Dion. Hal. *Comp.* 14). This phonological study built on treatments of grammar in classical and Stoic philosophy that had divided sounds into φωνήεντα and ἄφωνα, voiced and voiceless sounds (Pl. *Cra.* 424c, *Tht.* 203b; Diog. Laert. *Zeno* 57).[17] Letters came to be classified in sound-based categories. Voiced sounds include what we would call vowels, sounds that can be pronounced alone. Sounds we would refer to as consonant sounds (γ, δ) were considered voiceless or mute because they were thought to have no sound of their own and to be audible only in combination with other sounds. A third category, ἡμίφωνον or semi-vowels, included sounds such as σ and ϱ that must be pronounced in combination with others but were thought to possess their own sound (Pl. *Philb.* 18b–c).[18] The three categories of sound were later amplified to include several subcategories: vowels were classified as long (η, ω), short (ε, ο), and common or variable (α, ι, υ); the semi-vowels as simple (ζ, μ, ν, ϱ, ς, σ) and double (ζ, ξ, ψ); mutes as smooth (κ, π, τ), rough (ϑ, φ, χ), and intermediate (β, γ, δ). Each of the three categories of mutes includes a labial (π, φ, β), dental (τ, ϑ, δ), and palatal consonant (κ, χ, γ) (Dion. Hal. *Comp.* 14).

In addition to their phonetic analysis of syllables into their component parts or στοιχεῖα, grammarians also examined the combination of syllables in sensible speech. While the various letters represent sounds, they amount to nonsense and have no rational explanation until properly combined in spoken syllables.[19] Plato argues that while the syllable is composed of various parts or elements (στοιχεῖα), it comprises the whole (τὸ ὅλον), a single form or concept (μία ἰδέα) (*Tht.* 204a).

Just as the elements of sound combine to form syllables, syllables combine to form nouns (ὀνόματα) and verbs (ῥήματα) (Pl. *Cra.* 424e–425a). Plato and Aristotle notice that like the mute element (consonant) in phonetics that could be articulated only with a voiced element (vowel), the noun when uttered alone does not comprise a sensible assertion, but requires predication (Pl. *Soph.* 262; Arist. *Int.* 3). Aristotle describes both the noun and verb as φωνὴ συνϑετή, a composite or synthesized sound (*Poet.* 20.7–9). The recombination of its elements occurred through the spoken word—either in spontaneous speech, reading written compositions aloud, reciting them from memory, or improvising with the aid of written texts. The interlacement of nouns and verbs (συμπλέκων τὰ ῥήματα τοῖς ὀνόμασι) creates language or discourse (ὁ λόγος) (Pl. *Soph.* 262d).

Writing in Greek made possible and even necessitated the analytical breakdown of speech into its component sounds. Plato uses διαλύειν—to separate, break up, or dissolve into elements (*LSJ s.v.* διαλύω)—to describe the phonetic analysis of sounds through which they are matched with letters (*Cra.* 425a–b). The sounds of the letters of the alphabet were construed as στοιχεῖα, or elements, referring to the elements of sound. Theoretical treatments of grammar clearly distinguish between the elements of sound (στοιχεῖα), the written symbols that represent these sounds (γράμματα), and a letter's name (e. g., alpha, beta).[20] Diogenes Laertius explains:

> Elements (στοιχεῖα) of language are the four-and-twenty letters (γράμματα). 'Letters,' however, has three meanings: (1) the particular sound or element of speech; (2) its written symbol or character; (3) its name, as Alpha is the name of the sound A (*Zeno* 7.56–57).[21]

In Plato's *Sophista,* Socrates explains that joining letters (τὰ γράμματα) takes place through the art of grammar (τέκνης τῆς γραμματικῆς) in the same way as a musician joins high-pitched and low-pitched sounds (τοὺς τῶν ὀξέων καὶ βαρέων φθόγγους) (*Soph.* 253 a–b). The joining of sounds into a syllable (ἡ συλλαβή) results in a single form (μία ἰδέα) arising out of the several conjoined elements (τῶν συναρμοττόντων στοιχείων) (Pl. *Tht.* 203e–204a). Various letters, representing sounds, comprise the parts (τὰ στοιχεῖα) that combine to form syllables (συλλαβάς), which combine to form verbs and nouns (ὀνόματα καὶ ῥήματα) (Pl. *Cra.* 424e).

Dionysius of Halicarnassus explains that the student learns "to write and to read, slowly at first and syllable by syllable" (*Dem.* 52).[22] He attests to the centrality of the syllable in the processes of reading and writing. Metzger points out that writing in *scriptio continua* necessitates this focus, since an undifferentiated block of text "is easiest to read when one is reading aloud, syllable by syllable" (1981, p. 31).[23] The terms συλλαβή (syllable) and στοιχεῖα (element) originally served as general terms for combination and part.[24] The root metaphor for συλλαβή is the notion of an intimate connection or joining. As applied to females it can signify conception or pregnancy; to males, a wrestling hold. When applied to speech it refers to the joining of the elements (στοιχεῖα) of sound by pronouncing a syllable aloud (*LSJ s.v.* συλλαβή). The syllable, not the letter or the word, functions as the basic linguistic unit in Greek.[25] The study of grammar facilitated both writing and reading by identifying spoken syllables and associating their sounds with written marks. Grammar's smallest components were the στοιχεῖα but its basic unit of analysis was the syllable. Writing analyzed speech sounds into their phonetic components and reading reconstituted speech by decoding written characters and recombining syllables in recitation.

Λέξις: VOICE IN WRITTEN FORM

Grammar supplied the tools and techniques to analyze speech according to its component sounds and therefore to capture and record speech in writing. The γραμματικὴ τέχνη (science of grammar) thus made possible writing in the sense of taking dictation. In so doing, the study of grammar provided the basis for formulating words and phrases, or writing in the sense of composition. Grammar's basic unit was the syllable, comprised of στοιχεῖα, the elements of speech sounds. Syllables combine to form larger clusters of sound, recognizable to us as words and phrases. According to the first extant systematic treatment of Greek grammar, the Γραμματική attributed to Dionysius Thrax, λέξις is the "minimal unit of grammatical description"[26] (Λέχις ἐστὶ μέρος τοῦ κατὰ σύνταξιν λόγου ἐλάχιστον) (633.31).

Λέχις describes the combination and arrangement of speech sounds to create sensible discourse, the beginnings of literary composition. Its primary concern was diction, including both the combination of words and word choice (ἐκλογή τῶν ὀνομάτων) for the construction of phrases (Grube 1952, pp. 257–58).[27] For Plato, λέχις referred to speech as opposed to song (ᾠδή) (*Lg*. 816d), but also to a particular style of writing (*Ap*. 17d). Aristotle uses λέχις to denote diction (*Rh*. 1410^{b}28, *Po*.1450^{b}13). He enumerates its elements, including letters, syllables, case, phrase, and the various parts of speech (*Poet*. 20.1).[28] Both Aristotle and, following him, Theophrastus, enumerated the λέξεως ἀρετή, the virtues or qualities of good diction. Aristotle identifies a single virtue (ἀρετή), perspicuity (σαφής), but he understands that virtue to contain clarity (σαφήνεια), propriety (πρέπον), and ornamentation (κατακσευή) (*Rh*. 1404b). Theophrastus's four virtues of style include these three, but he adds correct speech (Ἑλληνισμός), also following Aristotle, to amplify the meaning of clarity (Cic. *Orat*. 79, Arist. *Rh*. 1407a).[29] The Stoics extended the list of virtues to five, adding brevity (συντομία) to Theophrastus's list (Diog. Laert. 7.59). They defined λέξις as "voice in written form" (Sandys 1921, p. 148), emphasizing its roots in sound and speech.[30] The author of *Περὶ ὕφους* (On the Sublime) simply prescribes good (or beautiful) words (κάλα ὀνομάτων) ([Longinus] *Subl*. 30.2).

WHAT IS A WORD?

Classical and Hellenistic Greek have no generic term for "word," referring to a lexeme (Small 1997, pp. 5–6). Although ὁ λόγος is frequently translated "word," our notion of a word is inadequate to the flexible sense of ὁ λόγος in classical and Hellenistic Greek. It could include what we would call a sentence, paragraph, or the overall message of a speech. Its usual meaning is the gist, main point, or overall message of a communication (Pl. *Soph*. 262a–d, Arist. *Rh*. 3.2.5).[31] This is typical of cultures heavily dependent on public, oral performance and aural reception rather than on the private, silent, and visual modes of reception that characterize cultures oriented primarily toward print.

Reflecting upon the oral culture of the South Slavic epic singer, Foley describes the conception of "word" in that context:

> Time and again the South Slavic *guslari* questioned by [the developers of the Oral Theory of composition, Milman] Parry and [Albert] Lord characterized a word not as a lexeme or a chirographically distinct item, but rather as a unit of utterance in performance. The minimal 'atom' in their compositional idiom was the poetic line, a ten-syllable increment whose integrity or wholeness is reinforced by recurrent vocal and instrumental melodies of the same length. They also spoke

> of a combination of lines, of a speech, of a scene, and of a whole song as a *rec* or 'word,' using the same term employed by contemporary linguists to denote something very different. It is striking that both Homer and the Anglo-Saxon poets also seem to conceive of the same kind of quantum, with Greek *epos* and Old English *word* both frequently employed to name units of utterance rather than the linguist's or the printer's conventions (1995, pp. 2–3).

The isolation of discrete lexical units reflects a literacy primarily oriented toward the visual perception of marks on a page. Kennedy (1989, p. 88) explains that only after the cultural shift away from primarily oral modes of publication of literature did "[a] 'word' become an entity, clearly distinguishable from and intermediate between authorial enunciation and reader reception." Havelock agrees. "Greek originally had no word for a word singly identified, but only various terms referring to spoken sound" (1982, p.8).

Small presents corroborating evidence from contemporary cognitive psychology, which shows that children and illiterate adults do not understand the word as a discrete unit until they become familiar with language in visual form in print. As long as they experience language primarily as speech, they have no need and develop no sensitivity to the lexeme as a unit of language (1997, pp. 5–6).

The usual textual format for Greek manuscripts is the undifferentiated block of text written in *scriptio continua*, depicting the linear flow of sound rather than the division of speech into lexical units. The Greek language certainly recognized the association of labels with things. The labels were called ὀνόματα καὶ ῥήματα, and referred to the names of things and the designators for their actions (Pl. *Soph.* 261e–262a, Arist. *Rh.* 3.2.5).[32] In English, ὀνόματα καὶ ῥήματα, is usually rendered as "nouns and verbs." Plato's definitions of ὀνόματα καὶ ῥήματα encompass a sentence's entire nominative or predicative clause (*Soph.* 262c). Plato defines discourse (λόγος) as a mingling of ὀνόματα καὶ ῥήματα to "indicate action or inaction or existence of anything that exists or does not exist." It is speech whereby one "does not merely give names, but . . . reaches a conclusion by combining verbs with nouns" (*Soph.* 262d).[33] In this sense lexemes were understood as units of meaning. But reflections on the Greek language and composition in classical and Hellenistic philosophy and literary criticism emphasized the sounded, spoken character of language and designated its components in these terms. Small explains, "Antiquity knew the concept of the word as a unit of speech, but did not consider the concept of the written word as a visual unit to be important" (1997, p.23).[34]

THE PARTS OF SPEECH

The lack of a clear delineation of the lexeme in Greek grammar is exhibited also in its fluid concept of the parts of speech (μέρος λόγου). Plato observes that every verbal affirmation requires at least a nominative and predicative component. He therefore recognizes only two lexical categories, nouns (ὀνόματα) and verbs (ῥήματα), which represent the two "vocal indications of being" (*Soph.* 261e). Plato describes the noun as a vocal sign applied to the doer of an action and the verb as a vocal sign indicating action, inaction, or a state of being (*Soph.* 262a–c). Aristotle distinguishes between nouns and verbs primarily according to whether or not a part of speech could stand on its own. As Aristotle describes them, the noun comes with resident meaning (καθ' αὑτὸ σημαντικόν) but no time reference, whereas the verb indicates time but has no meaning in itself, even though it has semantic content (*Poet.* 20.7–9). These early classifications of the parts of speech focus on the combined effect of nouns and verbs when articulated in some sensible unit of discourse rather than their discrete, abstract identity.

More complex classifications of the parts of speech developed only gradually. Classification of the various parts of speech became fixed only with the Latin grammarians, who considered Greek speech from the viewpoint of a different language (Robins 1967, p. 33). Although Plato concerns himself solely with nouns and verbs, Aristotle recognizes the noun, verb, conjunction (connectives and particles, σύνδεσμος), and joint (the article, ἄρθρον) (*Poet.* 20.6–9). Yet Aristotle, typically notable for his precision in classification, equivocates on the delineation of parts of speech:

> Verbs by themselves, then, are nouns, and they stand for or signify something, for the speaker stops his process of thinking and the mind of the hearer acquiesces. However, they do not as yet express positive or negative judgments. For even the infinitives 'to be,' 'not to be,' and the participle 'being' are indicative only of fact, if and when something further is added. They indicate nothing themselves but imply a copulation or synthesis, which we can hardly conceive of apart from the things thus combined (*Int.* 3).

The Stoic Chrysippus reckoned five parts of speech, separating common and proper nouns. He distinguished between word classes on the basis of sound as well as function. Conjunctions and joints are so classed, for example, because joints are inflected whereas conjunctions are not (Diog. Laert. *Zeno,* 7.58). Dionysius of Halicarnassus considers the various parts of speech the elements of diction (στοιχεῖα τῆς λέξεως) (*Comp.* 2, 7). The manner in which the elements are arranged distinguishes poetry from prose (τεζήν λέξιν) (Dion Hal. *Comp.* 11). Dionysius Thrax developed the eight classifications that ultimately became canonical, including the noun, verb, participle, article, pronoun, preposition, adverb, and conjunction.[35] Dionysius of Halicarnassus and Quintilian both rehearse the historical development of eight classifications without mentioning the Γραμματική of Dionysius Thrax (Dion. Hal. *Comp.* 2, Quint. *Inst.* 1.4.17–21). Notably, Quintilian preserves the Greek list of eight parts of speech while recognizing that one of them, the article, does not apply to his own native Latin (*Inst.* 1.4.18–21). Although Dionysius Thrax's classifications eventually established the norm, his scheme did not enjoy universal acceptance in his own time. Some sixty years later, Dionysius of Halicarnassus gives a history of word classification that describes several prevailing schemes without claiming orthodoxy for any one. After describing word classification systems that contain three, four, five, six and more parts of speech, Dionysius writes:

> The subject could be discussed at considerable length, but it is enough to say that the combination or juxtaposition of these primary parts, whether there be three, four or any number of them, forms what are called clauses (κῶλα).[36] Next, the joining together of these clauses constitutes what are called the "periods", and these make up the complete discourse (τελειοῦσι λόγον). (*Comp.* 2).

Dionysius places primary emphasis on the synthetic combination of sound into speech, not the definitive classification of lexical units (*Comp.* 2). He also designates the primary units of composition, the colon and period. If the syllable served as the basic unit of phonetics, the colon fulfilled this function for λέξις (speech, style) , and the period for σύνθεσις (composition). Because the definitions of colon and period are intimately interconnected, they will be discussed and defined below.

Σύνθεσις: PUTTING IT ALL TOGETHER

The elements of sound as analyzed in ἡ τέκνη γραμματική (the science of grammar) and the parts of speech analyzed as ἡ λέξις (speech, style) become interwoven in ἡ συμπλοκή (weaving) through the actual process of literary composition, which Greek authors conceived of as ἡ σύνθεσις.[37] The word signifies in Greek many kinds of composition (Arist. *Metaph.* 5.1013b, 1014b; 6.1027b). It frequently refers to fitting stones together in building a temple or other structure (Arist. *Eth. Nic.* 1174a23), and sometimes to an agreement (Pind. *Pyth.* 4.168), the arrangement of a marriage (Diod. Sic. 9.10.4), or a peace treaty (Diod. Sic. 11.26.3, 12.8.1). Ἡ σύνθεσις also has various technical senses in mathematics, logic, physics, and medicine (LSJ s.v. σύνθεσις). In Greek grammar and literary criticism, ἡ σύνθεσις applies to the fitting together of the various elements of language to create a whole literary composition. The component parts are variously conceived, depending on the subject under consideration. Σύνθεσις can be crafted through the combination of letters, syllables, words, parts of speech, or word groups. Aeschylus (*PV* 460) depicts Prometheus as the one who taught humans to compose literature by combining letters (γραμμάτων τε συνθέσις) while Aristotle refers to the synthesis of syllables (*Metaph.* 14.1092a) and Plato to the combination of nouns and verbs (σύνθεσις ἔκ τε ῥημάτων . . . καὶ ὀνομάτων) (*Soph.* 263d). Dionysius of Halicarnassus defines σύνθεσις in terms of the arrangement of the parts of speech (τῶν τοῦ λόγου μορίων) or other word groups (ἅ δὴ καὶ στοιχεῖά τινες τῆς λέξεως καλοῦσιν) (*Comp.* 1).

Application of σύνθεσις (composition) to various components of language reflects no imprecision in the term's use; rather, the reverse is true. Irrespective of the level of discourse, ἡ σύνθεσις emphasizes the combination of elements to create an integral whole, at the phonetic, morphological, and syntactic levels, as well as at the level of a complete literary composition. In every case, σύνθεσις refers to the whole that emerges and not to the mere juxtaposition of parts. Σύνθεσις can therefore designate a particular kind of discourse. For example, Aeschines (*On the Embassy* 2.153) inveighs against the dishonest discourse of an opponent in the embassy who, he claims, could not put reliable words together even by mistake (ὅτι πρὸς τῇ τερατεῖα τοῦ τρόπου καὶ τῇ τῶν ὀνομάτων συνθέσει νοῦν οὐκ ἔκει) and he thrusts one of his many ironic jabs at τὴν τῶν ὀνομάτων σύνθεσιν τῶν Δημοσθένους ἀγαπήσοντας (the overly-elegant speech of Demosthenes) (*In Ctes.* 3.142). Theophrastus defines gossip (ἡ λογοποιία) as the σύνθεσις of false statements (ψευδῶν λόγων) (*Char.* 8.1).

At a higher level of abstraction, Aristotle refers to the structure (τὴν σύνθεσιν) of a tragedy (*Poet.* 1485a). He provides in the *Politics* an elaborate example of this notion of σύνθεσις as the structure of a composition, in which he compares the political structure of the state to that of drama and music. Aristotle claims that citizens produce different political structures according to how they agree to govern themselves, in the same way that a play becomes either a comedy or a tragedy according to the manner in which the chorus executes their part, even though the choruses for tragedies and comedies are composed of the same persons, or as a melody can exist in different modal structures, even though it consists of the same musical notes. These synthetic structures are characterized by the harmonization (ἁρμονίαν) of their various parts, as with musical modes (3.1276b).

Ἡ ἁρμονία (harmony) is another way of expressing the synthetic combination of syllables and phrases to create a pleasing and meaningful composition. Its meaning overlaps with that of the English word harmony.[38] Ἡ ἁρμονία (harmony) is a common term for music (Pl. *Tht.* 145d) or musical melody and its beauty (Arist. *Poet.* 1447a, Plut. *Vit. Per.* 15.1) and is sometimes paired with rhythm (ῥυθμός) (Arist. *Poet.* 1448b). When ἡ ἁρμονία refers to musical harmony, it is frequently described in terms of the various Greek modes or scales, each of which expresses a different sequence of intervals between tones.[39] Aristotle applies ἡ ἁρμονία to the musical modes to focus on the (mathematical) ratio of tonal intervals in a scale (*Metaph.* 1.986a, 1.985b, 5.1024a). Pindar appeals to the lyre to weave (ἐξύφαινε) a song with Lydian harmony (ἁρμονία) (*Nem.* 4.44). He also uses ἁρμονία metaphorically to signify a kind of inner concord (*Pyth.* 8.67).

Musical harmony also serves as a metaphor for other kinds of order and concord. For example, Aristotle uses musical harmony as a figure for the state (*Pol.* 1.1254a) and elsewhere quotes an aphorism of Heraclitus, "The faintest harmony comes from difference" (*Eth. Nic.* 1155b.1). Euripedes alludes to the easily disturbed harmony of a woman's nature (*Hipp.* 162). Strabo recalls that Plato and the Pythagoreans classed philosophy with music and held that the universe was organized in an harmonious arrangement (*Geography* 10.3.10). Plato entertains a lengthy discussion of whether the human soul animates the body in a manner analogous to the way harmony characterizes the music from the strings of the lyre.[40]

Other usages of ἡ ἁρμονία that are not generally echoed in the English word harmony apply to the joining of physical materials, especially in ship building (Herodotus *Histories* 2.96.2) and construction,[41] especially stone masonry (Josephus *BJ* 5.156, 175).[42] Together with the explicit connection of ἁρμονία with beautiful musical sound, these usages explain the application of ἁρμονία to literary composition. Plato refers to the harmony of speech (ἁρμονίν λόγων)[43] (*Tht.* 175e) and Aristotle to the harmony of ordinary conversation (λεκτικῆς ἁρμονίας δεόμενος) (*Rh.* 1408b). Aristotle lists harmony (ἁρμονία), volume (μέγεθος) and rhythm (ῥυθμός) as the three necessary qualities of speech, both in drama and in oratory

(*Rh.* 1403b). Plato combines the notions of harmonious speech and inner concord by describing the ideal of a speaker whose words are not only musically beautiful but are also consistent with his deeds (*Lach.* 188).

These notions cohere with typical usages of ἡ σύνθεσις (composition) to describe the harmonious combination of syllables, words, and phrases that form a beautiful and integral whole. Dionysius of Halicarnassus presents an extended treatment of σύνθεσις in his treatise *Περὶ συνθέσεως ὀνομάτων* (On Literary Composition), written in Rome in the first century BCE to rectify what he perceived to be corruptions of Hellenistic usage in favor of Attic rhetoric. His definition states that ἡ σύνθεσις (composition) is "a certain process of arranging the parts of speech (τῶν τοῦ λόγου μορίων) or the elements of diction (στοιχεῖὰ . . . τῆς λέξεως)" (*Comp.* 2, 6).

Dionysius compares literary composition to the construction of other kinds of structures, such as building, carpentry, ship-building and embroidery (*Comp.* 2, 6). Although he distinguishes σύνθεσις (composition) from ἐκλογή (word choice) and elevates the importance of σύνθεσις,[44] he explains that all these sorts of composition are similar in that, while the selection of materials is chronologically prior to their assembly, the manner in which they are combined is primarily responsible for the power of the resulting structure (*Comp.* 2). And while no rigid logical scheme governs the placement of various parts, literary compositions that are well-composed (συνετίθεσαν εὖ) conform to a definite system (τέκνη) (*Comp.* 5).[45] Both prose and poetry are subject to this τέκνη (science) and both can confer beauty on ideas. But both are also equally capable of miscarrying or lacking rhetorical impact because their form of expression is ineffective (*Comp.* 3, 20, 26).

Dionysius' treatise is the only complete ancient work extant in Greek concerning word order and euphony. He prescribes the beautiful harmonization (καλὴ ἁρμονία) of four elements of literary composition (σύνθεσις). These are noble melody (μέλος εὐγενές), dignified rhythm (ῥυθμὸς ἀξιωματικός), impressive variation (μεταβολὴ μεγαλοπρεπὴς), and the appropriateness of all these (τὸ πᾶσι τούτους παρακολοθοῦν πρέπον) (*Comp.* 13). He considers melody primarily as a function of phonetics and euphony (*Comp.* 14–16), whereas rhythm derives primarily from vowel quantity and applies equally to poetry and prose.[46] Melody and rhythm supply the raw materials that must be varied and used appropriately. Dionysius envisions interweaving both of these materials in σύνθεσις. He summarizes the gist of his argument concerning melody:

> The varied effect of the syllables is produced by the interweaving of letters (τὰς τῶν γραμμάτων συμπλοκὰς), that the diverse nature of words is produced by the combination of syllables (τῶν συλλαβῶν σύνθεσιν), and that the multiform character of a discourse is produced by the arrangement of words (τὰς τῶν ὀνομάτων ἁρμονίας) (*Comp.* 16).

Rhythm furnishes the character and impact of prose, whether rhythms are used individually or whether various rhythms are interwoven (ἐὰν τι ἀλλήλοις κατὰ τὰς ὁμοζυγίας συμπλέκωνται) (*Comp.* 18). Variation gives prose its great advantage over poetry, since it entails the freedom to employ whatever changes seem pleasing (ἡ δὲ πεζὴ λέξις ἅπασαν ἐλευθερίαν ἔχει καὶ ἄδειαν ποικίλλειν ταῖς μεταβολαῖς τὴν σύνθεσιν), whereas poetry's meter constrains word choice and phrase length by specifying vowel quantities in measured lines (*Comp.* 19). Appropriateness is the most important principle of all. Since each of the many types of composition exhibits its distinct character (χαρακτήρ), the form of expression should match the nature of the message to be conveyed (*Comp.* 20–21).

Σύνθεσις denotes the results of literary composition at both micro and macro levels. It can be analyzed into various component parts. Λέξις describes its diction and λόγος its gist. The ultimate function of all the elements and principles of σύνθεσις, Dionysius states, is

> to arrange words in a proper relationship to one another, to fit [word groups] together properly (τά τε ὀνόματα οἰκείως θεῖνει παρ' ἄλληλα), and to divide the whole discourse suitably into periods (τοῖς κώλοις ἀποδοῦναι τὴν προσήκουσαν ἁρμονίαν καὶ ταῖς περιόδοις διαλαβεῖν εὖ τὸν λόγον) (*Comp.* 2).

Dionysius thus indicates that the basic units of σύνθεσις are the colon and the period.

BASIC SOUND GROUPS

Structure, then, is achieved primarily through the arrangement of a Greek prose composition's basic building blocks, the colon (κῶλον) and period (περίοδος). These are the prose analogs to the poetic verse and metric line,[47] whose significance as speech and sound is now widely recognized.[48] Demetrius begins his treatise *On Style*, with this statement: "Just as poetry is organized by metres (such as half-lines, hexameters, and the like), so too prose is organized and divided by what are called clauses (κῶλα)" (*Eloc.* 1).

Vocal articulation provided the primary criterion for delineating both the colon and the period. Aristotle defines the colon and period in relation to each other: "A period may be composed of cola or simple. The former is a complete statement, distinct in its parts and easy to repeat in a breath."[49] The criterion of the duration of breath to delineate cola and periods persists in Latin criticism. In a passage quoted by Quintilian, Cicero explains this requirement:

> It was failure or scantiness of breath that originated periodic structure and pauses between words, but now that this has once been discovered, it is so attractive, that even if a person were endowed with breath that never failed, we should still not wish him to deliver an unbroken flow of words; for our ears are only gratified by a style of delivery which is not merely endurable but also easy for the human lungs (Cic. *De Or.* 3.46.181; Quint. *Inst.* 9.4.125).

Aristotle limits the number of cola in a period to two and prescribes that component cola, when more than one exist, should either be antithetical or set in parallel (*Rh.* 3.9.6–9). Demetrius, too, allows for simple periods containing only one colon, but permits up to four cola in a period (*Eloc.* 16).[50] But the duration of a breath remains the most important criterion.[51] Without cola to organize it, Demetrius writes, a speech "would otherwise continue at length without limit and simply run the speaker out of breath" (*Eloc.* 1).

A composition's colometric structure was available to the ancient reader through its grammar, which encodes its aural organization. Cola "mark out the boundaries [of what is being said] at frequent points" (ἐν πολλοῖς ὁρίζοντα τὸν λόγον) (Demetr. *Eloc.* 1). In Latin criticism, the colon is called a *membrum*, signaling its grammatical dependence on other cola. Like the members of a body, the "colon is meaningless if detached from the whole body (*a toto corpore*) of the sentence" (Quint. *Inst.* 9.4.123). The colon spans a single grammatical segment and usually combines with other cola to express a complete thought. The colon is "brief and complete" yet "does not express the entire thought, but is in turn supplemented by another colon" (*Rhet. Her.* 4.19.26).

Cola were combined into periods (περίοδοι), whose structure was also governed by sound. Like cola, periods were defined functionally, not formally. A period consists of cola that can be spoken in a single breath and easily comprehended by hearing. They are units of discourse that are balanced, rounded, and grammatically complete. Aristotle's definition of the period makes this clear: "[B]y period I mean a [statement] (λέξιν) that has a beginning and end in itself and a magnitude that can be easily grasped" (*Rh.* 3.9.3). If a period is too short, Aristotle cautions, the hearer stumbles, but if too long the speaker leaves the hearer behind (*Rh.* 3.9.6).

Derived from πέρι (around) and ὁδός (path, road, or way), the term period suggests a circular path or a complete circuit (Lausberg 1998, p. 414). Citing Aristotle's description of a period as a portion of speech with a beginning and an end, Demetrius compares the structure of a period to the out-and-back path taken by a runner of the δίαυλος:

> The very use of the word 'period' implies that there has been a beginning at one point and will be an ending at another, and that we are hastening towards a definite goal as runners do when they leave the starting place. For at the very beginning of their race the end of the course is before their eyes (*Rh.* 3.9.2; Demetr. *Eloc.* 11).

Rounding (περιάγω) was considered to be the period's distinguishing mark. Rounding implies some echo at the end of the period of its beginning sounds. The period's conclusion is understood to return to the beginning or indicate closure in some way. The most frequently recommended aural devices to signal a period's closure are rounding, concentration, and elongation, or length at the end. Concentration (συστροφή) signifies a density or coiling together of strong signals. Elongation or length can be achieved phonetically or rhythmically through the use of long vowels, or the sheer addition of syllables (Demetr. *Eloc.* 17–18). Cola were unified into periods by means of repeated similar sounds in their final syllables, similar beginning words, or repeated inflections of the same word (Arist. *Rh.* 3.9.8–10).

The period signals through sound its beginning, end, and structural completeness. Its clearest structural signal is an indication of closure. Aristotle's prescription for a rhythmic signal for closure demonstrates that the period is aurally and not graphically defined. He writes, "[T]he end [of the period] should be clearly marked, not by the scribe nor by a punctuation mark, but by the rhythm itself" (*Rh.* 3.8.6). To this end, periods ought to be balanced, meaning that they should sustain a modulated rhythm over a manageable scope. Quintilian retains this emphasis on rhythm at the period's end. He explains:

> Rhythm pervades the whole body of prose through all its extent. For we cannot speak without employing the long and short syllables of which feet are composed. Its presence is, however, most necessary and most apparent at the conclusion of the period, firstly because every group of connected thoughts has its natural limit and demands a reasonable interval to divide it from the commencement of what is to follow: secondly because the ear, after following the unbroken flow of the voice and being carried along down the stream of oratory, finds its best opportunity of forming a sound judgment on what it has heard,

> when the rush of words comes to a halt and gives it time for consideration. Consequently all harshness and abruptness must be avoided at this point, where the mind takes breath and recovers its energy (*Inst.* 9.4.61).

A smaller grammatical unit, the comma, comprises an abbreviated form of the colon.[52] The comma is a grammatical fragment defined by its brevity (Demetr. *Eloc.* 1.8). Its name signifies a chip or segment, something chopped or cut, and may consist of a single word. Commas (κόμματα) typically occur as interjections, exclamations, or introductions to speeches and occur "when single words are set apart by pauses in staccato speech" (*Rhet. Her.* 4.19.26).[53] While the comma is considered suitable for apothegms, maxims and other short figures, it is typically associated with a forceful style (Demetr. *Eloc.* 241–3; Quint. *Inst.* 9.4.126). Commas occur relatively infrequently. Kleist summarizes:

> In writing colometrically, the one great purpose agreed upon by all ancient rhetoricians is to enable the reader to read intelligently, and properly to husband his breath in speaking. The all-essential thing is that both colon and comma, when taken by themselves, make sense and admit of proper breathing (1928, p.26).[54]

The power of the period as a structuring device establishes two poles of a gradient from a highly periodic structure in which the boundaries of each period are clear, to a non-periodic structure in which cola are distinguishable but not blended into periods (Arist. *Rh.* 3.9.1).[55] Ancient commentators analyzed compositions colon by colon to evaluate their structure and determine whether they effectively achieved their pragmatic objectives. The sound and structure of a composition's cola figured as prominently in σύνθεσις (composition) as the meaning of its words. Elements of structure included the relative length of cola within a period, the means of connecting cola with each other, and parallelism in sound or grammatical construction. Some commentators even insisted on the primacy of sound over sense, since unmusical cola could controvert a speech's meaning. Dionysius of Halicarnassus claims, "[J]ust as fine thought is of no use unless one invests it with beautiful language, so here too it is pointless to devise pure and elegant expression unless one adorns it with the proper arrangement" (*Comp.* 3).

LITERARY STYLE

Based upon the structure and character of a composition's cola and periods, compositions were said to exhibit particular styles that were associated with distinct pragmatic effects. Aristotle analyzed diction (λέξις),[56] Dionysius of Halicarnassus evaluated harmony (ἁρμονία) and different ways of weaving (ὑφαίνω) a literary fabric (συμπλοκή), while Demetrius wrote of various types of expression (ἑρμηνεία); but all advanced overlapping typologies of style based upon the types and arrangements of cola and periods. Each type was described in terms of its stylistic "character" (χαρακτήρ).[57] The term derives from smithing, and refers to striking an image on coins.[58] Χαρακτήρ is metaphorically applied to persons and things to signify a standard, typical, or ideal form or type. The classical commentators on style evaluated the effect of a literary composition according to its characteristic aural stamp.

CONTINUOUS AND PERIODIC STYLE

Aristotle and, following his schema, Demetrius,[59] distinguished periodic (κατεστραμμένην δὲ ἡ ἐν περιόδος) from continuous (εἰρομένην) style (λέξις).[60] Demetrius uses different labels, but his prescriptions cohere with Aristotle's. Demetrius prefers ἑρμηνεία (interpretation, explanation) to Aristotle's λέξις (speech, style). He refers to the periodic and continuous styles as "compact (κατεστραμμένη οἷον ἡ κατὰ περιόδους ἔχουσα)" and "disjointed (ἡ διῃρημένη ἑρμηνεία)" (*Eloc.* 12). Demetrius employs the metaphor of building construction to contrast periodic and continuous style:

> The clauses (κῶλα) in the periodic style may in fact be compared to the stones which support and hold together the roof which encircles them, and the clauses of the disjointed style to stones which are simply thrown about near one another and not built into a structure (*Eloc.* 13).

Both Aristotle and Demetrius associate the continuous style with an older or more antique type of diction,[61] and more often define it in terms of what it lacks than by any positive characteristics. Aristotle furnishes this definition: "By a continuous style I mean that which has no end (τέλος) in itself and only stops when the sense is complete" (*Rh.*1409a). The component cola of the continuous style exhibit little grammatical subordination and instead seem tacked onto one another in a series.[62] Non-periodic structure was considered suitable for historical narrative, demonstrative oratory, or the communication of facts (*Rh.* 9.4.129–30). Quintilian comments:

> History does not so much demand full, rounded rhythms as a certain continuity of motion and connexion of style. For all its cola are closely linked together, while the fluidity of its style gives it great variety

> of movement; we may compare its motion to that of men, who link hands to steady their steps, and lend each other mutual support (*Inst.* 9.4.129).

Aristotle finds the continuous style "unpleasant, because it is endless, for all wish to have the end in sight" (*Rh.* 3.9.2). Others simply note the lack of grandeur in this style and indicate where its use is appropriate (Quint. *Inst.* 9.4.129; Cic. *De Or.* 3.49.199). Aristotle and Demetrius provide the following examples.

CONTINUOUS STYLE

Aristotle (*Rh.*1409a):
Ἡροδότου Θουρίου ἥδ᾽ ἱστορίης ἀπόδειξις[63]

Demetrius (*Eloc.* 12):
Ἑκαταῖος Μιλήσιος ὧδε μψθεῖται·
τάδε γράφω,
ὥς μοι δοκεῖ ἀληθέα εἶναι
οἱ γὰρ Ἑλλήνων λόγοι πολλοί τε καὶ γελοῖοι, ὡς ἐμοὶ φαίνονται, εἰσίν.[64]

Aristotle's example contains only one colon. Presumably, the string of genitives gives the passage its sequential, endless, or continuous quality. Demetrius's illustration contains multiple cola of uneven length with few such structural markers as grammatical subordination or parallelism.

PERIODIC STYLE

Periodic style consists of balanced cola linked by such grammatical connections as subordination, or such structural connections as parallelism or antithesis. Aristotle provides an example of periods with cola that are "divided (ἡ διῃρημένη)" or "opposed (ἡ ἀντικειμένη)."

Divided cola (*Rh.* 1409b):
πολλάκις ἐθαύμασα τῶν τὰς πανηγύρεις συναγόντων
καὶ τοὺς γυμνικοὺς ἀγῶν -ας καταστρησάντων[65]

Opposed cola (*Rh.* 1410a):
ἀμφοτέρους δ᾽ ὤνησαν,
καὶ τοὺς ὑπομείναντας **καὶ** τοὺς ἀκολουθήσαντας

τοῖς μὲν γὰρ πλείω τῆς οἴκοι πορσεκτήσαντο,
τοῖς δὲ ἱκανὴν τὴν οἴκοι κατέλιπον[66]

Classical literary criticism contains an apparent contradiction about the periodic character of prose. On the one hand, commentators explain that all prose is comprised of periods, and that rounding and balance are the period's hallmarks, reflecting its structural unity. On the other hand, commentators observe that not all periods are equally rounded or balanced. In fact, classical Latin literary critics admit that the possible variance among periods is so great that the periods in some prose are so poorly delineated as to be nearly undetectable. In other words, the commentators know on grammatical grounds where a period's boundaries should be, even when little rounding or balance exists. The commentators therefore seem to equivocate by indicating that periods organize all prose, but that some prose is characterized by a non-periodic quality. In the case of non-periodic or "continuous" prose, they recognize that periods technically exist but are detectable only on the basis of grammatical completeness and do not exhibit the rounding or balance that characterize highly periodic prose (Arist. *Rh.* 3.9.2; Quint. *Inst.* 9.4.129). Such non-periodic quality is itself a characterizing aspect of a composition's sound signature.

AUSTERE, POLISHED, AND BLENDED STYLES

Dionysius of Halicarnassus outlines a threefold typology of style that characterized prose theory in the late Hellenistic period (Kennedy 1989, p. 195). He distinguishes three types of style: the austere, the polished, and the blended or mixed style.[67] Austere style (τῆς αὐστηρᾶς ἁρμονίας), as the name suggests, sounds harsh and stark. At the level of the syllable, it employs harsh consonants, long vowel sounds, and multi-syllabic words. It admits of hiatus and consonant clash. These give the impression of words standing on their own, with space around them. At the level of the colon, it exhibits dignified rhythm and lacks parallelism. At the level of the period, it can fall short of or exceed the length of a breath, often lacks rounding and balance, and uses few particles and connectives. The period's boundaries may not necessarily coincide with sense. They should be simple and independent. Simplicity means avoidance of ornamentation, spectacular or polished endings, and affectation. Independence means that periods need not blend with surrounding periods. This stylistic type aims at dignity rather than elegance. It employs the cadences of ancient writing and conveys a slow, settled quality. Its beauty lies not in adornment but in sounding noble and impressive. The beauty of this style "consists in its patina of antiquity" (*Comp.* 22) Dionysius singles out Pindar in poetry, Aeschylus in tragedy, Thucydides in history, and Antiphon in oratory as exemplary proponents (*Comp.* 22, *Dem.* 38–39). Dionysius analyzes the following passage from Thucydides by way of illustration.

AUSTERE STYLE

Period 1:

θουκυδίης Ἀθηναῖος # ξυνέγραψε τὸν # πόλεμον # τῶν #Πελοποννησίων #

καὶ Ἀθηναίων ὡς ἐπολέμησαν πρὸς ἀλλήλους,

Period 2:

ἀρξάμενος εὐθὺς καθισταμένου,

καὶ * ἐλπίσας μέγαν τε * ἔσεσθαι

καὶ * ἀξιολογώτατον **τῶν προγεγενημένων**,

Period 3:

τεκμαιρόμενος

ὅτι * ἀκμάζοντές τε * ἦσαν ἐς αὐτόν ἀμθότεροι παρασκευῇ τῇ τάσῃ,

καὶ τὸ * ἄλλο Ἑλληνικόν ὁρῶν # ξυνιστάμενον # πρὸς ἑκατέρους,

τὸ μέν εὔθυς,

τό δέ καὶ διανοούμενον. (Thuc. 1.1.)[68]

Dionysius judges this passage as austere primarily on the basis of frequent hiatus (marked above by asterisks) and consonant clashes, (marked above by pound signs), the lack of rounding at the period's end (bold-faced type above), and unbalanced cola (note the significant differences in cola length) (*Comp.* 22).

Dionysius's second type is polished style (ἡ γλαφυρὰ σύνθεσις). The primary aesthetic goal of the polished style is euphony and a pleasant musical effect. It is characterized at the level of the syllable with an avoidance of harsh consonants and hiatus. It employs multiple balanced cola that flow together in a melodious arrangement, often in parallel. Its cola can be compared to a finely woven net because of the smoothness with which they are fitted together. Whereas in the austere style words stand apart, they flow together smoothly in the polished style. Words superfluous to the sense of the composition can be added in the polished style to smooth out the sound and unify the periods. The polished style has a fluid, mellifluous quality. This style uses clearly defined, well-rounded periods with multiple cola and strong endings. Its periods keep pace with the space of a breath. Figures such as antithesis, paronomasia, antistrophe, and anaphora are appropriate techniques for arranging cola into periods (*Comp.* 23, *Dem.* 40).

> It requires that the words shall keep on the move, swept forward and riding along on top of one another, all sustained in their movement by mutual support, like the current of a stream that never rests. It sets out to blend together and interweave its component parts, and to make

them convey as far as possible the effect of a single utterance. This result is achieved by the exact fitting together of the words, so that no perceptible interval between them is allowed. In this respect the style resembles finely-woven net, or pictures in which the lights and shadows melt into one another. It requires all its words to be melodious, smooth and soft and like a maiden's face. It shows a sort of repugnance towards rough and dissonant syllables, and careful avoidance of everything rash and hazardous (*Comp.* 23).

Dionysius mentions Hesiod and Sappho from poetry and Isocrates from oratory as favored proponents of this style (*Paneg.* 96–99). He furnishes this example from Isocrates (*Dem.* 40).

POLISHED STYLE

Period 1:

Ἐπειδὴ γὰρ οὐχ οἷοί τε ἦσαν πρὸσ ἀμφοτέρας
ἅμα παρατάξασθαι τὰς δυνάμεις,
παραλαβόντες ἅπαντα τόν ὄχλον
ἐκ τῆς πόλεως
εἰς τὴν ἐχομένην νῆσον ἐξέπλευσαν,
ἵν᾽ ἐν μέρει καὶ μὴ ποός ἑκάτερα κινδυνεύωσι.

Period 2:

καίτοι πῶς ἄν ἐκείνων ἄνδρες ἀμείνους
ἢ μᾶλλον φιλέλληνες ὄντες ἐπιδεχθεῖεν,
οἵτινες ἔτλησαν ἐπιδεῖν,
ὥστε μὴ τοῖς πολλοῖς αἴτιοι γενέσθαι τῆς δουλείας,
ἐρήμην **μὲν** τὴν πόλιν γιγνομένην,
τῆν **δὲ** χώραν πορθουμένην,
ἱερὰ **δὲ** συλώμενα καὶ νεὼς ἐμπιμπραμένους,
ἅπαντα **δὲ** τόν πόλεμον περὶ τὴν πατρίδα τὴν αὐτῶν
γενόμενον;[69]

Smooth sounds and parallel cola are evident in both periods. In the second period the final three cola are placed in parallel and get progressively longer, contributing to the period's rounding and balance.

Dionysius's third stylistic type, the mixed (μικτήν), blended, or tempered style (τὴν εὔκρατον), is not distinctive in itself, but employs features from both the austere and polished styles. Dionysius recommends the blended style above all others because it mediates between two extremes.[70] Representatives of the blended style represent the pinnacle of Greek literature, including Homer from the poets, Sophocles from the tragedians, Plato and Aristotle from the philosophers, Herodotus from the historians, and, ultimately, Demosthenes from the orators (*Comp.* 24, *Dem.* 41–42). Dionysius (*Dem.* 43) offers the following example from Demosthenes.

BLENDED STYLE

Period 1:
Εἰ δέ τις ὑμῶν, ὦ * ἄνδρες Ἀθηναῖοι, τὸν # Φίλιππον εὐτυχοῦντα *
ὁρῶν ταὐτῃ φοβερὸν # προσπολεμῆσαι νομίζει,
σώφρονος μὲν ἀνθρώπου προνοίᾳ χρῆται

Period 2:
μεγάλη γὰρ # ῥοπή, **μᾶλλον δὲ ὅλον ἡ τύχη** παρὰ πάντ᾽ ἐστὶ τὰ τῶν
ἀνθρώπων #πράγματα.

Period 3:
οὐ μήν ἀλλ᾽ ἔγωγε,
εἴ τις αἵρεσίν # μοι δοίη,
τὴν #τῆς ἡμετέρας πόλεως τύχην ἂν ἑλοίμην ἐθελόντων,
ἃ προσήκει, ποιεῖν ὑμῶν καὶ κατὰ μικρόν, ἢ τὴν ἐκείνου.

Period 4:
Πολὺ γὰρ πλείους ἀφορμὰς εἰς τὸ τὴν # παρὰ τῶν θεῶν εὔνοιαν
ἔχειν ὁρῶ ὑμῖν ἐνούσας ἢ ἐκείνῳ.[71]

Dionysius mentions the hiatus (noted above with asterisks) and consonant clash (noted above with pound signs) characteristic of the austere style that punctuate the otherwise smooth sounds in this example. Dionysius singles out the phrase in boldface type in the second period as one in which short vowel sounds are sustained for too long a time for the polished style. He states that the fourth period reverts to the austere style by virtue of its harsh sounds and disjointed cola (*Dem.* 43).

OTHER TYPOLOGIES

The stylistic classifications outlined above do not exhaust the categories that ancient literary critics devised, but represent well the schemes in common use. Dionysius of Halicarnassus writes that standardized names for the various stylistic types do not exist, but "anyone who likes may assign the appropriate names when he has heard their characteristics and their differences" (*Comp.* 21). Among the other Greek typologies not discussed above, Demetrius's is notable for its complexity and detail. *Περὶ ἑρμηνείας* (*On Interpretation*) contains schemes similar to both of those illustrated above. He identifies two kinds of expression (ἑρμηνείας), the compact and disjointed, much like Aristotle's classification of periodic and continuous style (λέξις), which is based primarily upon the construction and arrangement of cola (*Eloc.* 12–14). Demetrius further delineates four stylistic types with distinctive characters (χαρακτῆρες)—similar to Dionysius's three-part classification of austere, polished, and blended style (ἁρμονία)—that are based primarily upon the various musical effects possible through the use of euphony, and the construction of periods (*Eloc.* 36). Demetrius's stylistic types include the grand, exhibiting characteristics of both the austere and the polished styles of Dionysius (*Eloc.* 36–126); the elegant (*Eloc.* 127–189), like Dionysius's polished style; the plain, like Aristotle's continuous style (*Eloc.* 190–239); and the forceful, which is similar to Dionysius's austere style (*Eloc.* 240–303).[72] Demetrius's lengthy and detailed descriptions contain specifications for grammatical construction, euphonic characteristics, colon length, periodic quality, word choice, and the use of figures.

Cicero and Quintilian illustrate the standard Latin typologies of literary style. Cicero's resembles that of Dionysius of Halicarnassus. It identifies three types, the full (*plena*) and rounded (*teres*), the plain that does not lack vigor and force (*tenuis non sine nervis ac viribus*), and one that combines elements of each (*ea quae particeps utriusque generis*) (*De Or.* 3.51.199). Quintilian, following Aristotle, identifies two stylistic types based upon the construction and arrangement of cola, the closely woven (*vincta atque contexta*) or periodic, and the loosely woven (*soluta*) or continuous (*Inst.* 9.4.19).

Precise distinctions among the various stylistic types seems less important for both the Greek and Latin commentators than the fact that the various ways of selecting and combining vocal sounds had definite and powerful effects. Certain rhythms and melodies were deemed appropriate for specific social occasions. For example, works composed of short cola marked by hiatus and phonetic dissonance were deemed suitable for noble, authoritative speech (Arist. *Rh.* 3.9.1–5; Demetr. *Eloc.* 38–78; Dion. Hal. *Dem.* 38–39; and *Comp.* 22), whereas phonetically fluid cola linked by paratactic connectives seemed appropriate for the historical narrative or the logical argument of philosophical discourse (Arist. *Rh.* 3.9.1; Demetr. *Eloc.* 190–91; Dion. Hal. *Dem.* 40; and *Comp.* 23). Longer cola marked by euphony and set in parallel with other cola exemplified the polished or elegant style, employed primarily to entertain or edify the audience (Demetr. *Eloc.* 128–88; Dion. Hal. *Dem.* 2). Above all, the length and character of the period's composite members must be appropriate, whether long or short (Demetr. *Eloc.* 4–8). Regardless of the stylistic scheme, analyses of style proceeded by listening to a text's aural units, its cola and periods, all of which exhibited grammatical integrity.[73]

APPLICATION OF STYLE

In recognition of these differences and their impact on the hearer, the classical stylebooks frequently advocate a mixture of both to obtain the advantages of each (Quint. *Inst.* 9.4.91).[74] Demetrius's prescriptions for the mixed style are typical:

> Discourse should neither . . . consist wholly of a string of periods, nor be wholly disconnected, but should rather combine the two methods. It will then be elaborate and simple at the same time, and draw charm from both sources, being neither too untutored nor too artificial (*Eloc.* 15).

Seeming "untutored" is the danger of continuous style, while highly periodic style risks sounding artificial. Demetrius's commentary implies that the original audiences of Hellenistic Greek compositions were keenly sensitive to their auditory elements.

Depending on how they were constructed, literary compositions created different kinds of music. The author of the first century CE treatise *Περὶ ὕψους* states, "Composition . . . is a kind of melody in words" ([Longinus], *Subl.* 39.3). Classical commentators required that a composition's language suit its purpose. The attention that ancient literary critics paid to the construction and arrangement of cola and periods illustrates their aural orientation. Their formal and aesthetic standards of composition fostered the production and blending of beautiful sounds that were supposed to be appropriate to the meanings they signified. Cicero compares words with wax, a material molded to form various shapes:

> Consequently at one moment we use a dignified style, at another a plain one, and at another we keep a middle course between the two; thus the style of our oratory follows the line of thought we take, and changes and turns to suit all the requirements of pleasing the ear and influencing the mind of the audience (*De Or.* 3.45.177).

All formal and aesthetic standards of composition were governed by the goal of appropriateness:

> In regard to style (λέξεως), one of its chief merits (ἀρετή) may be defined as perspicuity (σαφῆ). This is shown by the fact that the speech (ὁ λόγος), if it does not make the meaning clear, will not perform its proper function; neither must it be mean, nor above the dignity of the subject, but appropriate (πρέπουσαν) to it (Arist. *Rh.* 3.2.2).[75]

Dionysius of Halicarnassus explains: "Just as certain clothes suit certain bodies, so certain language fits certain thought" (*Dem.* 18). Aristotle insists on certain propriety of style:

> A different style is suitable to each kind of Rhetoric. That of written compositions is not the same as that of debate; nor, in that latter, is that of public speaking the same as that of the law courts (*Rh*. 3.12.1).[76]

These stylistic differences were thought to be appropriate to the topic at hand:

> Propriety of style will be obtained by the expression of emotion and character, and by proportion to the subject matter. Style is proportionate to the subject matter when neither weighty matters are treated offhand, nor trifling matters with dignity, and no embellishment is attached to an ordinary word (Arist. *Rh*. 3.7.1–2).

Quintilian elaborates:

> Our rhythm must be designed to suit our delivery. . . . [D]o we not adapt our voice and gesture to the nature of the themes on which we are speaking? There is, therefore, all the less reason for wonder that the same is true of the feet employed in prose, since it is natural that what is sublime should have a stately stride, that what is gentle should seem to be led along, that what is violent should seem to run and what is tender to flow (*Inst*. 9.4.138–39).

Hellenistic history writing was governed by the requirement both that historical narratives should be plainly laid out without flourishes or undue artifice, and that the speeches embedded in those narratives should be written in a style appropriate to the speaker and the occasion. Thucydides, for example, affirms that his narrative is reliable because his conclusions ". . . will not be disturbed either by the ways of a poet displaying the exaggeration of his craft, or by the compositions of the chroniclers that are attractive at truth's expense . . ." (1.21). And because it was difficult for him to remember word for word after the Peloponnesian war ended the speeches that he heard before and during the war, Thucydides endeavored to "make the speakers say what was in my opinion demanded of them by the various occasions, of course adhering as closely as possible to the general sense of what they really said" (1.22). Thucydides's practice became accepted as the norm[77] and was reiterated by Lucian (*c*. 115– after 180 CE):[78]

> The body of the history is simply a long narrative. So let it be adorned with the virtues proper to narrative, progressing smoothly, evenly and consistently, free from humps and hollows. Then let its clarity be limpid, achieved, as I have said, both by diction and the interweaving of the matter (*Hist. conscr*. 55).[79]

Concerning speeches in historical narrative, Lucian prescribes, "let his language suit his person and his subject, and next let these also be as clear as possible. It is then, however, that you can play the orator and show your eloquence" (*Hist. conscr.* 58).

Different stylistic effects are achieved by careful crafting that attends to the characteristics of speech as sound. Quintilian explains:

> No one will deny that some portions of our speech require a gentle flow of language, while others demand speed, sublimity, pugnacity, ornateness or simplicity, as the case may be, or that long syllables are best adapted to express dignity, sublimity and ornateness. [But] passages of an opposite character, such as those in which we argue, distinguish, jest or use language approximating to colloquial speech, are better served by short syllables (*Inst.* 9.4.130–31).

Ancient theorists upheld the requirement of an appropriate fit between a compositional strategy or technique and its pragmatic objective, and they specifically applied this requirement to their compositional art.

LEVELS OF COMPOSITION

The foregoing survey of composition's elements indicates that Greek authors crafted their works with their auditory impact in mind at every level of construction. They analyzed works after the fact to evaluate and also to improve the sounded quality of their compositions. The levels of construction and analysis are summarized below.

Hellenistic Greek boasts the significant advantage of providing a vast body of literature that reflects on its own literate culture. Reflections on γραμματική, λέξις, and σύνθεσις provide a comprehensive system of categories and criteria for literary analysis. Their system is founded upon the grounding of Hellenistic Greek literature in a culture primarily dependent upon oral performance for

Levels of Composition

	γραμματική **Grammar**	λέξις **Speech**	σύνθεσις **Composition**
Goal	ἡ εὐφωνία pleasing sounds	ἀρετὴ λέξεως good diction	ἡ ἁρμονία harmony
Function	capture speech sounds	join sounds to form phrases	harmonize sounds into an effective whole
Linguistic arena	phonology	syntax	semantics
Primary concern	grammar	diction	style
Basic unit	syllable	colon	period

publication and memory for storage and recall. Modern interpreters of Hellenistic Greek texts must evaluate such texts according to the standards and criteria with which they were composed before it is possible to appreciate the proper meaning of these texts.

ENDNOTES

1. Schmidt (1985, pp. 28, 30) notes the emphasis on the spoken character of the language in the contemporary study of Hellenistic Greek, especially in the work of Winer and Moulton.
2. "Publication throughout antiquity always had a large oral component." (Small 1997, p. 40). See chapter 1, "The Technology of Writing in the Greco-Roman World," above.
3. The limited role of instrumentation in ancient Greek music indicates the primacy of the human voice in all forms of communication and public performance in classical and Hellenistic Greece. "Greek music was fundamentally vocal—and hence literary—in character" (Mathiesen 1999, p. 159). Mathiesen also notes that Plato and Aristotle "regarded instrumental music as inferior to vocal music" (1999, pp. 159–60). "Instruments were sometimes played on their own, but mostly they served to accompany the human voice. There normally was such accompaniment . . . but its role was subordinate" (West 1992, p. 39).
4. Achtemeier (1990, pp. 3, n. 2) argues that ". . . we need to keep in mind the essentially oral communication of the written texts of the NT and shape our examination of those texts, and their interpretation, accordingly."
5. See the extensive argument in Lentz (1989), especially chapter 4, "Orality and Literacy in Basic Education" (pp. 46–70).
6. Kaster (1993, p. 337) shows that, while our information concerning the format and curriculum of education in antiquity is still debated, considerable attrition would have occurred in the transition from the earliest to the latest educational stages, whatever system is proposed.
7. Although Cribiore's evidence comes primarily from Egypt, there is no reason to think that the usefulness of learning to inscribe one's name differed in Egypt from the rest of the Mediterranean world.
8. Pottery fragments inscribed with sequences of syllables that pair successive consonants with each vowel also offer evidence of this educational practice. A typical example preserved in the British Museum illustrates this kind of writing exercise. For a photograph, see Beck (1975, p. 16).

9. "The division of words into syllables was a fundamental step in education. One of the practical effects of the syllabic method of instruction was to teach how to break words at line end, and the extreme consistency of scribes in literary and documentary papyri shows that education succeeded at this" (Cribiore 1996, p.87).
10. See also Marrou (1956, p. 150–52).
11. Robins (1957, pp. 102–103) documents what little dissension exists with this "generally held view," based primarily upon concerns about authenticity arising from a scholiast's comments and some potentially spurious later additions to the treatise. Thrax's grammar deals primarily with phonology and grammar but not with syntax, which was not systematized until the second century CE with the Alexandrian grammarian Apollonius Dyscolus, whose syntax built on Thrax's Γραμματική.
12. This is in spite of Thrax's description of grammar as ἐμπειρία (skill), which ranked below τέχνη (science) in a hierarchical scale of intellectual activity. Thrax's description focused the pragmatic aspects of his grammar, which were aimed at the larger goal of correct reading aloud (Robins 1957, pp. 79–80).
13. Robins continues, "Later in antiquity the term also encompassed correct Greek (Ἑλληνισμός), a good written style, and the general study of literature" (1957, 78).
14. Plato states: ". . . by the science of grammar we assign these letters—alpha, beta, and the rest—to names. . . ." (*Cra.* 431e–432a). See also *De Musica* (1131d), where grammar is classified with music as a vocal art. Aristotle cites as an example of a comprehensive science the science of grammar, which "studies all articulate sounds. (*Metaph.* 4.2.6).
15. Although traditionally atttibuted to Plutarch, the pseudonomous attribution of *De Musica* is now generally recognized.
16. The organization of these disciplines governed the old Athenian education that held sway until the intellectual revolution of the fifth century BCE. The study of letters and music were then separated in the formal academic curriculum. (Marrou 1956, pp. 41–43, 69–72). For a discussion of the influence of orality and sound on basic education in ancient Greece, see Lentz (1989, pp. 49–51).
17. For a discussion of the grammar of the Stoics see Sandys (1921, pp. 146–50).
18. See also Aristotle (*Poet.* 20.3–4). For a description of these phonetic categories according to modern phonetic theory, see Allen (1987, pp. 12–61).

19. This is not to say that the elements of sound have no meaning. Aristotle (*Int.* 2) clarifies the point by distinguishing between nonsense and noise. Noise has meaning, he explains, but not in the sense of articulate sound. Nor does Plato deny the elements of sound any meaning. For example, he argues (*Cra.* 405–406) for a word's meaning based on the meaning of its component sounds.
20. But Ryle (1960, pp. 431–51) contends that Plato sometimes used γράμματα (letters) for phonetic elements as well.
21. For examples of writings that make use of this distinction, see Pl. *Plt.* 277; Arist. *Metaph.* 5.3.1–4; and Dion. Hal. *Comp.* 14. Both στοιχεῖον and γράμμα are frequently translated into English as "letter," but this is misleading since it fails to specify, as the Greeks did, whether the term refers to the written sign or its phonetic value.
22. Note that this progress coheres with the material evidence, especially that cited in Cribiore (1996, p. 137), indicating that students typically could not read their written marks as they learned to write, and that they learned about syllables only as they learned later to read.
23. For illustrations and an expanded description, see Metzger (1992, pp. 10–13).
24. Aristotle (*Metaph.* 5.3.1) defines στοιχεῖον as "the primary immanent thing, formally indivisible into another form, of which something is composed." In the same passage, he specifically invokes the example of sound: "the elements (στοιχεῖα) of sound are the parts of which that sound is composed and into which it is ultimately divisible, and which are not further divisible into other sounds formally different from themselves. If an element be divided, the parts are formally the same as the whole: e.g., a part of water is water; but it is not so with the syllable (συλλαβῆς)."
25. Aristotle (*Poet.* 20.5) denies the syllable any semantic meaning, but recognizes it as a complete articulate sound, φωνή.
26. Translation by Robins (1967, p. 33).

    Even in the classical era the Greeks certainly knew how to distinguish the lexical unit, but their emphasis on its sounded character continued through the Hellenistic age and after Dionysius Thrax. Both before and after the clear distinction of the various parts of speech, the focus on sound and the primacy of speech prevailed.
27. Grube (1952, pp. 257–58) correctly notes that λέξις can refer to style in a general sense or a particular quality of style, but it most

often refers to diction as opposed to composition or to the treatment of a topic. Its meaning is therefore determined by context.

28. Robins finds it odd that the grammar that evolved from the Greek language does not "proceed first with the formal identification of the word unit, then with the classes of words, and finally with the categories relevant to them" (1967, p. 25). But this phenomenon is anomalous only from the point of view of a print culture that understands the lexeme as the building block of prose because words are primarily apprehended visually on the printed page as discrete units surrounded by white space.
29. Innes (1985, p. 260) shows that Theophrastus stands firmly in Aristotle's camp and that his expansion of Aristotle's definition amplifies it without altering its fundamental meaning.
30. Modern linguistics continues to stress the primacy of sound in communication. Ferdinand de Saussure writes: "The linguistic sign unites, not a thing and a name, but a concept and a sound-image. The latter is not the material sound, a purely physical thing, but the psychological imprint of the sound, the impression that it makes on our senses" (1966, p. 66). More recently, it has been shown that Saussure's model is too simple because "the actual relation between language and writing is far more complex . . . [and] reading can actually be divorced from language entirely . . ." (Fischer 2003, p. 330). But in the Hellenistic world, reading and writing were essentially linked to speech and sound, as Fisher himself affirms: "Reading and writing did not exist as autonomous domains of activity. They were minimal appendages to speech" (2003, p. 14–15).
31. See also *LSJ s.v.* λόγος. Small (1997, p. 204) claims that Jerome's Latin Vulgate translation of John 1:1 is probably responsible for the mistranslation of ὁ λόγος as "the word" in English.
32. Occasionally ὀνόματα occurs alone (see Dion. Hal. *Comp.* 1), but in such cases it should be understood as a kind of shorthand for ὀνόματα καὶ ῥήματα.
33. Plato (*Soph.* 263a) gives two examples of a subject: "Theatetus," in the sentence, "Theatetus sits," and "Theatetus, with whom I am now talking," in the sentence, "Theatetus, with whom I am now talking, flies."
34. As evidence, Small (24) points to the phonetic method of teaching reading in antiquity outlined above. "The unit of the word . . . is not considered from the point of view of its meaning, but rather of its pronunciation."
35. "Τοῦ δὲ λόγου μέρη ὀκτώ, ὄνομα, ῥῆμα, μετοχή, ἄρθρον,

ἀντωνυμία, πρόθεσις, ἐπίῤῥημα καὶ σύνδεσμος" (13). Robins (1957, pp. 97–102) notes that Thrax's categories remain useful even today, although a few aspects of Thrax's system diverge from modern grammatical categories, including the separation of the participle into its own word class, the inclusion of the adjective with nouns, and the inclusion of the relative pronoun with the article.

36. The Loeb edition's translation of κῶλα as "clauses" is potentially misleading because "clause" connotes in modern grammar a technical meaning that does not match precisely the meaning of κῶλα in Hellenistic Greek grammar.
37. Kelber (1994, pp. 193–216), one of the first to appreciate the importance of the technology of communication in biblical study, has called for a thorough re-examination of literary composition in the Greco-Roman world in view of the close association of composition and performance.
38. In Harmony's mythical personification (Hes. *Theog*. 901, 963; Aesch. *PV*. 545, *Supp*. 1034; Strabo *Geography* 7.7.8.), she is the daughter of Ares and Aphrodite and the wife of Cadmus, legendary founder of Thebes who was said to have civilized the Boeotians by teaching them to write in Phoenician letters.
39. See, for example, Pl. *Phdr*. 268.
40. Ultimately, he argues that the analogy does not hold. The soul governs the body's actions but the lyre's strings and the way they are strung and plucked determine the quality of harmony they produce. Musical harmony can exist in degrees, whereas the soul either is or is not present in the body (*Phd*. 85–96).
41. Josephus (*AJ* 8.69, 12.76) describes the harmonious construction of the Jerusalem temple. Pausanias (2.27.5) praises Polycleitus' pleasing architectural design of the theater at Epidaurus.
42. Pausanias (2.25.8) marvels at the stonework in the Cyclopean walls of Tiryns.
43. See also Joseph. *AJ* 14.2.
44. Dionysius offers a famous example from Homer, arguing that Homer uses very ordinary words but achieves powerful and moving effects, thus his power to persuade lies in συνθέσις (composition) rather than ἐκλογή (word choice) (*Comp*. 3).
45. The author of *Περὶ ὕψους* ([Longinus] *Subl*. 2.2, 36.3) also affirms that nature and art are inextricably linked in composition.
46. Both have rhythm, he explains (*Comp*. 17–18), but poetry also has meter.
47. Ancient literary critics delineated prose and poetic units on similar terms, with close attention to their effectiveness as units

of sound. Aristotle (*Rh.* 3.8) introduces his discussion of literary style with analyses of prose rhythm, based upon poetic forms. Quintilian (*Inst.* 9.4.2) names rhythms as one of the three essential components of artistic structure and describes its importance and application (9.4.91–116). The nearest analogs in modern English to the colon and period are the grammatical clause and the complete sentence, but this comparison should be qualified. In modern English, clauses and sentences are delineated according to formal criteria concerning grammatical content and independence.

48. Lord (1960) articulates his Oral-Formulaic theory, which was refined and extended by Foley (1988).
49. "Περίοδος δὲ μὲν ἐν κώλοις, ἡ δ᾽ ἀδφελής. ἔστι δ᾽ ἐν κώλοοις μὲν λέξις ἡ τετελειωμένη τι καὶ διῃρημένη καὶ εὐανάπνευστος" (*Rh.* 3.9.5). I have adapted the LCL translation to make it more literal. John Henry Freese's translation uses "clause" and "sentence," which are confusing terms in this discussion because of their technical meanings.
50. Various lengths are possible. Demetrius (*Eloc.* 1–7) offers a twenty-seven syllable phrase to illustrate a long colon and an eleven-syllable phrase as a short colon.
51. "The length of a period is limited by the length of breath, and by the intellectual capacity for overview ('memory')." (Lausberg 1998, p. 416).
52. But Lausberg cautions: "In the study of meter something quite different is understood by colon and comma; the colon is part of a verse which respects the boundaries of the metrical foot, whereas the comma does not respect the boundaries of the metrical foot." (1998, pp. 416–17).
53. Quintilian (*Inst.* 9.4.122) observes that most writers consider a comma as a portion of a colon.
54. Kleist (1928, p.26) elaborates: " In view of this lack of more precise information from ancient sources we are justified in allowing ourselves a certain latitude in applying the colometric system to ancient texts."
55. While from a technical standpoint all prose could be understood to consist of periods, well-rounded and balanced periods could be distinguished from periods that merely met certain minimal technical requirements. The wide range available for periodic structure explains why the period could be classified as a figure, as in *Rhet. Her.* 4.19.27.
56. Λέξις can denote syle in a general sense but it more often refers to diction, or to the contribution to style made by appropriate

word choice (see Grube 1952, pp. 257–58). Likewise, σύνθεσις can refer to the harmonious blending of syllables to form cola, of cola to form periods, and of periods to form compositions.

57. Λέξις: Arist. *Rh.* 3.4.5. Χαρακτήρ: Demetr. *Eloc.* 36; Dion. Hal. *Dem.* 37. Latin critics also classify various stylistic types, each suited to its own pragmatic purpose. See, for example, *Rhet. Her.* 4.8.11 and Quint. *Inst.* 9.4.19.
58. The term derives from χαράσσω, to make pointed, sharpen, or whet, to furnish with notches or teeth like a saw, or to smite or brand (*LSJ s.v.* χαράσσω). The noun χαρακτήρ refers to an engraver, an engraving tool, or its resulting stamp (*LSJ s.v.* χαρακτήρ).
59. "Demetrius" in this discussion refers to the author of *Περὶ ἑρμηνείας*. A tenth century manuscript falsely attributes this work to Demetrius of Phaleron (c. 360–280 BCE), a student of Aristotle. The author of *Περὶ ἑρμηνείας* is unknown and dating is debated. References to historical persons in the text indicate the work cannot be earlier than the first half of the third century BCE, and the author's apparent ignorance of Cicero and of Dionysius of Halicarnassus' typology of styles suggests a date before 30 BCE (Innes 1995, pp. 312–15). Possible references to Philodemus would require a date before the first century BCE but the work's content is consistent with that of the early Peripatetics (Kennedy 1989, p. 196).
60. As Grube (1952) properly points out, the two-type classification proposed by Aristotle refers specifically to the construction of periods rather than to literary style in the sense of the pragmatic effect of a composition as a whole. This distinction helps to interpret Demetrius's preservation both of Aristotle's two-type theory and of Dionysius's three-type theory, which he expands to four types. The distinction between the construction of periods and a composition's overall stylistic tone is also helpful when confronting the apparent contradiction in Greek literary theory posed by "non-periodic" or continuous style, since all literature is composed of periods, even if a period consists of only one colon. But Grube overcomplicates the point by distinguishing too sharply between "sentence structure" and "literary style" in Aristotle and Theophrastus, primarily because "sentence" and "literary" in our senses of these terms do not exist in Hellenistic Greek prose theory. Hellenistic Greek does not have sentences, but only periods. And style is never "literary" in the sense of a separate genre of (silently read) literature divorced from oral performance. As the historical development of stylistic classifications

in antiquity shows, Aristotle's distinction between periodic and continuous prose helped eventually to sharpen a growing awareness of various stylistic effects in subsequent literary criticism, even if Aristotle did not propose a typology of two literary styles in the modern sense, or even in the sense used by Dionysius of Halicarnassus. For Aristotle, continuous and periodic prose remain at the level of λέξις (speech, diction, style), not σύνθεσις (composition).

61. "ἡ μέν οὖν εἰρομένη λέξις ἡ ἀρχαία ἐστίν" (Arist. *Rh.* 1409a). Demetrius (*Eloc.* 14) compares the "disjointed" (continuous) style with archaic statues with sharp, clean lines, and the "compact" (periodic) style with the grander, more polished sculptures of Phidias.
62. Both Aristotle and Demetrius state that their cola are combined using connecting particles, but their examples do not illustrate this.
63. "This is the exposition of the investigation of Herodotus of Thurii."
64. "Hecataeus of Miletus speaks as follows. I write these things as they seem to me to be true. For the stories told by the Greeks are, as it appears to me, many and absurd."
65. "I have often wondered at those who gathered together the general assemblies and instituted the gymnastic contest."
66. "They were useful to both, both those who stayed and those who followed; for the latter they gained in addition greater possessions than they had at home, for the former they left what was sufficient in their own country."
67. Origination of the threefold classification of style is often attributed to Aristotle's student and his successor as head of the Lyceum, Theophrastus, most of whose works are not extant but can be partially reconstructed from quotations by Dionysius of Halicarnassus, Demetrius, Cicero, Quintilian, Ammonius, and Simplicius. The attribution is made on the basis of Dionysius of Halicarnassus (*Dem.* 3) in which Dionysius reports that Theophrastus credits the invention of a third, middle, style to Thrasymachus. Grube (1952, pp. 251–67) refutes the view that the three-style theory comes to Dionysius from Thrasymachus through Theophrastus on the grounds that Dionysius's topic in the passage in question is word choice (ἐκλογὴ ὀνομάτων), not style. Theophrastus is generally understood to "continue and extend" the work of Aristotle (Sharples 1996, pp. 1504–05). Thus Innes (1985, pp. 251–67) argues that Theophrastus advocated a Peripatetic mean between the extremes of plain and grand style,

consistent with his promotion of the paean as a mean between the dactyl and the iamb in prose rhythm and of terseness (συστροφή) as a mean between the unstructured and overly structured periods. The threefold classification of Dionysius of Halicarnassus can even be interpreted in terms of a Peripatetic mean between the extremes of plain (austere) and grand (polished) style (Bonner 1938, pp. 257–66). It may be that Theophrastus's extension of Aristotle's twofold typology eventually evolved into the three-type theory of Dionysius of Halicarnassus (Kennedy 1989). For our purposes it is sufficient to observe that Dionysius's threefold typology is not inconsistent with Aristotle's two types. Both argue for a stylistic gradient from unadorned plain style to ornamented, elaborate style, and both require that a composition's style should be appropriate to the composition's topic and purpose.

68. "[Period 1:] Thucydides, an Athenian, wrote this history describing the war which the Peloponnesians and the Athenians waged against one another, [period 2:] beginning the work as soon as the way broke out because he expected that it would be great and memorable above all previous wars. [Period 3:] He inferred this from the fact that both sides were entering upon it at the height of their military power, and from the realization that the rest of the Greek races were ranging themselves on one side or the other at the outset, or were intending to do so before long." Divisions into cola and periods are from Dionysius.
69. "[Period 1:] For when they were not able to draw themselves up against both the land and the sea forces at once, they took with them the entire population, abandoned the city, and sailed to the neighbouring island, in order that they might face the threat from each of the two forces in turn and not from both at once. [Period 2:] And yet how could men be shown to be braver or more fervent lovers of Greece than our ancestors who, to avoid bringing slavery upon the rest of Greece, endured seeing their city made desolate, their land plundered, their sanctuaries rifled, their temples burned, and the whole weight of the war pressing upon their country?" Dionysius does not analyze this passage into cola and periods but attributes of the style as described by Dionysius are noted in the illustration above.
70. Bonner (1938, pp. 257–66) argues convincingly that Dionysius's approval of the blended style derives from his following the peripatetic values of Aristotle and Theophrastus in favoring a moderate path between stylistic extremes.
71. "[Period 1:] If any of you, Athenians, regards Philip as a formidable opponent because you see him enjoying good fortune, that

is sound reasoning. [Period 2:] Fortune is of great importance—or rather, she is all-important—in all human affairs. [Period 3:] But that is not to say that, given the choice, I should not prefer our city's fortune to Philip's, if only you would do your duty even to a slight degree. [Period 4:] For I see that you have many more claims to divine favour than he has. But we sit, I presume, doing nothing; and a man who is himself idle cannot require even his friends to help him, much less the gods." Dionysius delineates the periods.

72. Roberts (1928, p.61) claims that Demetrius is the only critic to classify separately the forcible or forceful style, apparently to find a suitable category for the style of Demosthenes, who stood in a class by himself.
73. The Hellenistic practice of analyzing style according to the sounded quality of a composition's grammatical units provides further evidence that the aural dimension of a composition was rooted in its grammatical structure and also supplied an essential component of meaning.
74. Dionysius of Halicarnassus, strong advocate for the mixed style, claims that the style emerged in the philosophical dialogues of Plato and developed with the works of Thrasymachus and the orator Isocrates, culminating with Demosthenes, its most accomplished exemplar (*Dem.* 1–4, 14a).
75. Quintilian (*Inst.* 1.5.1) also refers to "the all-important quality of appropriateness (*apte, quod est praecipuum*)."
76. Aristotle's distinction between "written compositions" (ἡ γραφική) and "debate" (ἀγωνιστική) does not suggest the existence of a literary genre or style designed for silent reading (ἡ γραφική). Kennedy's commentary on this passage is helpful: "Before the end of the fifth century B.C. [*sic*] most oratory was extempore and not published in written form; but sophists like Gorgias began the writing and publishing of epideictic speeches, and this was continued by Isocrates. In judicial oratory, speechwriters (*logographoi*)—of whom Antiphon is perhaps the earliest and Lysias the most famous—had made a profession for themselves in ghostwriting speeches for clients to memorize and deliver in court, and some of these speeches were published. By Aristotle's time, political orators, including Demosthenes, were publishing written, polished versions of speeches they had earlier delivered. Though writing had been introduced into Greece in the ninth century, 'publication' long remained a matter of oral presentation. . . . Rhetoric gave increased attention to the study of written composition. The radical effects of greater reliance on writing

can, however, be exaggerated; ancient society remained oral to a much greater degree than modern society, and the primary goal of the teaching of rhetoric was consistently an ability to speak in public" (1991, p. 254).

77. "Thucydides' methodological statements . . . were likely the best-known in the Greek literary world" (Sacks 1984, p. 133).
78. "Lucian reflects the general criteria for history writing expressed in the classical, Hellenistic, and Roman periods" (Sacks 1984, p. 124). Sacks (1984, pp. 125–132) further traces the evolution of the requirement of appropriateness in history writing through the rhetorical work of Dionysius of Halicarnassus.
79. Note that Lucian employs the metaphor of woven fabric for the craft of history writing, referring as quoted above to "the interweaving of the matter (τῇ συμπεριπλοκῇ τῶν πραγμάτων)."

WORKS CONSULTED

Achtemeier, Paul J. 1990. *Omne Verbum Sonat*. *JBL* 109:3–27.

Allen, W. S. 1987. *Vox Graeca: A Guide to the Pronunciation of Classical Greek*. 3d ed. Cambridge: Cambridge University.

Beck, Frederick A. G. 1975. *Album of Greek Education: The Greeks at School and Play*. Sydney: Cheiron.

Bonner, S. F. 1938. Dionysius of Halicarnassus and the Peripatetic Mean of Style. *CP* XXXIII:257–66.

Cribiore, Raffaella. 1996. *Writing, Teachers, and Students in Graeco-Roman Egypt*. Atlanta: Scholars.

Fischer, Steven Roger. 2003. *A History of Reading*. Edited by J. Black, *Globalities*. London: Reaktion Books.

Foley, John Miles. 1988. *The Theory of Oral Composition: History and Methodology*, *Folkloristics*. Bloomington: Indiana University Press.

———. 1995. *The Singer of Tales in Performance*. Bloomington and Indianapolis: Indiana University Press.

Grube, G. M. A. 1952. Thrasymachus, Theophrastus, and Dionysius of Halicarnassus. *American Journal of Philology* 73:251–67.

Havelock, Eric A. 1982. *The Literate Revolution in Greece and its Cultural Consequences*. Princeton: Princeton University Press.

Innes, Doreen C. 1985. Theophrastus and the Theory of Style. *Rutgers University Studies* 2:251–67.

———. 1995. Introduction to Demetrius, On Style. In *Aristotle XXIII*, edited by G. P. Goold. Cambridge and London: Harvard.

Kaster, Robert A. 1993. Notes on Primary and Secondary Schools in Late Antiquity. *TAPA* 113:223–46.

Kelber, Werner. 1994. Modalities of Communication, Cognition, and Physiology of Perception: Orality, Rhetoric, Scribality. *Semeia* 65:193–216.

Kennedy, George A. 1989. The Evolution of a Theory of Artistic Prose. In *The Cambridge History of Literary Criticism*, edited by G. A. Kennedy. Cambridge: Cambridge University Press.

———. 1989. Language and Meaning in Archaic and Classical Greece. In *The Cambridge History of Literary Criticism*, edited by G. A. Kennedy. Cambridge: Cambridge University Press.

———. 1991. *Aristotle On Rhetoric: A Theory of Civic Discourse*. Translated by G. A. Kennedy. New York, London: Oxford University Press.

Kleist, James A. 1928. Colometry and the New Testament (Concluded). *Classical Bulletin* 4:26–27.

Kloppenborg Verbin, John S. 2000. *Excavating Q: The History and Setting of the Sayings Gospel*. Minneapolis: Fortress.

Lausberg, Heinrich. 1998. *Handbook of Literary Rhetoric*. Translated by M. T. Bliss, A. Jansen and D. E. Orton. Leiden: Brill.

Lentz, Tony. 1989. *Orality and Literacy in Hellenic Greece*. Carbondale, IL: Southern Illinois University Press.

Lord, Albert B. 1960. *The Singer of Tales, Harvard Studies in Comparative Literature, 24*. Cambridge: Harvard University Press.

Marrou, Henri-I. 1956. *A History of Education in Antiquity*. Translated by G. Lamb, *Wisconsin Studies in Classics*. Madison, WI: University of Wisconsin Press, [1982].

Mathiesen, Thomas J. 1999. *Apollo's Lyre: Greek Music and Music Theory in Antiquity and the Middle Ages*. Lincoln: University of Nebraska Press.

Metzger, Bruce M. 1981. *Manuscripts of the Greek Bible: An Introduction to Greek Paleography*. New York: Oxford University Press.

———. 1992. *The Text of the New Testament: Its Transmission, Corruption, and Restoration*. 3d ed. New York, Oxford: Oxford University Press.

Roberts, W. Rhys. 1928. *Greek Rhetoric and Literary Criticism*. London: Longmans.

Robins, R. H. 1957. Dionysius Thrax and the Western Grammatical Tradition. *TPS*:67–106.

Robins, Robert Henry. 1951. *Ancient and Mediaeval Grammatical Theory in Europe*. London: Bell.

———. 1967. *A Short History of Linguistics, Indiana University Studies in the History and Theory of Linguistics*. Bloomington: Indiana University Press.

Ryle, Gilbert. 1960. Letters and Syllables in Plato. *Philosophical Review* LXIX:431–51.

Sacks, K. 1984. Rhetorical Approaches to Greek History Writing in the Hellenistic Period. In *SBLSP*, edited by K. Richards. Chico: Scholars.

Sandys, John Edwin. 1921. *A History of Classical Scholarship*. Reprint of the Cambridge edition Vol. 1: From the Sixth Century B.C. to the End of the Middle Ages. New York: Hafner.

Saussure, Ferdinand de. 1966. *Course in General Lingusitics*. Translated by W. Baskin. New York: McGraw-Hill.

Schmidt, Daryl. 1985. The Study of Hellenistic Greek Grammar in the Light of Contemporary Linguistics. In *Perspectives on the New Testament: Essays in Honors of Frank Stagg*, edited by C. H. Talbert. Macon, GA: Mercer University Press.

Sharples, Robert William. 1996. *Theophrastus*. In *The Oxford Classical Dictionary*, edited by S. Hornblower and A. Spawforth. Oxford: Oxford.

Small, Jocelyn Penny. 1997. *Wax Tablets of the Mind: Cognitive Studies of Memory and Literacy in Classical Antiquity*. London and New York: Routledge.

Stanford, W. B. 1967. *The Sound of Greek: Studies in the Greek Theory and Practice of Euphony, Sather Classical Lectures*. Berkeley, CA.

West, M. L. 1992. *Ancient Greek Music*. New York: Oxford University Press.

Yates, Francis. 1966. *The Art of Memory*. Chicago: University of Chicago Press.

Chapter 4

Repetition

Sound's Structuring Device

STRUCTURE

Structure makes literary compositions comprehensible. In modern literature typographical conventions visually organize the surface structures of a printed composition. Conceptual structures that organize what is signified take the form of narrative patterns, literary themes, and logical connections. A silent reader accepts a printed composition's surface structure as given and so has no need to construct it. The meaning-making project of silent readers focuses on insight into the significations of various words and phrases. Successful interpretation depends on a silent reader's ability to discern relationships among abstract concepts at the level of semantics. Recurrence of concepts and ideas as signified by various words engages silent readers in the construction of a written composition and thus increases reading satisfaction and enriches the quest for meaning. Printed compositions can be read and reread at will to deepen understanding.

In memorial cultures dependent on speech, the dynamics of comprehension differ because they depend on sound. Auditory signals organize a spoken composition's surface instead of the visual marks that interpret print.[1] Audiences must process compositions in "real time," whereas "readers can refer backward and forwards in the text" (Stubbs 1980, p. 13). An audience cannot afford to rely primarily on semantic meaning to make sense of a spoken composition because real time processing does not afford the opportunity to register every word's full semantic force. Listeners cannot even identify a series of syllables as a lexeme until after the sounds have been spoken and no longer exist as sound but only as memory. Audiences must therefore rely on structural clues to find meaning. In real-time auditory reception, hearers must be guided by a composition's auditory cues to focus on selected items. The audience of John F. Kennedy's 1961 inaugural address instinctively listened for "Ask," as soon as they had heard and comprehended "Ask not."

Spoken compositions must employ different techniques than those communicated through the silent reading of print. Lacking visual surface structures to organize its signifiers—e. g., spaces between words, punctuation, paragraphing, headings, and page layout—audiences of spoken performances construct a composition's surface structure from auditory signals. They must perceive organizational structures as those structures emerge in real time through sound patterns built up syllable by syllable. Each syllable becomes comprehensible only in relation to other sounds.

COLOMETRY

The grammar of sound in Hellenistic Greek unveils the architecture of συμπλοκή and exposes its structural units. Greek grammar analyzes discourse progressively at the level of the syllable, colon, and period. These basic speech units build on each other: syllables form cola, cola form periods, periods build compositions. Each type of speech unit controls a different level of discourse with its unique dynamics. Phonology, syntax and semantics interrelate because they share a common foundation, the syllable. Together the syllable, colon, and period comprise composition's building blocks and account for organizational structure.

Compositions read aloud are declaimed breath by breath. As composition's basic breath unit, the colon serves as composition's structural foundation. Displaying compositions in colometric form simulates their breath-by-breath delivery and allows their structural outlines to emerge.

COLOMETRY IN MANUSCRIPTS

Presenting ancient compositions in colometric form is not a new technique, but an ancient accommodation to the demands presented by reading aloud. Indeed, some New Testament manuscripts are arranged colometrically to aid public reading. Metzger defines colometric transcription:

> Colometry is the division of a text into κῶλα and κόμματα, that is, sense lines of clauses and phrases so as to assist the reader to make the correct inflection and the proper pauses (1981, p. 39).[2]

Gamble has also described the practice:

> The same considerations [*i.e.*, the accommodation of written manuscripts to the demands of effective public reading] resulted eventually in the practice of transcribing scriptural texts per *cola et commata*, that is, in sense lines, each semantic unit (phrase [*comma*] or clause [*colon*]) being written on a separate line (yet still without separating words).

> Such colometric transcription was a departure from the more common stichometric method of scriptio continua, according to which the lines of texts were written out to a standard number of syllables, regardless of the sense units comprised by them. The colometric method attended closely to sense, while the stichometric was merely a matter of space. The transcription of a manuscript in sense-lines anticipated and obviated some of the main difficulties of reading and especially of public reading: a good part of the reader's normal work was done by the manuscript itself, which showed the reader exactly what the sense units were and prescribed the pauses or breaths between (1995, pp. 229–30).[3]

Kleist points out that such manuscripts attest to the importance of the colon as the basic compositional unit in Greek:

> It goes without saying that the colometric presentation of a text was not a purely subjective adjustment made without rhyme or reason. The objective basis for it lay in the building up of the text itself. It was because the ancient writer knew how to compose colometrically that the ancient reader was enabled to recite colometrically (1928, p. 26).

Most early texts arranged to facilitate reading are multilingual manuscripts that may have been read aloud in both languages successively (Gamble 1995, p. 230–31). Perhaps the best examples of such arrangements of the New Testament can be found in Codex Bezae (the gospels and Acts) and Codex Claromontanus (the Pauline corpus) (Schütz 1922, p. 168).[4] Both are diglots, displaying the biblical text in Greek and Latin on facing pages (Aland and Aland 1987, pp. 109–110).

MODERN EFFORTS IN COLOMETRY

In recognition of the importance of the colon as the organizational unit inherent in ancient Greek texts, others have called for the incorporation of colometric analysis into methodologies for modern biblical interpretation. Kleist's articles in 1927 and 1928 made this appeal, based on his understanding of the New Testament as a collection of spoken compositions. He writes:

> If a translation of the New Testament different from the versions in common use were at all desirable, I think I should be for presenting the sacred text in colometric form. In the present-day movement for modernized translation of the New Testament, the first step forward might in my opinion be a step backward, back to the days of the early Christian centuries when the origin of the scriptures was still fresh in the minds of men [*sic.*]. . . . Colometry would do away with two somewhat disturbing things in reading the Bible, first, with that artificial

> division of the text by chapter and verse, and second, with division of the text by paragraph: neither verse nor paragraph was known to the ancient writers. And to the classical teachers I would like to say that, if the early professors of rhetoric saw an advantage in using colometric texts for Demosthenes and Cicero, it may perhaps be to our advantage if we too begin to read and analyze Cicero and Demosthenes with the help of colometry (1928, p. 27).[5]

Two other studies during this time period have observed the importance of colometry in classical and Hellenistic literature and have noted the potential for colometric analysis of the New Testament. Debrunner surveys then-recent critical literature and adduces brief examples from the New Testament, including a colometric display of Luke 9:1–4 (1926, pp. 231–33). Schütz (1922, p. 180) notes the colon's importance for Greek prose rhythm and emphasizes the similarity between the metric line in Greek poetry and the colon in Greek prose.[6]

Despite these calls for colometric analysis of the New Testament, few attempts at such analysis have been made. Perhaps this is because assertions about the structural importance of the colon have not been accompanied by a clear, systematic methodology for identifying and analyzing a composition's colometric structure. A notable effort was undertaken from 1977–1983 by the New Testament Society of South Africa to analyze colometrically the entire Gospel of Matthew. Their goal was a colon-by-colon analysis of the gospel that would provide a foundation for a fresh interpretation of the gospel's structure and meaning. The Society devoted two volumes of *Neotestamentica* to the results of this comprehensive effort in which various scholars each analyzed a chapter of the gospel from the perspective of discourse analysis (Nuwe-Testamentiese Werkgemeenskap van Suid-Afrika 1977 and Nuwe-Testamentiese Werkgemeenskap van Suid-Afrika 1983). It proved a noteworthy effort, even though the variety of scholars engaged in the *Neotestamentica* project and their different perspectives and interests resulted in some fragmentation in method and findings. The *Neotestamentica* project applies to an ancient composition a grammatical approach derived from modern analytical methods. Similarly and more recently, Davis (1999) has analyzed Philippians by cola. Like the *Neotestamentica* project, his "oral biblical criticism" defines "colon" according to the insights of discourse analysis and modern linguistics rather than employing ancient understandings of grammar as a science of sound. Thus both projects miss the primary dynamic that organized compositions for their ancient author and audiences—that of sound.

Davis has employed a three-stage method for "oral biblical criticism" that searches for compositional units. His method employs George Kennedy's six-step method of rhetorical criticism, supplemented by insights drawn from discourse analysis and by the exigencies of "orality," based upon both "oral characteristics" of literature and "characteristics of oral composition" (Davis 1999, 44–63). Davis' three stages of oral biblical criticism are, respectively, analysis of the author's rhetorical style, identification and analysis of units, and analysis of the method of progression from unit to unit (Davis 1999, p. 63).

Davis' oral biblical criticism quite properly emphasizes the spoken character of New Testament literature, but speech is not synonymous with "orality." Davis acknowledges a "blending of orality and literacy" beginning with Plato (Davis 1999, p. 26). His discussion indicates that by such "blending" he means that written materials were used in a social context where oral performance was normal.[7] In recognition of this blending and in response to the methodological problems it poses to critical methods based on "orality," Davis turns to theories of ancient rhetoric, which study written compositions that were publicly declaimed out loud.

Davis' turn to rhetoric is quite appropriate, but his use of rhetorical theory does not take account of sound's role in rhetoric and oral performance. And since writing remained a secondary process in the ancient world, rhetoric's success in serving the communication needs of the Greco-Roman world is not attributable to its blending of speech and writing, but rather derived from its establishment of "common places" for communication where the society's topics and values could be shared. These common places were stored neither in writing nor in speech, but in the wax tablets of the mind and the storehouses of memory—and the storage process depended on sound.

Appropriate critical approaches must account for a composition's organization for storage in memory. Davis' methodological starting point, an author's rhetorical style, begins at the highest level of discourse, the stylistic, at which a host of organizational strategies are assumed, such as the literary characteristics of various rhetorical genres, and catalogs of rhetorical figures. Davis next proceeds to unit identification and analysis armed with expectations to find such conventional devices. Missing is any explicit recognition of the foundation in sound and memory for building such organizational features, beginning at the level of grammar with the colon. As we have argued, ancient compositional techniques built literary style syllable by syllable, colon by colon through the artful manipulation of sound. It is not possible reliably to identify an author's rhetorical style before analyzing a composition's component cola, defined as breath units.

A well-grounded analysis must discern the boundaries of compositional units according to the dynamics of sound, not by abstract, logical schemes or the traditions represented by a printed text. Chapter and verse numbers, titles, and paragraphing must be removed so as not to obstruct the composition's structural features. Sound itself trains an audience's ear, enabling a listener to discern the beginnings and endings of a composition's component units. Often these boundaries differ from those demarcated by chapter divisions or labeled with topical headings in printed texts.

Stowers elucidates the hermeneutical problem caused by artificial divisions that were imposed long after composition by concerns not native to those compositions. He decries the effects of chapter and paragraph divisions imposed upon Paul's letter to the Romans:

> Divisions always impose interpretations upon the text. Whatever criteria are used to divide the text into paragraphs and chapters are necessarily related to what the editor believes about the genre of Romans. The division of Romans in this way forms a kind of outlining according to a certain perception of the argumentation, rhetoric, and contents of the letter. If the editor conceives of Romans as a document to instruct Christians in right doctrines, then that assumption will be reflected in the way that the editor introduces paragraphs. The very concept of a paragraph or a chapter is foreign to Paul's way of writing and obscures his rhetoric (Stowers 1994, pp. 10–11).[8]

As Kleist has remarked, "It was because the ancient writer knew how to compose colometrically that the ancient reader was enabled to recite colometrically" (Kleist 1928, p. 26).

COLOMETRY IN NEED OF SOUND

Because modern attempts to analyze New Testament compositions colometrically have applied modern linguistic categories to ancient literature, they have not produced compelling interpretative results. These efforts have analyzed New Testament compositions as print, not as speech. Missing is a theoretical foundation for analyzing New Testament compositions on their own terms, as woven fabrics of sound. As for ancient manuscripts that have displayed the New Testament colometrically to facilitate public reading aloud, this format can become a useful analytical tool only when supported by a theory for the way sound builds structure in spoken compositions.

Because the ancient Greek τέχνη (science) of grammar served primarily as science of sound, it can supply this missing theoretical foundation. Combined with Hellenistic literary criticism, which analyzed the dynamics of sound in performance, these ancient sources provide a basis for understanding sound as a sequence of events in time.[9] The analysis of sound begins with the ancient definition of a colon as a breath unit and seeks to account for sound's linear character and reception in real time. And just as Hellenisitic literary criticism analyzed how cola were blended into periods and built a unified composition, so a skillful analysis examines compositions colometrically, sound by sound and breath by breath, to discern a composition's structure and meaning.

Fundamental to a theory of sound's structuring function is the observation that sounds uttered singly and sequentially must be comprehended in groups. Sounds are incomprehensible if they seem unrelated. To be comprehended and recalled from memory after being heard, sounds must be organized into patterns.[10] Empirical assessments of perception demonstrate that "groups are perceived in terms of the proximity and the similarity of the elements available to be grouped" (Lerdahl and Jackendoff 1983, p. 41). Repetition makes it possible to perceive sounds as proximate and similar, and therefore to organize sounds into groups. Sounds are grouped when they resemble each other and occur within a time span brief enough to be held intact in memory.

HOW REPETITION CREATES STRUCTURE

Repetition associates sounds, grouping similar sounds together and establishing relationships among sound groups. Repetition distinguishes meaningful sounds from noise by organizing sounds into sensible patterns. This is true for music as well as speech, since both forms of expression are communicated through a linear stream of sound.[11] In Hellenistic Greek, similar inflectional suffixes organize sound groups, such as prepositional phrases or a noun and its article and modifiers. Proximity associates sounds that occur together, especially when they are repeated, as in the case of introductory formulae or epithets. Additional acoustic effects and syntactic strategies build on this basic grouping device to form larger compositional structures.

Repetition serves as sound's most basic structuring device because it accounts for the dynamics of listening: "*attention* to the salient aspects of a complex stimulus, and *memory* of past events which stand in important relationships to present material" (Sloboda 1985, pp. 165–66).[12] Repeated sounds draw attention. A repeated set of auditory signals recalls their previous articulation and invites an audience to reinterpret current sounds in light of sounds that have already occurred. Sounds are remembered in terms of the contributions they make to the emerging aesthetic whole. Sounds must occur in memorable sequences, since each sound must exert its influence on meaning at the moment of utterance and reception to be recorded in memory. Repetition enables audiences to organize a composition's sounds into groups and store them in memory economically, for accurate recall. Ong explains listening dynamics in a memorial culture:

> [T]o solve effectively the problem of retaining and retrieving carefully articulated thought, you have to do your thinking in mnemonic patterns, shaped for ready oral recurrence. Your thought must come into being in heavily rhythmic, balanced patterns, in repetitions or antitheses, in alliterations and assonances, in epithetic and other formulary expressions, in standard thematic settings (the assembly, the mean, the duel, the hero's 'helper', and so on), in proverbs which are constantly heard by everyone so that they come to mind readily and which themselves are patterned for retention and ready recall, or in other mnemonic form. Serious thought is intertwined with memory systems (1982, pp. 33, 34).

In the linear dynamics of auditory reception, sounds heard one at a time are comprehended in relation to other sounds occurring earlier or later in sequence. Listeners hold sound groups in memory to comprehend them, mentally reaching backward in memory to previous sounds and forward to anticipated sounds. As with music, comprehension of speech and its retention in memory is enhanced by an "economy of coding," wherein repeated sound patterns can draw attention and be stored in memory just once, then recalled as repetitions or variations of the pattern (Sloboda 1985, p. 190). To understand a repetition of sounds as a repetition, a listener must perceive their similarity and recall previous sounds based on their proximity to subsequent sounds.

Aural patterns established through repetition influence the reception of subsequent sounds. As remembered patterns accumulate in memory, they acquire structure and build expectations for future sounds. A composition's sounds train the ear, both to attend to particular rhythms, patterns, and topics as the composition progresses and to retain them in memory. Sound shapes audience expectations and trains the ear to expect a pattern's repetition, variation, or completion. Sound also motivates an audience to listen for the resolution of aural tension and to attend to the relation between a sound's acoustic quality and its reference or semantic meaning. Repetition unifies a linear stream of sounds and enables them to be comprehended as a unified whole. Repetition structures sounds, enabling listeners to transcend sound's linear character.

REPETITION AND THE SILENT READER

Repetition of signifiers often seems unimportant, redundant and unimaginative to silent readers because of their heavy dependence on semantic meaning signified by a composition's words. A modern reader's apprehension of lexemes as units of meaning is automatic because the medium of print presents symbols for sounds in prearranged groups separated by spaces. The possibility of multiple re-readings enables silent readers to consider each word's meaning at a self-determined pace. Signifiers do not need to be repeated to reinforce their meaning. Silent readers therefore generally view the repetition of signifiers negatively as an artistic weakness or flaw.[13]

Silent critics must determine how to recognize a repetition as a repetition in compositions whose audiences depend on sound for their organization. As Nidich points out,

> Repetition is not a simple-minded stylistic device that allows an audience to follow a story that is heard rather than read [silently] or that offers a composer a quick way to create content without varying the vocabulary or the syntax. Repetition is a means of metonymically emphasizing key messages and moods in a work of literature as in a musical composition (1996, p.13).[14]

Silent readers have access to repetition's dynamics through contemporary forms of communication that depend on sound, such as advertising jingles and popular vocal music. These compositions successfully employ repeated signifiers because their reception takes place in real time inasmuch as they are typically heard and seldom silently read. Repeated sounds sometimes occur as lexemes and groups of lexemes, but frequently they do not. Two famous lyrics by the American songwriter Cole Porter illustrate this dynamic:

> Every time I look down on this timeless town,
> Whether blue or gray **be her skies**,
> Whether loud be her cheers, or whether soft be her tears,
> More and more do I **realize**
> That I love Paris in the springtime . . . (1983, pp. 304–5).

"I Love Paris" employs simple rhymes of individual words ("down" and "town," "cheers" and "tears"), as well as the more complex rhyme of "be her skies" and "realize." This latter rhyme exceeds the boundaries of the single word and relies upon the similar rhythm of the successive syllables in "be her skies" and "realize," irrespective of the boundaries of the lexemes that comprise the rhyming sequences. Such rhymes suggest that the connections forged by rhyme derive their mnemonic and aesthetic power from the repetition of sounds, not the reiteration of ideas signaled by words.

Still more complex schemes are possible, as the following lines from "You're the Top" illustrate. Rhymes not only transcend the boundaries of the lexical unit, but they repeat sequences of syllables that represent incomplete parts of words and reduplicate rhythmic patterns. For the sake of illustration, two lines from the end of a verse and two lines from a subsequent refrain are shown:

> You're **a rose**, you're infer**no's** Dante
> You're **the nose** on the great Durante
> . . .
> I'm a lazy lout who is just about to stop
> But if baby I'm the bottom, you're the top! (1983, pp. 119–21).

The simple rhymes of "stop" and "top" at the end of the refrain exhibit the most basic kind of repetition. In a more complex rhyming scheme, "a rose" not only rhymes with "the nose" but it is also echoed in interior rhyme with the last syllable of "inferno's." The second line reinforces the sequence of syllables in "inferno's" by rhyming "-no's Dante" with "Durante." Similarly, rhyming "-zy lout" with "about" associates sequences of syllables that do not correspond with the boundaries of lexemes. The alliteration of "lazy lout" and "But if baby I'm the bottom," intensifies the effect of the simple end rhyme in the refrain's final two lines.

Because repeated sound groups in "You're the Top" transcend the boundaries of individual words, they connect otherwise unrelated elements. The association of a rose with inferno and Jimmy Durante's nose seem unlikely, even whimsical. These playful sound effects capture the joy the singer takes in the unlikely and gratuitous romantic connection between his "baby" and himself, a "lazy lout."

THE FUNCTIONS OF REPETITION

Similar dynamics organize ancient, spoken compositions and shape their meaning. The Sermon on the Mount (Mt 5–7) facilitates analysis of repetition's functions, since it organizes disparate sayings from Q into a unified speech.[15] Examples from the Sermon will illustrate the dynamics of repetition.[16]

FUNCTION 1: REPETITION DELINEATES SOUND GROUPS

The syllable and not the lexeme is the basic sound unit of speech in Greek. The most basic repetition is therefore the recurrence of a phoneme or syllable. Syllables can be arranged in meaningful sound patterns that can include more or fewer sounds than those that comprise the isolated lexeme. Repetition of syllables and phonemes organizes proximate sounds into groups on the basis of similarity. Grouping according to proximate, similar sounds forms the foundation of repetition's structuring function.[17] Techniques include alliteration (the repetition of initial sounds), assonance (the repetition of internal vowel sounds or approximate rhyme), and *homoioteleuton* or rhyme (the repetition of terminal sounds). These techniques organize sounds in clusters and function at an auditory level, not at the level of semantic meaning.

In inflected languages, rhyme frequently associates syntactically related words. Conversely, non-inflected words, such as conjunctions and particles, divide related sound groups, since the sounds of non-inflected words frequently do not conform to the sounds of surrounding words and therefore stand out as distinct.

A brief example illustrates sound's structuring dynamics. No words or phrases recur in the following passage from the Sermon on the Mount, except the article and personal pronouns:

Mt 5:16

οὕτως λαμψάτω τὸ φῶς ὑμῶν ἔμπροσθεν τῶν ἀνθρώπων, ὅπως ἴδωσιν ὑμῶν τὰ καλὰ ἔργα καὶ δοξάσωσιν τὸν πατέρα ὑμῶν τὸν ἐν τοῖς οὐρανοῖς.[18]

Yet clusters of similar sounds unify the passage and enhance its meaning. First, repeated ω(ς) sounds reinforce the passage's key image, φῶς, light.

οὕτ**ως** λαμψάτω τὸ **φῶς** ὑμῶν ἔμπροσθεν τῶν ἀνθρώπων, ὅπ**ως** ἴδ**ωσ**ιν ὑμῶν τὰ καλὰ ἔργα καὶ δοξάσ**ωσ**ιν τὸν πατέρα ὑμῶν τὸν ἐν τοῖς οὐρανοῖς.

Proximity is established by the repeated pronoun, ὑμῶν, which divides each colon into two groups of contiguous sounds.

οὕτως λαμψάτω τὸ φῶς	**ὑμῶν**	ἔμπροσθεν τῶν ἀνθρώπων,
ὅπως ἴδωσιν	**ὑμῶν**	τὰ καλὰ ἔργα
καὶ δοξάσωσιν τὸν πατέρα	**ὑμῶν**	τὸν ἐν τοῖς οὐρανοῖς.

The repeated -ῶς/ω phonemes cluster in the first section of each colon.

οὕτ**ως** λαμψάτω τὸ φ**ῶς**	ὑμῶν	ἔμπροσθεν τῶν ἀνθρώπων,
ὅπ**ως** ἴδ**ωσ**ιν	ὑμῶν	τὰ καλὰ ἔργα
καὶ δοξάσ**ωσ**ιν τὸν πατέρα	ὑμῶν	τὸν ἐν τοῖς οὐρανοῖς.

Repeated phonemes of inflectional suffixes organize each colon's ending.

οὕτως λαμψάτω τὸ φῶς	ὑμῶν	ἔμπροσθεν **τῶν** ἀνθρώπ**ων**,
ὅπως ἴδωσιν	ὑμῶν	**τὰ** κα**λὰ** ἔργ**α**
καὶ δοξάσωσιν τὸν πατέρα	ὑμῶν	τὸν ἐν **τοῖς** οὐραν**οῖς**.

Even though these acoustic clues carry little or no semantic load in themselves, the central placement of ὑμῶν (your), coupled with echoes of the key word φῶς (light) at the beginning of each colon and rhyming inflectional endings at each colon's end, carry the passage's message: you should let *your light* shine. Such sound effects are not evident to a silent reader, whose sense of meaning relies almost exclusively on semantics. The recurrence of speech sounds, however, conveys the passage's gist, its λόγος.

In addition to repeating a specific *quality* of sound, such as the recurrence of a phoneme or syllable, repetition can also function by repeating the *quantity* or duration of a series of sounds. Two frequently occurring types of sound quantity repetition include παρίσωσις, successive cola of approximately equal lengths, and παρομοίωσις, parallelism of sound between corresponding parts of approximately equivalent cola (Smyth 1984, p. 681).[19]

The following example from the Sermon exhibits both equivalent colon length (παρίσωσις) and parallelism of corresponding elements (παρομοίωσις):

Mt 5:34–35

ἐγὼ δὲ λέγω ὑμῖν μὴ ὀμόσαι ὅλως·

μήτε	ἐν τῷ οὐρανῷ,	ὅτι θρόνος	ἐστὶν τοῦ θεοῦ·
μήτε	ἐν τῇ γῇ,	ὅτι ὑποπόδιόν	ἐστιν τῶν ποδῶν αὐτοῦ·
μήτε	εἰς Ἱεροσόλυμα,	ὅτι πόλις	ἐστὶν τοῦ μεγάλου βασιλέως[20]

Cola of roughly equivalent length (παρίσωσις) follow the initial prohibition, μὴ ὀμόσαι ὅλως. The cola are also set in parallel (παρομοίωσις). Each colon begins with μήτε followed by a prepositional phrase beginning with ἐν or εἰς, the particle ὅτι, a predicate nominative, the predicate ἐστίν, then a genitive modifier with repeated –ου or -ων sounds. Placement of these distinctive elements in corresponding positions within parallel cola unifies the parallel elements and draws attention to the terms that are different: Heaven, throne, God; earth, footstool, his feet; Jerusalem, city, great king. This example illustrates that sound quantity, in addition to sound quality, can designate sound groups within a linear stream of sounds.

FUNCTION 2: REPETITION ORGANIZES SOUNDS INTO STRUCTURAL UNITS

Besides organizing sounds into groups, repetition can delineate larger structural units by repeating basic sound groups. Just as the repetition of phonemes organizes sounds into groups, the recurrence of sound groups creates larger structural units within a composition.[21]

REPETITION ESTABLISHES PATTERNS

The initial sounds of the Sermon on the Mount do not immediately emerge as a pattern.

Mt 5:3
Μακάριοι οἱ πτωχοὶ τῷ πνεύματι, ὅτι αὐτῶν ἐστιν ἡ βασιλεία τῶν οὐρανῶν.[22]

A pattern can be apprehended only after it has been repeated. These sounds of 5:3 ultimately create a template for the Sermon's entire structural scheme, but their structuring effect is not evident at this point. A structural unit can be discerned only after the reprisal of a sound sequence:

Mt 5:3–4
Μακάριοι **οἱ** πτωχοὶ τῷ πνεύματι, **ὅτι αὐτῶν** ἐστιν
ἡ βασιλεία τῶν οὐρανῶν.
μακάριοι **οἱ** πενθοῦντες, **ὅτι αὐτοὶ** παρακληθήσονται.[23]

When a sound group is repeated, the two groups of similar sounds can be perceived as parallel. Repetition of a group of sounds enables a hearer to assign significance to previous and future sounds and construe them as a pattern. When new sounds echo previous sounds stored in memory, the repeated sound cluster functions as a unit. Empirical tests of auditory pattern recognition show

> . . . that pattern perception is a hypothesis testing activity that starts at the beginning of the stimulus. . . . Once a hypothesis is chosen, it is coded into memory: consequently, pattern violations are less serious at the beginning of a pattern than internally (Devine and Stephens 1993, p. 395).

Repetitions need not precisely duplicate previous sounds to be so apprehended. Grouping requires only similarity, not identity. Enough sounds must be repeated to invoke the previously articulated sound group, but differences add interest and sustain attention. The repeated elements in a sound group indicate a pattern's essential features. In the example above, the emerging pattern's characteristic elements include: μακάριοι οἱ [substantive] ὅτι [third person pronoun] [predicate].

The nine beatitudes in Mt 5:4–12 are not identical, yet they are readily understood as repetitions of the pattern set forth in 5:3.[24] Each iteration of the emerging pattern strikes the audience as a beginning. Yet the repetitions are not entirely new, since each reiteration also recalls a sound pattern that previously has been stored in memory.

VARIATION

Established patterns furnish templates for subsequent sounds and shape a listener's expectations. Once established by repetition, patterns may be varied, modified, and transformed. Variations entail minor pattern changes that leave the basic form intact. The second beatitude (5:4) furnishes a helpful example:

Mt 5:3–4

Μακάριοι οἱ πτωχοὶ τῷ πνεύματι, ὅτι **αὐτῶν** ἐστιν ἡ βασιλεία τῶν οὐρανῶν.
μακάριοι οἱ πενθοῦντες, ὅτι **αὐτοὶ** παρακληθήσονται.

In the second line, the occurrence of the third person pronoun αὐτοί in the ὅτι clause indicates its importance in the structural pattern. The shift from the genitive case in the ὅτι clause of 5:3 to the nominative case in the parallel clause in 5:4 changes that structural element's component sounds and necessitates a change in syntax: the verbal idea of the ὅτι clause is arranged differently in the second beatitude where its subject occurs in the initial position. The second beatitude (i.e., the first repetition) clearly reiterates the first beatitude's essential structural elements; so much so that these elements help to establish the beatitudes' pattern. Nevertheless, a syntactical shift comprises a variation in the pattern.

The same sort of variation recurs after the seventh beatitude. The eighth beatitude reverts to the first beatitude's use of the genitive form of the third person pronoun and the placement of the predicate in initial position in its ὅτι clauses:

Mt 5:9–10

μακάριοι οἱ εἰρηνοποιοί,
ὅτι **αὐτοὶ** υἱοὶ θεοῦ κληθήσονται.
μακάριοι οἱ δεδιωγμένοι ἕνεκεν δικαιοσύνης,
ὅτι **αὐτῶν ἐστιν** ἡ βασιλεία τῶν οὐρανῶν.[25]

The return to the form of the first beatitude rounds the beatitudes into a larger compositional unit and generates an expectation of an upcoming structural shift. Thus the eight beatitudes rehearse a single, simple structural pattern, beginning with μακάριοι and a predicate nominative, followed by a brief ὅτι clause. The ὅτι clause, however, occurs in two variations: a ὅτι αὐτῶν ἐστιν form in the first and eighth beatitudes and a ὅτι αὐτοί form in the intervening beatitudes 2–7.

MODIFICATION

Pattern modifications change or rearrange one or more pattern components while preserving the pattern's essential form. Again, Matthew's beatitudes supply a helpful illustration. After an eight-fold iteration of the beatitude pattern, the ninth beatitude modifies it. The ninth beatitude's form differs substantially from the form as initially presented, reproducing only the pattern's essential elements, μακάριοι . . . ὅτι, the sound signatures for the pattern's two component parts:

Comparison of Mt 5:3 and 5:11–12

Mt 5:3

Μακάριοι οἱ πτωχοὶ τῷ πνεύματι,
ὅτι αὐτῶν ἐστιν ἡ βασιλεία τῶν οὐρανῶν.[26]

Mt 5:11–12

μακάριοί ἐστε

ὅταν	ὀνειδίσωσιν		ὑμᾶς
καὶ	διώξωσιν		
καὶ	εἴπωσιν	πᾶν πονηρὸν καθ'	ὑμῶν[ψευδόμενοι]ἕνεκενἐμοῦ·

χαίρετε καὶ ἀγαλλιᾶσθε,
ὅτι ὁ μισθὸς ὑμῶν πολὺς ἐν τοῖς οὐρανοῖς·
οὕτως γὰρ ἐδίωξαν τοὺς προφήτας τοὺς πρὸ ὑμῶν.[27]

The sound patterns established in 5:3–10 remain in 5:11, but they undergo significant modification. Although the primary organizing auditory signals remain (μακάριοι and ὅτι), the ninth beatitude is substantially longer than the previous eight. It changes to the second person (ἔστε), directly addressing the audience. Its predicate is expressed in the μακάριοι clause but implied in the ὅτι clause, reversing the pattern of beatitudes 1 and 8. Yet a listener properly apprehends the passage as the ninth beatitude, a modification of the previously established pattern, μακάριοι . . . ὅτι (See table: Comparison of Sound Patterns in Mt 5:3 and 5:11).

Secondary signals indicate that the established pattern remains in force. In 5:11 the expected ὅτι clause does not occur immediately. Instead, a clause beginning with the similar-sounding ὅταν intervenes. Although the ὅταν clause substantially elongates the μακάριοι

Comparison of Sound Patterns in Mt 5:3 and 5:11

Pattern element	Established pattern: 5:3	Modified pattern: 5:11
Opening sound signature:	**μακάριοι οἱ** πτωχοὶ τῷ πνεύματι	μακάριοί ἐστε
Intervening phrase:		**ὅταν** ὀνειδίσωσιν ὑμᾶς καὶ διώξωσιν καὶ εἴπωσιν πᾶν πονηρὸν καθ᾽ ὑμῶν [ψευδόμενοι]
Second sound signature:	**ὅτι αὐτῶν** ἐστιν ἡ βασιλεία τῶν οὐρανῶν	ὅτι ὁ μισθὸς ὑμῶν πολὺς ἐν τοῖς οὐρανοῖς· οὕτως γὰρ ἐδίωξαν τοὺς προφήτας τοὺς πρὸ ὑμῶν.

section, its repeating verb endings (ὀνειδίσωσιν, διώξωσιν, εἴπωσιν) (they denounce, persecute, spread . . . gossip) unify the intervening sounds. Then, a pair of imperatives follows, χαίρετε and ἀγαλλιᾶσθε (rejoice and be glad), linked by καί (and), the same connector employed to link the previous series of predicates. The imperative verbs reiterate the mode of direct address in μακάριοί ἐστε (congratulations to you), which had distinguished this beatitude's opening from all the preceding ones. After this reprisal of the beatitude's beginning sounds, the expected ὅτι clause occurs. The inflectional ending -ων closes both ὅτι clauses, even though the same words do not recur.

Repetition requires not only memory but also insight. To identify patterns and recognize variations and modifications, listeners must be able to discriminate a pattern's characteristic features and select its essential elements. In this way, the dynamics of repetition enlist an audience's participation in the construction of a composition as it is spoken aloud.

TRANSFORMATION

In addition to establishing, varying, and modifying sound patterns, repetition can transform a pattern to adapt its structure to a new purpose. The transition from the beatitudes to the next section of the Sermon provides a helpful illustration:

Mt 5:11–14

1 **Original pattern:**

1.1 **μακάριοι** οἱ δεδιωγμένοι ἕνεκεν δικαιοσύνης,

1.2 **ὅτι** αὐτῶν ἐστιν ἡ βασιλεία τῶν οὐρανῶν.

2 Modified pattern:

2.1 **μακάριοί ἐστε**
2.2 ὅταν ὀνειδίσωσιν ὑμᾶς
2.3 καὶ διώξωσιν
2.4 καὶ εἴπωσιν πᾶν πονηρὸν καθ' ὑμῶν [ψευδόμενοι] ἕνεκεν ἐμοῦ·

2.5 χαίρετε καὶ ἀγαλλιᾶσθε,
2.6 **ὅτι** ὁ μισθὸς ὑμῶν πολὺς ἐν τοῖς οὐρανοῖς·
2.7 οὕτως γὰρ ἐδίωξαν τοὺς προφήτας τοὺς πρὸ ὑμῶν.

3 Transformed pattern:

3.1 **Ὑμεῖς ἐστε** τὸ ἅλας τῆς γῆς·
3.2 ἐὰν δὲ τὸ ἅλας μωρανθῇ, ἐν τίνι ἁλισθήσεται;
3.3 εἰς οὐδὲν ἰσχύει ἔτι εἰ μὴ βληθῆναι ἔξω καὶ καταπατεῖσθαι ὑπὸ τῶν ἀνθρώπων.

4 New pattern repeated:

4.1 **Ὑμεῖς ἐστε** τὸ φῶς τοῦ κόσμου.
4.1 οὐ δύναται πόλις κρυβῆναι ἐπάνω ὄρους κειμένη·[28]

The pattern modifications that occur at the end of the beatitudes become the basis for a transformation to a new auditory scheme in the Sermon's second section (5:13–16). The original and now familiar pattern of the beatitudes organizes period 1 above. The switch to the second person provides the distinguishing feature of the pattern as modified in period 2. In period 3, the initial sounds reiterate the previous second person pronoun and predicate to establish a new, two-part structure. The new pattern begins with ὑμεῖς ἐστε and a metaphorical image, followed by clauses that elaborate the image and develop the comparison with the audience. This new structure becomes definitively confirmed and established as an organizing pattern when repeated in period 4.

FUNCTION 3: REPETITION SELECTS SOUNDS FOR EMPHASIS

By assigning priority to certain sounds, repetition serves as a primary tool for guiding interpretation. Sounds can be selected for emphasis and made more memorable by virtue of their acoustic quality as well as their placement within sound groups.[29] The placement of sounds within sound groups or structural units derives from repetition's structural role.

SOUND PLACEMENT

Sounds receive special attention when they occur at the beginning or end of a sound group. Repeated sounds within a structural unit also attain special attention. The repetition of sounds in separate structural units can assign importance if the repeated sounds are related to other privileged sounds. Sounds are selected as important if they occur in corresponding places in parallel sound groups, as well as when they differ from the repeated sounds within a structural unit. In any case, the influence that sound exerts on meaning logically and chronologically precedes semantics.

BEGINNING AND ENDING SOUNDS

The reason beginning and ending sounds receive particular attention is that they help to define the sound group and orient an audience to a composition's organizational patterns. The repetition of μακάριοι at the beginning of each beatitude serves this function. The frequent repetition of μακάριοι at the beginning of the Sermon not only draws attention to μακάριοι itself, but it also prepares an audience to listen for repeated beginning sounds as organizational devices throughout the Sermon.

Ending sounds can also serve as auditory signals. The repetition of ἡ βασιλεία τῶν οὐρανῶν at the end of the first and eighth beatitudes assigns importance to this phrase:

Mt 5:3, 10

Opening phrase	Middle phrase	Ending
Μακάριοι οἱ πτωχοὶ τῷ πνεύματι,	ὅτι αὐτῶν ἐστιν	ἡ βασιλεία τῶν οὐρανῶν.
μακάριοι οἱ δεδιωγμένοι ἕνεκεν δικαιοσύνης	ὅτι αὐτῶν ἐστιν	ἡ βασιλεία τῶν οὐρανῶν.

The sound sequence ἡ βασιλεία τῶν οὐρανῶν at the end of the first and eighth beatitudes functions as a bracket for the first section of the Sermon. This patterned repetition of ἡ βασιλεία τῶν οὐρανῶν in the beatitudes also evokes previous occurrences of this phrase in Matthew[30] and signals an emerging primary theme in Matthew's gospel.

THEMATIC SOUNDS

The Sermon develops the theme of ἡ βασιλεία τῶν οὐρανῶν (heaven's domain) by associating this formulaic phrase with other distinctive sound groups. The term ὁ οὐρανός (heaven/sky) achieves significance in the beatitudes because of its relation to the key term, ἡ βασιλεία τῶν οὐρανῶν.[31] Of the 82 occurrences of ὁ οὐρανός in Matthew, it is used only 18 times to refer to the sky or heavens.[32] By contrast, ὁ οὐρανός occurs with ἡ βασιλεία (domain) 33 times.[33] Seven of these occur in the Sermon on the Mount.[34] In 31 of the remaining 49 occurrences of ὁ οὐρανος in Matthew, the term occurs with ὁ πατήρ (father), ἡ γῆ (the earth), or both.[35] Twelve of these usages occur in the Sermon on the Mount.[36] The auditory association of ὁ οὐρανός with ὁ πατήρ and ἡ γῆ reinforces their semantic relationship: ἡ βασιλεία τῶν οὐρανῶν (heaven's domain) belongs to ὁ πατήρ (the father), creator of ὁ οὐρανός καὶ ἡ γῆ (heaven and earth). Each iteration of these sounds triggers a whole complex of associations of the father's kingdom that prevails in heaven and on earth. As these terms recur they suggest and imply each other because their frequent association in sound is retained in memory, even when the terms occur alone.

Mere repetition of a phrase does not in itself privilege a sound sequence, since other terms that lack thematic meaning are also frequently repeated. For example, the word ὁ ἄνθρωπος (man) occurs more than twice as often in Matthew (116 occurrences) as does ἡ βασιλεία (domain) (55 occurrences). Nevertheless, ὁ ἄνθρωπος does not function as a theme in the gospel, whereas ἡ βασιλεία does, by virtue of its structural placement. Conversely, ἡ δικαιοσύνη (righteousness) functions as a strong theme in Matthew, yet the gospel exhibits only 7 occurrences of this term, and only 26 occurrences of words with the same lexical stem (δίκαιος, 17; δικαιοσύνη, 7; δικαιόω, 2). These examples indicate that frequency alone is not sufficient to designate a theme or to privilege a sound group as important. Repetition assigns importance to selected sound groups by virtue of their organization and placement.

Repetition of sounds throughout a structural unit also assigns importance to the recurring sounds. After Matthew's beatitudes, the threefold repetition of τὸ ἅλας/ἁλισθήσεται (salt/salty) in the section on salt and light (5:13–16) reinforces the image.

Mt 5:13

Ὑμεῖς ἐστε τὸ ἅλας τῆς γῆς·
ἐὰν δὲ τὸ ἅλας μωρανθῇ,
ἐν τίνι ἁλισθήσεται;
εἰς οὐδὲν ἰσχύει ἔτι εἰ μὴ βληθῆναι ἔξω καὶ καταπατεῖσθαι
ὑπὸ τῶν ἀνθρώπων.[37]

Reinforcement is especially strong since the first occurrence of τὸ ἅλας in 5:13 is coupled with τῆς γῆς (the correlative term to ὁ οὐρανός). The vowel sounds α and η characterize this brief phrase.

Although the final line does not repeat τὸ ἅλας or τῆς γῆς, it does frequently reiterate α, η, and its allophone, ει, evoking the governing vowel sound of the two key terms.

Similarly, we have seen that the repetition of the phoneme ως in 5:14–16 reinforces that period's prevailing image, φῶς, in the same way:

Mt 5:16

οὕτως λαμψάτω τὸ **φῶς** ὑμῶν ἔμπροσθεν τῶν ἀνθρώπων,
ὅπως ἴδωσιν ὑμῶν τὰ καλὰ ἔργα
καὶ δοξάσωσιν τὸν πατέρα ὑμῶν τὸν ἐν τοῖς οὐρανοῖς.[38]

Recurrence of the whole lexical unit, τὸ φῶς, is not required to invoke the image. The recurring ως/ω phoneme is sufficient to sustain the image and thus designate this sound as significant.

PARALLEL SOUNDS

Sounds that occur in corresponding places within parallel sound groups frequently claim special attention. We have seen the effect of the phrase ἡ βασιλεία τῶν οὐρανῶν at the beginning and end of the beatitudes. The opening of the Lord's prayer supplies another helpful illustration:

Mt 6:9b–10

Πάτερ ἡμῶν ὁ ἐν τοῖς οὐρανοῖς,
ἁγιασθήτω τὸ ὄνομά σου,
ἐλθέτω ἡ βασιλεία σου,
γενηθήτω τὸ θέλημά σου, ὡς ἐν οὐρανῷ καὶ ἐπὶ γῆς.[39]

Several dynamics converge to confer special importance on selected sounds in this passage. The Sermon's auditory signals have already trained an audience to attend to opening sounds. Here, πάτερ ἡμῶν (our father) opens a new section in which other sounds occur that have previously been designated as thematic by virtue of their structural placement: ἡ βασιλεία (domain), οὐρανοῖς (-ῷ) (heaven), and γῆς (earth). These sounds, in turn, occur in privileged positions: references to heaven and earth bracket parallel clauses, and ἡ βασιλεία (domain) occurs in the center, in the middle of the second parallel clause. As in the beatitudes, the structural placement of these terms carries semantic force: God's kingdom is depicted at the center and in the midst of heaven and earth. The association of πατέρ ἡμῶν (our father) with these important thematic sounds establishes this sound group and its variants (ὁ πατὴρ ὑμῶν ὁ οὐράνιος, ὁ πατὴρ ὑμῶν ἐν τοῖς οὐρανοῖς) (our father in heaven, our father in the heavens) as thematic.

The repetition of ἐν τοῖς οὐρανοῖς/ἐν οὐρανῷ (in the heavens, in heaven) helps to delineate the prayer's first structural unit. Parallel phrases within the unit employ imperative predicates at the beginning and σοῦ at the end. The phrases differ in their middle terms. The terms τὸ ὄνομα (name), ἡ βασιλεία (domain), and τὸ θέλημα (will) stand out and become associated as related terms. The veneration of the father's name as sacred, the coming of the kingdom, and the realization of the father's will emerge as related notions that imply each other. In such instances, terms attract attention not merely because they are repeated but because they are placed in parallel positions in repeated sound sequences.

DISTINCTIVE SOUNDS

Established sound patterns shape a listener's expectations. Distinctive sounds that diverge from an established pattern can also receive special importance because they surprise a hearer. In the ninth beatitude, the switch from third to second person deviates from the established pattern and therefore receives emphasis:

Comparison of Auditory Signals in Beatitudes 1–8 and 9

Beatitudes 1–8	Μακάριοι **οἱ**	ὅτι
Beatitude 9	Μακάριοί **ἐστε**	ὅτι

The Sermon's section on the law and the prophets exhibits a different dynamic, whereby distinctive sounds deviate from the listener's expectation:

Mt 5:17

1 Μὴ νομίσητε ὅτι ἦλθον καταλῦσαι τὸν νόμον ἢ τοὺς προφήτας·
2 οὐκ ἦλθον καταλῦσαι
3 ἀλλὰ πληρῶσαι.[40]

In this example, parallel elements in successive cola are progressively abbreviated to emphasize contrasting elements. The phrase τὸν νόμον ἢ τοὺς προφήτας does not recur in the two parallel lines that follow. The second colon substitutes οὐκ for the phrase μὴ νομίσητε ὅτι, emphasizing the negation. Colon 3 includes only the adversative ἀλλά, which contrasts with οὐκ in line 2, and the new infinitive πληρῶσαι, which replaces καταλῦσαι in the parallel position in the previous two cola. While colon 3 avoids explicit mention of all other terms, it also implies the parallel elements from the previous cola that complete the meaning of colon 3. This brachiological reduction of sound groups emphasizes the final line's distinctive element—the concluding and contrasting term πληρῶσαι.

SUMMARY OF THE FUNCTIONS OF REPETITION

Repetition's power to confer meaning derives from its organizing influence on sound and the resulting impact on a composition's structure. Sound organizes compositions one sound at a time into structural units and guides their comprehension by assigning distinctive sound signatures to larger sound units. Repetition's first and most basic function is the delineation of sound groups. It takes place at the most elementary level of repetition, the recurrence of phonemes and syllables. The repetition of these basic sound units organizes sounds into comprehensible groups and memorable sound patterns. Just as the syllable is the basic unit of analysis for the dynamics of repetition, the colon and period are the basic units of analysis for sounds organized into elementary groups that conform to grammatical boundaries and mark pauses for the breath in declamation.

As these sound patterns emerge, repetition's second function becomes possible: the organization of sounds into structural units. The creation of structural units is a cumulative process. Newly emerging sound patterns enable listeners to apprehend larger sound groups, to store sound patterns in memory, and to both recall and employ those patterns in creating meaning. By means of repetition, various sound patterns are initially established, then varied, modified, and transformed. This cumulative process trains the listener's ear to comprehend sounds in real time.

As listeners process long sequences of sound patterns, repetition guides the listener's comprehension through its third function: the selection of certain sounds for emphasis. In real time listeners cannot dwell on the full semantic implication of every sound, and must therefore focus attention on selected sounds. Repetition guides this selection process by privileging certain sounds through their quality and placement. Sound quality makes sounds distinctive and memorable. Sound placement privileges sounds that occur in certain locations. Sounds receive emphasis when they occur at the beginning or end of a structural unit, in recurring thematic refrains, in parallel configurations, or some other distinctive arrangement. (See table: The Functions of Repetition.)

STRUCTURE AND INTUITION

Perception of sound patterns is an intuitive process based on multiple auditory signals. Repetition's grouping function, the basis of its structuring power, depends upon the intuition of similarity and proximity.

The Functions of Repetition

Functions	Devices
1: Delineate sound groups	• Repeated phonemes • Repeated syllables
2: Create structural units	• Pattern establishment • Pattern variation • Pattern modification • Pattern transformation
3: Select sounds for emphasis	• Sound quality • Beginning and ending sounds • Thematic sounds • Parallel sounds • Distinctive sounds

These are relative concepts. How much resemblance is required for sounds to be perceived as similar? How closely must sounds succeed each other to be perceived as proximate? Are sounds successfully grouped when they are similar but not proximate, or proximate but not similar? The answer is that sound patterns are perceived relative to surrounding sounds and that sound signals must be confirmed by multiple clues. Listening in real time requires several sound clues for each structural signal to avoid misleading an audience. Still, exact predictions are not possible and rigid rules do not apply. Sometimes sound effects are ambiguous because various sound signals conflict. Apprehension of sound patterns is an interpretative process that requires attention and insight as an audience participates creatively in the construction of a spoken composition. Sound's dynamics have a cumulative effect and they take shape in relation to other sounds. Patterns supported by multiple sound signals are less ambiguous and more likely to reflect a composition's organic structure.

COLOMETRY, STRUCTURE, AND SOUND MAPS

Colometry divides compositions into breaths that represent a linear stream of speech. Repeated sounds organize patterns that build a composition's structure. Sound mapping begins by dividing a composition colometrically, then moving both up and down the hierarchy of discourse to analyze syllables and periods. This accordion-style motion oscillating within and beyond colometric boundaries ensures that acoustic analysis discerns sounds' proper relationships and constantly re-evaluates sounds and sound groups in relation to other relevant sounds and sound patterns. Sound mapping detects the organic boundaries of a composition's structure and depicts its acoustic patterns. Chapter 5, Developing Sound Maps, will explain how to develop sound maps by dividing compositions into cola and plotting out sound patterns established by repetition.

ENDNOTES

1. Fischer (2003, pp. 12–14) explains that our very definition of reading has expanded over the course of civilization as reading competency has increased with the availability of print. Two different types of reading can be distinguished: "literal, or mediate" reading and "visual or immediate" reading. Literal reading relates to the process of attaching sounds to written signs to decode a composition's meaning, whereas visual, immediate reading involves attaching sense to sign directly and without recourse to sound, as in "fluent adult reading" today. Fluent reading builds on proficiency at literal reading, but "[f]or want of longer texts and a reading audience, reading as we know it today did not exist before classical antiquity" (14).
2. Additional reading aids besides the display of colometric structure were also employed. "Because reading was known to be a matter of interpretation and because it was so important to convey the right interpretation in public reading, early manuscripts of scriptural texts are often written in a somewhat larger hand, with few letters to the line and fewer lines to the page, than other texts and were more often furnished with reading aids" (Gamble 1995, p. 229).
3. Kleist describes the stichometric system: "In the stichometric style the text was measured by the stichos which is the Greek term for our English *line*, and the length of the MS. was determined by the number of the stichoi it contained. In this style the text was written straight on without a break until the stichos was filled up. Each page of a MS. done in this fashion presented a solid block of written matter more or less uniform in length and width. In this arrangement no regard was had for such divisions of the text as the sense might require" (1927, p. 19). Metzger provides a more detailed description of stichometric transcription: "From ancient times the average hexameter line of writing (στίχος), comprising sixteen syllables of about thirty-six letters, was taken as a stan-

dard measure for literary works. The number of στίχοι served (a) to show the length of a treatise or book, (b) to provide a standard for payment to the scribe and the pricing of the book, (c) to guard against later interpolations and excisions, and (d) to permit, through the notation in the margin of the στίχοι by fifties, the general location of citations" (1981, pp. 38–39). See also Schutz (1922, pp. 164–72) for a comparison of stichometry and colometry.

4. According to Metzger (1981), the oldest New Testament manuscript transcribed stichometrically is the Chester Beatty papyrus of the Pauline Epistles, P^{46}. See also Dahl (1979) and Gamble (1995, pp. 229–30), for a discussion of colometry in manuscripts of the New Testament.
5. See also Kleist (1927, p. 19).
6. "Die kolometrische Form schafft dem poetischen Element der neutestamentlichen Prose die verdiente Geltung wieder. Das Kolon ist für die Kunstprosa, was der Vers für die Poesie ist: Mittel zur Umgrenzung der künstlerischen Form. Nicht sind beide, Kolon und dichterischer Vers, identisch. Denn der letztere wird da abgeschlossen, wo es der Rhythmus erheischt, der über die Sinnteilung hinausgreifen kann."
7. But see chapter 1, "The Technology of Writing in the Greco-Roman World," and chapter 2, "The Woven Composition," which explain that speech is not "orality" and the presence of writing does not necessarily imply literacy.
8. Stowers (1994, p. 11) also dismisses as inappropriate the division of Romans into cola and commata, but his definitions of these terms are incorrect. Stowers understands colometric divisions to be arbitrary, according to numbers of syllables. Admittedly, theoreticians disagree concerning the precise definition of the colon (See chapter 3, "The Grammar of Sound," and Lausberg 1998, p. 418). Nevertheless, the method Stowers describes as colometry more closely approximates the stichometric method of textual display described above, not colometric display. Stowers is also incorrect in his understanding of the division of biblical texts into cola and commata as a process imposed mechanically upon texts centuries after their composition (1994, p. 11). As we have seen, cola and commata were the basic building blocks of the compositions themselves.
9. See chapter 3, "The Grammar of Sound."
10. Based upon their study of Greek prosody and experimental psychology, Devine and Stephens note, "pattern induction is such a basic cognitive activity that we have a propensity to look for and 'find'

patterns even when they are objectively not there" (1993, p. 391).

11. Grouping is "common to many aspects of cognition" and remains "the most basic component of musical understanding" (Lerdahl and Jackendoff 1983, p. 13); "the grammar that describes grouping structure seems to consist largely of general conditions for auditory pattern perception that have far broader application than for music alone" (p.36).
12. Emphasis in the original.
13. Modern students have learned that "vigorous writing is concise. A sentence should contain no unnecessary words, a paragraph no unnecessary sentences, for the same reason a drawing should have no unnecessary lines and a machine no unnecessary parts." (Strunk and White 1972, p.14). Here, "unnecessary" means words superfluous to the meaning or sense. Contemporary, silent readers generally construe repeated words as unnecessary. Ong (1982, p. 37) cites an example from the first creation story in Genesis as a Hebrew text from an oral culture. He notes that its "additive oral style," with repeated connectors between sentences, seems redundant to our ears. Those connectors are therefore omitted from modern English translations of the text.
14. Nidich adds, "Scholars with a taste for a particular sort of literate aesthetic have sneered at repetition [and find it] boring and tedious" (1996, p. 13).
15. See chapter 10, Sound and Structure: The Sermon on the Mount, for a sustained analysis of the Sermon on the Mount.
16. A sound map of the Sermon on the Mount in its entirety and a discussion of its interpretative implications are set forth in Lee (2005, pp. 125–312).
17. By contrast, some recent New Testament studies have charted recurring words and phrases to determine patterns of meaning. See Robbins (1996, pp. 65–91) for an analysis of 1 Corinthians 9; and Horsley (1999, pp. 190–91). Davis (1999, pp. 85–89) lends considerable weight to word repetition, although he recognizes other kinds of repetition.
18. "That's how your light is to shine in the presence of others, so they can see your good deeds and acclaim your Father in the heavens."
19. The inclusion of such devices in lists of compositional techniques and literary figures attests to their importance for ancient auditors. See, for example, Aristotle (*Rh.* 3.9.9).
20. "But I tell you: Don't swear at all. Don't invoke heaven, because it is the throne of God, and don't invoke earth, because it is God's

footstool, and don't invoke Jerusalem, because it is the city of the great king."

21. Parunak (1981, pp. 153–68) argues that "oral typesetting" also takes place in the literature of the Hebrew Bible and organizes its compositions.
22. "Congratulations to the poor in spirit! Heaven's domain belongs to them."
23. "Congratulations to the poor in spirit! Heaven's domain belongs to them. Congratulations to those who grieve! They will be consoled."
24. Critics differ in the way they enumerate Matthew's beatitudes because they ignore sound and therefore misconstrue structure. When read silently in a printed text, the differences between Mt 5:11–12 and the preceding eight beatitudes are more apparent than their similarities. The extensive discussion in the critical literature of this shift primarily considers Matthew's redaction of Q and other sources and notes especially the shift to the second person in 5:11. See especially Zahn (1922, p. 193) and Kloppenborg (1986, pp. 36–56). Most commentators count nine beatitudes but note the shift in 5:11. Davies (1988, pp. 460–61) and Luz (1989, p. 242), are representative. Betz (1995, pp. 147–53) finds ten beatitudes, counting 5:12, which begins with χαίρετε καὶ ἀγαλλιᾶσθε (rejoice and be glad) as the tenth. Daube (1956, pp. 196–201) notes that the formal shift in 5:11 does not argue against the section's unity; for not only does Q also includes 5:11, but other ancient literature, including the Hebrew Bible, frequently employs the "pleasant and effective pattern" of elongating the final element in a list.
25. "Congratulations to those who work for peace! They will be known as God's children. Congratulations to those who have suffered persecution for the sake of justice! Heaven's domain belongs to them."
26. "Congratulations to the poor in spirit! Heaven's domain belongs to them."
27. "Congratulations to you when they denounce you and persecute you and spread malicious gossip about you because of me. Rejoice and be glad! In heaven you will be more than compensated. Remember, this is how they persecuted the prophets who preceded you."
28. "Congratulations to you when they denounce you and persecute you and spread malicious gossip about you because of me. Rejoice and be glad! In heaven you will be more than compen-

sated. Remember, this is how they persecuted the prophets who preceded you. You are the salt of the earth. But if salt loses its zing, how will it be made salty? It then has no further use than to be thrown out and stomped on. You are the light of the world. A city sitting on top of a mountain can't be concealed."

29. See chapter 5, Developing Sound Maps, for a discussion of the power of sound quality to draw attention.
30. Mt 3:2 and 4:17 announce ἡ βασιλεία. Mt 4:8 draws a contrast with the kingdom of heaven and the kingdoms of the world, and Mt 4:23 declares the good news of the kingdom.
31. Interpreters observe that ὁ οὐρανός (heaven) occurs more frequently in Matthew than elsewhere in the New Testament, and that Matthew prefers the plural to the singular form (Aland 1987, s.v. οὐρανός). The expression ἡ βασιλεία τῶν οὐρανῶν (heaven's domain) and the plural form in general is usually explained as a Semiticism (Davies and Allison 1988, p. 329); (Luz 1989, p.169). This explanation derives from the frequency of the plural in LXX relative to secular Greek literature (Traub 1967, p. 510). The plural does not occur in classical literature. (*LSJ s.v.* οὐρανός). Betz (1985, pp. 118–19) argues that in the Sermon on the Mount the singular refers to the sky, whereas the plural refers to the heavenly firmament as the realm of God the Father. This may be the case, but the differential occurrence in Matthew of singular and plural forms of ὁ οὐρανός is not unique to the Sermon but rather is typical of New Testament usage (*BDAG s.v.* οὐρανός). Betz does not claim that such differential usage is atypical of Matthew, but he draws conclusions about the usage of ὁ οὐρανός in the plural in the Sermon because he posits separate authorship for the Sermon and the rest of Matthew's gospel. In secular Greek prose, ὁ οὐρανός does indeed have two meanings. It can indicate the sky, as well as the firmament of heaven and the dwelling of the gods. These meanings are closely related in secular Greek, and in classical usage are almost never clearly distinguishable because both senses are always implied (Traub 1967, pp. 497–500). In any case, the argument above concerning thematic usage of ὁ οὐρανός in Matthew does not depend on whether different semantic meanings are implied by the singular and plural. My claim is simply that in its various inflections ὁ οὐρανός functions thematically in Matthew at the level of sound because of its frequent association with other key terms.
32. Mt 8:20, 11:23, 14:19, 16:1, 2, 3; 19:21, 21:25 (two occurrences), 22:30, 23:22, 24:29, 30 (two occurrences), 31; 26:64, 28:2.

33. Mt 3:2, 4:17, 5:3, 10, 19 (two occurrences), 20; 7:21, 8:11, 10:7, 11:11, 12; 13:11, 24, 31, 32, 44, 45, 47, 52; 16:19, 18:1, 3, 4, 23; 19:12, 14, 23; 20:1, 22:2, 23:13, 25:1.
34. Mt 5:3, 10, 19 (two occurrences), 20; 7:21.
35. Mt 3:16, 17; 5:12, 16, 18, 34, 45; 6:1, 9, 10, 20, 26 (two occurrences); 7:11, 10:32, 11:25, 12:50, 13:32, 16:17, 19 (two occurrences); 18:10, 14, 18 (two occurrences), 19; 24:35, 36; 28:18.
36. Mt 5:12, 16, 18, 34, 45; 6:1, 9, 10, 20, 26 (two occurrences); 7:11.
37. "You are the salt of the earth. But if salt loses its zing, how will it be made salty? It then has no further use than to be thrown out and stomped on."
38. "That's how your light is to shine in the presence of others, so they can see your good deeds and acclaim your Father in the heavens."
39. "Our Father in the heavens, your name be revered. Impose your imperial rule, enact your will on earth as you have in heaven."
40. "Don't imagine that I have come to annul the Law or the Prophets. I have come not to annul but to fulfill."

WORKS CONSULTED

Aland, Kurt, ed. 1987. *Concordance to the Novum Testamentum Graece*. 3d ed. Berlin: De Gruyter.

Aland, Kurt, and Barbara Aland. 1987. *The Text of the New Testament, An Introduction to the Critical Editions and to the Theory and Practice of Modern Textual Criticism*. Translated by E. F. Rhodes. Grand Rapids: Eerdmans.

Betz, Hans Dieter. 1985. The Sermon on the Mount (Matt 5:3–7:27): Its Literary Genre and Function. In *Essays on the Sermon on the Mount*, edited by H. D. Betz. Philadelphia: Fortress.

———. 1995. *The Sermon on the Mount, Hermeneia*. Minneapolis: Fortress.

Dahl, N. A. 1979. 0230 (=PSI 1306) and the Fourth-Century Greek-Latin Edition of the Letters of Paul. In *Text and Interpretation*, edited by E. Best and R. McL. Wilson. Cambridge: Cambridge University Press.

Daube, D. 1956. The Last Beatitude. In *The New Testament and Rabbinic Judaism*. London: Athlone.

Davies, W.D., and D.C. Allison. 1988. *A Critical and Exegetical Commentary on the Gospel According to Matthew*. 3 vols. Vol. 1, *International Critical Commentary*. Edinburgh: T & T Clark.

Davis, Casey Wayne. 1999. *Oral Biblical Criticism: The Influence of the Principles of Orality on the Literary Structure of Paul's Epistle to the Philippians*. Edited by S. E. Porter. Vol. 172, *JSNTSup*. Sheffield: Sheffield Academic Press.

Debrunner, Albert. 1926. Grundsätzliches über Kolometrie im Neuen Testament. *TBl* 5:231–33.

Devine, A. M., and Laurence D. Stephens. 1993. Evidence from Experimental Psychology for the Rhythm and Metre of Greek Verse. Paper read at Transactions of the American Philological Association.

Fischer, Steven Roger. 2003. *A History of Reading*. Edited by J. Black, *Globalities*. London: Reaktion Books.

Gamble, Harry Y. 1995. *Books and Readers in the Early Church: A History of Early Christian Texts*. New Haven and London: Yale University Press.

Horsley, Richard, and Jonathan A. Draper. 1999. *Whoever Hears You Hears Me: Prophets, Performance, and Tradition in Q*. Harrisburg, PA: Trinity.

Kleist, James A. 1927. Colometry and the New Testament. *Classical Bulletin* 3:18–19.

———. 1928. Colometry and the New Testament (Concluded). *Classical Bulletin* 4:26–27.

Kloppenborg, John S. 1986. Blessing and Marginality: The 'Persecution Beatitude' in Q, Thomas and Early Christianity. *Foundations and Facets Forum* 2:36–56.

Lausberg, Heinrich. 1998. *Handbook of Literary Rhetoric*. Translated by M. T. Bliss, A. Jansen and D. E. Orton. Leiden: Brill.

Lee, Margaret E. 2005. A Method for Sound Analysis in Hellenistic Greek: The Sermon on the Mount as a Test Case. D.Theol., Melbourne College of Divinity, Melbourne.

Lerdahl, Fred, and Ray Jackendoff. 1983. *Generative Theory of Tonal Music*. Cambridge, MA: MIT.

Luz, Ulrich. 1989. *Matthew 1–7: A Commentary*. Translated by W. C. Linss, *EKKNT*. Minneapolis: Augsburg.

Metzger, Bruce M. 1981. *Manuscripts of the Greek Bible: An Introduction to Greek Paleography*. New York: Oxford University Press.

Nidich, Susan. 1996. *Oral World and Written Word: Ancient Israelite Literature*. Edited by D. A. Knight, *Library of Ancient Israel*. Louisville, KY: Westminster John Knox.

Nuwe-Testamentiese Werkgemeenskap van Suid-Afrika. 1977. *The Structure of Matthew 1–13: An Exploration into Discourse Analysis*. Vol. 11, *Neotestamentica*. Pretoria: University Pretoria.

———. ed. 1983. *Structure and Meaning in Matthew 14–28*. Vol. 16, *Neotestamentica*. Stellenbosch: University of Stellenbosch.

Ong, Walter J. 1982. *Orality and Literacy: The Technologizing of the Word*. Edited by T. Hawkes, *New Accents*. London and New York: Methuen.

Parunak, H. 1981. Oral Typesetting: Some Uses of Biblical Structure. *Bib* 62:153–68.

Porter, Cole. 1983. *The Complete Lyrics of Cole Porter*. New York: Knopf.

Robbins, Vernon K. 1996. *The Tapestry of Early Christian Discourse: Rhetoric, Society and Ideology*. London and New York: Routledge.

Schütz, Roland. 1922. Die Bedeutung der Kolometrie für das Neuen Testament. *ZNW* 21:161–84.

Sloboda, John A. 1985. *Musical Mind: The Cognitive Psychology of Music*. Oxford: Clarendon.

Smyth, Herbert Weir. 1984. *Greek Grammar*. Cambridge: Harvard University Press.

Stowers, Stanley K. 1994. *A Rereading of Romans: Justice, Jews, and Gentiles*. New Haven: Yale University Press.

Strunk, William Jr., and E. B. White. 1972. *The Elements of Style*. 2d ed. New York: Macmillan.

Stubbs, Michael. 1980. *Language and Literacy: The Sociolinguistics of Reading and Writing, Routledge Education Books*. London: Routledge and Kegan Paul.

Traub, Helmut. 1967. οὐρανός. In *TDNT*, edited by G. Friedrich. Grand Rapids, MI: Wm. B. Eerdmans.

Zahn, Theodor. 1922. *Das Evangelium des Mätthaus, Kommentar zum Neuen Testament*. Leipzig: Deichert.

Chapter 5

Developing Sound Maps

READING TO HEAR

Having begun to appreciate Hellenistic literature as speech and as sound, we can now turn to a silent, printed copy of the New Testament to develop sound maps. We cannot, of course, duplicate the listening experiences of ancient audiences nor achieve the kind of listening fluency that audiences in the Greco-Roman world enjoyed. Some features of ancient oral performances are irretrievably lost; others can only be approximated but never fully recreated. We can, however, attend to sound in a systematic way and thus discover a composition's organic structure according to the linear dynamics of sound. This is especially true for compositions in Hellenistic Greek. The invention of the phonetic alphabet and the practice of writing *scriptio continua* demonstrate that Greek writing was especially adapted to capturing the language's sounds and preserving its spoken character. As chapter 3 has shown, Greek grammar encodes sound, which organizes compositions and thus guides their reception and interpretation. The flexible word order of Hellenistic Greek permits acoustic manipulation to achieve various sound effects, and inflectional patterns associate syntactically related words through rhyming suffixes. Repetition of sound groups creates patterns that organize compositions into structural units. Ancient readers of manuscripts written in *scriptio continua* presented those compositions meaningfully in oral performance by decoding the written marks syllable by syllable without the aid of such modern organizational devices as topical headings, chapter and verse divisions, punctuation, and even spaces between words.

Listening for a composition's aural characteristics begins by recapturing the linearity of auditory reception and thus recapitulating the process of reading aloud. Analyzing a composition syllable by syllable makes it possible to discover how sound builds a composition's structure and guides the meaning-making process. Chapter 4 has shown the importance to a silent reader of visually displaying a composition's colometric structure and analyzing its patterns of repetition. Sound mapping and ancient reading both begin with a graphic presentation of syllables in a linear stream.[1] Ancient readers used manuscripts written in *scriptio continua*; modern readers use printed or electronic Greek versions. Mapping sound requires a reader to attend to a composition one syllable at a time and to organize a composition's sounds according to the auditory patterns that emerge.

In order to recover some feeling for a composition's impact upon an ancient audience and thereby gain a better sense of the meaning it presumably had for that audience, modern, silent readers must abandon reading strategies that rely on typographical conventions in favor of organizational schemes established and implemented through sound. Abandonment of logical and conventional organizational schemes inevitably disorients a modern reader, but such disorientation is both necessary and desirable precisely because the conventions of print obscure the organic structure achieved through auditory devices as sounds are articulated and apprehended in a linear stream. Sound mapping enables a reader to submit to the ear training exerted by a composition's sounds and thus gradually to achieve a better understanding of the composition through a more lively appreciation of structures built up by sound.

Becoming reoriented by sound requires first the mapping and then the analysis of a composition's sounds as a prelude to exegesis. Rediscovering the New Testament as it is organized by sound opens new doors for exegesis and sheds light on stubborn interpretive problems. To compensate for a modern, silent readers' inability to process sounds in real time, sound mapping graphically represents sound features thereby presenting new data for analysis and creating new possibilities for interpretation. Criteria for the development and analysis of a sound map are outlined below.

WHAT IS A SOUND MAP?

A sound map is a visual display that exhibits a literary composition's organization by highlighting its acoustic features and in doing so depicts aspects of a composition's sounded character in preparation for analysis. Just as geographic spaces can be mapped in various ways to highlight different features of a landscape, so sound maps can employ many methods of presentation to exhibit various sound patterns, but in any case function according to criteria that arise from ancient experiences of reading, writing, and listening. Analysis proceeds colon by colon, breath by breath, with the sound data indicating a composition's structure, sound quality, and distinctive sound effects.

BEGIN WITH THE COLON

The colon is the basic building block of analysis because it represents a breath unit, a unit of speech. Sound maps divide compositions colometrically to exhibit these basic speech units, one colon to a line. Numbering cola makes reference easier. Manipulating an electronic version of the composition under review facilitates its rearrangement into colometric form as well as permitting the addition of such other visual clues as boldface and italic type, underscoring, and even color to highlight the composition's acoustic features.

Dividing a composition colometrically demands the identification of the colon's boundaries. Cola span sense units. Sometimes a colon can be identified as a predicate and all of its related elements, as in the passage below from Mark's gospel.[2]

Mark 15:16–17

1 Οἱ δὲ στρατιῶται ἀπήγαγον αὐτὸν ἔσω τῆς αὐλῆς,
ὅ ἐστινπραιτώριον,
2 καὶ συγκαλοῦσιν ὅλην τὴν σπεῖραν.
3 καὶ ἐνδιδύσκουσιν αὐτὸν πορφύραν
4 καὶ περιτιθέασιν αὐτῷ πλέξαντες ἀκάνθινον στέφανον·[3]

When a colon exceeds the length of a line, a hanging indent can indicate its continuation on the line below.

Mark 15:27

1 Καὶ σὺν αὐτῷ σταυροῦσιν δύο λῃστάς,
ἕνα ἐκ δεξιῶν
καὶ ἕνα ἐξ εὐωνύμων αὐτοῦ.[4]

Sometimes cola definition seems more problematic. As chapter 3 has shown, in antiquity cola were defined pragmatically, neither logically nor in conformity with a set of abstract linguistic principles. In compositions with complex syntax and multiple levels of grammatical subordination, colometric boundaries frequently circumscribe a sense unit controlled by a finite verb or some other verbal element, such as a participle or infinitive, as in this passage from Luke's gospel.[5]

Luke 2:1

1 Ἐγένετο δὲ ἐν ταῖς ἡμέραις ἐκείναις
2 ἐξῆλθεν δόγμα παρὰ Καίσαρος Αὐγούστου
3 ἀπογράφεσθαι πᾶσαν τὴν οἰκουμένην.[6]

Conversely, sometimes a colon contains more than one finite verb. This frequently occurs with brief cola and compound predicates, as in Matthew's performance of this Q saying.[7]

Matt 7:7

1 Αἰτεῖτε, καὶ δοθήσεται ὑμῖν·
2 ζητεῖτε, καὶ εὑρήσετε·
3 κρούετε, καὶ ἀνοιγήσεται ὑμῖν.[8]

Sometimes no verbal element is present but εἶναι is implied, as in this passage from Luke's birth narrative.[9]

Luke 2:14

1 Δόξα ἐν ὑψίστοις θεῷ
2 καὶ ἐπὶ γῆς εἰρήνη ἐν ἀνθρώποις εὐδοκίας.[10]

At other times, the verbal element is implied elliptically in parallel cola, as in this passage from the Sermon on the Mount.[11]

Matt 5:15

1	οὐδὲ καίουσιν λύχνον καὶ	**τιθέασιν** αὐτὸν	ὑπὸ τὸν μόδιον
2	ἀλλ'	[**missing verb**]	ἐπὶ τὴν λυχνίαν,
3	καὶ λάμπει πᾶσιν τοῖς ἐν τῇ οἰκίᾳ[12]		

Occasionally, cola can be analyzed in more than one way. Just as musicians interpret a musical score in various ways, different readers might declaim a passage at different paces and with different pauses. And although choosing a particular phrasing for a particular performance is an interpretive process, it is not arbitrary. Audiences can usually discern whether an interpretation is true to a musical composition. Similarly, different sound maps might display colometric divisions of the same passage differently, depending on the particular sound features to be exhibited. Provided that breath units are sensibly and consistently discerned, a composition's aural structure will emerge and can be variously displayed to highlight selected acoustic features.

For example, a passage containing two predicates might be analyzed as a single colon to emphasize its brevity, as in this passage from the Sermon on the Mount.

Matt 5:34a

1 ἐγὼ δὲ **λέγω** ὑμῖν μὴ **ὀμόσαι** ὅλως·[13]

Alternatively, the same passage might be exhibited as two cola to emphasize its connection with subsequent cola.

Matt 5:34–36

1	**ἐγὼ δὲ λέγω ὑμῖν**	
2	**μὴ ὀμόσαι ὅλως·**	
3	**μήτε** ἐν τῷ οὐρανῷ,	ὅτι θρόνος ἐστὶν τοῦ θεοῦ·
4	**μήτε** ἐν τῇ γῇ,	ὅτι ὑποπόδιόν ἐστιν τῶν ποδῶν αὐτοῦ·

5 **μήτε** εἰς Ἱεροσόλυμα, ὅτι πόλις ἐστὶν τοῦ μεγάλου βασιλέως·
6 **μήτε** ἐν τῇ κεφαλῇ σου ὀμόσῃς, ὅτι οὐ δύνασαι μίαν τρίχα λευκὴν ποιῆσαι ἢ μέλαιναν.[14]

In any case, cola would not be accurately described if their boundaries were assigned arbitrarily. For example, colon divisions assigned to achieve roughly equivalent line lengths would be incorrect.

An incorrect colometric division of Matt 5:34a

1 ἐγὼ δὲ λέγω
2 ὑμῖν μὴ ὀμόσαι
3 ὅλως· μήτε ἐν τῷ
4 οὐρανῷ, ὅτι θρόνος
5 ἐστὶν τοῦ θεοῦ·

The hypothetical example above can be shown to be improper because it separates related elements. Predicates are divorced from their subjects (θρόνος / ἐστὶν, "cola" 4–5) (throne/is) and indirect objects (λέγω / ὑμῖν, "cola" 1–2) (I say/to you); an infinitive from a modifying adverb (ὀμόσαι / ὅλως, "cola" 2–3) (swear/at all); and an article from its noun (τῷ / οὐρανῷ, "cola" 3–4) (heaven).

ARRANGE THE PERIODS

When cola are combined into periods a sound map should cluster those cola to exhibit the methods of joining and blending cola into periods. To depict periodic boundaries on a sound map, one may either leave a blank line between cola or number them separately. Setting off each period facilitates analysis of its internal structure and the relations among its component cola.

Cola can be combined paratactically or by means of grammatical subordination. Well-formed periods are typically characterized by rounding (the repetition at the period's end of sounds heard at the beginning), balance (parallel or antithetical cola) and elongation (long final colon and/or multiple long vowel sounds), such as this passage from Paul's letter to Philemon.[15]

Philemon 4–6

1 Εὐ**χαριστῶ** τῷ θεῷ μου πάντοτε
2 μνείαν σου ποιούμενος ἐπὶ τῶν προσευχῶν μου,
3 ἀκούων σου τὴν ἀγάπην καὶ τὴν πίστιν
4 ἣν ἔχεις πρὸς τὸν κύριον Ἰησοῦν καὶ εἰς πάντας τοὺς ἁγίους,
5 ὅπως ἡ κοινωνία τῆς πίστεώς σου ἐνεργὴς γένηται
ἐν ἐπιγνώσει παντὸς ἀγαθοῦ τοῦ ἐν ἡμῖν εἰς **Χριστόν**[16]

This period is rounded by the repetition of beginning sounds at the end of the period, including the semantically significant syllables –χαριστ-/χριστ, παν-, and the phoneme ω. Balance is achieved by means of the paired participles in cola 2 and 3. The period's final colon is elongated by its longer duration and many long vowel sounds.

Often, not all indications of periodic structure need be present for periodic boundaries to remain nonetheless clear, as in this passage from John's gospel.[17]

John 20:6–9

1.1 ἔρχεται **οὖν** καὶ Σίμων Πέτρος ἀκολουθῶν αὐτῷ,
1.2 καὶ εἰσῆλθεν εἰς τὸ μνημεῖον·
1.3 καὶ θεωρεῖ τὰ ὀθόνια κείμενα,
1.4 καὶ τὸ σουδάριον, ὃ ἦν ἐπὶ τῆς κεφαλῆς αὐτοῦ,
1.5 οὐ μετὰ τῶν ὀθονίων κείμενον
1.6 ἀλλὰ χωρὶς ἐντετυλιγμένον εἰς ἕνα τόπον.

2.1 τότε **οὖν** εἰσῆλθεν
2.2 καὶ ὁ ἄλλος μαθητὴς ὁ ἐλθὼν πρῶτος εἰς τὸ μνημεῖον,
2.3 καὶ εἶδεν καὶ ἐπίστευσεν·
2.4 οὐδέπω γὰρ ᾔδεισαν τὴν γραφὴν ὅτι δεῖ αὐτὸν ἐκ νεκρῶν ἀναστῆναι.[18]

The usual indications of periodic structure are missing from the passage displayed above. No clear rounding or balance occurs in either period, although period 2 does have an elongated ending. But periodic boundaries are evident in structural elements that are parallel in the two periods, such as the initial οὖν, the additional time indicator marking the beginning of period 2, the containment of paratactically joined cola within the period (neither period begins nor ends with cola joined by καί), and the syllable ου at the beginning the colon following the paratactic cola in both periods.

Occasionally periods will exhibit some signals of periodic structure but in other ways seem to breach the conventions, as in this exerpt from Luke's birth narrative.[19]

Luke 2:8–12

1.1 Καὶ ποιμένες ἦσαν ἐν τῇ χώρᾳ τῇ αὐτῇ ἀγραυλοῦντες
1.2 καὶ φυλάσσοντες φυλακὰς τῆς νυκτὸς ἐπὶ τὴν ποίμνην αὐτῶν.
1.3 καὶ ἄγγελος κυρίου ἐπέστη αὐτοῖς
1.4 καὶ δόξα κυρίου περιέλαμψεν αὐτούς,
1.5 καὶ ἐφοβήθησαν φόβον μέγαν.
1.6 καὶ εἶπεν αὐτοῖς ὁ ἄγγελος,

2.1 Μὴ φοβεῖσθε,

2.2 ἰδοὺ γὰρ εὐαγγελίζομαι ὑμῖν χαρὰν μεγάλην ἥτις ἔσται παντὶ
τῷ λαῷ,
2.3 ὅτι ἐτέχθη ὑμῖν σήμερον σωτὴρ ὅς ἐστιν Χριστὸς κύριος
ἐν πόλει Δαυίδ·
2.4 καὶ τοῦτο ὑμῖν τὸ σημεῖον,
2.5 εὑρήσετε βρέφος ἐσπαργανωμένον καὶ κείμενον ἐν φάτνῃ.[20]

Period 1 above is tightly unified at the narrative level, in that the quick succession of statements joined by *καί* all focus the shepherds' experience and take their point of view. Cola 3 and 4 are balanced by close parallelism. The period's colometric structure builds tension and increases suspense. But the period has a shortened final colon instead of an elongated ending. Even more unusual is the separation of the introduction to the angel's speech from the speech itself, which begins in the following period. Yet the integrity of the periodic structure indicates that the periodic boundary should be drawn as shown.[21]

Not all Greek composition is highly periodic, and even in passages with well-defined periods, single-colon periods can occur. The paratactic, even choppy narrative style of Mark's gospel has often been observed.

Mark 15:25–27

1 ἦν δὲ ὥρα τρίτη καὶ ἐσταύρωσαν αὐτόν.

2 καὶ ἦν ἡ ἐπιγραφὴ τῆς αἰτίας αὐτοῦ ἐπιγεγραμμένη, Ὁ βασιλεὺς
τῶν Ἰουδαίων.

3 Καὶ σὺν αὐτῷ σταυροῦσιν δύο λῃστάς, ἕνα ἐκ δεξιῶν καὶ ἕνα ἐξ
εὐωνύμων αὐτοῦ.[22]

Much of Mark's narrative is composed of simple periods, periods containing only one colon, such as the passage displayed above.

Even in the highly structured Sermon on the Mount, simple periods can occur.

Matt 6:21–22

1.1 ὅπου γάρ ἐστιν ὁ θησαυρός σου,
1.2 ἐκεῖ ἔσται καὶ ἡ καρδία σου.

2 **Ὁ λύχνος τοῦ σώματός ἐστιν ὁ ὀφθαλμός.**

3.1 ἐὰν οὖν ᾖ ὁ ὀφθαλμός σου ἁπλοῦς,
3.2 ὅλον τὸ σῶμά σου φωτεινὸν ἔσται·[23]

The aphorism that comprises period 2 above stands alone between two brief periods with paired cola. Neither continuous style nor simple periods prevent proper discernment of periodic boundaries, since sound reliably establishes a composition's structure.

IDENTIFY SOUND PATTERNS

As readers become oriented to a composition's sounds, submitting to the composition's ear training and dispensing with externally imposed organizational schemes, organic sound patterns emerge. Repetition organizes sounds into groups, and sound groups into phrases and larger structural units. Chapter 4 has outlined the dynamics of listening to compositions in real time to discover patterns established through repetition of phonemes, syllables, and larger sound groups. Sound maps plot out patterns of repetition, exhibiting structural features and distinctive sound effects in a visual display. To present visually a composition's structural features crafted by sound and stored in memory, various strategies can be employed, including the use of boldface type for repeating sounds, alignment of parallel elements and underscoring thematic phrases.

IDENTIFY COMPOSITIONAL UNITS

Oral performance and auditory reception depend on memory as the primary vehicle for information storage and retrieval. This means that compositions must be declaimed aloud, apprehended in real time through listening, and stored in memory in distinct units with mnemonic tags that enable recall. Compositional units can be discerned by virtue of their auditory boundaries and mnemonic tags, evident in their distinctive sound signatures. Sound maps exhibit compositions divided into units designated by sound.

To map the sounds of a composition under review, one must determine the proper boundaries of a compositional unit on the basis of sound. No single set of guidelines for discerning unit division can be prescribed for two reasons. First, as chapter 1 has shown, compositional practice in the ancient world did not place a high value on crafting large, architectonic schemes to organize compositions from beginning to end, primarily because it was physically difficult. Instead, attention is paid to joining smaller compositional units that represent chunks of material from the τόποι (places) of a memorial ϑησαύρος (treasury). As chapter 3 has shown, this does not mean that compositions lacked unity or artistry. Bits of material drawn from memory were not merely strung together like beads, but neither were overarching schemes imposed, arranging compositional units into an ordered hierarchy. Rather, well-selected units of remembered material that could be held in memory and viewed in the confined space of a writing surface were crafted and blended together using various artistic devices. The concern for structuring intermediate compositional units according to some abstract logic derives much more from the conventions of print and the practice of silent reading. These concerns were not native to ancient literature.

Second, the demands of genre, audience, and authorial idiolect create virtually limitless possibilities for compositional organization and argue against prescribed guidelines. Greek literary taste permitted wide-ranging freedom of artistic expression. All compositional concerns were subordinated to the success of an oral performance and the persuasiveness of rhetorical argument. Admittedly, rhetorical literature followed more prescriptive patterns than other genres because its social contexts were more predictable and constrained. But even in the rhetorical arena wide latitude was permitted within rhetorical types.

As with the discernment of colometric and periodic boundaries, identification of compositional elements such as units, sections, and parts is an interpretative task. An interpreter must submit to a composition's ear training to become oriented to the structures established and implemented by sound. Outcomes cannot always be predicted. Instead, results must arise organically from the composition's acoustic features. Like the discernment of boundaries for cola and periods, unit boundary delineation is neither subjective nor arbitrary. Because sound imposes structure on compositions at both the micro and macro levels, it organizes speech into comprehensible units and is therefore the most reliable guide to compositional structure.

At the macro level of unit definition and compositional organization, sound remains fundamental but operates in concert with other literary devices. For example, the scene-setting strategies of narrative, such as indications of time and place, help to organize the plot and facilitate the audience's visualization of narrated action.[24] Grammatical signals like verbal aspect and changes of grammatical person and number guide reception by signaling point of view.[25] Even more, ear training can embed structural devices in a composition to accomplish a pragmatic purpose.[26] All such devices are implemented at the level of sound, although they also entail the dimensions of semantics, syntax, poetics, and rhetoric.

Because compositions exhibit a wide range of organizational formats, the examples of sound mapping and analysis presented in this book are not entirely consistent in their schemes for numbering and labeling of cola, periods, units, sections, and parts. For example, the discussion of Mark's crucifixion narrative in chapter 6 will show that periodic structure, while evident, is not a strong feature of Mark's literary style. Instead, continuous cola advance the narrative in a style consistent with Hellenistic historical narration. And thus in the sound map of Mk 15:25–41 cola are numbered sequentially throughout the narrative, but periods are numbered within each of its parts, beginning with 1. Conversely, in the highly periodic letter to Philemon examined in chapter 8, periods are numbered sequentially from the beginning to the end of the letter, and cola are numbered within periods, beginning with 1. This scheme facilitates the analysis of Paul's complex periodic organization. The Sermon on the Mount presents yet another arrangement with its hierarchical organization of units within sections. Thus our sound map of Matt 5–7 in chapter 10 adopts a hierarchical scheme. Sections are numbered sequentially throughout the Sermon, and each section's component units are numbered with the section's designation. So, for example, in the antitheses (section 4 of the Sermon), the first antithesis comprises a unit and is numbered 4.1. The second is numbered 4.2, and so on. Periods are numbered within units and cola are numbered within periods.

DESCRIBE SOUND QUALITY

Sound quality refers to the character of individual sounds, to the ways sounds are combined, and to the relation between sound and meaning. Concern for euphony and the mellifluous flow of language in classical and Hellenistic Greek sharpened audience appreciation of each sound's unique character. Whereas modern writers strive for aptness in word choice based primarily on semantics, Hellenistic authors strove for harmony (ἁρμονία). A well-spoken (εὔγλωσσον) composition contained harmonized sounds that were sweet in the ears (μελιχρὸν ἐν ταῖς ἀκοαῖς) (Dion. Hal. *Comp.* 1). Quintilian justifies the importance of sound quality in this way: "[I]n the first place nothing can penetrate to the emotions that stumbles at the portals of the ear, and secondly man is naturally attracted by harmonious sounds" (*Inst.* 9.4.10). The auditory characteristics of speech sounds and their various combinations affect their reception. Distinctive sound qualities include euphony, cacophony, and onomatopoeia. Phonemes and syllables draw attention both when they are especially pleasant and when they are cacophonous. They also strike the ear with particular force when the speech sounds imitate the phenomenon they describe.

EUPHONY AND HARMONY

Euphony refers to the aesthetic quality of phonemes and syllables and the overall auditory impact of a series of sounds. Harmony refers to the way sounds are combined. The semantic field of ἁρμονία (harmony) includes notions of joining or fastening—either in a literal sense referring to a ship's planks or the connection of anatomical parts, or figuratively to refer to a covenant or government order. The term has several technical meanings. In music, for instance, it refers to the stringing together of tones in a scale or mode, while in literary composition it signifies an arrangement of words so well combined that that it is fit to be set to music (*LSJ s.v.* ἁρμονία).[27] The appeal of euphony and harmony was strong in Hellenistic Greek, which regarded certain sounds as beautiful in themselves (Demetr. *Eloc.* 173–77; Dion. Hal. *Comp.* 3). The author of the treatise *Περὶ ὕφους* (On the Sublime) states as an obvious fact that melody provides "a natural instrument of persuasion and pleasure" ([Longinus] *Subl.* 39.1). The treatise asks:

> Must we not think, then, that composition, which is a kind of melody in words—words which are part of man's nature and reach not his ears only but his very soul—stirring as it does myriad ideas of words, thoughts, things, beauty, musical charm, all of which are born and bred in us, and by the blending of its own manifold tones, bringing into the hearts of bystanders the speaker's actual emotion so that all who hear him share in it, and by piling phrase on phrase builds up one majestic whole—must we not think, I say, that by these very means it casts a spell on us and always turns our thought towards what is majestic and dignified and sublime and all else that it embraces, winning a complete mastery over our minds? (39.3)

Euphony and harmony were frequently achieved through the use of smooth consonants and open vowel sounds.[28] The opening of the Lord's prayer illustrates this dynamic:

Example of euphony

Mt 6:9b–10

1 Πάτερ ἡμῶν ὁ* ἐν τοῖς οὐρανοῖς,
2 ἁγιασθήτω τὸ ὄνομά σου,
3 ἐλθέτω ἡ βασιλεία σου,
4 γενηθήτω τὸ θέλημά σου,
5 ὡς ἐν οὐρανῷ καὶ ἐπὶ γῆς.[29]

This passage is memorable partly because of its harmonious sounds. Smooth consonants such as γ, λ, μ, ν, and ρ connect many of the syllables. Harsher consonant sounds such as ζ, κ, ξ, π, τ, χ are rare. Hiatus, which was considered inharmonious because it interrupts sound with a glottal stop between words,[30] occurs in this passage only once, in the first line (ὁ ἐν; marked with an asterisk above).

Rhyming inflectional suffixes (the repeated genitive pronoun σου and the repeated verb ending -θητω and -τω) enhance the parallelism of lines 2–4. The recurrence of οὐρανοῖς/οὐρανῷ in the first and last lines serves to unify the passage. The phrase καὶ ἐπὶ γῆ at the end of the passage elongates the final line and allows time for the repetition to register with the audience. The passage makes for pleasant and easy listening.

CACOPHONY AND DISSONANCE

Cacophony refers to unpleasant sounds or a displeasing overall auditory effect. Dissonance refers to unpleasant sound combinations. Sounds that stand apart from surrounding sounds through consonant clash or hiatus make a stronger impression than aurally nondescript or unrepeated sounds:[31]

Example of cacophony
Mk 16:29b–30

1 Οὐὰ*ὁ καταλύων τὸν ναὸν καὶ*οἰκοδομῶν ἐν τρισὶν ἡμέραις,
2 σῶσον σεαυτὸν καταβὰς ἀπὸ τοῦ σταυροῦ.[32]

Frequent σ/ζ sounds imitate hissing, and frequent κ/τ/π/χ phonomes evoke spitting sounds. Onomatopoeia for hissing and spitting provides a distinctive sound signature for these cola.[33]

Example of dissonance
Mt 7:23

1 καὶ τότε ὁμολογήσω*αὐτοῖς ὅτι*Οὐδέποτε*ἔγνων ὑμᾶς·
2 ἀποχωρεῖτε ἀπ'*ἐμοῦ οἱ*ἐργαζόμενοι τὴν ἀνομίαν.[34]

Frequent harsh-sounding consonants create dissonance, especially when combined with hiatus.[35] The resulting auditory effect supports this passage's brutal message. The stern statements οὐδέποτε ἔγνων ὑμᾶς (I never knew you) and ἀποχωρεῖτε ἀπ᾽ ἐμοῦ (get away from me) remain unrelieved by any euphonic or organizing impact of parallel structure or internal rhyme.

ONOMATOPOEIA

Onomatopoeia privileges sounds by imitating sounds of the entity or event being described, thus placing the signifier and signified in concert (Demetr. *Eloc.* 94). The following section of the Sermon that adduces images from nature provides a useful illustration:

Example of onomatopoeia
Mt 6:26

1 ἐμβλέψατε εἰς τὰ πετεινὰ τοῦ οὐρανοῦ ὅτι
2 οὐ σπείρουσιν

3 οὐδὲ θερίζουσιν
4 οὐδὲ συνάγουσιν εἰς ἀποθήκας[36]

This description of the birds of the air is arranged in rhythmic, parallel lines that employ frequent sigma sounds (including σ, ζ, and ψ) and the repeated syllable ου, imitating birdsong. Internal rhyme in the parallel predicates of cola 2, 3, and 4 (σπείρουσιν, θερίζουσιν, συνάγουσιν) (plant, harvest, gather) intensifies this effect. This euphonic effect advances the aptness of the image of birds as a figure for the divine.

ANALYZE THE RELATION BETWEEN STYLE AND SUBJECT

The blending of sounds in various literary styles is important because stylistic conventions shaped audience expectations. Noting a composition's literary style and its relation to the composition's subject is an important aspect of sound analysis. Because of the value ancient audiences placed on the appropriateness of literary style to a composition's content, sound analysis should include careful examination of the relation between style and subject. Since sound and semantics make independent contributions to a composition's meaning, they can either reinforce each other or be placed in tension for a disturbing or ironic effect. The classical commentators suggest this possibility in their discussions of styles gone awry. The various stylistic types are achieved by artful blendings of the sounds and significations of words. To be sure, the intended affect is not always achieved; Demetrius explicitly associates a faulty style with each of the stylistic types he identifies. When faulty, the grand style becomes frigid (*Eloc.* 114–15), the elegant style affected (*Eloc.* 186), the plain style arid (*Eloc.* 236), and the forceful style repulsive, disgusting, or obscene (*Eloc.* 302). Some examples from Matthew's gospel and Lukan parallels will suggest the range of possibilities for communicating meaning through literary style.

PERIOD FORMATION

At the level of λέξις (speech, diction), compositions can exhibit continuous or periodic style, or a mixture of the two. "Style" in this sense refers to the manner of combining cola into periods. The power of the period as a structuring device establishes two poles of a gradient from highly periodic structure in which the boundaries of each period are clear, to a non-periodic style in which cola are distinguishable but not blended into periods (Arist. *Rh.* 3.9.1).[37] While from a technical standpoint all prose could be understood to consist of periods, well-rounded and balanced periods could be distinguished from those that merely met certain minimal technical requirements. Highly periodic compositional form and less periodic, continuous, or disjointed style achieve very different stylistic effects. Long cola were thought best suited for an elevated style or complex subject, whereas a simple subject or forcible style required short cola. Above all, the length and character of the period's composite members must be appropriate, whether long or short (Demetr. *Eloc.* 4–8). In recognition of these differences and their impact on the hearer, the classical stylebooks frequently advocate a mixture of both to obtain the advantages of each.

Continuous style

The verses immediately preceding the Sermon on the Mount exemplify a relatively non-periodic or continuous style appropriate to historical narration.

4:23–25

Period 1

Καὶ περιῆγεν ἐν ὅλῃ τῇ Γαλιλαίᾳ,

	διδάσκων	ἐν ταῖς συναγωγαῖς αὐτῶν
καὶ	κηρύσσων	τὸ εὐαγγέλιον τῆς βασιλείας
καὶ	θεραπεύων	πᾶσαν νόσον
καὶ		πᾶσαν μαλακίαν ἐν τῷ λαῷ.

Period 2

καὶ ἀπῆλθεν ἡ ἀκοὴ αὐτοῦ εἰς ὅλην τὴν Συρίαν·
καὶ προσήνεγκαν αὐτῷ πάντας τοὺς κακῶς ἔχοντας ποικίλαις νόσοις

καὶ βασάνοις	συνεχομένους	
καὶ	δαιμονιζομένους	
καὶ	σεληνιαζομένους	
καὶ	παραλυτικούς,	
καὶ ἐθεράπευσεν		αὐτούς.

Period 3

καὶ ἠκολούθησαν αὐτῷ ὄχλοι	πολλοὶ ἀπὸ τῆς	Γαλιλαίας
καὶ		Δεκαπόλεως
καὶ		Ἱεροσολύμων
καὶ		Ἰουδαίας
καὶ	πέραν τοῦ	Ἰορδάνου.[38]

Although these three verses string cola together without balancing or rounding cola into periods, periodic boundaries can be discerned by the sound patterns that emerge. The predominant aural patterns consist of the repeated paratactic connector καί, the repeated medial -ων in period 1, the fivefold repetition of terminal -ους in period 2, and the five locations named at the ends of the cola in period 3. These weak structural signals do not contribute to periodic delineation, rounding, or balance. Nevertheless, despite its continuous style, periods in the passage are clearly delineated.

Periodic style

By contrast, Matthew's performance of the Lord's prayer illustrates how cola can be combined into periods that demonstrate the structural ideals of rounding and balance and create a more elegant, polished tone.

6:9b–15

Period 1 (6:9–10)

1	Πάτερ ἡμῶν	ὁ ἐν τοῖς **οὐρανοῖς,**	
2		ἁγιασθήτω	τὸ ὄνομά σου,
3		ἐλθέτω	ἡ βασιλεία σου,
4		γενηθήτω	τὸ θέλημά σου,
5		ὡς ἐν **οὐρανῷ**	καὶ ἐπὶ **γῆς.**[39]

The first period is balanced by the three central cola set in parallel with rhyming structural elements, including aorist imperative verbs ending in –ήτω/έτω, their subjects ending in identical -a sounds because of their inflectional suffixes, and their identical genitive modifier, σου. And with their common term (ὁ οὐρανός), the first and fifth cola bracket the parallel elements. Rounding is achieved by the repetition in the fifth colon of the heavens, mentioned previously in colon 1, and elongation by the addition of its complement, the earth. This return to an element in the period's beginning and the pairing of the repeated element with its complementary term, the earth, lends a sense of wholeness, return, or completion.

Period 2 (6:11–13)

1	Τὸν ἄρτον	ἡμῶν τὸν ἐπιούσιον δὸς		ἡμῖν σήμερον·
2	καὶ **ἄφες**	ἡμῖν τὰ	ὀφειλήματα	ἡμῶν,
3	ὡς καὶ	ἡμεῖς **ἀφήκαμεν** τοῖς	ὀφειλέταις	ἡμῶν·
4	καὶ μὴ εἰσενέγκῃς	ἡμᾶς εἰς	πειρασμόν,	
5	ἀλλὰ ῥῦσαι	ἡμᾶς ἀπὸ τοῦ	πονηροῦ.[40]	

Repeated occurrences of the first person plural pronoun unify the second period. Similar sounding inflections of τὸ ὀφείλημα and ὁ ὀφειλέτης are paired near the end of cola 2 and 3. These two cola are also paired by recurrences of ἀφίημι and the ὡς καί construction at the beginning of colon 3. This construction recalls the ὡς construction in the last colon of period 1. The repeated consonants π and ϱ in the final syllables of cola 4 and 5 create a second pairing of cola in period 2 with similar endings. These final two cola, joined by ἀλλά at the beginning of cola 5, form an antithesis that balances the preceding three cola with their unifying terminal personal pronouns.

Period 3 (6:14–15)

1 Ἐὰν γὰρ ἀφῆτε τοῖς **ἀνθρώποις** τὰ παραπτώματα αὐτῶν,
2 ἀφήσει καὶ ὑμῖν ὁ πατὴρ ὑμῶν ὁ οὐράνιος·
3 ἐὰν δὲ μὴ ἀφῆτε τοῖς **ἀνθρώποις,**
4 οὐδὲ ὁ πατὴρ ὑμῶν ἀφήσει τὰ παραπτώματα ὑμῶν.[41]

The third period consists of paired conditional statements: A variation in the final colon's order of terms rescues the period from the predictability of strict parallelism. The fourth colon's abbreviated epithet, ὁ πατὴρ ὑμῶν, supplies its first term, whereas the more expansive version of the epithet in colon 2 comes at the colon's end. The resulting chiastic arrangement of subject and predicate in cola 2 and 4 supply interest, while the period's final phrase, τὰ παραπτώματα ὑμῶν, repeats the ending of the period's first colon. This repetition contributes to the period's rounded quality, while the paired conditional statements balance the period.

The periodic character of Matt 6:9b–15 contrasts with Luke's version of the Lord's Prayer which is briefer, exhibits fewer periodic features, and depends heavily on the paratactic connector καί to join cola.

Luke 11:2b–4
Period 1

1 Πάτερ,
2 ἁγιασθήτω τὸ ὄνομά σου·
3 ἐλθέτω ἡ βασιλεία σου

Period 2

1 τὸν ἄρτον ἡμῶν τὸν ἐπιούσιον δίδου ἡμῖν τὸ καθ' ἡμέραν·
2 καὶ **ἄφες** ἡμῖν τὰς ἁμαρτίας ἡμῶν,
3 καὶ γὰρ αὐτοὶ **ἀφίομεν** παντὶ ὀφείλοντι ἡμῖν·
4 καὶ μὴ εἰσενέγκῃς ἡμᾶς εἰς πειρασμόν.[42]

After the address in period 1 a parallel couplet follows, with rhyming sounds. The cola are balanced but not rounded, nor is the ending elongated. The second period has fewer cola than the parallel passage in Matthew and they are joined paratactically. It is unified by the repeated first person pronoun but there are fewer occurrences than in Matthew's rendition. Luke's version also lacks the reference to the father and the paired occurrences of τὰ ὀφειλήματα. Its final colon is slightly elongated by including relatively more syllables and long vowel sounds. Because Luke's prayer lacks the paired conditional statements that conclude Matthew's version, its periodic structure is simpler and more straightforward, and thus more clearly reflects the prayer's survival concerns.

This comparison of Matthew's and Luke's different performances of what was presumably the same Q passage is especially noteworthy in its illustration that a composition's dynamics are not solely determined by its semantic content or the abstract ideas it invokes. Rather, such dynamics are shaped by the author's creative management of periodic structure.

LITERARY STYLE

Chapter 3 has shown that typologies of literary style classified the various sound effects available when blending periods together. Several New Testament examples illustrate these possibilities.

Austere style

The austere or grave style (ὁ χαρακτὴρ τῆς αὐστηρᾶς ἁρμονίας) conveys an antique-sounding tone that evokes a noble severity. Cacophony and hiatus are acceptable in the austere style because these unpleasant aural effects rivet the hearer's attention. The grave style employs few connectives and uses the article only sparingly. Periods are independent and simple. Independence means that periods need not blend with surrounding periods nor remain consistent within themselves. Simplicity means the avoidance of spectacular or polished endings, ornamentation, and affectation. Cola seldom exhibit parallel structure, but impressive rhythms and noble figures are often employed, along with long syllables and long words that are separated by a time interval from neighboring words.

This stylistic type aims at dignity rather than elegance. It employs the cadences of ancient writing and conveys a slow, settled quality. Its beauty lies not in adornment but in lending a composition "a patina of antiquity" (Dion. Hal. *Comp.* 22–23). The short, independent periods in Matthew's beatitudes create such a patina.[43] Their repeated pronouncement of blessing rings with authority by virtue of the composition's stately, austere style.

5:3–10

1.1 Μακάριοι οἱ πτωχοὶ τῷ πνεύματι,
1.2 ὅτι*αὐτῶν ἐστιν ἡ βασιλεία τῶν οὐρανῶν.

2.1 μακάριοι οἱ πενθοῦντες,
2.2 ὅτι*αὐτοὶ παρακληθήσονται.

3.1 μακάριοι οἱ πραεῖς,
3.2 ὅτι*αὐτοὶ κληρονομήσουσιν τὴν γῆν.

4.1 μακάριοι οἱ πεινῶντες καὶ διψῶντες τὴν δικαιοσύνην,
4.2 ὅτι*αὐτοὶ χορτασθήσονται.

5.1 μακάριοι οἱ*ἐλεήμονες,
5.2 ὅτι*αὐτοὶ*ἐλεηθήσονται.

6.1 μακάριοι οἱ καθαροὶ τῇ καρδίᾳ,
6.2 ὅτι*αὐτοὶ τὸν θεὸν ὄψονται.

7.1 μακάριοι οἱ*εἰρηνοποιοί,
7.2 ὅτι [*αὐτοὶ] υἱοὶ θεοῦ κληθήσονται.

8.1 μακάριοι οἱ δεδιωγμένοι ἕνεκεν δικαιοσύνης,
8.2 ὅτι*αὐτῶν ἐστιν ἡ βασιλεία τῶν οὐρανῶν.[44]

The periods that comprise the beatitudes are not linked with connecting particles or by any other means but remain grammatically independent. The article occurs infrequently. Each period includes relatively long words, usually at the period's beginning (μακάριοι) and end (παρακληθήσονται, period 2; χορτασθήσονται, period 4; ἐλεηθήσονται, period 5). And while κληρονομήσουσιν does not occur at the end of period 3, it is followed by τὴν γῆν, a construction marked by rhyming, long syllables that slow the period's pace and steady its rhythm. The first and last periods in this passage close with a thematic phrase, ἡ βασιλεία τῶν οὐρανῶν, instead of a long word, but the phrase functions as a single term and is marked by long syllables. Furthermore, each period includes a repeating formula that encodes hiatus (marked by asterisks). Although the component periods closely parallel each other, cola within periods are not set in parallel. In this setting the repetition of the initial formula creates an austere effect, and the frequent occurrence of hiatus lends gravity by prefacing sounds with silence.

Because of its smoother sounds and infrequent use of hiatus, the parallel passage in Luke's gospel sounds less grave.

Luke 6:20b–21

1.1 Μακάριοι οἱ πτωχοί,
1.2 ὅτι ὑμετέρα*ἐστὶν ἡ βασιλεία τοῦ θεοῦ.

2.1 μακάριοι οἱ πεινῶντες νῦν,
2.2 ὅτι χορτασθήσεσθε.

3.1 μακάριοι οἱ κλαίοντες νῦν,
3.2 ὅτι γελάσετε.[45]

Elegant style

The polished or elegant style (ἡ γλαφυρὰ σύνθεσις) aims at decoration rather than dignity. This style uses clearly defined, well-rounded periods with multiple cola and strong endings. In the elegant style, cola are blended into periods through antithesis, anaphora, parallelism of length and sound, and other poetic devices. The polished style avoids vowel clashes and harsh combinations of semivowels and consonants. Words superfluous to the sense of the composition can be added in the polished style to smooth out the sound and unify the periods. The primary aesthetic goal of the polished style is the creation of euphony and a pleasant musical effect (Dion. Hal. *Dem.* 40; *Comp.* 23; and Demetr. *Eloc.* 128–88). The rhetorical proposition of the Sermon on the Mount furnishes a good example. Its sophisticated style adorns its complex governing idea.

Matt 5:17–20

1.1 Μὴ νομίσητε ὅτι* ἦλθον καταλῦσαι **τὸν νόμον** ἢ τοὺς προφήτας·
1.2 οὐκ ἦλθον καταλῦσαι
1.3 *ἀλλὰ πληρῶσαι

2.1 *ἀμὴν γὰρ *λέγω ὑμῖν*,
2.2 ἕως ἂν παρέλθῃ ὁ*οὐρανὸς καὶ ἡ γῆ,
2.3 ἰῶτα ἓν ἢ μία κεραία*οὐ μὴ παρέλθῃ*ἀπὸ **τοῦ νόμου**
2.4 ἕως ἂν πάντα γένηται.

3.1 **ὃς ἐὰν οὖν λύσῃ** μίαν τῶν ἐντολῶν τούτων τῶν ἐλαχίστων
3.2 **καὶ διδάξῃ** οὕτως τοὺς ἀνθρώπους,
3.3 ἐλάχιστος **κληθήσεται** *ἐν τῇ βασιλείᾳ τῶν οὐρανῶν·

4.1 **ὃς δ' ἂν ποιήσῃ**
4.2 **καὶ διδάξῃ**
4.3 οὗτος μέγας **κληθήσεται** *ἐν τῇ βασιλείᾳ τῶν οὐρανῶν.

5.1 *λέγω γὰρ ὑμῖν* ὅτι*
5.2 ἐὰν μὴ περισσεύσῃ ὑμῶν ἡ δικαιοσύνη πλεῖον τῶν γραμματέων καὶ Φαρισαίων,
5.3 οὐ μὴ*εἰσέλθητε *εἰς τὴν βασιλείαν τῶν οὐρανῶν.[46]

Sophisticated devices are employed in this passage to combine cola into periods. Little parataxis occurs and is never used to connect one period to the next. Instead, cola are combined by means of antithesis (marked by the οὐκ/ἀλλά construction in period 1), and parallelism (paired ἦλθον καταλῦσαι cola in period 1, paired ἕως ἄν clauses in period 2, and parallel ἐὰν μή and οὐ μή cola in period 5). Not only are cola combined into periods, but periods are connected to each other through parallelism and repeated sound groups. The first two periods are linked by the repetition of ὁ νόμος, and the final three periods by their repetition of ἐν τῇ βασιλεία (εἰς τὴν βασιλείαν) τῶν οὐρανῶν. Λέγω ὑμῖν connects periods 2 and 5. Periods 3 and 4 are structurally parallel despite the abbreviation by ellipsis in period 4.

Syllables are smoothly connected, with few occurrences of hiatus or clashing consonant combinations. Where hiatus does occur, it draws attention to the section's proposition (periods 1 and 5) and emphasizes key Matthean thematic phrases (ὁ οὐρανὸς καὶ ἡ γῆ, period 2; ἡ βασιλεία τῶν οὐρανῶν, periods 3, 4, and 5). Euphony and ornamentation characterize this passage. The aesthetic value of euphony is served by the minimal use of the paratactic connector καί, the presence of rhyme in the first two periods due to the aorist infinitive with its -αι ending, and the repeated terminal -ων at the end of periods 3, 4, and 5. Notable ornaments include the occurrence of both antithesis and parallelism in period 1, the unifying effect of repeated phrases (τὸν νόμον in periods 1 and 2; βασιλεία in periods 3, 4, and 5), the variety of periodic structures, and hendiadys in periods 2 and 5.

Plain style

By its lack of ornamentation, the plain literary style creates an unaffected tone. Luke's prohibition of anxiety provides an example.[47] Its opening periods illustrate this style's distinctive character.

Luke 12:22b–26

1.1	μὴ μεριμνᾶτε	τῇ ψυχῇ		τί φάγητε,	
1.2	μηδὲ		τῷ σώματι	τί ἐνδύσησθε.	
1.3		ἡ γὰρ ψυχὴ		πλεῖόν ἐστιν	τῆς τροφῆς
1.4	καὶ		τὸ σῶμα		τοῦ ἐνδύματος.

2.1 κατανοήσατε τοὺς κόρακας
2.2 ὅτι **οὐ** σπείρουσιν
2.3 **οὐδὲ** θερίζουσιν,
2.4 οἷς **οὐκ** ἔστιν ταμεῖον **οὐδὲ** ἀποθήκη,
2.5 καὶ ὁ θεὸς τρέφει αὐτούς·
2.6 πόσῳ μᾶλλον ὑμεῖς διαφέρετε τῶν πετεινῶν.

3 τίς δὲ ἐξ ὑμῶν μεριμνῶν δύναται ἐπὶ τὴν ἡλικίαν αὐτοῦ προσθεῖναι πῆχυν;[48]

These periods are clearly distinguishable, but they are not highly adorned nor do they have an elegant tone. The first period is balanced by pairs of statements about ἡ ψυχή and τὸ σῶμα. Period 2 contains two balanced pairs, cola 2 and 3, and the οὐκ/οὐδέ statement in colon 4. Its sixth colon is slightly elongated. Period 3 is independent, consisting of one long colon.

The parallel passage in Matthew shows slightly more elegance with few semantic differences.

6:25–27

1.1 μὴ μεριμνᾶτε τῇ ψυχῇ **ὑμῶν** τί φάγητε [ἢ τί πίητε],
1.2 μηδὲ τῷ σώματι **ὑμῶν** τί ἐνδύσησθε·
1.3 οὐχὶ ἡ ψυχὴ πλεῖόν ἐστιν τῆς τροφῆς
1.4 καὶ τὸ σῶμα τοῦ ἐνδύματος;

2.1 ἐμβλέψατε εἰς τὰ πετεινὰ **τοῦ οὐ**ρανο**ῦ**
2.2 ὅτι **οὐ** σπείρ**ου**σιν
2.3 **οὐδὲ** θερίζ**ου**σιν
2.4 **οὐδὲ** συνάγ**ου**σιν εἰς ἀποθήκας,
2.5 καὶ ὁ πατὴρ ὑμῶν ὁ **οὐ**ράνιος τρέφει αὐτά·
2.6 **οὐ**χ ὑμεῖς μᾶλλον διαφέρετε αὐτῶν;

3 τίς δὲ ἐξ ὑμῶν μεριμνῶν δύναται προσθεῖναι ἐπὶ τὴν ἡλικίαν αὐτοῦ πῆχυν ἕνα;[49]

Although Matthew's rendition of this Q passage is nearly identical to Luke's, its few differences significantly alter its tone. In period 1, the occurrences of ὑμῶν connect the first two cola, disturbing the parallelism of the ψυχή and σῶμα statements and complicating its balanced cola. In period 2, the addition of τοῦ οὐρανοῦ at the end of colon 1 emphasizes the repeated ου sound of the repeating negative particle. The occurrence of ἐμβλέψατε εἰς τὰ πετεινά instead of Luke's κατανοήσατε τοὺς κόρακας omits the harsh, repeating κ sounds and introduces ψ and τ. These consonants, especially when combined with the repeating ου sounds, emphasize repeating τ and σ phonemes throughout the period. The combined effect is a sustained onomatopoeia imitating birdsong. In period 3, the occurrence of ἕνα, places rhythmic emphasis at the end of the period, intensifying its point. Luke's rendition, lacking this word, instead emphasizes the rhythmic progress of the line, creating a more reflective tone. Thus the tone of Luke's version is closer to the plain style of philosophic discourse, whereas Matthew's version subtly introduces additional figures and rhetorical flourishes that invoke a relatively more tendentious point of view.

Appropriateness

Generally, the criterion of appropriateness requires that form and content function in concert. Yet depending upon a speaker's rhetorical objective, an apparently unsuitable style might be employed to achieve a particular effect. Indeed, the earliest definition of a figure in Greek rhetoric, by Zoilus of Amphipolis, is "to pretend one thing and to say another" (*[Rh. Al.]* 1437a17). Zoilus' student, Anaximenes, defined irony similarly: "saying something while pretending not to say it" (*[Rh. Al.]* 1434a17). Strategies such as ridicule, irony, and parody could be employed to discredit or demean an opponent, and their authors were praised for their cleverness and subtlety.[50]

The beginning of Matthew's gospel demonstrates this persuasive potential of setting form and content at odds:

Mt 1:1–3a

Βίβλος γενέσεως Ἰησοῦ Χριστοῦ υἱοῦ Δαυὶδ υἱοῦ
Ἀβραάμ.
Ἀβραὰμ ἐγέννησεν τὸν Ἰσαάκ,
Ἰσαὰκ δὲ ἐγέννησεν τὸν Ἰακώβ,
Ἰακὼβ δὲ ἐγέννησεν τὸν Ἰούδαν καὶ τοὺς ἀδελφοὺς αὐτοῦ,
Ἰούδας δὲ ἐγέννησεν τὸν Φάρες καὶ τὸν Ζάρα ἐκ τῆς Θαμάρ,[51]

Three aural characteristics emerge from this brief excerpt from the gospel's opening sounds. First, it exhibits an austere style, identifiable by its brief cola in a repetitive format. The weak, postpositive δέ supplies the connections between cola. The connector neither subordinates cola in a complex grammatical structure, nor does it create an obvious paratactic link, since the connector takes secondary position after the initial proper name in each colon, each of which repeats the terminal syllables of the preceding colon. Internally, the repeated iota sound at the beginning of each name in the genealogy links the first four cola. These austere sound sequences suit the genealogy form, which serves to establish the subject's claim to honor and social position.[52]

The repeated -ου in the inflectional suffixes at the ends of the first and fourth cola bracket these cola together and set the final colon apart. This fifth colon supplies the first hint that something is amiss. It follows the parallel pattern established in the preceding four cola, each of whose concluding element begins with the name of someone begotten. In the preceding cola, the name begins with Ἰ. But in the fifth colon, Φάρες breaks this sequence, alerting the audience to listen for something important. Thus when it occurs at the colon's end, Tamar's name creates a jarring effect. Women's names do not belong in genealogies because they cannot contribute to a subject's honor. Tamar is particularly problematic—both because she is Canaanite, and because she had to resort to the disguise of a prostitute to exact justice from Judah, the father of her son, Perez. Such scandalous elements run counter to the purpose of a genealogy. Moreover, the genealogy proceeds in this fashion, detailing in austere style the lineage of Jesus through illegitimacy and other tainted sexual unions.[53]

Finally, the genealogy broaches Jesus' conception:

Mt 1:18

1 Τοῦ δὲ Ἰησοῦ Χριστοῦ ἡ γένεσις οὕτως ἦν.
2 μνηστευθείσης τῆς μητρὸς αὐτοῦ Μαρίας τῷ Ἰωσήφ,
πρὶν ἢ συνελθεῖν αὐτοὺς
εὑρέθη ἐν γαστρὶ ἔχουσα ἐκ πνεύματος ἁγίου.[54]

Here the style shifts to a more elegant and grammatically sophisticated tone. Colon 2 is lengthy, including a complexity of verbal constructions (a genitive absolute, an articular infinitive, and a finite verb). Repeated α[ς], ει[ς], and η[ς] sounds unify the two cola internally, while repeated ου and ευ sounds mark the beginning and end. The problematic nature of Jesus' origins comes framed in this elegant style. In both the genealogy and the ensuing narrative, form and content send conflicting signals.

SOUND AND MEANING

Sound contributes to an audience's meaning-making project by organizing a composition's sounds into structures that guide interpretation. In spoken compositions, sound and semantics make independent contributions to meaning. Not only does sound's communicative power often support and work in concert with semantic meaning, but sound effects can influence meaning independently by virtue of their acoustic quality and structuring functions. Sound maps facilitate identification and analysis of such structural features and prepare an interpreter for exegesis.

ENDNOTES

1. Similarly, Stowers advises, "Without diminishing the helpfulness of critical editions, I suggest that scholars also ought to work with

a text in *scriptio continua*. Then it will be more difficult to forget that to have a text at all is an act of interpretation" (1994, p. 16).

2. See chapter 6, "Listening to the Centurion: Mark's Crucifixion," for a sound map and analysis of this passage in context.
3. "And the Roman soldiers led him away to the courtyard of the governor's residence, and they called the whole company <of Roman troops> together. And they dressed him in purple and crowned him with a garland woven of thorns."
4. "And with him they crucify two rebels, one on his right and one on his left."
5. See chapter 9, "Sound and Narrative: Luke's Nativity," for a sound map and analysis of this passage in context.
6. "In those days it so happened that a decree was issued by Emperor Augustus that a census be taken of the whole civilized world."
7. See chapter 10, "Sound and Structure: The Sermon on the Mount," for a sound map and analysis of this passage in context.
8. "Ask—it'll be given to you; seek—you'll find; knock—it'll be opened for you."
9. See chapter 9, "Sound and Narrative: Luke's Nativity," for a sound map and analysis of this passage in context.
10. "Glory to God in the highest,and on earth peace to people whom he has favored!"
11. See chapter 10, "Sound and Structure: The Sermon on the Mount," for a sound map and analysis of this passage in context.
12. "Nor do people light a lamp and put it under a bushel basket but rather on a lampstand, where it sheds light for everyone in the house."
13. "But I tell you: Don't swear at all."
14. "But I tell you: Don't swear at all. Don't invoke heaven, because it is the throne of God, and don't invoke earth, because it is God's footstool, and don't invoke Jerusalem, because it is the city of the great king. You shouldn't swear by your head either, since you aren't able to turn a single hair either white or black."
15. See chapter 7, Persuasion and Conversion, Paul's Letter to Philemon," for a sound map and analysis of this passage in context.
16. "I always thank my God when I remember you, Philemon, in my prayers, because I keep hearing about the confidence you have with regard to the lord Jesus and your love for all God's people. I pray that the sharing of your confident trust in God will result in a recognition of all of the good that we are capable of in the service of the Anointed. Your love has brought me great joy and

encouragement, because the hearts of God's people have been refreshed because of you, dear friend."

17. See chapter 8, "Hearing is Believing: John 20," for a sound map and analysis of this passage in context.
18. "Then Simon Peter comes along behind him and went in. He too sees the strips of burial cloth there, and also the cloth they had used to cover his head, lying not with the strips of burial cloth but rolled up by itself. Then the other disciple, who had been the first to reach the tomb, came in. He saw all this, and he believed. But since neither of them yet understood the prophecy that he was destined to rise from the dead, these disciples went back home."
19. See chapter 9, "Sound and Narrative: Luke's Nativity," for a sound map and analysis of this passage in context.
20. "Now in the same area there were shepherds living outdoors. They were keeping watch over their sheep at night, when a messenger of the Lord stood near them and the glory of the Lord shone around them. They became terrified. But the messenger said to them, 'Don't be afraid: I bring you good news of a great joy, which is to benefit the whole nation; today in the city of David, the Savior was born to you—he is the Anointed, the Lord. And this will be a sign for you: you will find a baby wrapped in strips of cloth and lying in a feeding trough.' "
21. This example also illustrates why it is important to remove chapter and verse markings, since the period above divides in the middle of a verse. Verse 10 begins with colon 1.6.
22. "It was 9 o'clock in the morning when they crucified him. And the inscription, which identified his crime, read, 'The King of the Judeans.' And with him they crucify two rebels, one on his right and one on his left."
23. "As you know, what you treasure is your heart's true measure. The eye is the body's lamp. It follows that if your eye is clear, your whole body will be flooded with light."
24. See chapter 9, "Sound and Narrative: Luke's Nativity," for an extended illustration.
25. See chapter 8, "Hearing is Believing: John 20," for an example of verbal aspect as a guide to reception.
26. See chapter 10, "Sound and Structure: The Sermon on the Mount," for a discussion of ear training and evolving structure.
27. See chapter 3, "The Grammar of Sound," for a fuller discussion of harmony.

28. See the discussion of phonetics in chapter 3, "The Grammar of Sound." Demetrius (*Eloc.* 173–77) describes the sound qualities that make words beautiful, including open vowels and smooth-sounding consonants.
29. "Our Father in the heavens, your name be revered. Impose your imperial rule, enact your will on earth as you have in heaven."
30. Hiatus is "the unpleasing succession of vowels in the final and initial sounds of adjoining words" (Blass, Debrunner, and Funk 1961, p. 256).
31. Dionysius of Halicarnassus (*Dem.* 40) finds clashing consonants and harsh sounds inimical to polished literary style.
32. "Ha! You who would destroy the temple and rebuild it in three days, save yourself and come down from the cross!"
33. See chapter 6, "Listening to the Centurion: Mark's Crucifixion," for a discussion of this passage in context.
34. "Then I will tell them honestly: 'I never knew you; get away from me, you subverters of the Law!' "
35. Hiatus, because it interrupts the flow of sound, is always notable but does not necessarily create cacophony. Dionysius of Halicarnassus (*Dem.* 38) finds hiatus acceptable in an antique style because the silence it creates lends dignity. Hiatus is deemed unpleasant when combined with clashing consonants and harsh sounds in a passage not meant to sound dignified (Demetr. *Eloc.* 68–72).
36. "Take a look at the birds of the sky: they don't plant or harvest, or gather into barns. Yet your heavenly Father feeds them. You're worth more than they, aren't you?"
37. See the discussion of literary style in chapter 3, "The Grammar of Sound."
38. Period 1: "And he toured all over Galilee, teaching in their synagogues, proclaiming the news of <Heaven's> imperial rule, and healing every disease and every ailment the people had." Period 2: "And his reputation spread through the whole of Syria. They brought him everyone who was ill, who suffered from any kind of disease or was in intense pain, who was possessed, who was epileptic, or a paralytic, and he cured them." Period 3: "And huge crowds followed him from Galilee and the Decapolis and Jerusalem and Judea and from across the Jordan."
39. "Our Father in the heavens, your name be revered. Impose your imperial rule,enact your will on earth as you have in heaven."
40. "Provide us with the bread we need for the day. Forgive our debts to the extent that we have forgiven those in debt to us. And

please don't subject us to test after test, but rescue us from the evil one."

41. "For if you forgive others their failures and offenses, your heavenly Father will also forgive yours. And if you don't forgive the failures and mistakes of others, your Father won't forgive yours."
42. Period 1: "Father, your name be revered. Impose your imperial rule. Period 2: Provide us with the bread we need day by day. Forgive our sins, since we too forgive everyone in debt to us. And please don't subject us to test after test."
43. Betz (1995, pp. 97–104) claims that beatitudes occur in two types of secular Greek sources, a ritual type associated with mystery cults and a philosophical type that is found in prooemia of didactic texts. Matthew's beatitudes, he claims, conform to the philosophical type because they introduce Jesus' ethical teaching in the Sermon on the Mount. Such a prooemium "is supposed to look archaic." I would argue rather that the form is designed to *sound* archaic.
44. "Congratulations to the poor in spirit! Heaven's domain belongs to them. Congratulations to those who grieve! They will be consoled. Congratulations to the gentle! They will inherit the earth. Congratulations to those who hunger and thirst for justice! They will have a feast. Congratulations to the merciful! They will receive mercy. Congratulations to those with undefiled hearts! They will see God. Congratulations to those who work for peace! They will be known as God's children. Congratulations to those who have suffered persecution for the sake of justice! Heaven's domain belongs to them."
45. "Congratulations, you poor! God's domain belongs to you. Congratulations, you hungry! You will have a feast. Congratulations, you who weep now! You will laugh."
46. "Don't imagine that I have come to annul the Law or the Prophets. I have come not to annul but to fulfill. I swear to you, before the world disappears, not one iota, not one serif, will disappear from the Law, until that happens. Whoever ignores one of the most trivial of these regulations, and teaches others to do so, will be called trivial in Heaven's domain. But whoever acts on <these regulations> and teaches <others to do so>, will be called great in Heaven's domain. Let me tell you: unless your religion goes beyond that of the scholars and Pharisees, you won't set foot in Heaven's domain."
47. See chapter 11, "Manuscript and Memory: Q on Anxiety," for a full analysis.

48. "That's why I tell you: Don't fret about life—what you're going to eat—or about your body—what you're going to wear. Remember, there is more to living than food and clothing. Think about the crows: they don't plant or harvest, they don't have storerooms or barns. Yet God feeds them. You're worth a lot more than the birds! Can any of you add an hour to life by fretting about it? So if you can't do a little thing like that, why worry about the rest?"
49. "That's why I tell you: Don't fret about your life—what you're going to eat and drink—or about your body—what you're going to wear. There is more to living than food and clothing, isn't there? Take a look at the birds of the sky: they don't plant or harvest, or gather into barns. Yet your heavenly Father feeds them. You're worth more than they, aren't you? Can any of you add one hour to life by fretting about it?"
50. Aristotle (*Rh.* 3.18.7) writes that irony is more gentlemanly (ἐλευθεριώτερον) than more direct jests. The author of *Περὶ ὕψους* ([Longinus] *Subl.* 34.2) includes wit, sarcasm, irony, and jests in a list of the excellences of Hyperides in comparison with Demosthenes.
51. "This is the family tree of Jesus the Anointed, who was a descendant of David and Abraham. Abraham was the father of Isaac, Isaac of Jacob, Jacob of Judah and his brothers, and Judah and Tamar were the parents of Perez and Zerah."
52. Instead of the austere style, Dionysuis of Halicarnassus (*Dem.* 2) finds the plain or continuous style suitable for genealogies as well as its typical applications in philosophy and historical narrative. "Being born into an honorable family makes one honorable, since the family is the repository of the honor of past illustrious ancestors and their accumulated acquired honor. One of the major purposes of genealogies in the Bible is to set out a person's honor lines and thus socially situate the person on the ladder of statuses" (Malina 1993, p. 29).
53. Brown (1977, pp. 71–74) reviews the scope of scholarly explanations for the presence of women in Matthew's genealogy. See also Schaberg (1987, pp. 20–34), for a discussions of the subversive impact of the presence of women in the genealogy. Scott (1990, p. 83) argues that the genealogy with its inclusion of problematic women gives the reader an "ideological orientation to the rest of the gospel." But Malina (1981, p. 98) finds that in Matthew's genealogy, "nearly the entire emphasis is on the male line of descent."
54. "The birth of Jesus the Anointed took place as follows: While his mother Mary was engaged to Joseph, but before they slept together, she was found to be pregnant by the holy spirit."

WORKS CONSULTED

Betz, Hans Dieter. 1995. *The Sermon on the Mount, Hermeneia.* Minneapolis: Fortress.

Blass, F., A. Debrunner, and Robert Funk. 1961. *A Greek Grammar of the New Testament and Other Early Christian Literature.* Translated by R. W. Funk. Chicago: University of Chicago Press.

Brown, Raymond E. 1977. *The Birth of the Messiah: A Commentary on the Infancy Narratives in Matthew and Luke.* Garden City: Doubleday.

Malina, Bruce J. 1981. *The New Testament World: Insights from Cultural Anthropology.* Atlanta: John Knox.

———. 1993. *The New Testament World. Insights from Cultural Anthropology.* revised ed. Louisville, KY: Westminster/Knox.

Schaberg, Jane. 1987. *The Illegitimacy of Jesus.* San Francisco: Harper and Row.

Scott, Bernard Brandon. 1990. The Birth of the Reader. *Semeia* 52:83–102.

Stowers, Stanley K. 1994. *A Rereading of Romans: Justice, Jews, and Gentiles.* New Haven: Yale University Press.

Part 2

Illustrations from the New Testament

Chapter 6

Listening to the Centurion

Mark's Crucifixion

In Mark's story of Jesus' crucifixion, the centurion's statement in 15:39 has long puzzled interpreters. Many have understood the centurion's declaration as a confession of faith (Taylor 1966, p. 597) and so taken the event as a climactic moment at the foot of the cross. Some, on the other hand, have interpreted the statement as ironic and ambiguous, the final insult in a brutal and degrading execution (Johnson 1987, p. 14–5; Fowler 1991, p. 203–8). It is tempting to imagine that we could properly interpret the centurion's declaration that Jesus is God's son, if only we could hear the centurion utter the words. Sound mapping indicates how the centurion's words sounded to the gospel's audience, since the story's cadences are encoded in its language. The rhythms of Mark's crucifixion narrative suggest the centurion's tone and help us better understand his dramatic role. Sound mapping and analysis cannot yield a final or inerrant interpretation of the passage, but provides a more ample foundation for exegesis because it observes signals integral to the composition and does not impose on the composition questions or ideologies external to it.

DELINEATION OF A UNIT

Once we have decided to hear the centurion's speech, we must determine at what point to tune in to the story. Certainly it is best to hear a whole gospel, but a gospel story, like all stories, contains episodes that tell their own tales. As we listen to the passion narrative, how do we know when the crucifixion episode begins? We expect sound to organize Mark's narrative. As we have seen in the theory of sound analysis outlined in Chapter 4, the repetition of phonemes, larger sound groups, and grammatical patterns organizes an audience's listening experience and shapes expectations. We can rely on sound's fundamental role as a structuring device when searching for an episode's boundaries.

Beginning in 15:11, cola begin with repeating patterns. In 15:11–15b, six successive cola begin with ὁ (οἱ) /δέ (and he [they]).

ὁ/οἱ δέ (15:11–15a)[1]

οἱ δὲ ἀρχιερεῖς ἀνέσεισαν τὸν ὄχλον ἵνα μᾶλλον
τὸν Βαραββᾶν ἀπολύσῃ αὐτοῖς.
ὁ δὲ Πιλᾶτος πάλιν ἀποκριθεὶς ἔλεγεν αὐτοῖς,
Τί οὖν [θέλετε] ποιήσω [ὃν λέγετε] τὸν βασιλέα τῶν Ἰουδαίων;
οἱ δὲ πάλιν ἔκραξαν, Σταύρωσον αὐτόν.
ὁ δὲ Πιλᾶτος ἔλεγεν αὐτοῖς, Τί γὰρ ἐποίησεν κακόν;
οἱ δὲ περισσῶς ἔκραξαν, Σταύρωσον αὐτόν.
ὁ δὲ Πιλᾶτος βουλόμενος τῷ ὄχλῳ τὸ ἱκανὸν ποιῆσαι ἀπέλυσεν
αὐτοῖς τὸν Βαραββᾶν,

Repeated opening sounds organize these cola into a unit. Beginning in 15:15b–24, different opening sounds create a new pattern of καί + [verb] + αὐτόν (and + [verb] + him), which occurs fifteen times.

καί (15:15b-24)[2]

καὶ παρέδωκεν τὸν Ἰησοῦν φραγελλώσας ἵνα σταυρωθῇ.
Οἱ δὲ στρατιῶται ἀπήγαγον **αὐτὸν** ἔσω τῆς αὐλῆς, ὅ ἐστιν
πραιτώριον,
καὶ συγκαλοῦσιν ὅλην τὴν σπεῖραν.
καὶ ἐνδιδύσκουσιν **αὐτὸν** πορφύραν
καὶ περιτιθέασιν **αὐτῷ** πλέξαντες ἀκάνθινον στέφανον·
καὶ ἤρξαντο ἀσπάζεσθαι **αὐτόν**, Χαῖρε, βασιλεῦ τῶν Ἰουδαίων·
καὶ ἔτυπτον **αὐτοῦ** τὴν κεφαλὴν καλάμῳ
καὶ ἐνέπτυον **αὐτῷ**,
καὶ τιθέντες τὰ γόνατα προσεκύνουν **αὐτῷ**.
καὶ ὅτε ἐνέπαιξαν **αὐτῷ**, ἐξέδυσαν **αὐτὸν** τὴν πορφύραν
καὶ ἐνέδυσαν **αὐτὸν** τὰ ἱμάτια τὰ ἴδια.
καὶ ἐξάγουσιν **αὐτὸν**
ἵνα σταυρώσουσιν **αὐτόν**.
Καὶ ἀγγαρεύουσιν παράγοντά τινα Σίμωνα Κυρηναῖον ἐρχόμενον
ἀπ᾽ ἀγροῦ, τὸν πατέρα Ἀλεξάνδρου καὶ Ῥούφου,
ἵνα ἄρῃ τὸν σταυρὸν **αὐτοῦ**.
καὶ φέρουσιν **αὐτὸν** ἐπὶ τὸν Γολγοθᾶν τόπον, ὅ ἐστιν
μεθερμηνευόμενον Κρανίου Τόπος.
καὶ ἐδίδουν **αὐτῷ** ἐσμυρνισμένον οἶνον, ὃς δὲ οὐκ ἔλαβεν.
καὶ σταυροῦσιν **αὐτὸν** καὶ διαμερίζονται τὰ ἱμάτια αὐτοῦ, βάλλοντες
κλῆρον ἐπ᾽ αὐτὰ τίς τί ἄρῃ.

The two repeating patterns overlap as the episode changes. Καί (and) opens the first colon of this new series (15:15b), then ὁ δέ (and he), the repeated opening of the previous series, recurs in the second colon (15:16). The fourth colon of this series (15:17) exhibits a paradigm of the pattern after several repetitions have established it:

καὶ	ἐνδιδύσκουσιν	αὐτὸν	πορφύραν[3]
καὶ +	**predicate +**	**αὐτὸν** +	(additional details)

Repeated opening sounds lend coherence to the cola in these two series. The pattern is not rigidly expressed in all instances but admits variation, as expected. Instead of αὐτόν (him), αὐτῷ (to him) occurs three times (vss. 17b, 19b, and 23) and αὐτοῦ (his) occurs twice (vss. 19a and 24b). In vs. 16b αὐτόν (him) is absent. Reiteration of this brief, single-colon pattern conveys the scene's brutality. Quintilian explains the convention: "Wherever it is essential to speak with force, energy and pugnacity, we shall make free use of commata and cola [that are not rounded into periods], since this is most effective, and our rhythmical structure must be so closely conformed to our matter, that violent themes should be expressed in violent rhythms to enable the audience to share the horror felt by the speaker" (*Inst.* 9.4.126).

When the pattern is first introduced in 15:16 its outlines are not yet completely clear:

Οἱ δὲ στρατιῶται ἀπήγαγον αὐτὸν ἔσω τῆς αὐλῆς, ὅ ἐστιν πραιτώριον[4]

The pattern's first iteration is not its definitive form because the pattern has not yet been established. Καί (and) is missing and instead οἱ δὲ (and they) occurs, echoing the organizational pattern from the previous section. The subject expressed in the pattern's first iteration, οἱ στρατιῶται (the soldiers), is implied in each subsequent iteration of the pattern. Repetition of the καί + [verb] + αὐτόν pattern fifteen times from 15:16–24 marks a narrative unit because their component cola reverberate with coherent sounds.

THE PATTERN BREAKS

Verse 25 does not follow the καί + verb + αὐτόν pattern, nor does the pattern resume after a brief interruption, as it does in verse 18 and verse 21. Instead, a new pattern emerges.

ἦν δὲ ὥρα τρίτη καὶ ἐσταύρωσαν αὐτόν.
καὶ ἦν ἡ ἐπιγραφὴ τῆς αἰτίας αὐτοῦ ἐπιγεγραμμένη, Ὁ βασιλεὺς τῶν Ἰουδαίων.[5]

The following cola become longer, the subject changes, and the hour is noted. Although καὶ (and) recurs in the second colon, a new repeated sound precedes it, ἦν (was). The new opening sound signals another structural shift. Beginning in 15:25, the narrative marks time not in days, but in hours, a chronological unit unprecedented in

Mark, who does not make prominent use of time markers. Instead, the author uses a variety of techniques to note shifts in scene, among them geographic markers, εὐθύς (immediately), and scene change. But beginning in 11:11–12, time markers expressed in days and parts of the day begin to appear with unusual frequency (11:19; 14:1; 14:12; 14:17; 15:1) to denote the events of "Holy Week." The shift in time in 15:25 from days to hours marks a shift in focus. In vs. 42 the time markers return to days, using a genitive absolute, καὶ ἤδη ὀψίας γενομένης, ἐπεὶ ἦν παρασκευή, ὅ ἐστιν προσάββατον.[6] Moreover, the events narrated in vss. 25–41 all take place at Golgatha.

These narrative signals, implemented and supported by sound, suggest the delineation of the unit at 15:25–41. This unit departs from the previous unit's sound signature, is governed by a new sound signature, and bounded by time markers expressed in hours. The unit's end, vss 40–41, is elongated by the list of the women, indicating closure. Sound does not operate independently of other indicators, but functions in concert with them to lay the foundation for other narrative signals.

Commentaries differ in the way they divide this section of Mark, and thereby attest to the confusion that ensues when sound signals are ignored and episode boundaries are imposed on the basis of external concerns. Taylor divides the unit at 15:21–41, noting:

> The narrative consists of short separate scenes strung together in rapid succession. From it one gains the impression of a comparatively brief foundation story, which has attracted to itself various items of tradition, some historical, and others legendary, out of which a kind of crucifixion drama has been compiled to meet the religious needs of a Gentile Church (Taylor 1966, p. 587).

Taylor notes the "short separate scenes strung together in rapid succession," but then places the unit boundaries based on an impression about its topic (crucifixion), the development of the tradition, and finally its purpose. That is, Taylor presents no unified description of the unit's structure. Collins in her Hermeneia commentary sees this section as part of the Passion Narrative (14:1–16:8). She starts the crucifixion of Jesus at 15:21 and ends it at 15:39. For her the witness of the women (15:40–41) is part of the burial (15:40–47). Her defense of this division largely relies on her reconstruction of a pre-Marcan passion narrative (2007, see esp. pp. 732–35). Taylor and Collins can represent an historical approach to the issue. Lohmeyer divides this section into two parts, the crucifixion (15:20b-32) and the death (15:33–41), on the basis of themes. Using this criterion, he takes 15:20b (καὶ ἐξάγουσιν αὐτὸν ἵνα σταυρώσουσιν αὐτόν)[7]—which in a sound map exhibits the καί + [verb] + αὐτόν pattern—as introducing the title for the next section, the crucifixion (1959, p. 341). Tolbert discerns a rhetorical or literary structure. For her the unit Mk 15:16–39 consists of a chiastic pattern that places the events of the third to ninth hour at the center (1989, p. 279). Although Tolbert notices the time markers, she discerns a chiasm organized around a theme. Against all these proposals is the fact that a sound map furnishes a better, more integral basis for discerning structure. Sound analysis attends to a composition's intrinsic features, the sounds that strike its hearers' ears, not to abstractions imposed from outside, such as a theoretical pre-Marcan passion narrative or a chiasm of themes or titles. To use a modern analogy, ignoring a sound map is like analyzing a modern novel by rearranging its paragraph marks and chapter divisions.

MARK'S CRUCIFIXION

Twenty six cola comprise the narrative unit delineated by sound, 15:25–41. Cola are arranged in simple periods (in which a single colon comprises the period) and complex periods (periods with more than one colon). Because of the frequency of simple periods, cola are numbered below in a single sequence from 1–26. The use of both simple and complex periods differs from the previous section of the gospel, which is composed almost exclusively of simple periods marked by the καί + [verb] + αὐτόν pattern. The alternation of simple and complex periods is not random in this passage but follows a repeating sequence. Our analysis will show that this unit is divided into three parts, each of which comprises a narrative scene with simple periods at the beginning and end, and complex periods in the middle. Periods and parts are labeled.

PART 1[8]

Period 1

1 ἦν δὲ ὥρα τρίτη καὶ ἐσταύρωσαν αὐτόν.

Period 2

2 καὶ ἦν ἡ ἐπιγραφὴ τῆς αἰτίας αὐτοῦ
ἐπιγεγραμμένη, Ὁ βασιλεὺς τῶν Ἰουδαίων.

Period 3

3 Καὶ σὺν αὐτῷ σταυροῦσιν δύο λῃστάς, ἕνα ἐκ δεξιῶν
καὶ ἕνα ἐξ εὐωνύμων αὐτοῦ.

As expected, the unit's opening cola accomplish a gradual transition from the sound signature of the previous unit to the new unit's distinctive sounds. In each of the first three cola, an echo occurs of the previous unit's sound signature. In the first two cola, ἦν (was) occurs at the beginning with a connector. (ἦν δὲ, then καὶ ἦν). The change in initial sounds in two successive cola signals an upcoming structural shift away from the καί + [verb] + αὐτόν pattern that organized 15:16–24. The terminal phrase of the unit's first colon echoes the pattern that had organized the previous unit: καὶ ἐσταύρωσαν αὐτόν (and they crucified them). In the previous unit, this organizing pattern occurred in initial position in each colon, whereas in colon 1 the pattern echo terminates the colon. Moreover, after fifteen cola with the same subject (στρατιῶται, soldiers), the initial phrase of colon 1 changes the subject to ὥρα and makes it specific: ἦν δὲ ὥρα τρίτη (it was the third hour). Marking time in days and hours recalls the prophecy of the Son of Man's coming (13:24–37) in which Jesus states that no one knows the day or the hour, so "you" should watch and stay alert. (Περὶ δὲ τῆς ἡμέρας ἐκείνης ἢ τῆς ὥρας οὐδεὶς οἶδεν, οὐδὲ οἱ ἄγγελοι ἐν οὐρανῷ οὐδὲ ὁ υἱός, εἰ μὴ ὁ πατήρ. βλέπετε ἀγρυπνεῖτε· οὐκ οἴδατε γὰρ πότε ὁ καιρός ἐστιν. 13:32–33)[9]. The close association of hours and days invokes this warning and catches the audience's attention. Both sound and narration signal a new unit. In colon 2, the royalty title Ὁ βασιλεὺς τῶν Ἰουδαίων (The king of the Jews) repeats the soldiers' mocking from the previous unit (15:18). The initial phrase of colon 3, καὶ σὺν αὐτῷ σταυροῦσιν (and with him they crucified), echoes the terminal phrase of colon 1 and the organizing pattern of the previous unit. But the pattern has been rearranged by placing αὐτῷ before the verb. The pattern could have been repeated with καὶ σὺνσταυροῦσιν αὐτῷ (and they co-crucified with him). The first three cola echo sounds from the previous unit, but with a difference, signaling change.

In addition to echoing previously established sound signals, the first three cola introduce new features that build this unit's distinctive sound signature. Its beginning and ending periods are simple (cola 1, 2, 3, and 10) and the intervening periods are complex (4–5–6, 7–8–9). The opening periods progressively become longer (the first one has 13 syllables, next two have 27 syllables each). As we have seen, colon 1 is brief, on the scale of the cola in the previous unit. Colon 2 contains opposed phrases:

καὶ ἦν ἡ ἐπιγραφὴ τῆς αἰτίας αὐτοῦ
ἐπιγεγραμμένη, Ὁ βασιλεὺς τῶν Ἰουδαίων

The lexeme γραφ-/γραμ- is paired with dishonor (τῆς αἰτίας αὐτοῦ) in the first phrase, and royalty (Ὁ βασιλεὺς τῶν Ἰουδαίων) in the second phrase.

Colon 3 contains parallel phrases indicating the placement of those crucified with Jesus:

3 Καὶ σὺν αὐτῷ σταυροῦσιν δύο λῃστάς, ἕνα ἐκ δεξιῶν
καὶ ἕνα ἐξ εὐωνύμων αὐτοῦ.

The parallel phrases are linked with the repetition of ἕνα and with repeating εκ / εξ and ων / ω sounds. The occurrence of parallelism and opposition within cola introduces figures typical of periodic structure, but these periods remain simple. Successively longer cola with hints of periodic structure cue the transition from the simple periods of the previous unit to the complex periods that follow and contribute to this unit's distinctive sound characteristics.

Period 4

4 Καὶ*οἱ παραπορευόμενοι*ἐβλασφήμουν αὐτὸν
κινοῦντες τὰς κεφαλὰς αὐτῶν καὶ λέγοντες,
5 Οὐὰ*ὁ καταλύων τὸν ναὸν καὶ*οἰκοδομῶν ἐν τρισὶν ἡμέραις,
6 σῶσον σεαυτὸν καταβὰς ἀπὸ τοῦ σταυροῦ.

Period 5

7 ὁμοίως καὶ οἱ ἀρχιερεῖς ἐμπαίζοντες
πρὸς ἀλλήλους
μετὰ τῶν γραμματέων ἔλεγον,
8 Ἄλλους ἔσωσεν, ἑαυτὸν οὐ δύναται σῶσαι·
9 ὁ Χριστὸς ὁ βασιλεὺς Ἰσραὴλ καταβάτω νῦν ἀπὸ τοῦ σταυροῦ, ἵνα
ἴδωμεν καὶ πιστεύσωμεν.

Following signals from the preceding cola, cola 4–6 combine to form a period characterized by a fluid stream of mixed sounds. In contrast with the terse diction of the unit's first three cola, colon 4 employs words with many syllables (παραπορευόμενοι, 6; ἐβλασφήμουν, 4; κινοῦντες, κεφαλὰς, and λέγοντες, 3).[10] Sound quality is blended throughout the period, with only four incidences of hiatus, two in colon 4 and two in colon 5 (marked by an asterisk in the sound map). One hiatus occurs before a κ, a harsh sound, and emphasizes the insult those-standing-by deliver with their derision (Οὐὰ*ὁ καταλύων, "Ha! You who would destroy . . .").

Like cola 4–5–6 (period 4), cola 7–8–9 also combine to form a period (5) with sound characteristics similar to those in period 4. The initial word, ὁμοίως (likewise), anticipates parallelism. Both periods contain speeches by those who taunt Jesus on the cross. Elements of the speech in period 4 by the confronters (οἱ παραπορευόμενοι) recur in period 5.

The Confronters (period 4)

5 Οὐὰ*ὁ καταλύων τὸν ναὸν καὶ*οἰκοδομῶν ἐν τρισὶν ἡμέραις,
6 σῶσον σεαυτὸν καταβὰς ἀπὸ τοῦ σταυροῦ.

Chief priests (period 5)

7 ὁμοίως καὶ οἱ ἀρχιερεῖς ἐμπαίζοντες
πρὸς ἀλλήλους
μετὰ τῶν γραμματέων ἔλεγον,
8 Ἄλλους ἔσωσεν, ἑαυτὸν οὐ δύναται σῶσαι·
9 ὁ Χριστὸς ὁ βασιλεὺς Ἰσραὴλ καταβάτω νῦν ἀπὸ τοῦ σταυροῦ,
ἵνα ἴδωμεν καὶ πιστεύσωμεν.

The taunts exhibit strong parallelism. Both are built around σωζώ (save) and καταβὰς ἀπὸ τοῦ σταυροῦ (come down from the cross). Both periods reverberate with the initial sounds of these two phrases. Frequent σ/ζ sounds imitate hissing, and frequent κ/τ/π/χ phonomes evoke spitting sounds. Onomatopoeia for hissing and spitting provides a distinctive sound signature for these periods. While the phrasing is not identical in the two periods, similar sounds connect them and characterize their similar taunts.

5 Οὐὰ ὁ **καταλύων τὸν ναὸν** καὶ*οἰκοδομῶν ἐν τρισὶν ἡμέραις,
6 σῶσον σεαυτὸν καταβὰς ἀπὸ τοῦ σταυροῦ.

7 ὁμοίως καὶ οἱ ἀρχιερεῖς ἐμπαίζοντες
πρὸς ἀλλήλους
μετὰ τῶν γραμματέων ἔλεγον,
8 Ἄλλους ἔσωσεν, ἑαυτὸν οὐ δύναται σῶσαι·
9 **ὁ Χριστὸς ὁ βασιλεὺς Ἰσραὴλ** καταβάτω νῦν ἀπὸ τοῦ σταυροῦ,
ἵνα ἴδωμεν καὶ πιστεύσωμεν.

The royalty title, ὁ βασιλεὺς Ἰσραὴλ, parallels the participle, ὁ καταλύων τὸν ναὸν (who would destroy the temple), which functions as a title. The two titles frame the taunts in the intervening cola: "Save yourself!" and, "He cannot save himself." These taunts are arranged chiastically:

σῶσον σεαυτὸν
ἑαυτὸν οὐ δύναται σῶσαι

The confronters mock Jesus as one who would tear down temple. The κατα of ὁ **κατα**λύων (c 5) parallels **κατα**βὰς (c 6). In colon 9 the royalty title is a variation of the soldiers' mocking (vs 18b) and Pilate's inscription (c 2) and part of Pilate's speech, 15:9, 12. The taunts of both groups convey the same ironic challenge: a person with a royal title cannot hang on a cross.

The words describing the taunts of the confronters and the chief priests reverberate throughout Mark's gospel. The confronters' action is depicted as ἐβλασφήμουν (*lit.*, They blasphemed). This word's root, βλασφή- (blaspheme), has deep resonances in Mark. In 2:7 the scribes say of Jesus, following his cure of the paralytic, Τί οὗτος οὕτως λαλεῖ; βλασφημεῖ· τίς δύναται ἀφιέναι ἁμαρτίας εἰ μὴ εἷς ὁ θεός;[11] In 3:29, Jesus pronounces the enigmatic saying, ὃς δ' ἂν βλασφημήσῃ εἰς τὸ πνεῦμα τὸ ἅγιον οὐκ ἔχει ἄφεσιν εἰς τὸν αἰῶνα.[12] Finally in the trial before the Sanhedrin the high priest exclaims after the witnesses, ἠκούσατε τῆς βλασφημίας (14:64).[13]

The participle ἐμπαίζοντες (making fun of), which describes the high priests' activity, recalls both ἐνέπαιξαν (they make fun of) in 15:20, which characterizes the soldiers' mockery, and ἐμπαίξουσιν αὐτῷ (they will make fun of him), which in 10:34 predicts his treatment by the Gentiles in the final Son of Man prophecy. The royal title repeats both the soldiers's mocking and Pilate's inscription. This repetition brings the chief priests to the side of and places them in allegiance with the gentiles. Drawing the circle even tighter, μετὰ τῶν γραμματέων signals a connection with οἱ ἀρχιερεῖς (the ranking priests). In the first and third Son of Man prophecies both groups are tied together: ἀποδοκιμασθῆναι ὑπὸ τῶν πρεσβυτέρων καὶ τῶν ἀρχιερέων καὶ τῶν γραμματέων[14] (8:31, see also 10:33). Again when Judas comes with those who arrest Jesus they are described as παρὰ τῶν ἀρχιερέων καὶ τῶν γραμματέων καὶ τῶν πρεσβυτέρων (14:43).[15] Finally at the beginning of the day that leads to Jesus' death, οἱ ἀρχιερεῖς μετὰ τῶν πρεσβυτέρων καὶ γραμματέων καὶ ὅλον τὸ συνέδριον[16] meet and hand Jesus over to Pilate (15:1). It should be noted that Mark in sound parallels τῶν γραμματέων (the scholars, *lit.*, the scribes)—which he alone among the evangelists uses exclusively in the genitive, see also 2:6, 7:1, 12:28, 38—with τῶν πρεσβυτέρων (the elders) and οἱ ἀρχιερεῖς / τών ἀρχιερων (the ranking priests) in order to identify the Jewish groups aligned against Jesus. They behave like the gentiles (ἐμπαίζοντες, making fun of) and repeat Pilate's and the soldiers' royal title. Thus in its use of sound the period identifies them with the gentiles.

Finally the terminal phrase in period 5 (ἵνα ἴδωμεν καὶ πιστεύσωμεν, so that we can see and trust for ourselves) adds a new dimension. The importance of this theme will emerge later. Because it has no parallel in the previous period, the use of this phrase to conclude a series of periods with strong parallelism draws attention to it.

Period 6

10 καὶ οἱ συνεσταυρωμένοι σὺν αὐτῷ ὠνείδιζον αὐτόν.

After two complex periods, a simple period occurs. The co-crucified had been introduced in period 3 (c 3). Cola 3 and 10 are strikingly parallel, without being identical.

3 καὶ σὺν αὐτῷ σταυροῦσιν δύο λῃστάς
10 καὶ οἱ συνεσταυρωμένοι σὺν αὐτῷ ὠνείδιζον αὐτόν.

The predicate in colon 3 (σταυροῦσιν, they crucified) becomes a participle in colon 10 (οἱ συνεσταυρωμένοι, those being crucified), with συν indicating their being co-crucified with Jesus. And like the first two groups, they too revile Jesus, but unlike ἐβλασφήμουν and ἐμπαίζοντες, which resonate in the gospel, ὠνείδιζον (abuse) occurs only here. Finally their taunt is not voiced. They remain speechless.

PART 2

Part 2 consists of cola 11–20; the opening (c 11) and concluding periods (c 20) are simple, and the other two periods are complex, each consisting of 4 cola (c 12–15 and c 16–19).

Period 1

11 Καὶ γενομένης ὥρας ἕκτης σκότος
ἐγένετο ἐφ' ὅλην τὴν γῆν ἕως ὥρας ἐνάτης.

Cola 11 and 1 are simple cola and indicate hours, but otherwise their structure is dissimilar. Colon 1 switches time from days to hours and connects to the previous unit's structure with καὶ ἐσταύρωσαν αὐτόν (and they crucified him), echoing the formula of the previous unit.

1 ἦν δὲ ὥρα τρίτη καὶ ἐσταύρωσαν αὐτόν.
11 Καὶ γενομένης ὥρας ἕκτης σκότος
ἐγένετο ἐφ' ὅλην τὴν γῆν ἕως ὥρας ἐνάτης.

Colon 11 emphasizes the time marker but in a different way than colon 1. Colon 11 contains two parts, both containing γεν- and an hour marker, and the second part is elongated with repeated long vowel sounds (η and ω). It notes the hour, the sixth, and proceeds to the ninth hour at the colon's end. The γεν- syllable is repeated before the named hour in each case (γενομένης ὥρας ἕκτης, ἐγένετο . . . ἕως ὥρας ἐνάτης)[17]. The long vowel in both numbers (ἕκτης, ἐνάτης, sixth, ninth) is repeated in the intervening phrase between markers (ὅλην τὴν γῆν, the whole land, reinforcing the focus on time and drawing the sixth and ninth hour together. The colon's balanced two-part structure tends toward periodic structure, which emerges in the subsequent period.

Period 2
12 καὶ τῇ ἐνάτῃ ὥρᾳ ἐβόησεν ὁ Ἰησοῦς φωνῇ μεγάλῃ,
13 *Ελωι*ελωι λεμα σαβαχθανι;
14 ὅ ἐστιν μεθερμηνευόμενον
15 Ὁ θεός μου ὁ θεός μου, εἰς τί*ἐγκατέλιπές με;

Colon 12 at the beginning of period 2 repeats the hour designation, with hour and number in reverse order, creating a chiasm (ὥρας ἐνάτης / ἐνάτῃ ὥρᾳ). Period 2 is divided into relatively short cola, two of which report Jesus' speech. Immediately following the time marker, ἐβόησεν (shouted) recalls the gospel's opening: φωνὴ βοῶντος ἐν τῇ ἐρήμῳ, Ἑτοιμάσατε τὴν ὁδὸν κυρίου (1:3).[18] Just as scripture described John the baptizer as a voice crying out, so here Jesus quotes the scriptures. The quotation is sounded first in Aramaic and then the narrator translates it into Greek. In colon 13, Jesus' speech is delivered in grave style marked by hiatus in the invocation of God's name (*ελωι*ελωι) and harsh consonant in σαβα**χ**θανι. The sound quality of Jesus' outcry stamps it as a genuine cry of dereliction.[19] In the translation of the speech in colon 15, sounds are smooth and more fluid, relieving the shock and austerity of colon 13 and elongating the period. The use of both austere and smooth style draws attention.

Period 3
16 καί τινες τῶν **παρεστώτων** ἀκούσαντες ἔλεγον,
17 Ἴδε*Ἠλίαν φωνεῖ.
18 δραμὼν δέ τις
καὶ γεμίσας σπόγγον ὄξους
περιθεὶς καλάμῳ
ἐπότιζεν αὐτόν, λέγων,
19 Ἄφετε ἴδωμεν εἰ ἔρχεται Ἠλίας καθελεῖν αὐτόν.

Period 3 is longer than period 2. It opens with new actors in colon 16. Οἱ παρεστηκότοι[20] (those standing nearby) in colon 16 are distinct from οἱ παραπορευόμενοι (those passing by) in part 1, period 4, the taunt scene. The words sound similar because of the same prepositional prefix, but they indicate different activities (Collins, p. 755). The speeches in period 3 (c 17, 19) are articulated by unnamed τινες τῶν παρεστώτων (some of those standing near by, c 16), while the action is performed by another unnamed τις (someone, c 18). The bystanders make a hearing mistake in colon 17. Ἠλίας is marked by hiatus as well as brevity, in contrast with the following colon. The bystanders correctly attend to this sound but incorrectly associate it with Jesus' utterance of Ελωι; thus they misconstrue Jesus' exclamation and fail to hear it as a cry of dereliction. Here, the bystanders follow a false sound signal that triggers incorrect associations. In colon 18 a string of participles (δραμών, γεμίσας, περιθεὶς, λέγων)[21] intervenes between iterations of his name, delaying the action and frustrating a hearer with the knowledge that Jesus' speech has been misinterpreted. Ἠλίας is repeated in the period's last colon and is therefore emphasized. This further misinterpretation following Jesus' cry reinforces the bystanders' mistake and makes hearers of the gospel witnesses to the bystanders' failure to apprehend Jesus' despair.

The final colon of this period (c 19) sets off various resonances. ἴδωμεν (let's see) recalls the ἵνα clause of the high priests, ἵνα ἴδωμεν καὶ πιστεύσωμεν (so that we can see and trust for ourselves). Finally, the expected coming of Elijah has bedeviled this gospel. Herod thinks Jesus might be John the Baptist *redividus*, or Elijah, or one of the prophets (6:15). The disciples note that some say Jesus is the John the Baptist or Elijah or one of the prophets (8:28). Following the transfiguration the scribes say Ἠλίαν δεῖ ἐλθεῖν πρῶτον (9:11).[22] Jesus responds, Ἠλίας ἐλήλυθεν (9:13)[23] and aligns Elijah's fate with that of the Son of Man. Unlike the disciples, the audience is expected to the draw the correct conclusion: Elijah is John the Baptist; the son of Man is Jesus. ἴδωμεν εἰ ἔρχεται Ἠλίας[24] indicates that these bystanders can neither hear nor understand.

The two complex periods of part 2 both report speech at the cross, Jesus' speech in period 2 and the speech of the unnamed in period 3. The paired speeches recall the paired instances of mockery in part 1, whose complex periods narrate derision from the confronters in period 4 and the priests in period 5. The mistaken identity is not a taunt but a misunderstanding. Repetition in part 2 of this pairing of complex periods sets up an expectation that subsequent complex periods also will be associated in some way. Even though the complex periods in part 2 are not paired through parallelism as are periods 4 and 5 in part 1, they are nevertheless connected by the doubling of the names of God and repetition of Elijah.

Period 4

20 ὁ δὲ Ἰησοῦς ἀφεὶς φωνὴν μεγάλην ἐξέπνευσεν.

Unlike the previous periods in this part and all the periods in the preceding part 1, period 4 fails to open with καί and instead employs the connector δέ. The period contains only one brief colon that depicts

Jesus' death with ἐξέπνευσεν (breathed his last), an onomatopoeia imitating the sound of breath going out. The period is set apart by its brevity and its unusual opening without καί. φωνὴν μεγάλην (great shout) repeats the phrase from colon 12, which narrates Jesus' speech, and rounds the part to a close. This colon's sound and subject set it apart and demand silence after the φωνὴν μεγάλην that accompanies Jesus' death. The death is a wordless sound.

The final colon of this part echoes other cola of this part. ἀφεὶς (let out) repeats the initial word of the previous colon. Ὁ δὲ Ἰησοῦς . . . φωνὴν[25] repeats the phrase from colon 12, forming an inclusio. Ἀφεὶς replaces ἐβόησεν because the mistaken identity of Jesus and John the Baptist has been resolved. The one new term is the appropriately terminal ἐξέπνευσεν.

PART 3

Period 1

21 Καὶ τὸ καταπέτασμα τοῦ ναοῦ ἐσχίσθη εἰς δύο ἀπ' ἄνωθεν ἕως κάτω.

Part 3 returns to the established opening device of καί. The initial cola of the two previous parts began with hour markers. This colon has no such marker, but its sounds signal the opening of a new part in several ways. Sound has trained the audience throughout this unit to associate simple cola with beginnings and endings. This is a simple colon, which follows a simple colon. Furthermore, the initial colon of part 2 had a double time marker, but following ὁ δὲ Ἰησοῦς . . . ἐξέπνευσεν time has ceased. Darkness and hours denote an apocalyptic image that is now spelled out. At the baptism (1:10), the heavens were σχιζομένους (torn open). But here it is the veil of the temple, divided in two, ἀπ' ἄνωθεν ἕως κάτω (from top to bottom). Κατα has been an important sound in the unit, associated with the taunt, καταβάτω νῦν ἀπὸ τοῦ σταυροῦ (come down from the cross). The word for veil, καταπέτασμα, also begins with this phoneme. The harsh consonant sounds and repetition of κ, τ, and σ sounds invoke through onomatopoeia the curtain's tearing.

Period 2

22 Ἰδὼν δὲ **ὁ** κεντυρίων **ὁ** παρεστηκὼς ἐξ ἐναντίας αὐτοῦ
ὅτι οὕτως ἐξέπνευσεν εἶπεν,
23 Ἀληθῶς οὗτος ὁ*ἄνθρωπος υἱὸς θεοῦ*ἦν.

Established patterns in the unit create an expectation that two complex periods will follow a simple initial colon. Period 2 conforms to this expectation. Although the period is brief, its long first colon delays the speech with narrative details. Period 2 introduces a new character, a Roman soldier who is identified by the Latin loan word κεντυρίων (*centurion*). In the parallel passage, Matthew (27:54) and Luke (23:47) use the Greek term, ἑκατόνταρχος. The Latin sound highlights his foreignness and brings hearers closer to the Roman executioner. He is characterized as ὁ παρεστηκὼς ἐξ ἐναντίας αὐτοῦ (standing opposite him). As ὁ παρεστηκὼς he is associated with those who offered Jesus something to drink, not with οἱ παραπορευόμενοι (those passing by) who blasphemed Jesus. Nor is he identified with the soldiers who have crucified Jesus, although logic (but not the sound or content of his utterance) would lead one to understand him as their commander. The soldiers have disappeared; the centurion appears neutral. Furthermore, he is first identified by the participle ἰδών (seeing), which recalls the ἵνα clause of the high priests, ἵνα ἴδωμεν καὶ πιστεύσωμεν,[26] and the "seeing" of those other bystanders who saw but did not understand. The centurion's position relative to the cross is emphasized by ἐξ ἐναντίας αὐτοῦ (opposite him), a detail that makes explicit the centurion's full frontal view and clear sight of the events being narrated. The ὅτι clause reiterates ὁ sounds, requiring exhalation and imitating the action narrated with the next word, ἐξέπνευσεν, which dramatizes Jesus' expiration.

Colon 23 contains the much-debated centurion's speech. The colon is brief, consisting of two instances of hiatus combined with fluid consonant sounds and well-blended long and short vowels. The utterance passes smoothly and closes quickly, avoiding both truncation and extended elongation. Notably, the colon lacks both the parallelism of the taunts and the onomatopoeia of hissing and spitting that characterized them in part 1. Nothing indicates that the centurion's declaration is a taunt. But neither is it a confession. Its fluid quality remains distinct from the grave, austere style that might be expected in a confession of faith from a Roman centurion. Around the sounds of the centurion's speech we find no creation of space that would call attention to such an unexpected turn as a confession from the accomplice of an executioner. Instead, the colon draws quickly to a close after only the slight elongation of the long vowel sounds of θεοῦ (God's) and ἦν (was).[27] Because ἦν is grammatically unnecessary and the concluding long vowel of the period, it catches the listener's attention and lends a sense of facticity to the centurion's speech. Further, that statement is introduced not by a participle like λέγων (saying), which is used with the other unnamed individual in colon 18, but by εἶπεν (he said), emphasizing with an aorist verb that Jesus' death is a completed and undisputed fact. "Seeing" is the subordinate activity, "speaking" is his main activity.

Period 3

24 Ἦσαν δὲ καὶ γυναῖκες ἀπὸ μακρόθεν θεωροῦσαι,
ἐν αἷς καὶ Μαρία ἡ Μαγδαληνὴ
καὶ Μαρία ἡ Ἰακώβου τοῦ μικροῦ
καὶ Ἰωσῆτος μήτηρ καὶ Σαλώμη,
25 αἳ ὅτε ἦν ἐν τῇ Γαλιλαίᾳ ἠκολούθουν αὐτῷ
καὶ διηκόνουν αὐτῷ,
26 καὶ ἄλλαι πολλαὶ αἱ συναναβᾶσαι αὐτῷ εἰς Ἱεροσόλυμα.

The final period moves toward closure with the list of women that elongates the period. It begins with Ἠσαν δέ (*lit.*, and there were) recalling the ἦν δέ (*lit.*, And there was) that began this unit (c 1). Repetitions of η, α, and αι characterize the first colon and, in fact, the entire period. The repeating vowel sounds in the women's list often occur with the phoneme μ from the women's names and also from μικροῦ and μήτηρ. Repetitions and variations of μα- / α / η give this period its distinctive sound signature. The list of women prolongs the colon, but does so in a different way than previous cola were sustained. Whereas in part 2 colon 18 was prolonged with a series of participles drawing out the narrative action and colon 22 was elongated with a participle, a prepositional phrase, and a ὅτι clause, colon 24 is sustained simply with καί, evoking the opening signal for periods in this unit and the gospel's overall paratactic style, which has been somewhat mitigated throughout this unit.

Like the centurion, the women introduced in colon 24 are designated as witnesses (θεωροῦσαι, observing) with a different word than was used for the centurion (ἰδων) but repeating its long vowel, ω. As noted earlier, the period's opening ἦσαν in colon 24 recalls the centurion's ἦν (c 23), thus associating the centurion with the women. The paired complex periods devoted to the centurion and the women support this association, especially since parts 1 and 2 have similarly contained paired complex periods. Grouping the centurion with the women confirms the status of the centurion's speech as a declaration of fact.[28]

The women are described as ἀπὸ μακρόθεν (from a distance) and so not associated with what has been going on. But since they are described as θεωροῦσαι (observing), the relation is not by sound but semantics; they are not characterized as ἴδουσα (seeing), a word that would recall the centurion's ἰδών. Will the second part of the ἵνα clause in the taunt ascribed to the chief priests and the scholars, ἵνα πιστεύσωμεν (so that we may trust), now be fulfilled? The period's ending offers several clues, beginning with colon 25.

25 αἳ ὅτε ἦν ἐν τῇ Γαλιλαίᾳ ἠκολούθουν αὐτῷ
καὶ διηκόνουν αὐτῷ,
26 καὶ ἄλλαι πολλαὶ αἱ συναναβᾶσαι αὐτῷ εἰς Ἱεροσόλυμα.

Colon 25 is balanced by a pair of verbs, ἠκολούθουν (followed) and διηκόνουν (assisted), which have similar sounds, occur with αὐτῷ (him), and thus create a parallel. Mark 1:18 announced the importance of following Jesus: καὶ εὐθὺς ἀφέντες τὰ δίκτυα ἠκολούθησαν αὐτῷ.[29] Likewise διηκονεῖν is an important theme in Mark: in 1:13 the angels διηκόνουν Jesus following his test in the wilderness, and Peter's mother-in-law διηκόνει Jesus and his disciples following her healing (1:31). Jesus describes the son of man as one who came not διακονηθῆναι ἀλλὰ διακονῆσαι,[30] and to give his life as a ransom for many (10:45).

Finally the many other women who have come with Jesus to Jerusalem are called αἱ συναναβᾶσαι (who had come up with). Because σύν (with) has also been important in the description of those who were co-crucified with Jesus, its recurrence here signals its importance. The recurrence of καταβαίνειν (come down) in the taunts gives a second indication of the importance of this description of the women with as αἱ συναναβᾶσαι. Not only does the term trigger a complex set of associations made possible by the sustained ear training the crucifixion episode imposes, but previously in this episode καταβαίνειν is selected for emphasis by virtue of its repetition and its strategic placement in each period where it occurs. These effects exploit sound's linear character, whereby successive repetitions make an impression when they strike the ear. Yet once a linear stream of sound enters the ear and is stored in memory, it functions multidimensionally. In the creative thesaurus of the mind, the images that sounds evoke can associate freely. In this passage, the description of the women with ἀναβαίνειν (coming up) invites an elaborate contrast between things that go up and things that go down. The rending of the temple curtain ἀπ' ἄνωθεν ἕως κάτω (from top to bottom), suggests that some of those associated with Jesus are κατα (down) and some are ανα (up). The women clearly line up with those who are ανα, and thus the opposite of those who taunted Jesus by using the word καταβαίνειν, challenging him to come down from the cross.

The women followed Jesus while he was in Galilee, and it is to them that the young man will announce that Jesus has gone before them to Galilee.

Colon 26 is not balanced by parallelism but instead provides an elongated stream of sound that draws the period to a close by repeating the α, η, and αι phonemes that have characterized this period and by naming a place, Ἱεροσόλυμα. The place name signals a narrative shift, repeats an emotionally charged word in the gospel, and elongates the period's end with its six syllables.

Part 3 contains all the structural elements that occur in parts 1 and 2, with the exception of the final simple period. As is typical of endings, the final element of the pattern is absent because it is unnecessary—the pattern's expectations have already been fulfilled. 16:1 and 2 return to day markers, finishing up seven days and so indicating the beginning of a new unit with a new distinctive tone.

CONCLUSION

Listening to the centurion has clarified his declaration that Jesus was υἱὸς θεοῦ (son of God). Hearing the centurion's declaration rules out certain interpretations of its meaning while it raises still more questions. More important, listening to the centurion has reframed fundamental questions about the crucifixion scene.

UNIT DEFINITION

Since the gospels were communicated primarily through sound, we should expect that sound would delineate compositional units and advance important interpretative questions. Sound builds a composition's structure. Discerning the organic boundaries of a compositional unit requires multiple auditory clues that signal a unit's beginning, end, and internal coherence. Often the boundaries that emerge differ from those that delimit a unit in an English bible, or even a critical edition of the Greek text. The conventions of print and the history of New Testament interpretation burden our perception of the text with sectional divisions imposed on the basis of theological assumptions about its meaning. Sound provides an important corrective to these imported assumptions by requiring sustained focus on the text itself in the concrete, physical form of its voiced articulation.

This analysis of Mark's crucifixion identifies the unit's boundaries as 15:25–41, the portion of the narrative in which time is marked in hours instead of days. Mention of the third hour in 15:25, where our analysis begins, is typically interpreted as a parenthetical reference to time embedded in the crucifixion scene (see for example, Collins, p. 746). Yet a sound analysis shows that the hour designation is not embedded but is structurally significant and fundamental to the narrative's organization. Recognition of the hour markers' structural importance requires an awareness of techniques for scene designation and markers for the passage of time throughout the gospel, at the level of the gospel's macro structure. The shift in colometric structure from the pattern καί + [verb] + αὐτόν to a sequence of alternating simple and complex cola creates a new sound pattern that confirms the hour marker's significance. These two units sound very different because of their different structures. Translation and the conventions of print obscure this sound difference.

Similarly, the listing of the women in 15:40–41 is sometimes treated as an isolated scene that intervenes between the crucifixion and burial. Yet sound indicates the list of women belongs to the crucifixion scene, not the burial scene, which has its own sound structure. Thus a sound map of the crucifixion must include 15:40–41, for the latter's parallel sound structure to that of the centurion's scene suggests that he too should be interpreted in conjunction.

Sound does more than signal a unit's beginning and end. It also organizes the unit into a coherent whole. In Mark's crucifixion narrative, sound delineates an alternating sequence of simple and complex periods that form three component parts with simple periods at the beginning and end, and two complex periods that are somehow associated with each other in the middle. Sharp divisions do not occur between parts. Although each part achieves through sound a sense of completion, the parts blend smoothly and sustain the narrative flow. At the beginning of the unit, three progressively longer cola make the transition to periodic structure and a new sound signature. At the unit's end, the absence of the expected concluding simple period softens the structural boundary and eases into the following scene. Similarly, the unit exhibits smooth transitions from the scenes preceding and following the crucifixion, as the sound analysis has demonstrated. The absence of sharp divisions between the composition's components derives from Mark's continuous narrative style, marked by frequent parataxis.

ASKING THE RIGHT QUESTIONS

Sustained focus on a composition's sounds should prompt questions for interpretation. Each part of Mark's crucifixion narrative suggests through sound its own particular issues.

THE TAUNTS

The taunts in part 1 are set in parallel and are sarcastic. Their sarcasm implies that Jesus cannot make good his claims, that he does not measure up to the standard of a χριστός (Christ) or a υἱὸς τοῦ θεοῦ (Son of God, Mk 1:1). Further, the parallelism of the taunts associates the role of ὁ βασιλεύς with destruction of the temple. The historic destruction of the Jerusalem temple by ὁ βασιλεύς (king) of the Roman Empire is the defining crisis of early Christianity, to which Mark's gospel issues a response (Mk 13). This suggests that Mark's gospel fundamentally redefines Christological categories. The sarcastic taunts comprise Mark's only reference in the crucifixion to soteriology.

ΕΛΩΙ ΕΛΩΙ

Since the taunts suggest in sound that Mark's gospel redefines Christology, Jesus' crying out in a great voice should be viewed as part of this process. Jesus' cry from the cross signals that Mark's Christology will not answer the sarcastic taunts. The word ἐβόησεν (cried out), with its echo of the opening scripture quotation of the gospel (1:3), indicates that the voice crying in the desert has been fulfilled but the crucifixion does not spell out how it has been fulfilled. Sound indicates directions for exegesis, but it also rules out interpretative attempts that contradict sound data or controvert their signals. For example, nothing in the sound of Jesus' outcry (Psalm 22:1a) supports the contention that it invokes the optimistic ending verses of the psalm. Piety may desire the soteriological implication of the psalm's conclusion, but sound rules it out.

THE COMING OF ELIJAH

The mistaken identity of Elijah is part of Mark's redefinition of Christology. In Part 1 the taunts of the confronters and the priests were paired and parallel. In Part 2, Jesus' loud outcry and the bystanders' mistaken identity are paired but not parallel. The mistake in identity warns the hearer against mistaking the meaning of Jesus' cry. The fact that Elijah has already come and is John the Baptist whom Herod put to death is the first step in Mark's redefinition. Sound makes Jesus' death the fundamental Christological datum.

ALLEGORICAL THINKING

Part 3 suggests a resolution to the dilemma posed in 4:12 when Mark has Jesus respond to a question about the parables with a puzzling quotation that the evangelist has freely adapted from Isaiah 6:9–10:

ἵνα βλέποντες βλέπωσιν καὶ μὴ ἴδωσιν,
καὶ ἀκούοντες ἀκούωσιν καὶ μὴ συνιῶσιν,
μήποτε ἐπιστρέψωσιν καὶ ἀφεθῇ αὐτοῖς.[31]

The repetition of βλέπ- anticipates the warning about the coming of the Son in 13:33, in which the audience is instructed to look and pay attention (βλέπετε ἀγρυπνεῖτε, Be on guard! Stay alert!). The beginning of the crucifixion narrative features those who taunt Jesus in Part 1; they see but do not see. Also in the section containing the chief priests' taunt (c 9), seeing and believing are introduced (ἵνα ἴδωμεν καὶ πιστεύσωμεν).[32] Those who stand around in part 2 hear but do not understand. Finally in part 3, the pattern breaks: the centurion sees and hears; the women see and understand. ἄφετε / ἀφείς (*lit.*, let or allow) also occurs in the quotation from Isaiah. Those who really see and understand are those who stand at the foot of the cross and witness Jesus' death. The centurion's colon is neither sarcastic, like the taunts, nor a confession of faith. For Mark, both the centurion and the women witness the reality of what happened. Their "Christology" does not demand that Jesus can destroy the temple, come down from the cross, or be a king. Nor do they mishear Jesus' last words. The centurion hears and states the fact. For Mark, this is the new Christology, and the women bear witness as those who have followed Jesus from the beginning until the end. This will be fresh in the hearer's memory when at the tomb the women are afraid and run away.

Appendix

Sound Map of Mark's Crucifixion

Mark 15:25-41

PART 1

Period 1

1 ἦν δὲ ὥρα τρίτη καὶ ἐσταύρωσαν αὐτόν.

Period 2

2 καὶ ἦν ἡ ἐπιγραφὴ τῆς αἰτίας αὐτοῦ
ἐπιγεγραμμένη, Ὁ βασιλεὺς τῶν Ἰουδαίων.

Period 3

3 Καὶ σὺν αὐτῷ σταυροῦσιν δύο λῃστάς, ἕνα ἐκ δεξιῶν
καὶ ἕνα ἐξ εὐωνύμων αὐτοῦ.

Period 4

4 Καὶ*οἱ παραπορευόμενοι*ἐβλασφήμουν αὐτὸν
κινοῦντες τὰς κεφαλὰς αὐτῶν καὶ λέγοντες,
5 Οὐὰ*ὁ καταλύων τὸν ναὸν καὶ*οἰκοδομῶν ἐν τρισὶν ἡμέραις,
6 σῶσον σεαυτὸν καταβὰς ἀπὸ τοῦ σταυροῦ.

Period 5

7 ὁμοίως καὶ οἱ ἀρχιερεῖς ἐμπαίζοντες
πρὸς ἀλλήλους
μετὰ τῶν γραμματέων ἔλεγον,
8 Ἄλλους ἔσωσεν, ἑαυτὸν οὐ δύναται σῶσαι·
9 ὁ Χριστὸς ὁ βασιλεὺς Ἰσραὴλ καταβάτω νῦν ἀπὸ τοῦ σταυροῦ, ἵνα
ἴδωμεν καὶ πιστεύσωμεν.

Period 6

10 καὶ οἱ συνεσταυρωμένοι σὺν αὐτῷ ὠνείδιζον αὐτόν.

PART 2

Period 1

11 Καὶ γενομένης ὥρας ἕκτης σκότος
ἐγένετο ἐφ' ὅλην τὴν γῆν ἕως ὥρας ἐνάτης.

Period 2

12 καὶ τῇ ἐνάτῃ ὥρᾳ ἐβόησεν ὁ Ἰησοῦς φωνῇ μεγάλῃ,
13 *Ελωι*ελωι λεμα σαβαχθανι;
14 ὅ ἐστιν μεθερμηνευόμενον
15 Ὁ θεός μου ὁ θεός μου, εἰς τί ἐγκατέλιπές με;

Period 3

16 καί τινες τῶν παρεστώτων ἀκούσαντες ἔλεγον,
17 Ἴδε Ἠλίαν φωνεῖ.

18 δραμὼν δέ τις
καὶ γεμίσας σπόγγον ὄξους
περιθεὶς καλάμῳ
ἐπότιζεν αὐτόν, λέγων,
19 Ἄφετε ἴδωμεν εἰ ἔρχεται Ἠλίας καθελεῖν αὐτόν.

Period 4
20 ὁ δὲ Ἰησοῦς ἀφεὶς φωνὴν μεγάλην ἐξέπνευσεν.

PART 3

Period 1
21 Καὶ τὸ καταπέτασμα τοῦ ναοῦ ἐσχίσθη εἰς δύο ἀπ' ἄνωθεν ἕως κάτω.

Period 2
22 Ἰδὼν δὲ **ὁ** κεντυρίων **ὁ** παρεστηκὼς ἐξ ἐναντίας αὐτοῦ
ὅτι **οὕ**τως ἐξέπνευσεν εἶπεν,
23 Ἀληθῶς οὗτος ὁ ἄνθρωπος υἱὸς θεοῦ ἦν.

Period 3
24 **Ἦσαν** δὲ **καὶ** γυν**αῖ**κες ἀπὸ μ**α**κρόθεν θεωροῦσ**αι**,
ἐν **αἷ**ς **καὶ** Μ**α**ρί**α** ἡ Μ**α**γδ**α**ληνὴ
καὶ Μ**α**ρί**α** **ἡ** Ἰ**α**κώβου τοῦ μικροῦ
καὶ Ἰωσῆτος μήτηρ **καὶ** Σ**α**λώμη,
25 **αἳ** ὅτε **ἦ**ν ἐν τῇ **Γ**α**λιλαί**ᾳ ἠκολούθουν αὐτῷ
καὶ δ**ιη**κόνουν αὐτῷ,
26 **καὶ** **ἄ**λλ**αι** πολλ**αὶ** **αἱ** συν**α**ν**α**β**ᾶ**σ**αι** αὐτῷ εἰς Ἱεροσόλυμ**α**.

English Translation

PART 1

Period 1
1 It was 9 o'clock in the morning when they crucified him.

Period 2
And the inscription, which identified his crime,
read, 'The King of the Judeans.'

Period 3
3 And with him they crucify two rebels, one on his right
and one on his left.

Period 4
4 Those passing by kept taunting him,
wagging their heads, and saying,
5 "Ha! You who would destroy the temple and rebuild it in three days,
6 save yourself and come down from the cross!"

Period 5

7 Likewise the ranking priests had made fun of him
to one another,
along with the scholars; they would say,
8 "He saved others, but he can't save himself!
9 'The Anointed,' 'the King of Israel,' should come down from the cross
here and now, so that we can see and trust for ourselves!"

Period 6

10 Even those being crucified along with him would abuse him.

PART 2

Period 1

11 And when noon came,
darkness blanketed the whole land until mid-afternoon.

Period 2

12 And at 3 o'clock in the afternoon Jesus shouted at the top of his voice,
13 "Eloi, Eloi, lema sabachthani"
14 (which means
15 "My God, my God, why did you abandon me?")

Period 3

16 And when some of those standing nearby heard, they would say,
17 "Listen, he's calling Elijah!"
18 And someone ran
and filled a sponge with sour wine,
stuck it on a pole,
and offered him a drink, saying,
19 "Let's see if Elijah comes to rescue him!"

Period 4

20 But Jesus let out a great shout and breathed his last.

PART 3

Period 1

21 And the curtain of the temple was torn in two from top to bottom!

Period 2

22 When the Roman officer standing opposite him saw
that he had died like this, he said,
23 "This man really was God's son!"

Period 3

24 Now some women were observing this from a distance,
among whom were Mary of Magdala,
and Mary the mother of James the younger and Joses, and Salome.

25 <These women> had regularly followed and assisted him when he was in Galilee,
26 along with many other women who had come up to Jerusalem in his company

ENDNOTES

1. ὁ/οἱ δέ (15:11–16 5a)
   But the ranking priests incited the crowd to get Barabbas set free for them instead.
   But in response <to their request> Pilate would again say to them,
   "What do you want me to do with the fellow you call 'the King of the Judeans'?"
   And they in turn shouted, "Crucify him!"
   Pilate kept saying to them, "Why? What has he done wrong?"
   But they shouted all the louder, "Crucify him!"
   And because Pilate was always looking to satisfy the crowd, he set Barabbas free for them,
2. καί (15:15b–24)
   had Jesus flogged, and then turned him over to be crucified.
   And the Roman soldiers led him away to the courtyard of the governor's residence, and they called the whole company <of Roman troops> together.
   And they dressed him in purple
   and crowned him with a garland woven of thorns.
   And the soldiers began to salute him: "Greetings, 'King of the Judeans'!"
   And they kept striking him on the head with a staff,
   and spitting on him;
   and they would get down on their knees and bow down to him.
   And when they had made fun of him, they stripped off the purple
   and put his own clothes back on him.
   And the Romans lead him out
   to crucify him.
   And they conscript someone named Simon of Cyrene,
   who was coming in from the country, the father of Alexander and Rufus,
   to carry his cross.
   And the Roman soldiers bring him to the place Golgotha
   (which means "Place of the Skull").
   And they tried to give him wine mixed with myrrh, but he didn't take it.

And the soldiers crucify him, and they divide up his garments, casting lots to see who would get what.

3. And they dressed him in purple.
4. And the Roman soldiers led him away to the courtyard of the governor's residence.
5. It was 9 o'clock in the morning when they crucified him.
   And the inscription, which identified his crime, read, 'The King of the Judeans.'
6. And when it had already grown dark, since it was preparation day (the day before the sabbath),
7. And the Romans lead him out to crucify him.
8. A translation for each Part, Period and Colon is provided in the appendix at end of the chapter.
9. As for that exact day or minute: no one knows, not even heaven's messengers, nor even the son, no one, except the Father. Be on guard! Stay alert! For you never know what time it is.
10. "Those passing by," 6; "they kept taunting," 4; "wagging," "heads," "saying" 3.
11. Why does that fellow say such things? He's blaspheming! Who can forgive sins except the one God?
12. But whoever blasphemes against the holy spirit is never ever forgiven, but is guilty of an eternal sin.
13. You have heard the blasphemy!
14. And be rejected by the elders and the ranking priests and the scholars.
15. Dispatched by the ranking priests and the scholars and the elders.
16. The ranking priests, after consulting with the elders and scholars and the whole Council
17. *Lit.*, And when it was the sixth hour, darkness was . . . until the ninth hour.
18. A voice of someone shouting in the wilderness: "Make ready the way of the Lord.
19. See Brown (1994, v. 2, pp. 1047–51) for a discussion of those rejecting this position in favor of seeing the end of the psalm with its more hopeful language as the intended point.
20. The textual problem does not affect the sound map. It is a spelling issue. See note in Nestle-Aland[27].
21. *Lit.*, running, filling, sticking, saying.
22. Elijah must come first.
23. Elijah in fact has come.
24. Let's see if Elijah comes?
25. But Jesus . . . shout.
26. So that we can see and trust for ourselves!

27. The lack of the article with υἱὸς θεοῦ has occasioned much comment. Recently Colllins (p. 767–8) has argued that the centurion's phrase employs the imperial title. From the point of view of sound (not grammar) the lack of the articles keeps the statement simple. With the imperial title listeners would expect more elaboration or grave style.
28. This will be confirmed once more in the following narrative scene in which Pilate, amazed (ὁ δὲ Πιλᾶτος ἐθαύμασεν εἰ ἤδη τέθνηκεν), seeks the centurion's report of Jesus' death (15:44), then the women see (ἐθεώρουν) where the corpse was laid (15:47).
29. And right then and there they abandoned their nets and followed him.
30. To be served, but to serve.
31. They may look with eyes wide open but never quite see, and may listen with ears attuned but never quite understand, otherwise they might turn around and find forgiveness!
32. So that we can see and trust for ourselves!

WORKS CONSULTED

Brown, Raymond E. 1994. *The Death of the Messiah: From Gethsemane to the Grave*. 2 vols, *Anchor Bible Reference Series*. New York: Doubleday.

Collins, Adela Yarbo. 2007. *Mark, A Commentary, Hermencia*. Minneapolis: Fortress.

Fowler, Robert M. 1991. *Let the Reader Understand: Reader-Response Criticism and the Gospel of Mark*. Minneapolis: Fortress Press.

Johnson, Earl S. 1987. Is Mark 15.39 the Key to Mark's Christology? *Journal for the Study of the New Testament* 31:3–22.

Lohmeyer, Ernst. 1959. *Das Evangelium des Markus. Kritisch-eregetischer Kommentar über das Neue Testament*. Göttingen: Vandenhock & Ruprecht.

Taylor, Vincent. 1966. *The Gospel According to Mark*. 2nd ed. London: Macmillan.

Tolbert, Mary Ann. 1989. *Sowing the Gospel, Mark's World in a Literary-Historical Perspective*. Minneapolis: Fortress Press.

Chapter 7

Persuasion and Conversion

Paul's Letter to Philemon

INTRODUCTION

Sound mapping yields its greatest benefit when applied to an entire composition because then it exhibits a complete structural skeleton and comprehensive catalog of sound devices. Paul's brief letter to Philemon offers an opportunity to illustrate sound mapping's benefits in a whole composition, not just a part.

Because Philemon is a short, occasional letter, it is often dismissed as inconsequential, or of lesser importance for Paul's theology. Sound mapping, however, controverts this conclusion and illustrates the independent contribution of sound to meaning apart from semantics. Paul's use of wordplays and other sound effects accomplishes a transformation of Onesimus from slave to beloved brother, based on Paul's implicit metaphor of the body of Christ. How Paul achieves this remarkable and artful effect has gone unnoticed in the literature about the letter.

In our sound map we have found it advisable to take the letter as presented and not to make assumptions drawn from outside the letter.[1] A letter always implies a narrative but its underlying story usually remains implicit. An interpreter's task is to make the letter's narrative explicit and resolve its interpretive issues in the context of that narrative. Traditionally, commentators have assumed that Onesimus is a runaway slave who has sought refuge with Paul (Lightfoot 1897, Reprinted 1968; Lohse 1971). According to this view, Paul writes to Philemon to negotiate the slave's return. The assumption that Onesimus is a runaway slave is probably based on a stereotyped notion of how slaves behave. Lightfoot (p. 312), for example, notes Terence's picture of slaves (*Phormio* 1.4.11–13). This understanding of the implied narrative is at least as old as John Chrysostom (Mitchell 1995, p. 136).

Recent challenges to this reconstruction demand reconsideration of the letter's implied narrative. Nowhere does the letter explicitly state or even imply that Onesimus has run away, nor are any of the technical terms for this situation invoked. Lampe has advanced the argument that Onesimus is not a runaway, but that he has sought Paul's intercession as an *amicus domini* with his master. He advances this case by means of documentary evidence from contemporary literature (Lampe 1985).[2] Finally, Callahan has argued that Onesimus is not a slave at all, but Philemon's brother. In this construction, Paul is asking Philemon to receive Onesimus back as his **beloved** brother—the accent falls on beloved (Callahan 1993, p. 373). Moreover, commentators have puzzled over what Paul is requesting from Philemon. Traditionally, the construal is that Paul wants Philemon to receive Onesimus back without punishment. Petersen has argued that Paul demands manumission, since slavery is incompatible with Paul's view of the gospel (1985).[3]

LETTER FORM

Because letters exhibit distinctive characteristics and sound reinforces letter conventions, we have indicated the standard letter division in the sound map itself. That the sound map supports letter conventions should not be surprising, since sound comprises these conventions, as in the use of conventional formulae. Paul's letter to Philemon follows letter-writing conventions, yet it reflects the form of the letter as modified by Paul. For example, Philemon includes an extended thanksgiving and an abbreviated form of the apostolic parousia ("prepare a room"). The only thing missing is the paraenesis.

STRUCTURAL OVERVIEW

Even though this is a short letter, the shortest of Paul's in the canon, its periods are elegant and complex. Throughout the letter cola are blended into periods through various techniques of grammatical subordination. Periods are less complex at the letter's beginning and end and more complex in the middle. The letter's climax (period 7, cola 1–2) is distinguished by brief cola set in parallel, with important elements surrounded by hiatus (designated with an asterisk (*) in the sound map) to set them apart and imbue the period with a serious tone.

ADDRESS[4]

PERFORMANCE SPACE

Period 1

1 Παῦλος δέσμιος Χριστοῦ Ἰησοῦ
καὶ Τιμόθεος ὁ ἀδελφὸς

2 Φιλήμονι τῷ ἀγαπητῷ καὶ συνεργῷ ἡμῶν
καὶ Ἀπφίᾳ τῇ ἀδελφῇ
καὶ Ἀρχίππῳ τῷ συστρατιώτῃ ἡμῶν
καὶ τῇ κατ' οἶκόν **σου** ἐκκλησίᾳ·
3 χάρις ὑμῖν καὶ εἰρήνη ἀπὸ θεοῦ πατρὸς ἡμῶν
καὶ κυρίου Ἰησοῦ Χριστοῦ

The letter's address establishes its performance space by naming its characters and designating their relationships. Paul identifies himself as δέσμιος Χριστοῦ Ἰησοῦ (prisoner of the anointed Jesus). This identification is consistent and reinforced throughout the letter. He identifies himself in no other way. Philemon is the only letter in which Paul uses this self-designation. Timothy is named as Paul's brother.

Philemon, the addressee, is named as a householder, *pater familias,* and the head of the ἐκκλησία (*lit.,* church) that meets in his house.[5] Paul thus addresses his letter not to a single addressee but to Philemon as part of an ἐκκλησία. Philemon's status is suggested in colon 2 by κατ' οἶκόν σου (who meet in your house). Family terms are used in the opening period: ὁ ἀδελφός (brother) occurs in colon 1, ἡ ἀδελφή (sister) and ὁ οἶκος (house) occur in colon 2 and πατρός (*lit.,* father) in colon 3, referring to God.

Philemon's ἐκκλησία is described at some length. Colon 2 names Apphia and Archippus, twice using ἡμῶν (our) to connect the group to Paul. In colon 3 ἡμῶν is repeated and associated with God. The repetition of ἡμῶν throughout the period gives the group a coherent identity. The third colon is elongated, signaling closure. Naming Ἰησοῦ Χριστοῦ at the colon's end rounds the period by returning to colon 1's reference to Jesus. Colon 3 reverses Jesus' name and title, creating a chiasm with colon 1. The role of Jesus' name and title in rounding the letter's opening brings attention to Jesus' defining identity for the ἐκκλησία.

The letter's performance space is defined as public space. Philemon is not reading the letter privately in his bedroom but publicly within the defined relationships established by the performance space. The space is occupied by those addressed, the whole ἐκκλησία, the larger group implied by Paul's designations of himself and Timothy, and the various addressees associated with the repeated ἡμῶν, including God. The unified period, rounded by the repeated and chiastically arranged name and title of Jesus, subsumes all the members of the group, including the addressees and also Paul and Timothy, under the identity of Jesus.

THANKSGIVING

PHILEMON IN THE κοινωνία

Period 2

1 Εὐχαριστῶ τῷ θεῷ μου πάντοτε μνείαν **σου** ποιούμενος ἐπὶ
τῶν προσευχῶν μου,
ἀκούων **σου** τὴν ἀγάπην καὶ
τὴν πίστιν

2 **ἦ**ν ἔχεις **πρὸς τὸ**ν κύριον Ἰησ**οῦ**ν
καὶ εἰς **πάντας το**ὺς ἁγί**ους**,

3 ὅπως ἡ κοινωνία τῆς πίστεώς **σου** ἐνεργὴς γένηται
ἐν ἐπιγνώσει παντὸς ἀγαθοῦ τοῦ ἐν ἡμῖν εἰς Χριστόν·

The thanksgiving shifts perspective within the performance space to Paul and Philemon. Paul zooms in on Philemon and Philemon's function in the κοινωνία (the sharing) using several sound devices. In period 2, colon 1 a pair of participial phrases focuses on Philemon by repeating σου (you, sing.). Philemon is praised for his ἀγάπη (love) and πίστις (confidence) in the community.[6] In colon 3 σου occurs again, associated with Philemon's πίστις as in colon 1. Colon 2 repeats η/εις sounds. Paired prepositional phrases in colon 2 also have similar sounds, with repeating π, τ, and υ/ουν(ς), setting the phrases in parallel. Colon 3 sustains the repeated -εις/-ης sounds. These cluster in the middle of colon 3, along with repeated εν/γεν/γη/γνω sounds, emphasizing Paul's hope that the sharing (κοινωνία) of Philemon's πίστις might bring forth an energy in the knowledge (ἐνεργὴς γένηται ἐν ἐπιγνώσει) of all good things that are ours in Christ. Repeated sounds from period 1 (ἐν ἡμῖν εἰς Χριστόν) make it clear that focus is not placed on Philemon as an isolated individual but on Philemon's function in the communal sharing, which had been associated in period 1 with Jesus' title and the first person plural pronoun. This elongated colon closes period 2 signaling closure of the Thanksgiving.

Schubert and White[7] agree with the letter's structure as depicted in the sound map, while most commentators (Lightfoot, Lohse, Fitzmyer, Dunn, Osiek [2000], Ryan) include period 3 (verse 7) as part of the thanksgiving. This finding is significant since Schubert's analysis is based on a comparative study of Paul's letters, while White's analysis is based on the analysis of the Greek letter form itself. That the analysis of sound agrees with Schubert and White is not surprising because it is consistent with relevant sound data from comparable literature. Sound supports convention because sound comprises it. Convention **is** sound.

BODY

PAUL AS PRISONER

As Paul focuses on Philemon in the thanksgiving by means of the repeated σου, he completes the dyad by referring to himself with singular pronouns as well. The thanksgiving is defined by its opening with the first person singular verb εὐχαριστῶ (I thank). The first person singular pronoun occurs twice in period 2, colon 1, once in the opening phrase and once at the colon's end. Paul telescopes his attention to focus on himself and Philemon as he begins to build the foundation for his main argument in the letter's body.

Period 3

1 χαρὰν γὰρ πολλὴν ἔσχον καὶ παράκλησιν ἐπὶ τῇ ἀγάπῃ **σου**,
2 ὅτι τὰ σπλάγχνα τῶν ἁγίων ἀναπέπαυται διὰ **σοῦ**, ἀδελφέ.

Period 4

1 Διό, πολλὴν ἐν Χριστῷ παρρησίαν ἔχων ἐπιτάσσειν **σοι** τὸ ἀνῆκον,
2 διὰ τὴν ἀγάπην μᾶλλον παρακαλῶ,
3 τοιοῦτος ὢν ὡς Παῦλος πρεσβύτης, νυνὶ δὲ καὶ δέσμιος Χριστοῦ Ἰησοῦ

Having drawn attention to Philemon's role in the κοινωνία in period 2, period 3 makes his role explicit. Repetition of the singular pronoun σου is sustained. Repeated α sounds draw together words that describe this role: τὰ σπλάγχνα τῶν ἁγίων ἀναπέπαυται.[8] Paul does not specify what Philemon does or how Philemon accomplishes the task of refreshing τὰ σπλάγχνα,[9] but this is the only description the letter offers of Philemon's role beyond implying his status as a householder. At the end of colon 2, Philemon for the first time is called brother, repeating the α sounds that have characterized period 3. Thus Philemon is recognized as brother by virtue of his contribution to the κοινωνία, which is his refreshment of τὰ σπλάγχνα.

The initial διό (So) indicates that Paul's joy is the basis for his request. White (p. 35) observes that this request is one of the longest requests he has observed in private papyri letters. Period 4 comprises brief cola exhibiting sustained repetition of π. Cola 1 and 2 repeat three lexemes from the the body's opening, Period 2: πολλήν, παράκλησις/παρακαλῶ and ἀγάπη.[10] The repeated π and α/ει/η sounds select important words for emphasis in period 4: πολλήν, παρρησία, ἐπιτάσσειν, ἀγάπη, παρακαλεῖν, Παῦλος, πρεσβύτης.[11] The recurring sounds draw attention to Paul's new topic, his preference for encouragement over command. As the π sound is repeated,

Paul weaves an ironic contrast between his expressed role and his right to authority. Paul claims the authority to command obedience, something more appropriate to the unexpressed title of apostle. Yet Paul prefers instead his status as old man and prisoner. Π repeats at the beginning of his name and πρεσβύτης (old man), a role amplified by the final colon's conclusion, νυνὶ δὲ καὶ δέσμιος Χριστοῦ Ἰησοῦ,[12] which repeats from the letter's address his status as prisoner.

Considerable discussion in the critical literature debates the meaning of πρεσβύτης, with some insisting that it means "ambassador."[13] "Ambassador" is the preferred meaning for those who find it necessary to find an explicit apostolic claim[14] in the letter but the sound map indicates otherwise. Paul never appeals to his role as apostle in this letter. Instead, he emphasizes his status as δέσμιος Χριστοῦ Ἰησοῦ. In period 4, νυνὶ δὲ implies that this status follows and extends his status as πρεσβύτης, suggesting an apparent weakness: he is an old man, and now has even been imprisoned. Paul exploits this apparent weakness by rejecting his prerogative of command. His choice implies a more fundamental strength, his latent prerogative. The sound map suggests that this latency is a potential source of strength because it is associated with Jesus Christ, whose name and title are appended to δέσμιος at the end of the period. Closing colon 3 with Χριστοῦ Ἰησοῦ rounds the period by echoing ἐν Χριστῷ in the period's opening. Like the opening periods of the address and the thanksgiving, this period that initiates Paul's request begins and ends with Jesus Christ. Rounding periods with Jesus' name and title enforce a sense that Christ Jesus encompasses the community and supplies its identity.

Period 5

1 παρακαλῶ **σε** περὶ τοῦ ***ἐμοῦ*** τέκνου,
2 ὃν ἐγέννησα ἐν **τοῖς** δεσμοῖς Ὀνήσιμον
τόν ποτέ **σοι*** ἄχρηστον
νυνὶ δὲ **σοὶ** καὶ****ἐμοὶ**** εὔχρηστον
3 ὃν ἀνέπεμψά **σοι,*** αὐτόν τοῦτ᾽ἔστιν τὰ* ***ἐμὰ*** σπλάγχνα
4 ὃν ἐγὼ ἐβουλόμην πρὸς ***ἐμαυτὸν*** κατέχειν,
5 ἵνα ὑπὲρ **σοῦ** ***μοι*** διακονῇ ἐν τοῖς δεσμοῖς τοῦ εὐαγγελίου,
6 χωρὶς δὲ τῆς σῆς γνώμης οὐδὲν ἠθέλησα ποιῆσαι,
7 ἵνα μὴ ὡς κατὰ ἀνάγκην τὸ ἀγαθόν **σου** ᾖ
ἀλλὰ κατὰ ἑκούσιον.

In period 5, Paul twice invokes his status as prisoner with the phrase ἐν τοῖς δεσμοῖς (in prison), once in colon 2 and once in colon 5. Like a drumbeat, four times in the first 5 periods, δεσμιος/δεσμοις defines Paul as prisoner, not as an apostle.

In period 5 Paul the prisoner and Philemon the householder face off concerning Onesimus. Σε, σοι, and σου, second person pronouns, are prominent sounds in this period. Like the thanksgiving in period 2, period 5 opens with a first person singular predicate, and ἐμοῦ, ἐμοὶ, ἐμά, ἐγώ and ἐμαυτόν are likewise prominent in the first part of the period. Colon 1 continues the π repetition of the previous 2 periods, with the emphasized παρακαλῶ (I would appeal) of period 4, colon 2 as the initial word of colon 1. This repetition of παρακαλῶ as Paul confronts Philemon accents Paul's preference, established in period 4, for encouragement over command. Since he has the power to command, Paul's rhetorical strategy is to reiterate his apparent weakness as an old man and a prisoner to create an implicit show of strength. At the period's end, cola 5–7 contrast Paul's prisoner status (ἐν τοῖς δεσμοῖς τοῦ εὐαγγελίου,[15] colon 5) with Philemon's freedom, as Paul again prefers to entreat κατὰ ἑκούσιον (of your own free will) instead of κατὰ ἀνάγκην (out of coercion) (colon 7).

THE TRANSFORMATION OF ONESIMUS

In period 5, colon 1 Paul entreats for τοῦ ἐμοῦ τέκνου (my child), using the first person singular pronoun in its emphatic form. Τοῦ ἐμοῦ τέκνου echoes δέσμιος Χριστοῦ Ἰησοῦ in the conclusion to the final colon of period 4, associating both Paul as prisoner and Paul's child, as yet unnamed, with Christ Jesus. Philemon first hears the person of concern identified emphatically as Paul's child in rhyme with Christ Jesus. Thus Paul reinforces his and Philemon's positions in a performance space defined as the arena encompassed by Jesus Christ. Paul is a prisoner of or on account of Christ (Παῦλος δέσμιος Χριστοῦ Ἰησοῦ, period 1, colon 1). Philemon is praised for τὴν ἀγάπην καὶ τὴν πίστιν ἣν ἔχεις πρὸς τὸν κύριον Ἰησοῦν (period 2, cola 1–2) and Philemon's πίστις (confidence, *lit.*, faith) energizes the community in the knowledge of the good things ἐν ἡμῖν εἰς Χριστόν[16] (period 2, colon 3). Jesus Christ is thus understood as the community's identifying element and its appropriate criterion for judgment.

Period 5, cola 2–4

2 ὃν ἐγέννησα ἐν **τοῖς** δεσμοῖς Ὀνήσιμον
τόν ποτέ **σοι*** ἄχρηστον
νυνὶ δὲ **σοὶ** καὶ* ***ἐμοὶ**** εὔχρηστον
3 ὃν ἀνέπεμψά **σοι,*** αὐτόν τοῦτ᾽ἔστιν τὰ* ἐμὰ σπλάγχνα
4 ὃν *ἐγὼ**ἐβουλόμην πρὸς ***ἐμαυτὸν*** κατέχειν,

In Period 5, cola 2–4 reverberate with the sounds of Paul's status as a prisoner (τοῖς δεσμοῖς, εμοι, σοι) and Onesimus' name.

Just as Onesimus' name begins and ends with ον sounds,[17] so does colon 2. Initial ον sounds also mark the beginnings of cola 2–4. A wordplay on Onesimus' name (ὄνησις, "use" or "profit") employing a different lexical stem organizes colon 2 (Ὀνήσιμον, ἄχρηστον ("Useless", εὔχρηστον ["Useful"]). The wordplay also evokes Jesus' title (Χριστός).[18] The concentrated rhymes and wordplays in colon 2 signal its importance. At the end of colon 2, νυνὶ δὲ (and now) repeats the phrase that occurs at the end of period 4, colon 3, which emphasizes Paul's status as a prisoner. Σοί ἄχρηστον is expanded at the colon's end to σοὶ καὶ ἐμοὶ. Hiatus emphasizes ἐμοὶ[19] and the expanded phrase draws Paul and Philemon together as Onesimus is declared useful.

In colon 2, Paul claims to have given birth to Onesimus in his imprisonment. He further describes Onesimus in colon 3 as τὰ ἐμὰ σπλάγχνα, using the possessive personal pronoun in its emphatic form and marking the pronoun with hiatus. Here the repetition of α sounds, concentrated at the colon's end, reprises a similar sound feature in period 3, colon 2, where Philemon is described as the brother who refreshes the σπλάγχνα of the holy ones.

The recurrence of τά σπλάγχνα here and the concentration of α sounds in both occurrences emphasize its importance. Whereas in period 3 the precise implication of the term remains ambiguous, here (period 5, colon 3) αὐτὸν[20] τοῦτ᾽ ἔστιν τὰ ἐμὰ σπλάγχνα follows Paul's description of Onesimus as Paul's very own little child, whom Paul has birthed. The names take the same form, with the emphatic form of the personal pronoun between the noun and its article, setting the names in parallel (τοῦ ἐμοῦ τέκνου / τὰ ἐμὰ σπλάγχνα). In this context, τά σπλάγχνα metaphorically depicts Onesimus as part of Paul's body. Hiatus and intensive personal pronouns (ἐμοῦ, ἐμά) reinforce this sense, connoting a visceral connection between Onesimus and Paul and invoking the intimacy and symbiosis of a mother and her infant.[21] Paul and Onesimus are thus to be construed as permanently connected and sustained by the same actions.

The complex rhymes and wordplays in these cola accomplish a transformation of Onesimus to Paul's child. Onesimus' own name, beginning and ending with ον, becomes the sound signature for this transformation, just as the naming of a child acknowledges paternity and recognizes the child's status in the family.

Period 6, cola 1–2

1 τάχα γὰρ διὰ τοῦτο ἐχωρίσθη πρὸς ὥραν
2 ἵνα αἰώνιον αὐτὸν ἀπέχῃς,
οὐκέτι ὡς δοῦλον

ἀλλὰ ὑπὲρ δοῦλον
ἀδελφὸν ἀγαπητόν

Period 6 preserves the crucial element of period 5's distinctive sound signature, the repeated ον sound that echoes the first and last syllable of Onesimus' name. Whereas in period 5 the repeated sounds accomplish a transformation of Onesimus to a child, in period 6 they transform Onesimus from slave to brother (ἀδελφὸν ἀγαπητόν, *lit.*, beloved brother). The transformation is now complete. Paul's child, Onesimus, is truly useful to both, and now is no longer a slave but a beloved brother. In the address, Paul had also used ἀγαπητός for Philemon so the bond is tightly tied. Paul asks Philemon to receive Onesimus not as slave but a brother.

The sound map of this period makes untenable Callahan's argument that Onesimus is Philemon's blood brother. Callahan reads ὡς δοῦλον of verse 16 as "as if he were a slave" (p. 373). This interpretation of ὡς as contrary to fact is impossible to sustain grammatically. Even more, the transformation accomplished by the period's sound signature of rhyming ον sounds draws attention to the transformation of Onesimus from slave to brother, just as period 5 drew attention to the transformation from useless to useful.[22]

Period 6, colon 3

3 μάλιστα ***ἐμοί***
πόσῳ δὲ μᾶλλον **σοὶ** καὶ ἐν σαρκὶ
καὶ ἐν κυρίῳ.

Lest the transformation of Onesimus from slave to child to brother be understood only in a religious sense, Paul makes his meaning clear in colon 3. The conjunction of ἐμοί/σοί (to me/to you) reinforces Paul's focus on the transaction between himself and Philemon. The final colon in period 6 makes explicit Paul's expectation that Onesimus undergo a real change in status, καὶ ἐν σαρκὶ καὶ ἐν κυρίῳ.[23] Although the Pauline letters often set these two phrases in contrast, here they are coordinates. Onesimus is to be a beloved brother both in the flesh and in the Lord.[24] The sound map suggests that this is precisely how Philemon should now refresh τὰ σπλάγχνα. Since Philemon and the community are all Paul's metaphorical children (τὰ σπλάγχνα), Philemon should now accept Onesimus as a new brother, and treat him as if he were in every way Philemon's own physical brother.

PAYMENT OF THE DEBT

Period 7

1 εἰ*οὖν με*ἔχεις κοινωνόν, προσλαβοῦ αὐτὸν ὡς ἐμέ*
2 εἰ δέ τι*ἠδίκησέν σε*ἢ*ὀφείλει, τοῦτο* ἐμοὶ*ἐλλόγα·

The structure of this period signals an important shift from the preceding, fully elaborated periods of the letter's body. White (p. 37) also sees a major shift in the letter's body based on his analysis of Greek letter forms. Once again, as expected, sound mapping supports the ancient conventions. This period contains only two brief cola marked by hiatus. As we have noted previously, hiatus is notable wherever it occurs and is unusual in Paul's typically smooth diction. Here as elsewhere in the letter, hiatus creates disjuncture in otherwise connected prose. The momentary stoppage of breath draws attention to what comes next. Paul's frequent use of hiatus in this passage slows the pace even more, creating space around its sounds and lending a grave tone. The shift is sudden and dramatic, signaling a turning point in the letter. The signal is not available at the semantic level of meaning but only at the level of sound.[25]

Period 7's cola are introduced by the conditional particle εἰ, which organizes both cola into two parts. Elements of both conditions are set in parallel. In contrast with the protasis of colon 1, which features the first person pronoun με, colon 2's protasis features the second person pronoun σε. Thus having a sharing with Paul (colon 1) is contrasted with any debt or injury to Philemon (colon 2). The first class conditions specify that the elements expressed in the protasis are real, consistent with fact. Having a sharing with (κοινωνόν) Paul is a present reality. Its occurrence recalls Paul's thanksgiving in period 3, colon 3 when Philemon was lauded for sharing his trust (ἡ κοινωνία τῆς πίστεώς σου). Likewise, Onesimus' debt to Philemon is genuine, even though it is downplayed with the indefinite particle τι. Repeated ει/η sounds in the protasis of both cola associate Onesimus with the debt, since they repeat the vowel sounds of ἢ ὀφείλει. The realities expressed in the protasis of both cola are made conditional upon alignment with Paul. The apodoses of both cola feature the first person pronoun in emphatic form, set apart by hiatus. Philemon's κοινωνόν with Paul depends upon Philemon's receiving Onesimus as if he were Paul (ὡς ἐμέ). Paul does not appeal to apostolic authority, but to the κοινωνία that Philemon and Paul share. Thus sound analysis lays bare Paul's intention. Philemon should set Onesimus free, making him a beloved brother, both in flesh and in the Lord. If there is a debt, Philemon should count it as Paul's, and should not call Onesimus to account.

Period 8

1 _ἐγὼ_ Παῦλος ἔγραψα τῇ*_ἐμῇ_ χειρί,*_ἐγὼ_*ἀποτίσω*·
2 ἵνα μὴ λέγω σοι ὅτι καὶ σεαυτόν μοι προσοφείλεις.
3 ναί,*ἀδελφέ,*

4 ***ἐγώ σου****ὀναίμην ἐν κυρίῳ·
5 *ἀνάπαυσόν μου τὰ σπλάγχνα*   ἐν Χριστῷ.

Period 8 sustains some of the sound features from the letter's turning point in the previous period. The repeated personal pronouns ἐγώ/ἐμῇ (colon 1) and σοι/σου/ σεαυτόν (cola 2, 4) drive home the point that the issue of Onesimus' debt is between Paul and Philemon. Notably, ἐγώ is grammatically unnecessary and ἐμῇ is emphatic. These first person pronouns also facilitate Paul's sustained use of hiatus to emphasize and lend gravity to his settlement of the debt.

Hiatus sets apart Paul's emphatic statement, ἐγὼ ἀποτίσω (I will pay you back), and also his insistence that he writes the statement with his own hand (ἔγραψα τῇ ἐμῇ χειρί). Along with the personal inscription, the sound and syntactic separation of ἐγὼ ἀποτίσω within the letter suggests the possibility that Paul is writing a physical promissory note. Although ἔγραψα τῇ ἐμῇ χειρί is sometimes taken as an indication that Paul has written the entire letter,[26] the sound map suggests that Paul has started writing at this point. Indeed, it tempts the interpreter to imagine the possibility that Paul himself has inscribed the words, ἐγὼ ἀποτίσω, legal terminology for repaying a debt, in a letter he has dictated to a scribe. Such activity would have been consistent with then-current letter writing practice.[27] Paul's handwriting would then function as his IOU to Philemon and the letter would provide a physical promise to pay,[28] a promise that is opposed to the apparently undesirable alternative articulated in colon 2, ἵνα μὴ λέγω σοι ὅτι καὶ σεαυτόν μοι προσοφείλεις.[29] Thus Paul reframes the relationships among himself, Philemon, and Onesimus in terms of two debts instead of one. In period 8 Paul places Onesimus' obligation to Philemon in the context of Philemon's debt to Paul. After mentioning Philemon's debt, Paul calls Philemon brother in colon 3, just as he has asked Philemon to accept Onesimus as a beloved brother in period 6, colon 2. In colon 4, Paul states that he expects a benefit (ὀναίμην) from Philemon, using a wordplay on Onesimus' name.[30] In exchange for Philemon's acceptance of Paul's promissory note, namely this letter, Paul offers to ignore Philemon's debt to Paul, Philemon's very self. Paul's promise to pay thus redeems Philemon and cancels his debt to Paul, just as Paul asks Philemon to redeem Onesimus and to settle Onesimus' debt with Paul himself.

The final colon of period 8 summarizes Paul's expectations for Philemon in terms that reprise the letter's thanksgiving. For the third time, repeated α sounds focus attention on τὰ σπλάγχνα. Its first occurrence refers to τὰ σπλάγχνα of the holy ones and praises

Philemon's function in the community as one who refreshes τὰ σπλάγχνα (period 3, colon 2). Its second occurrence (period 5, colon 3) names Onesimus as Paul's σπλάγχνα, suggesting a physical, bodily connection between them. In period 8, colon 5, Paul delivers the imperative that Philemon refresh Paul's σπλάγχνα, which is Onesimus. Philemon must follow Paul's directions about Onesimus in order to participate in the κοινωνία, to remain ἐν Χριστῷ.

In English translations of Philemon, τὰ σπλάγχνα is frequently rendered figuratively as "heart" in all three occurrences, spiritualizing the term and giving it a remote and abstract meaning. Uses of τὰ σπλάγχνα in Philemon are thus generally regarded as parenthetical remarks that convey a vague sense of closeness. Such renderings do not explain why Paul would employ this relatively rare word[31] three times in the letter, in three distinct contexts to express a casual observation. In all its occurrences, the sound map selects τὰ σπλάγχνα for particular emphasis, signaling its importance. In all three usages, Paul appeals to the defining element of the community, Christ Jesus, and to the community's status ἐν κυρίῳ καὶ ἐν Χριστῷ. Thus the sound map suggests that τὰ σπλάγχνα is somehow related to the letter's core message. It is best understood in Philemon as a metonym that implies the whole, construed as a human body.[32] The metaphor is visceral and concrete, not a remote abstraction.[33] Sound demonstrates that the bodily metaphor of τὰ σπλάγχνα betrays more than a personal sense of warmth toward the holy ones or Onesimus ("the hearts," "my heart") but rather conveys the very gist of Paul's argument about the integrity in Christ of the κοινωνία, construed as a physical body.[34]

Period 9

1 Πεποιθὼς τῇ ὑπακοῇ σου ἔγραψά σοι,
2 εἰδὼς ὅτι καὶ ὑπὲρ ἃ λέγω ποιήσεις.
3 ἅμα δὲ καὶ ἑτοίμαζέ μοι ξενίαν,
4 ἐλπίζω γὰρ ὅτι διὰ τῶν προσευχῶν ὑμῶν χαρισθήσομαι ὑμῖν.

The final colon of period 9 is elongated, signaling closure. The relatively simple structure is consistent with the trend begun in period 7 when Paul's style became briefer and more direct. The gradual simplification of periodic structure signals that the letter is coming to an end.

THE CLOSING

Period 10

1 Ἀσπάζεταί σε Ἐπαφρᾶς ὁ συναιχμάλωτός μου ἐν Χριστῷ Ἰησοῦ,
2 Μᾶρκος, Ἀρίσταρχος, Δημᾶς, Λουκᾶς, οἱ συνεργοί μου.
3 Ἡ χάρις τοῦ κυρίου Ἰησοῦ Χριστοῦ μετὰ τοῦ πνεύματος ὑμῶν.

The letter's final two periods employ balanced cola with repeating σ/ψ/ζ sounds. Two groups of people are identified in period 10. Epaphras is a fellow prisoner, while four others are identified as co-workers. Συνεργός was used in the address to identify Philemon. Ὁ συναιχμάλωτος designates one taken with a spear (αἰχμή), and thus a captive. This term for captivity is strikingly different from the one Paul uses in the address, and a noteworthy departure from the δεσμ-words accented throughout the letter. Previously Paul has drawn himself, Philemon and Onesimus together, binding them, consistent with the root meaning of δεῖν (to bind). The letter's several spiritual evolutions—the birthing that takes place ἐν τοῖς δεσμοῖς, the transformation from slave to child and from child to beloved brother, and finally the celebrations implicit in τὰ σπλάγχνα and κοινωνία—all stress the binding together that the letter seeks to accomplish. Sound therefore signals that, although the semantic fields of the two terms overlap, the words associated by sound function for a single purpose—and ὁ συναιχμάλωτός stands apart from this purpose.

CONCLUSION

The gains from our analysis of a sound map of Philemon include the following.

1. The sound map agrees with White's formal analysis of the letter based on Greek letter forms, and frequently disagrees with modern commentators who appear to ignore the formal characteristics of Greek letters. That sound mapping would support the formal analysis of the Greek is to be expected, since the Greek letter form was conveyed in sound and Greek literary criticism consistently affirms the constructive role of sound in composition.

2. Paul circumscribes the performance space as the κοινωνία identified with Jesus Christ. Frequent occurrence of the name and title of Jesus labels the community's identity. The label's structural placement focuses the community's purpose. Sound selects for emphasis and elaboration several metaphors that define the performance space in terms of the community's integrity. The use of δεσμ- lexemes furnishes one such metaphor, since Paul identifies himself not as an apostle but as a prisoner for Christ Jesus. The repetition of δεσμ- lexemes bind together Paul, Philemon and Onesimus in the context of the community. The recurrence of τὰ σπλάγχνα also supports this construction. The sound map shows that τὰ σπλάγχνα is no vague, figurative term. It contributes to the letter's primary purpose by serving as a metonym for the community. Τὰ σπλάγχνα functions in Philemon like Paul's σῶμα (body) language in his other letters.

3. The sound map clearly indicates how the transformation of Onesimus takes place. The use of Onesimus' name with its repeated ου sound to structure that transformation makes the point. Onesimus is Paul's child, transformed from slave to beloved brother.

4. Period 7 is the letter's climax. Thus Paul's point is twofold: to maintain κοινωνόν Philemon must receive Onesimus as Paul and whatever debt remains is to be charged to Paul's, not to Onesimus' account.

Do these gains from sound mapping help to adjudicate debates about the letter's implied narrative? The way Onesimus is transformed clearly indicates that he is a slave. This is another reason to lay aside Callahan's argument that Onesimus was not a slave but Philemon's brother.

Onesimus obviously owes a debt to Philemon, but Paul now assumes responsibility for that debt, putting himself in Onesimus' place. In period 8, colon 2 maneuvers Philemon into the debtor's role. This reversing of debtor's roles and the emphasis placed through sound on παρακαλῶ lend support to the assumption that Paul is acting as an *amicus domini*.

Multiple sound map features indicate that Paul wants Philemon to act voluntarily in setting Onesimus free. Philemon must accept Onesimus as a beloved brother—not just in the Lord, but also in the flesh. If Philemon wants to remain in κοινωνίον with Paul, he would appear to have no choice. Furthermore, Philemon should receive Onesimus as he would Paul and he should refresh Paul's τὰ σπλάγχνα, that is Onesimus. By framing the performance space as the κοινωνία identified with Jesus Christ, Paul requires Philemon to relinquish his claim on Onesimus if he would remain in that space. Clearly in the new creation, the κοινωνία of Christ Jesus, there is no place for Philemon's continued acceptance of slavery.[35]

Appendix
Sound Map of Philemon

ADDRESS

Period 1

1 Παῦλος δέσμιος Χριστοῦ Ἰησοῦ
καὶ Τιμόθεος ὁ ἀδελφὸς
2 Φιλήμονι τῷ ἀγαπητῷ καὶ συνεργῷ ἡμῶν
καὶ Ἀπφίᾳ τῇ ἀδελφῇ
καὶ Ἀρχίππῳ τῷ συστρατιώτῃ ἡμῶν
καὶ τῇ κατ᾽ οἶκόν **σου** ἐκκλησίᾳ·
3 χάρις ὑμῖν καὶ εἰρήνη ἀπὸ θεοῦ πατρὸς ἡμῶν
καὶ κυρίου Ἰησοῦ Χριστοῦ

THANKSGIVING

Period 2

1 Εὐχαριστῶ τῷ θεῷ μου πάντοτε
μνείαν **σου** ποιούμενος ἐπὶ τῶν προσευχῶν μου,
ἀκούων **σου** τὴν ἀγάπην καὶ τὴν πίστιν
2 ἣν ἔχεις πρὸς τὸν κύριον Ἰησοῦν
καὶ εἰς πάντας τοὺς ἁγίους,
3 ὅπως ἡ κοινωνία τῆς πίστεώς **σου** ἐνεργὴς γένηται
ἐν ἐπιγνώσει παντὸς ἀγαθοῦ τοῦ ἐν ἡμῖν εἰς Χριστόν·

BODY

Period 3

1 χαρὰν γὰρ πολλὴν ἔσχον καὶ παράκλησιν ἐπὶ τῇ ἀγάπῃ **σου**,
2 ὅτι τὰ σπλάγχνα τῶν ἁγίων ἀναπέπαυται διὰ **σοῦ**, ἀδελφέ.

Period 4

1 Διό, πολλὴν ἐν Χριστῷ παρρησίαν ἔχων ἐπιτάσσειν **σοι** τὸ ἀνῆκον,
2 διὰ τὴν ἀγάπην μᾶλλον παρακαλῶ,
3 τοιοῦτος ὢν ὡς Παῦλος πρεσβύτης, νυνὶ δὲ καὶ δέσμιος Χριστοῦ
Ἰησοῦ

Period 5

1 παρακαλῶ **σε** περὶ τοῦ *ἐμοῦ* τέκνου,
2 ὃν ἐγέννησα ἐν **τοῖς** δεσμοῖς Ὀνήσιμον
τόν ποτέ **σοι*** ἄχρηστον
νυνὶ δὲ **σοὶ** καὶ****ἐμοὶ**** εὔχρηστον
3 ὃν ἀνέπεμψά **σοι,*** αὐτόν τοῦτ᾽ ἔστιν τὰ****ἐμὰ***
σπλάγχνα·
4 ὃν ἐγὼ ἐβουλόμην πρὸς ***ἐμαυτὸν*** κατέχειν,

5 ἵνα ὑπὲρ **σοῦ** ***μοι*** διακονῇ ἐν τοῖς δεσμοῖς τοῦ εὐαγγελίου,
6 χωρὶς δὲ τῆς σῆς γνώμης οὐδὲν ἠθέλησα ποιῆσαι,
7 ἵνα μὴ ὡς κατὰ ἀνάγκην τὸ ἀγαθόν **σου** ᾖ
ἀλλὰ κατὰ ἑκούσιον.

Period 6

1 τάχα γὰρ διὰ τοῦτο ἐχωρίσθη πρὸς ὥραν
2 ἵνα αἰώνιον αὐτὸν ἀπέχῃς,
οὐκέτι ὡς δοῦλον
ἀλλὰ ὑπὲρ δοῦλον
ἀδελφὸν ἀγαπητόν
3 μάλιστα ***ἐμοί***
πόσῳ δὲ μᾶλλον **σοὶ** καὶ ἐν σαρκὶ
καὶ ἐν κυρίῳ.

Period 7

1 εἰ*οὖν ***με****ἔχεις κοινωνόν, προσλαβοῦ αὐτὸν ὡς ***ἐμέ****
2 εἰ δέ τι*ἠδίκησέν **σε***ἢ*ὀφείλει, τοῦτο* ***ἐμοὶ****ἐλλόγα·

Period 8

1 ***ἐγὼ*** Παῦλος ἔγραψα τῇ****ἐμῇ*** χειρί,****ἐγὼ****ἀποτίσω*·
2 ἵνα μὴ λέγω **σοι** ὅτι καὶ σεαυτόν μοι προσοφείλεις.
3 ναί,*ἀδελφέ,*
4 ***ἐγώ*** **σου***ὀναίμην ἐν κυρίῳ·
5 *ἀνάπαυσόν μου τὰ σπλάγχνα* ἐν Χριστῷ.

Period 9

1 Πεποιθὼς τῇ ὑπακοῇ σου ἔγραψά σοι,
2 εἰδὼς ὅτι καὶ ὑπὲρ ἃ λέγω ποιήσεις.
3 ἅμα δὲ καὶ ἑτοίμαζέ μοι ξενίαν,
4 ἐλπίζω γὰρ ὅτι διὰ τῶν προσευχῶν ὑμῶν χαρισθήσομαι ὑμῖν.

CLOSING

Period 10

1 Ἀσπάζεταί σε Ἐπαφρᾶς ὁ συναιχμάλωτός μου ἐν Χριστῷ Ἰησοῦ,
2 Μᾶρκος, Ἀρίσταρχος, Δημᾶς, Λουκᾶς, οἱ συνεργοί μου.
3 Ἡ χάρις τοῦ κυρίου Ἰησοῦ Χριστοῦ μετὰ τοῦ πνεύματος ὑμῶν.

English Translation

ADDRESS

Period 1

1 Paul, a prisoner because I serve the Anointed Jesus,
and Timothy, my associate,
2 to Philemon, our dear colleague—
also to Apphia our sister,
to Archippus who joined up with us

and to the Anointed's people who meet in your house.
3 May you have favor and peace from God, our creator and benefactor,
and from our lord, Jesus, God's Anointed

THANKSGIVING

Period 2

1 I always thank my God when I remember you, Philemon, in my
prayers, because I keep hearing about your love and the confidence
2 you have with regard to the lord Jesus
and for all God's people.
3 I pray that the sharing of your confident trust in God will result in a
recognition of all of the good that we are capable of in the service of
the Anointed.

BODY

Period 3

1 Your love has brought me great joy and encouragement,
2 because the hearts of God's people have been refreshed because of you,
dear friend.

Period 4

1 So, although in my capacity as an envoy of the Anointed I could
order you to do what is fitting,
2 I would rather appeal to you out of love,
3 just as I am, Paul, an old man and now even a prisoner because of the
Anointed Jesus.

Period 5

1 I appeal to you on behalf of my child,
2 the one whose father I became while I was in prison, Onesimus.
At one time he was "Useless" to you,
but now he has become "Useful" both to you and to me.
3 In sending him back to you I am sending my own heart.
4 I really wanted to keep him here with me,
5 so that he could assist me on your behalf while I am in prison for
proclaiming God's world-transforming message;
6 but I did not wish to do anything without your consent,
7 so that your good deed would not be done out of coercion
but of your own free will.

Period 6

1 Perhaps the reason that Onesimus was separated from you for a
while is
2 so that you could have him back forever,
no longer as your slave,
but more than a slave,

a beloved friend.
3 He is that special to me,
but even more to you, both as a man
and as one who belongs to our lord.

Period 7

1 So, if you consider me your partner, welcome him as you would welcome me.
2 And if he has wronged you in any way or owes you anything, charge that to my account.

Period 8

1 I, Paul, am putting this in my own handwriting: *I will pay you back,*
2 in order to avoid saying to you that you owe me your life.
3 Yes, my friend,
4 I am asking you for something "useful" in the service of our lord.
5 Refresh my heart as one who belongs to the Anointed.

Period 9

1 I am writing like this to you because I am confident that you will comply with my wishes.
2 I know that you will do even more that I am asking.
3 And, by the way, prepare a guest room for me,
4 because I am hoping that, through your prayers, I will be restored to you.

CLOSING

Period 10

1 Epaphrus, who is imprisoned with me because of his service to the
Anointed Jesus, sends greetings to you,
2 as do Mark, Aristarchus, and Luke, my colleagues.
3 May all of you be conscious that the gracious favor of the lord Jesus,
God's Anointed, is present among you.

ENDNOTES

1. Thus we have set aside the relationship to Colossians. Colossians is most probably not from Paul, but rather composed later. What its author knows about the situation surrounding or growing out of the letter to Philemon is unknown. To explain the similarity in the names between the letters one may assume either that the author of Colossians knows the situation or that he knows the letter and borrows the names. There is no way to decide between these options.
2. This argument has recently received strong support from Fitzmyer (2000, pp. 19–23) and Dunn (1996, pp. 304–5).

3. Strong critique by Horsley (1988, pp.178–80), apparent acceptance by Ryan (2005, pp. 175–76).
4. A full translation is in the Appendix at end of chapter.
5. *Pace* Knox who sees the σου as referring to Archippus (1935, Reprinted 1959, p. 62). The paratactic καί argues against this.
6. Schubert (1939, pp. 65–66) classifies this thanksgiving as what he calls type 1a. It has 7 parts. 1) principal verb Εὐχαριστῶ; 2) personal object τῷ θεῷ μου; 3) temporal adverb πάντοτε; 4) object phrase 5) Participle clause with temporal adverbial phrase μνείαν σου ποιούμενος ἐπὶ τῶν προσευχῶν μου; 6) causal clause ἀκούων σου τὴν ἀγάπην . . .; 7) final clause ὅπως . . .
7. White (1971, p. 35), provides evidence for the use of a joy phrase as the opening for a body of a letter.
8. The hearts of God's people (*lit.*, of the saints) have been refreshed
9. Τὰ σπλάγχνα has both literal and metaphorical meanings. It almost always occurs in the plural and refers to inward parts or internal organs, especially the heart, lungs, liver and kidneys, the parts of an animal reserved for consumption by persons offering animal sacrifice. It also denotes any inner organ, and occasionally the belly, womb, or loins, referring to the procreative functions of the lower parts of the body. Koester (1971, p. 555) observes that this is "a very strong and forceful term." Derived from this sense, the term occasionally describes children. It is also used metaphorically for the seat of emotion and impulsive feelings, especially anger. Koester notes that "Greek usage, at any rate in the pre-Christian period, does not view the σπλάγχνα as the seat of heart-felt mercy, as in later Jewish and the first Christian writings. There is no developed transferred use [to indicate "heart" or the center of personal feeling], and the word is never employed for mercy itself. This rather rough term seems none too well adapted to express Christian virtue or the divine dealings." (Koester 1971, p. 555; LSJ s.v. τὸ σπλάγχνον). Fitzmeyer (p. 100) among others, recognizes a problem in determining the precise meaning of τὰ σπλάγχνα in this passage. He notes the literal meaning as the viscera and summarizes various figurative usages of the term in LXX, Paul, other New Testament documents and early Christian writings, but without explanation he leaves unchallenged the typical translation of "hearts."
10. Great/capacity (*lit.*, enough), encouragement, and love.
11. Capacity, to order, love, to appeal, Paul, and old man.
12. And now even a prisoner because of the Anointed Jesus.
13. Lightfoot (p. 338–39) seems responsible for this suggestion. He bases his argument on Ephesians 6:20 and argues that πρεσβύτης

was mistaken for πρεσβεύτης. Peterson (p. 125–28) makes a strong argument for this, and while Ryan (p. 233–4) supports the proposal, Fitzmyer (p. 105–6) just as strongly argues against it. He has a good summary of recent literature on the topic.

14. Lohse (p. 199) forcibly makes this case.
15. *Lit.,* in prison for the good news.
16. That we are capable of in the service of the Anointed (*lit.,* which is ours in Christ).
17. Fitzmyer (p. 108) joins a long list of commentators who consider the grammatical issue with Ὀνήσιμον in the accusative case. This means that it is not in apposition with τοῦ ἐμοῦ τέκνου. He follows Lightfoot's suggestion that is in the accusative because of attraction to the relative pronoun ὃν. But the sound map also indicates that this facilitates the elaborate rhyme based on ον.
18. Lightfoot (p. 340) refers to this as "far too recondite to be probable." Fitzmyer (p. 109) rejects this word play as "far-fetched" because he thinks it would have to be "*a-christianos,*" but this is being too wooden and literal minded. τοῦ ἐμοῦ τέκνου has already been associated in rhyme with Χριστοῦ Ἰησοῦ, so added word play seems quite reasonable. Besides, "*Christianos*" was almost certainly not in play during Paul's lifetime. Lohse (p. 200) and Osiek (p. 136) are among those in support of the wordplay.
19. Normal Greek word order would place the first person in first position. The unusual placement, combined with hiatus, draw attention to ἐμοί.
20. αὐτόν is grammatically difficult to explain, but the sound map demonstrates the advantage of carrying on the ον rhyme as well as highlighting τὰ ἐμὰ σπλάγχνα.
21. Fitzmyer (p. 100) notes late Greek usages of τὰ σπλάγχνα that reflect Hebrew terms for belly and womb. He also notes Lightfoot's comparison of σπλάγχνα here with its usage in Artemidorus, in which it refers to one's children. Fitzmeyer also cites the use of τὰ σπλάγχνα for children in Eusebius *Historica ecclesiastica* 7.21.3. (p. 109). Thus Fitzmeyer recognizes the connection between the use of τὰ σπλάγχνα here with Paul's designation of Onesimus as τοῦ ἐμοῦ τέκνου.
22. Horsley (1988, pp. 181–3) strongly in support of Callahan fails to explain the grammar; Fitzmyer (p. 114), strongly rejecting. This construction is not only grammatically difficult, but given ὡς ἐμέ in period 7, colon 1, makes no sense. If Philemon is to receive Onesimus as Paul, then brother should be used in an equivalent sense.

23. *Lit.*, both in the flesh and in the Lord.
24. In fairness to Callahan, this colon is his strongest evidence that Onesimus is Philemon's brother. But the καὶ . . . καὶ construction fits better in the period as binding Paul and Philemon together and Paul's rhetorical argument.
25. Osiek (p. 140), for example, does not notice the turning point that sound indicates but instead finds ambiguity. "Verse 17 may have some connection to the above discussion, but perhaps not."
26. Lightfoot (p. 344) thinks Paul inscribed the whole letter because the reference here he says is "incidental."
27. This phrase is a formulaic phrase in papyrus letters for the signature of the sender.
28. Lohse (p. 204) refers to this a "promissory note" and Fitzmyer (p. 118) calls it an "IOU."
29. In order to avoid saying to you that you owe me your life.
30. Ὀνίνημι means to help or profit. Lightfoot (p, 345) and Osiek (p. 141) in support; BDF §488.1b against and Fitzmyer (p. 119) uncertain. Given the other wordplays in this letter, this one would also seem probable.
31. Τὸ σπλάγχνον occurs only 11 times in the New Testament. The verb σπλαγχνίζομαι occurs 12 times, for a total of 23 occurrences of this lexical stem in the New Testament. Only the noun occurs in Paul. Koester (1971, p. 550) observes that the term is also rare in LXX. "The noun is mostly restricted to later portions," usually when the Hebrew equivalent is not available. The verb occurs only twice, in Prv. 17:5 and 2 Macc. 6:8.
32. Koester (1971, p. 555) notes that τὸ σπλάγχνον in Paul has "lost completely the sense of creaturely or natural emotion; it also shows no traces here of the later Jewish sense of 'mercy. . . .'" Rather, "the word is used by Paul for the whole man."
33. Koester (1971, p. 555) insists that for Paul σπλάγχνα "remains a very strong and forceful term.".
34. Osiek, after noting that σπλάγχνα is "difficult to translate" in Philemon (p. 135, p. 137), concludes that in this instance it relates "explicitly to their [Paul's, Philemon's, and Onesimus'] common incorporation into Christ. (p. 141).
35. It is unclear what this means for slavery in general. Although Petersen has argued that the letter draws a more systematic conclusion, we find nothing in the sound map to require that interpretation.

WORKS CONSULTED

Callahan, Allen Dwight. 1993. Paul's Epistle to Philemon: Toward an Alternative *Argumentum*. *Harvard Theological Review* 86:357–76.

Dunn, James D. G. 1996. *The Epistles to the Colossians and to Philemon*. Edited by I. H. Marshall, W. W. Gasque and D. Hagner, *New Interntinal Greek Testament Commentary*. Grand Rapids: Eerdmans.

Fitzmyer, Joseph A. 2000. *The Letter to Philemon, Anchor Bible*. New York: Doubleday.

Horsley, Richard A. 1988. Paul and Slavery: A Critical Alternative to Recent Readings. *Semeia* 83/84:153–202.

Knox, John. 1935, Reprinted 1959. *Philemon Among the Letters of Paul*. Nashville: Abindgdon.

Koester, Helmut. 1971. σπλάγνον. 7: 548–59 In *Theological Dictionary of the New Testament*, edited by G. Kittel and G. Friedrich. Grand Rapids: Wm. B. Eerdmans.

Lampe, Peter. 1985. Keine 'Sklavenflucht' des Onesimus. *Zeitschrift für Neutestamentliche Wissenschaft* 76:135–37.

Lightfoot, J.B. 1897, Reprinted 1968. *St. Paul's Epistles to the Colossians and To Philemon*. Grand Rapids: Zondervan.

Lohse, Eduard. 1971. *Colossians and Philemon*. Translated by W. R. Poehlmann and R. J. Karris, *Hemeneia*. Philadelphia: Fortress Press.

Mitchell, Margaret M. 1995. John Chrysostom on Philemon: A Second Look. *Harvard Theological Review* 88:135–48.

Osiek, Carolyn. 2000. *Phillipians, Philemon*. Edited by V. P. Furnish, *Abingdon New Testament Commentaries*. Nashville: Abingdon.

Petersen, Norman. 1985. *Rediscovering Paul, Philemon and the Sociology of Paul's Narrative World*. Philadelphia: Fortress Press.

Ryan, Judith M. 2005. Philemon. In *Philippians and Philemon*, edited by B. B. Thurston and J. M. Ryan. Collegeville: Liturgical Press.

Schubert, Paul. 1939. *Form and Function of the Pauline Thanksgivings, Beihefte zur Zeitschrift für die neutestamentliche Wissenschaft und die Kunde der älteren Kirche*. Berlin: Töpelmann.

White, John L. 1971. The Structural Analysis of Philemon: A Point of Departure in the Formal Analysis of the Pauline Letter. *Society of Biblical Literature Seminar Papers 1971* 1:1–47.

Chapter 8

Hearing is Believing

Resurrection in John 20

INTRODUCTION

The resurrection appearances are distinctive features in John's gospel and as such have long attracted critical attention. The different portrayals of seeing the risen lord and coming to faith provide an interpretative key to the gospel. When understood only in terms of the gospel's plot, its characters' different experiences of the risen lord are muted, underplayed, and often misinterpreted. But a spoken performance conveys meaning that is independent of the words' semantic content. A sound map picks up these additional frequencies and tunes in to dimensions of meaning available only in sound. The author of John's gospel artfully employs a feature of the Greek language, verbal aspect, as scaffolding for his the gospel's unique theological perspective.

One of the real advances in Greek grammar in recent years concerns the elaboration of verbal aspect (Porter 1989; Fanning 1990; Porter 1994). Grammarians have long understood that the Greek tenses do not function primarily as temporal markers, as English tenses do. This difference has recently been clearly formulated in terms of verbal aspect, "how the verbal action was perceived to unfold" (Porter 1994, p 22).[1] Verbal aspect is one of the ways sound initiates an audience's visualization of narrated action. This is a difficult notion for us speakers of English to grasp, because for us tense signals time. Not for Greek speakers. It signals aspect—how to view an action.

The aorist aspect in Greek views an action as an entirety. Its name signals its meaning. From ὁριστός/ὁρίζειν, it designates something unlimited, whole or entire. The name also implies the horizon, or boundary against which something is viewed.[2] The present aspect views an action as durative or in progress, and draws attention to the action; the perfect views an action as reflecting a given, unchangeable, and often complex state of affairs, virtually always with implications for the future. The aorist is used when there is no reason to select the present or perfect. As the default aspect it has the least semantic load.

Verbal aspect can be understood in terms of stage directions to an audience as they construct a narrative. Imagine a stage in an amphitheater. The present aspect places the action in the foreground at center stage, while an aorist provides background. Action expressed in the perfect bridges the stage and the audience. The perfect takes place at the stage's apron, closing the distance between the narrative and the audience.

John 20, as well as the whole of the gospel of John, exploits the aspectual system's potential for a theological purpose. John 1:29–34 offers a simple example. John initially βλέπει (sees) Jesus and λέγει (says). This foregrounds his seeing and speech, to use a visual metaphor, and thereby underlines it. In v. 32 his witness is in the aorist, setting up the background. In the conclusion (v. 34) his climactic speech moves to the perfect, out on the apron, as he testifies to what he has seen: κἀγὼ ἑώρακα, καὶ μεμαρτύρηκα (I have seen this and I have certified that) "This is God's son." This confession, introduced in the perfect aspect, is the same one that will conclude chapter 20. To repeat, the present aspect foregrounds the action (seeing Jesus and saying "behold, the Lamb"); the aorist views the action in its entirely (John witnessed—this is what John does); while the perfect describes realities that impinge on the future and, in John, on the audience ("I have seen and bear witness that this one is the son of God").

NARRATIVE STRUCTURE

Chapter 20 represents a complete narrative in the fourth gospel's resurrection story. Its unified sounds, structure, themes and location designate the narrative's boundaries. It divides into two major sections, each with its own but similarly constructed introduction. Chapter 21, which employs a very different structure and takes place in a different location, can be clearly differentiated from chapter 20.[3]

The introductions to Chapter 20's two sections have multiple time references, including a repeated day marker. Each section has a thematic sound: τὸ μνημεῖον in section 1 and εἰρήνη ὑμῖν in section 2.

Section 1 (20:1)[4]

Τῇ δὲ μιᾷ τῶν σαββάτων Μαρία ἡ Μαγδαληνὴ ἔρχεται πρωῒ
σκοτίας ἔτι οὔσης εἰς τὸ μνημεῖον,

Section 2 (20:19)

Οὔσης οὖν ὀψίας τῇ ἡμέρᾳ ἐκείνῃ **τῇ μιᾷ σαββάτων**,
καὶ τῶν θυρῶν κεκλεισμένων
ὅπου ἦσαν οἱ μαθηταὶ διὰ τὸν φόβον τῶν Ἰουδαίων,
ἦλθεν ὁ Ἰησοῦς
Εἰρήνη ὑμῖν.

The section introductions exhibit many similarities. The repetition of τῇ μιᾷ (τῶν) σαββάτων (*lit.*, on the first day of the week) draws attention to the day of the week. The use of the cardinal instead of the ordinal number is normal in the New Testament and based on the LXX, yet is unusual in Hellenistic Greek.[5] In addition, the genitive absolute clauses, both employing οὔσης, indicate opposite ends of a day, from before sunrise to sunset. The action in each period is initiated by a form of ἔρχεσθαι (ἔρχεται, ἦλθεν, to come).

SECTION 1

UNIT 1

An Empty Tomb: Three Points of View

Section 1 contains two units with several signals noting a shift from one unit to the next. Unit 1 deals with the tomb's discovery (periods 1–6), while unit 2 concerns Mary Magdelene (periods 7–14).

In unit 1 every period repeats the phrase τὸ μνημεῖον (the tomb). Τὸ μνημεῖον occurs seven times, always at the end of a colon. Five times the phrase is εἰς (into) τὸ μνημεῖον and twice ἐκ (out of) τοῦ μνημείου.[6] Variation of the phrase from εἰς το ἐκ in the first three periods creates an ABBA pattern. Εἰς τὸ μνημεῖον is always used with some form of ἔρχεσθαι. The repetition of the lexeme μνημει- furnishes a unifying sound, theme and focal point for the unit. A minimal description of the tomb occurs in the previous story (19:41), but here its description is left to the imagination. As μνημει- repeats with a regular rhythm at the end of selected cola, the tomb's emptiness and the responses of the characters come to the fore.

The unit also employs additional sound clues to concentrate an audience's attention. The cola are short with few dependent or subordinate clauses. Except for the first period, each subsequent period of Section 1 is introduced by οὖν (*lit.*, then) in postpositive position.[7] The paratactic connector καί gives the unit an overall impression of simplicity and directness. This style is typical for historical narration.

Period 1[8]

1 Τῇ δὲ μιᾷ τῶν σαββάτων
Μαρία ἡ Μαγδαληνὴ ἔρχεται πρωῒ σκοτίας ἔτι οὔσης εἰς τὸ μνημεῖον,
2 καὶ βλέπει τὸν λίθον ἠρμένον ἐκ τοῦ μνημείου.

Mary Magdalene initiates the action. She has been mentioned only once before in the gospel with the beloved disciple, the mother of Jesus, and Mary the wife of Clopas at the foot of the cross (19:25). Period 1 contains a double time marker (Τῇ δὲ μιᾷ τῶν σαββάτων;

πρωῒ σκοτίας ἔτι οὔσης)[9] denoting a shift from the previous scene and a beginning of a new unit. Both cola of period 1 end with a μνημει-phrase, focusing attention on the tomb. Mary approaches under cover of σκοτία (darkness). Nicodemus (3:1–2) had come to Jesus at night (νύκτος), and since the gospel's prologue σκοτία (darkness) has functioned thematically.[10] The mention of darkness in period 1, occuring in the only subordinate phrase, indicates time while sounding symbolic overtones in the gospel.[11]

Period 2

1 τρέχει **οὖν**
2 καὶ ἔρχεται πρὸς Σίμωνα Πέτρον
καὶ πρὸς τὸν ἄλλον μαθητὴν ὃν ἐφίλει ὁ Ἰησοῦς,
3 καὶ λέγει αὐτοῖς,
4 Ἦραν τὸν κύριον ἐκ τοῦ μνημείου,
5 καὶ* οὐκ οἴδαμεν ποῦ*ἔθηκαν αὐτόν.

Period 2 begins with action. Its first colon includes only a predicate and the postpositive particle οὖν. Strong consonants (τ and χ) punctuate the action at the beginning of cola 1 and 2. Paratactic style takes hold in colon 2. No grammatical subordination occurs. The quick succession of verbs moves the action towards the two disciples. The double occurrence of πρός is unusual, but sets up a parallel between the unnamed disciple and Peter. Unlike Mary Magdalene, Peter has played an important narrative role since the gospel's early scenes, so the suggested elevation of the unnamed disciple to Peter's stature is provocative.

The other disciple, who surely corresponds to the beloved disciple (so, e.g., Bultmann 1971, p. 684; Brown 1970, v. 2, p. 983) has made only recent (though indeed significant) appearances in the narrative: first in 13:23 and then in 19:26 with Mary Magdalene at the cross. This unidentified disciple first appears at the last supper while the disciples are trying to ferret out the betrayer. He is identified only as ὃν ἠγάπα ὁ Ἰησοῦς. In his next[12] appearance at the cross where Jesus entrusts his mother to him, he is identified as τὸν μαθητὴν . . . ὃν ἠγάπα. Ὁ μαθητὴς ὃν ἀγάπα ὁ Ἰησοῦς[13] functions as a thematic phrase and a metonym that references and summarizes a narrative value.[14] In the Fourth Gospel this thematic phrase stands for the ideal disciple (Brown 1979, p. 31).[15] Despite efforts to solve the puzzle of the beloved but unnamed disciple's identity, it remains a mystery because we are not fully a part of the performance arena (Foley 1995, pp. 47–49) of the Fourth Gospel. The thematic phrase ὁ μαθητὴς ὃν ἀγάπα ὁ Ἰησοῦς is recast as τὸν ἄλλον μαθητὴν ὃν ἐφίλει ὁ Ἰησοῦς in period 2, colon 2.[16]

Mary's report to Peter and the other disciple in colon 4 reiterates the reference to the tomb and so keeps ἐκ τοῦ μνημείου alive in memory. The description of Jesus as ὁ κύριος (*lit.*, master/lord) is unusual for this Gospel.[17] Given the context of her report that "they have taken" him, it is surely not a christological title. Her report initially seems to confirm a rumor like that in Matthew's Gospel (27:64) that the body of Jesus was stolen.

The use of the plural οἴδαμεν (we [don't] know) in colon 5 has occasioned much comment (Brown, 1970, 2:984). But the gospel previously has employed the technique of the unexpected first person plural to engage an audience in the narrative. At the conclusion of the prologue, at its climactic moment, "the Word became flesh and lived ἐν ἡμῖν, καὶ ἐθεασάμεθα[18] his glory" (John 1:14). Likewise, when Nicodemus first addresses Jesus, he says, Ῥαββί, οἴδαμεν "that you are a teacher sent from God" (3:2).[19] Similarly here, the use of the first person plural draws an audience to Mary's point of view. Hers becomes the first response to the evidence of the missing ὁ κύριος.

Period 3

1 Ἐξῆλθεν **οὖν** ὁ Πέτρος καὶ ὁ ἄλλος μαθητής,
2 καὶ ἤρχοντο εἰς τὸ μνημεῖον.
3 ἔτρεχον δὲ οἱ δύο ὁμοῦ·
4 καὶ ὁ ἄλλος μαθητὴς προέδραμεν τάχιον τοῦ Πέτρου
5 καὶ ἦλθεν πρῶτος εἰς τὸ μνημεῖον,
6 καὶ παρακύψας βλέπει κείμενα τὰ*ὀθόνια,*
7 οὐ μέντοι*εἰσῆλθεν.

The recurrence of a predicate followed by οὖν signals the opening of a new period and suggests the emergence of a pattern. Period 3 continues in paratactic style. Verbs of motion introduced in period 2 (τρέχειν, ἔρχεσθαι, to run, to come) continue to plot the action. Both ὁ ἄλλος μαθητὴς (the other disciple) and εἰς τὸ μνημεῖον (into the tomb) occur twice in a patterned arrangement, with εἰς τὸ μνημεῖον in terminal position in cola 2 and 4, continuing the pattern established at the unit's beginning in period 1. The ὁ μαθητὴς ὃν ἀγάπα ὁ Ἰησοῦς, which had been recast in period 2, varies again in period 3 to become ὁ ἄλλος μαθητὴς προέδραμεν τάχιον τοῦ Πέτρου. The variation is reinforced in colon 5 with πρῶτος (first).This associates the προ/πρω sound with the other disciple, moving him into the tomb ahead of Peter and therefore able to be described as seeing the linen wrappings lying there. Κείμενα (lying) echoes the repeated tomb reference with its similar ending sound (κείμενα, μνημεῖον).

The shortness of the final colon and the hiatus in cola 6 and 7 draw attention to his action.

Period 4

1 ἔρχεται **οὖν** καὶ Σίμων Πέτρος ἀκολουθῶν αὐτῷ,
2 καὶ εἰσῆλθεν εἰς τὸ μνημεῖον·
3 καὶ θεωρεῖ τὰ*ὀθόνια κείμενα,
4 καὶ τὸ σουδάριον, ὃ*ἦν ἐπὶ τῆς κεφαλῆς αὐτοῦ,*
5 οὐ μετὰ τῶν ὀθονίων κείμενον
6 ἀλλὰ χωρὶς ἐντετυλιγμένον εἰς ἕνα τόπον.

In period 4, οὖν recurs at the beginning of the period, reinforcing its role as a period marker in this unit. Period 4 continues patterns established in this unit's previous periods. In colon 1, two verbs of motion plot the action, ἔρχεσθαι, as in periods 2 and 3, and ἀκολουθεῖν (*lit.*, to follow) instead of ἔρχεσθαι, emphasizing the recent designation of the other disciple as προ- and πρῶτος. The tomb phrase (εἰς τὸ μνημεῖον) at the end of colon 2 echoes the repeated phrase at the ends of cola 2 and 5 in the previous period. It reverberates again here in period 4 at the ends of cola 3 and 5 with the similar-sounding phrases τὰ ὀθόνια κείμενα and τῶν ὀθονίων κείμενον, repeating this sound from 3.6. The loose rhyme among μνημεῖον, κείμενα, and κείμενον associates related semantic ideas, tomb and lying. Simon Peter is the main actor in this period, but is described as "following him," sustaining the suggestion of his subordination to the other disciple.

Beginning in colon 3, the action shifts from verbs of motion to what Peter sees, with the repetition of τὰ ὀθόνια κείμενα from 3.6. The verb is θεωρεῖ, instead of βλέπει,[20] which was used for Mary in 1.2 and the other disciple in 3.6. The new predicate for seeing echoes the medial consonant ὀθόνια and focuses attention to what Peter sees. Peter becomes a witness to the body's not having been stolen, for the threefold reference to "linen lying about" and the neatly rolled up head covering implies that the body is missing but not stolen, otherwise the burial garments also would be missing.

Period 5

1 τότε***οὖν** εἰσῆλθεν καὶ ὁ*ἄλλος μαθητὴς ὁ*ἐλθὼν πρῶτος εἰς τὸ μνημεῖον,
2 καὶ*εἶδεν
3 καὶ*ἐπίστευσεν·
4 οὐδέπω γὰρ ᾔδεισαν τὴν γραφὴν ὅτι δεῖ*αὐτὸν ἐκ νεκρῶν ἀναστῆναι.

Period 5 continues the unit's established paratactic style with the postpositive οὖν marking a new period as previously in periods 2,

3, and 4. Now in period 5 the predicate follows οὖν, whereas before the predicate preceded it. Instead, οὖν is preceded by an adverb and separated from it by hiatus. Hiatus recurs in cola 2–4. The delayed verb at the period's beginning and the frequency of hiatus create listening space, a dramatic pause, while the other disciple approaches and enters the tomb, marked by repetition of the terminal εἰς τὸ μνημεῖον, repeating the phrase that has become this unit's distinctive sound signature.

The designation of the other disciple is varied here as ὁ*ἐλθὼν πρῶτος,[21] a transformation of the thematic ὁ μαθητὴς ὃν ἀγάπα ὁ Ἰησοῦς. This thematic phrase was initially varied in period 2 to ὁ ἄλλος μαθητὴς ὃν ἐφίλει ὁ Ἰησοῦς (2.2). Now in 5.1 the relative clause is transformed to ὁ*ἐλθὼν πρῶτος, again emphasizing the designation of the other disciple as προ- and πρῶτος in 3.4–5. The transformed phrase not only accents the disciple's (and by extension the community's) closeness to Jesus, but now places him ahead of Peter. This distancing from Peter continues with the next two verbs—καὶ*εἶδεν καὶ*ἐπίστευσεν (he saw and believed). These two verbs occur without objects, unlike the verbs of seeing in periods 1, 3, and 4. The dramatic pause created by the delayed predicate in colon 1 and frequent hiatus emphasize the extremely brief cola 2 and 3, composed solely of predicates and καὶ. The lack of elaboration and even physical movement stops the action momentarily, lending gravity to disciple's act of belief, which is the unit's narrative climax.

Colon 4 breaks the period's paratactic style. The colon is long, especially compared with the two preceding cola, and it includes a subordinate clause with frequent long vowel sounds. This stylistic shift sets colon 4 apart from the story line. By this change in style and intrusion into the narrative, the narrator's aside allows the listener time to register the full import of the disciple's action in the previous cola.[22]

Period 6

1 ἀπῆλθον οὖν πάλιν πρὸς αὐτοὺς οἱ μαθηταί.

A simple period concludes the unit. Οὖν is once again repeated to mark its beginning, and again the predicate, a form of ἐρχεσθαι, occurs in initial position. The colon's brevity and lack of embellishment, along with the usual form of period marker of οὖν preceded by a predicate, draws the unit to a close.

Verbs supply the driving force in this unit with a majority of verbs derived from compound forms of ἔρχεσθαι. Periods 1 and 2 use the present aspect in simple forms: ἔρχεται (1.1) . . . βλέπει (1.2) . . . τρέχει

(2.1) . . . ἔρχεται (2.2) . . . and λέγει (2.3).[23] Five present verbs in a row clearly place the story's action in the foreground.

In 3.1 when Peter and the other disciple arrive on stage, verbal aspect shifts to the aorist, moving the action into the background. Because the verbs of coming and running in 3.2, 3 are imperfects, they stretch out the action and thus create an interlude between the initial action of Mary and the paired pacing of the other two characters. The verbs τρέχει and ἔρχεται give the story a driving quality. Cola 3.4–5 which describe the activity of the other disciple maintain the background, elaborating the thematic phrase that identifies the disciple and reiterating εἰς τὸ μνημεῖον, focusing attention on the tomb as the narrative setting.

Peter's scene in period 4 indicates the ambivalence of his character in the Fourth Gospel. The verbs describing his action jump back and forth between present, aorist, and present, thus making it difficult for an audience to focus on the action. The description of what he observes links the linens lying there (τὰ ὀθόνια κείμενα) with both the verb in the present aspect (θεωρεῖ) and the tomb setting (εἰς τὸ μνημεῖον).These sound features draws attention to the linens, the head wrapping, and the tomb—and thus away from Peter.

The aorist aspect in period 5 for the disciple—εἰσῆλθεν, εἶδεν, ἐπίστευσεν[24]—describes the default, an action to be taken for granted from the beloved disciple. In contrast to Peter, his narration is strongly focused. Rather than say what the disciple believes or why he believes, the narrator presents an image of belief.[25] The beloved disciple thus becomes the first example of faith—a faith that becomes a model for the community claiming his heritage, and one that is not based on hearing, seeing, or touching the resurrected Jesus.[26]

This first unit presents three points of view on the empty tomb: Peter draws no conclusion; Mary Magdalene assumes that someone has stolen the body; only the beloved disciple, comes, sees, and has faith.

UNIT 2
A Voice in the Garden

Unit 2 is constructed as a dialogue. Fittingly, λέγει (*lit.*, she says) is one of its dominant sounds and becomes a period marker. Since the verb of saying is in the present aspect, it places the event in the foreground, not the remote past.[27]

The formula (λέγει αὐτῇ Ἰησοῦς, Period 9, 11, and 13) introduces Jesus' dialogue, thus setting speech in a prominent position. While parataxis is still present, the structure of its dialogue becomes a stronger organizing feature than parataxis, as in unit 1. Οὖν, a sound feature of the previous unit, recurs but no longer marks the beginning of periods.

Mary Magdalene

Period 7

1 Μαρία δὲ εἱστήκει **πρὸς τῷ μνημείῳ** ἔξω κλαίουσα.
2 ὡς **οὖν** ἔκλαιεν παρέκυψεν **εἰς τὸ μνημεῖον,**
3 καὶ θεωρεῖ δύο ἀγγέλους ἐν λευκοῖς καθεζομένους,
    ἕνα πρὸς τῇ κεφαλῇ
  καὶ ἕνα πρὸς τοῖς ποσίν,
4 ὅπου ἔκειτο τὸ σῶμα τοῦ Ἰησοῦ.
5 καὶ λέγουσιν αὐτῇ ἐκεῖνοι,
6 Γύναι, τί κλαίεις;

Following the paratactic unit 1, period 7 becomes stylistically more complex. Sound signals from unit 1 recur, but with a different structural placement. Unit 1's period marker οὖν does not occur until colon 2. The tomb phrase occurs in varied form in the first colon (πρὸς τῷ μνημείῳ), but in the middle of the colon, not at its end. It occurs in its established form at the end of colon 2, but is not repeated—and for the first time is not used with a form of ἔρχομαι. These reprisals of sound signals from unit 1 help ease the transition to a new unit. They no longer function structurally, but because they have become familiar, they tie the new period to the previous unit until new structural markers are established.

Period 7's opening cola twice describe Mary as weeping. The period's middle cola, 3 and 4, vividly depict the scene of angels at the tomb. Repeated ου/ευ and λ sounds focus attention on the angels themselves in colon 3 (δ**ύο** ἀγγέ**λους** ἐν **λευ**κοῖς) and parallel phrases (ἕνα πρὸς . . . ἕνα πρὸς) make explicit their placement relative to each other. Colon 4 employs repeated ο/ου/ω to shift attention back to the absent Jesus (**ὅπου** ἔκειτ**ο τὸ** σῶμα **τοῦ** Ἰησ**οῦ**).[28] Colon 5 introduces the unit's dialogue with a simple colon, καὶ λέγουσιν αὐτῇ ἐκεῖνοι.[29] Their question in colon 6 reiterates the theme that was stated in cola 1–2, thus drawing renewed attention to Mary's weeping and rounding the period to signal closure.[30]

Period 8

1 **λέγει*αὐτοῖς**
2 ὅτι*Ἦραν τὸν κύριόν μου,
3 καὶ*οὐκ οἶδα ποῦ*ἔθηκαν αὐτόν.
4 ταῦτα εἰποῦσα ἐστράφη εἰς τὰ ὀπίσω,

5 καὶ θεωρεῖ τὸν Ἰησοῦν ἑστῶτα,
6 καὶ οὐκ ᾔδει ὅτι Ἰησοῦς ἐστιν.

Period 8 reports Mary's response. The opening colon repeats the short introduction to direct speech introduced in 7.5, this time at the beginning of a period and marked by hiatus. Three short cola repeat Mary's report to the disciples, indicating that Mary draws no implication of a heavenly presence. Mary's speech differs slightly from her report to the disciples in 2.4–5, in that the verb is singular (οἶδα [I] instead of οἴδαμεν [we]) and μου substitutes for ἐκ τοῦ μνημείου. Frequent hiatus in Mary's speech, as in period 5 dealing with the other disciple, creates listening space for an audience and allows time to record it in memory. Colon 4 employs a participial phrase that delays and creates a transition to Mary's seeing Jesus. Cola 5 and 6 are set in parallel, reminiscent of the parallel phrases describing the angels. The singular οὐκ οἶδα (I don't know) in colon 3 is reinforced in colon 6 with οὐκ ᾔδει (she didn't know), emphasizing that Mary recognizes neither the angels nor Jesus.

Mary's turning is described in colon 4 in the aorist, and thereby placed in the background. Her seeing (θεωρεῖ, in the present aspect) in colon 5, is foregrounded and contrasts with Peter's θεωρεῖ (4.3) in that rather than discarded grave-cloths, she sees Jesus standing there. Ἑστῶτα (standing, in the perfect) is the first description of the risen Jesus. The perfect suggests that Jesus is still standing, waiting to be recognized by the audience, who have been presented the beloved disciple as a model for what they should do. While using verbs of seeing for Mary and the disciples, the author does not use "appearance" for Jesus. Instead, in this first case, a physical term is employed and is framed in the perfect aspect, suggesting that Jesus remains equally "standing" for the audience; they do not need an appearance.

Period 9

1 **λέγει*αὐτῇ** Ἰησοῦς,
2 Γύναι, τί κλαίεις;
3 τίνα ζητεῖς;

Period 9 repeats the speech introduction from the previous periods in this unit, this time including hiatus and the feminine pronoun. Jesus repeats the angels' question with an addition. Τίνα ζητεῖς (Who is it you're looking for?) The repetition of the angel's question in Jesus' speech replicates for the audience Mary's confusion about Jesus' identity. The addition of τίνα ζητεῖς in colon 3 signals a difference and leads their dialogue toward elaboration and resolution.

Period 10

1 ἐκείνη δοκοῦσα ὅτι*ὁ κηπουρός ἐστιν **λέγει*αὐτῷ**,
2 Κύριε,*
3 εἰ σὺ*ἐβάστασας **αὐτόν**,
4 εἰπέ μοι ποῦ*ἔθηκας **αὐτόν**,
5 κἀγὼ* **αὐτὸν** ἀρῶ.

In period 10 the opening formula λέγει*αὐτῷ, which has become a period marker, is delayed until the end of the first colon. The intervening phrase delays the action and intensifies the dramatic irony of Mary's inability to recognize the speaker. In colon 2, Mary's use of κύριε to address the one she takes to be the gardener indicates that the word is understood as the normal address for a male.[31] Hiatus again marks Mary's speech in cola 2–5. The consistent use of hiatus in Mary's speech resists the cultural tendency to dismiss women's speech and instead creates listening space for an audience, thereby marking Mary's speech as important. Repetition of αὐτόν balances cola 3–5 and places emphasis on Jesus. The final colon, although brief, employs balance, symmetry, hiatus and rhyming of κἀγὼ (so I) and ἀρῶ (take away) to draw attention to Mary's desire to be present with Jesus (αὐτόν, him).

Period 11

1 **λέγει*αὐτῇ** Ἰησοῦς,
2 Μαρία.

Period 12

1 στραφεῖσα*ἐκείνη **λέγει*αὐτῷ** Ἑβραϊστί,
2 Ραββουνι ὃ λέγεται Διδάσκαλε.

Period 11 opens with λέγει αὐτῇ reinforcing the unit's period marker. Jesus' speech has been marked by brevity throughout the unit but 11.2 consists of a single word, Mary's name. Period 12 repeats the period marker λέγει*αὐτῷ and relates Mary's one-word response, but the cola are elongated by an introductory participle (as in 8.4 and 10.1) and the narrator's translation of her appellation for Jesus.[32] Only their brief dialogue is narrated, not their actions nor Mary's emotional response, which an audience must supply. Mary did not recognize the physical body, but she does recognize the voice or λόγος. Voice, like breath (τὸ πνεῦμα), is a perfect model for spirit. It has body, but it is not physical (John 3:8).

Period 13

1 **λέγει*αὐτῇ** Ἰησοῦς,
2 Μή μου ἅπτου,*

3 οὔπω γὰρ ἀναβέβηκα πρὸς τὸν πατέρα·
4 πορεύου δὲ πρὸς τοὺς ἀδελφούς μου
5 καὶ εἰπὲ*αὐτοῖς,
6 Ἀναβαίνω πρὸς τὸν πατέρα μου καὶ πατέρα ὑμῶν
καὶ θεόν μου καὶ θεὸν ὑμῶν

Period 13 again employs the unit's period marker, λέγει αὐτῇ. Following a dialogue carried out previously in the unit with extremely brief cola, Jesus' speech in 13.2–6 is comparatively long. The period repeats ου/ευ/υ and η/α sounds throughout unifying the period and emphasizing the vowel sounds in colon 2, the first statement of Jesus' speech, Μή μου ἅπτου.[33] Colon 3 elaborates Jesus' prohibition in colon 2. Cola 4–5 sustain those vowel sounds as Jesus issues new instructions. In colon 6, he tells Mary to repeat his message to the disciples. The final rhyming around μου (my) and ὑμῶν (your) elongates the parallel, signals the period's closure and unites Jesus with those who believe.

The parallel elements in cola 3 and 6 are built around forms ἀναβαίνειν and πρὸς τὸν πατέρα. Jesus tells Mary not to continue clinging to him οὔπω γὰρ ἀναβέβηκα πρὸς τὸν πατέρα.[34] The perfect aspect views an action as perfected. The use of the negative indicates that the process of resurrection is not yet perfected. Ἀναβαίνειν functions significantly in the gospel. It has two primary uses. In the aorist it frequently narrates going up to Jerusalem to a feast (2:13. 5:11, 7:8, 10, 14; 11:55, 12:20). On three other occasions ἀναβαίνειν is associated with the son of man. In answer to Nathaniel, Jesus responds (λέγει):

Ἀμὴν ἀμὴν λέγω ὑμῖν,
ὄψεσθε τὸν οὐρανὸν ἀνεῳγότα
καὶ τοὺς ἀγγέλους τοῦ θεοῦ ἀναβαίνοντας
καὶ καταβαίνοντας ἐπὶ τὸν υἱὸν τοῦ ἀνθρώπου (1:51).[35]

This enigmatic statement is also programmatic and looks forward to the gospel's conclusion. Again in Jesus' dialogue with Nicodemus ἀναβαίνειν is associated with the son of man and ὑψωθῆναι (elevated or exalted).

καὶ οὐδεὶς ἀναβέβηκεν εἰς τὸν οὐρανὸν
εἰ μὴ ὁ ἐκ τοῦ οὐρανοῦ καταβάς, ὁ υἱὸς τοῦ ἀνθρώπου.
καὶ καθὼς Μωϋσῆς ὕψωσεν τὸν ὄφιν ἐν τῇ ἐρήμῳ,
οὕτως ὑψωθῆναι δεῖ τὸν υἱὸν τοῦ ἀνθρώπου,
ἵνα πᾶς ὁ πιστεύων ἐν αὐτῷ ἔχῃ ζωὴν αἰώνιον (3:13–15).[36]

Besides bringing together ἀναβαίνειν and ὑψωθῆναι, this passage also incorporates πιστεύειν. Thus when Jesus tells Mary that οὔπω γὰρ ἀναβέβηκα, he is indicating that the process laid out in the programatic statements in 1:51 and expanded upon in 3:13ff is not yet perfected. Faith is required to finish it.

Mary is to tell the disciples, Ἀναβαίνω πρὸς τὸν πατέρα. The present aspect depicts the process as in progress. The process is ongoing. Coming to faith is part of the process of ascending, lifting up.

Jesus' name initiates the ου sounds in period 13 and colon 2 immediately picks up on them. Colon 6 ends with the internal rhyme of μου/ὑμῶν, with Father and God being interchanged. The ου sounds are repeated in parallel phrases built on τὸν πατέρα **μου** (my father) and θεόν **μου** (my God). The reference to the disciples as **τοὺς** ἀδελφ**ούς** **μου** (my brothers) recalls the early Christian address. Those who believe in the ascending are a new family. Jesus acknowledges this by solemnly proclaiming Ἀναβαίνω πρὸς τὸν πατέρα μου καὶ πατέρα ὑμῶν καὶ θεόν μου καὶ θεὸν ὑμῶν. The balance of this phrase and τοὺς ἀδελφούς μου joins them together into the family of the divine fellowship.

Period 14

1 ἔρχεται Μαρία ἡ Μαγδαληνὴ ἀγγέλλουσα τοῖς μαθηταῖς
2 ὅτι Ἑώρακα τὸν κύριον,
3 καὶ ταῦτα εἶπεν αὐτῇ.

Period 14 sustains the α/η/ου sounds from the previous period; but its opening colon, elongated with a participle, marks the beginning of a new period. Unlike the previous period in unit 2 (8–13), period 14 does not include the period marker, λέγει αὐτῷ/αὐτῇ. Each successive colon is briefer than the preceding one and they reprise aspects of the unit's dialogue. These structural features draw the periods and unit to a close. Notably, all the periods in unit 2 except periods 12 and 13 end with brief cola instead of elongated ones, as expected in elegant prose. Period 12 is elongated by the narrator's translation and period 13 is elongated by the parallel based on ἀναβαίνειν and πρὸς τὸν πατέρα. The unit's the narrative climax occurs with one-word exchanges between Jesus and Mary, when he utters her name and she responds. Their clipped speech, peppered with hiatus, takes on an unusual sound signature. Like the empty tomb, the unit's speeches become important for what they do not contain, for what is absent.

Period 14 begins with Mary's action still in the present, but the last two cola shift. Colon 2 reports her speech directly, in first person and in the perfect aspect. Colon 3 is indirect speech by the narrator. The use of the perfect Ἑώρακα (I have seen) emphasizes the wholeness of

Mary's seeing and its continuing endurance. Mary becomes a model of faith. In this regard τὸν κύριον now refers to the risen Jesus and has become a christological title.

SECTION 2

UNIT 3

Εἰρήνη ὑμῖν

Period 15

1 Οὔσης οὖν ὀψίας τῇ ἡμέρᾳ ἐκείνῃ τῇ μιᾷ σαββάτων,
καὶ τῶν θυρῶν κεκλεισμένων
ὅπου ἦσαν οἱ μαθηταὶ διὰ τὸν φόβον τῶν Ἰουδαίων,
ἦλθεν ὁ Ἰησοῦς
2 καὶ ἔστη εἰς τὸ μέσον
3 καὶ λέγει αὐτοῖς,
4 **Εἰρήνη ὑμῖν.**

Period 15 exhibits multiple signs of a structural shift, marking not just a new period, but a new unit. A genitive absolute signals a time shift to evening (Οὔσης οὖν ὀψίας).[37] The paratactic style of unit 1 returns and οὖν recurs as a marker for a period's beginning. The reference to τῇ μιᾷ σαββάτων repeats the phrase introduced in 1.1, although in a new position. Unit 3's first colon contains several subordinate phrases before the main verbs, a style the previous units have not trained the ear to hear. A second genitive absolute in the perfect not only notes but accents the locked doors (τῶν θυρῶν κεκλεισμένων) and the disciples' fear (τὸν φόβον τών Ἰουδαίων). In colon 2, λέγει αὐτοῖς, the period marker from unit 2, occurs in the middle of the period. Although the phrase does not function structurally here, it invokes the earlier dialogue between Jesus and Mary, and focuses attention on Jesus' upcoming speech. Εἰρήνη ὑμῖν (*shalom*) is the normal Jewish greeting. As in his dialogue with Mary, his speech is extremely brief. Thus, as in periods 7, 9, and 11 in the previous unit, Jesus' speech in colon 2 ends the period with an abbreviated colon rather than an elongated one.

The verbs of cola 1 and 2 occur in the aorist, signaling the background or default modality, and Jesus' speech moves immediately to the foreground with the present aspect (λέγει). In period 9.2, verbs in the perfect aspect described Jesus' standing; now at the end of the elongated first colon and the beginning of colon 2, Jesus ἦλθεν καὶ ἔστη (came and stood). Just as forms of ἔρχομαι gave the sound signal in section 1, now ἦλθεν καὶ ἔστη form the background for describing Jesus' resurrection experience for the disciples.

Period 16

1 **καὶ τοῦτο εἰπὼν** ἔδειξεν τὰς χεῖρας καὶ τὴν πλευρὰν αὐτοῖς.
2 ἐχάρησαν οὖν οἱ μαθηταὶ ἰδόντες τὸν κύριον.
3 εἶπεν οὖν αὐτοῖς πάλιν,
4 Εἰρήνη ὑμῖν·
5 καθὼς ἀπέσταλκέν με ὁ πατήρ,
6 κἀγὼ πέμπω ὑμᾶς.

After Jesus' single-colon speech, period 16 begins with an introductory, subordinate phrase. The colon's narrated action is silent. The reference to the hands and side reverberate with images from earlier episodes in the gospel. The hands and the side show that the risen Jesus is the crucified Jesus, a theme implied before, now forcibly proclaimed. "Side" also points back to the passion's conclusion (19:31–7), in which the truth of what was reported was attested by the beloved disciple "that you also may believe" (19:35), and a passage from Zechariah 12:10 is quoted: "They shall look on him whom they have pierced" (19:37).

Cola 2 and 3 employ οὖν, the period marker from unit 1 that was repeated in period 15.1. It does not mark the beginning of a period, as in unit 1, but its twofold repetition in cola 2 and 3 suggests a sense of beginning, indicating that the silent actions narrated at the beginning of the period are preliminary to Jesus' upcoming speech. The elongated first and second cola suggest a progression of responses to the resurrected Jesus. The beloved disciple saw only an empty tomb and believed; Mary heard Jesus' voice and believed. Now the disciples see the hands and side of Jesus and they believe. The images become progressively more physical.

Colon 4 repeats Jesus' brief greeting. Cola 5 and 6 elaborate the greeting with parallel phrases (καθὼς . . . κἀγὼ). Such parallel elaboration has become typical of Jesus' speech in this episode, having occurred in the previous unit in periods 9 and 13, where the elaborated parallels become progressively longer.[38]

Period 17

1 **καὶ τοῦτο εἰπὼν** ἐνεφύσησεν
2 καὶ λέγει αὐτοῖς,
3 Λάβετε πνεῦμα ἅγιον·
4 ἄν τινων ἀφῆτε τὰς ἁμαρτίας
ἀφέωνται αὐτοῖς,
5 ἄν τινων κρατῆτε
κεκράτηνται.

Period 17 opens with a phrase repeated from the previous period, καὶ τοῦτο εἰπών (*lit.*, and saying this). The phrase has become this unit's period marker. In periods 16 and 17, the phrase emphasizes a previous speech by Jesus, introduces new narrated action and finally a closing speech by Jesus. The action narrated in colon 1 is brief—Jesus breathes, inviting an audience to anticipate speech.[39] Jesus' speech in cola 3–5 again includes a brief statement elaborated by cola set in parallel. As in Jesus' previous speeches in this episode, its introductory statement is notable for its brevity. Πνεῦμα ἅγιον (holy spirit) is rare in John (normally John uses πνεῦμα). Jesus was introduced by John the Baptist in 1:29 as "the Lamb of God ὁ αἴρων τὴν ἁμαρτίαν τοῦ κόσμου."[40] In this commission, that announcement finds its fulfillment. This unit began with a reference to the disciples' fear of the Judeans and Jesus showing them his side. The audience now begins to put the pieces together. The first part of the quotation from Zechariah 12:10—"And I will pour out on the house of David and the inhabitants of Jerusalem a spirit of compassion and supplication, so that when they look on him whom they have pierced they shall mourn for him as one mourns for an only child, and weep bitterly over him as one weeps over a first-born"—is now fulfilled in the disciples' commission. The Zechariah quotation and the announcement of John the Baptist form the context in which this commission is to be understood. Cola 4 and 5 employ an ellipsis in the last colon (τὰς ἁμαρτίας, αὐτοῖς) and elongation by frequent long vowel sounds. The structure of Jesus' speech signals closure by invoking the format of Jesus' previous speeches to Mary and elongating the parallel cola.

UNIT 4
Touching and Feeling

Period 18

1 Θωμᾶς δὲ εἷς ἐκ τῶν δώδεκα,
2 ὁ λεγόμενος Δίδυμος,
3 οὐκ ἦν μετ' αὐτῶν ὅτε ἦλθεν Ἰησοῦς.
4 ἔλεγον **οὖν** αὐτῷ οἱ ἄλλοι μαθηταί,
5 *Ἑωράκαμεν τὸν κύριον.

In the first colon of period 18, δέ, together with the elaborate naming of a new character and a note about his absence, indicate a scene shift and a new unit. Naming and place are among the techniques the author has employed to indicate scene shift in each of this episode's units. The scene-changing signals are weaker here than previously, suggesting a minor scene shift. Repeated ω sounds in colon 1 associate Thomas' name with his status as one of the Twelve (εἷς ἐκ τῶν δώδεκα), while the explanatory phrase in colon 2 offers an alternative name.

Thomas has appeared twice before in the Gospel. In his first appearance (11:16) the translation ὁ λεγόμενος Δίδυμος[41] was also given. In his second appearance, he is identified only as Θωμᾶς (14:5). In this third appearance, an additional phrase is used to identify him: εἷς ἐκ τῶν δώδεκα.

Even though "the Twelve have little role" in fourth gospel (Brown, 1970, 2.10224),[42] the term functions as a conventional title. The Twelve make only one other appearance in the gospel: in chapter 6 a serious schism occurs among the disciples and Jesus questions the twelve about whether they, too, wish to depart. This leads to a version of Peter's confession in the fourth gospel.

Κύριε,
πρὸς τίνα ἀπελευσόμεθα;
ῥήματα ζωῆς αἰωνίου ἔχεις,
καὶ ἡμεῖς πεπιστεύκαμεν
καὶ ἐγνώκαμεν
ὅτι σὺ εἶ ὁ ἅγιος τοῦ θεοῦ (6:68–9).[43]

This provokes the fourth gospel's version of Jesus' "get behind me, Satan" speech.

Οὐκ ἐγὼ ὑμᾶς τοὺς δώδεκα ἐξελεξάμην,
καὶ ἐξ ὑμῶν εἷς διάβολός ἐστιν;
ἔλεγεν δὲ τὸν Ἰούδαν Σίμωνος Ἰσκαριώτου·
οὗτος γὰρ ἔμελλεν παραδιδόναι αὐτόν, εἷς [ὢν] ἐκ τῶν δώδεκα (6:70–1).[44]

Thus the title εἷς ἐκ τῶν δώδεκα in the fourth gospel has not only the connotation of having been chosen by Jesus, but also of being identified with Judas. Accordingly, its reference is ambiguous.

The explanation of his name, ὁ λεγόμενος Δίδυμος, is also somewhat ambiguous. Thomas' first appearance in this gospel (11:16) comes at the end of the Lazarus story. Immediately after Thomas' name (from the Hebrew *thoma,* twin) is translated, he says, "Let's go along too, so we can die with him." His statement indicates that he does not understand. The second appearance of Thomas is in the last discourse, where he responds to Jesus' statement that he must depart.

Κύριε,
οὐκ οἴδαμεν ποῦ ὑπάγεις·
πῶς δυνάμεθα τὴν ὁδὸν εἰδέναι (14:5).[45]

But as we have seen, οὐκ οἶδα appears in Mary's initial response to the angels' question of why she is weeping. Once again, then, Thomas is made to appear uncomprehending.[46]

Having introduced Thomas into the narrative, period 18 closes (colon 5) with an echo of Mary Magadelene's confession in 14.2–3. Again in colon 4, οὖν continues to function as an introduction to an important speech rather than as a period marker. In colon 5, the disciples' report is brief and set apart from the period by hiatus. Their seeing maintains the perfect aspect, consistent with Mary's speech in period 14. They have seen the whole process and their seeing will endure.

Period 19

1 ὁ δὲ εἶπεν αὐτοῖς,
2 Ἐὰν μὴ * ἴδω *ἐν ταῖς χερσὶν αὐτοῦ τὸν τύπον τῶν ἥλων
3 καὶ βάλω τὸν δάκτυλόν μου* εἰς τὸν τύπον τῶν ἥλων
4 καὶ βάλω μου τὴν χεῖρα* εἰς τὴν πλευρὰν αὐτοῦ,
5 *οὐ μὴ πιστεύσω.

Thomas' response to the disciples' declaration is a balanced period with cola set in parallel with frequent long vowel sounds, and the ω sound of the verbs tying the four cola of his speech together. Colon 2 introduces the sound with ἴδω (I see), which is set apart in the colon by hiatus at the beginning and end. The repetition of τὸν τύπον τῶν ἥλων (*lit.*, mark of the nail) at the end of cola 2 and 3, and the sandwiching of χερσὶν / δάκτυλόν / χεῖρα[47] between the first person verbs and the repeated phrase, tie the first three cola of his speech together. The negative particle in colon 2, the marking of seeing with hiatus and the double negative in colon 5, introduced by hiatus, give a strong negative cast to the whole speech. The οὐ μὴ with the aorist subjunctive, a classical form,[48] emphasizes an emphatic negative in the future: "Never will I." The colon's shortness in comparison to the length of the other cola in the period draws attention to this negative declaration. The period's conclusion recalls the conclusion of Mary's speech to the person she took to be a gardener in period 10. Mary's speech also contained balanced cola with a repeated medial sound (αὐτὸν) and a brief ending: κἀγὼ αὐτὸν ἀρῶ. Mary's conclusion, however was framed positively, whereas Thomas' concluding statement is emphatically negative.

UNIT 5

Period 20

1 Καὶ μεθ' ἡμέρας ὀκτὼ πάλιν ἦσαν ἔσω οἱ μαθηταὶ*αὐτοῦ
καὶ Θωμᾶς μετ' αὐτῶν.

2 ἔρχεται ὁ Ἰησοῦς τῶν θυρῶν κεκλεισμένων,
3 καὶ*ἔστη*εἰς τὸ μέσον
4 καὶ*εἶπεν,
5 **Εἰρήνη ὑμῖν**.

Period 20 begins with a time indicator that suggests another unit division, although it surely continues the narrative begun in period 15. A week has passed. Period 20 echoes period 15 and the beginning of unit 3, with its time marker, introductory phrases, and concluding cola with Jesus' greeting of the disciples. Colon 3 creates listening space around Jesus' standing through hiatus, a sound device that has marked the important moments in Jesus' appearances. As in 8.5 and 15.2, Jesus' standing is expressed in the perfect, suggesting Jesus' continuing presence in the community. Jesus' speech continues the pattern of concluding a period with a brief colon.

Period 21

1	εἶτα λέγει τῷ Θωμᾷ,			
2		Φέρε τὸν δάκτυλόν	**σου**	ὧδε
3	καὶ	*ἴδε τὰς χεῖράς	**μου**	
4	καὶ	φέρε τὴν χεῖρά	**σου**	
5	καὶ	βάλε εἰς τὴν πλευράν	**μου**	
6	καὶ μὴ		γίν**ου**	*ἄπιστος
7	ἀλλὰ			πιστός.

In period 21, Jesus elaborates his brief greeting, and again the elaboration is set in balanced, parallel cola that match the parallelism of Thomas' speech and respond to each of Thomas' demands. But whereas Thomas' speech consisted of three parallel cola with a concluding statement (οὐ μὴ πιστεύσω, I'll never believe), Jesus speech answers Thomas' conditions with four parallel cola (2–5) with a concluding invitation to belief, also set in parallel (cola 6–7). Jesus' speech doubles Thomas' use of χείρ, first referring to Jesus' hands (colon 3), then Thomas' (colon 4). Hiatus in Jesus' speech creates listening space around seeing and believing, as in Thomas' speech in period 19. Rhyming pronouns at the ends of these cola form an ABAB pattern of σου, μου, σου, μου. This ου sound is then repeated in the final imperative γίνου, tying all five cola together and uniting Thomas with Jesus. His negative statement in colon 6 (with μή) softens Thomas' negative statement (with ού μὴ).[49] The final colon of Jesus speech (7) is balanced with the contrast ἄπιστος ἀλλὰ πιστός.[50] Such elongated parallelism has become typical of Jesus' speech when it expands on a short initial statement.

Period 22

1 ἀπεκρίθη Θωμᾶς καὶ*εἶπεν αὐτῷ,
2 Ὁ κύριός **μου** καὶ ὁ θεός **μου**.

Period 22 reports Thomas' response in a format that conforms to Jesus' speech, with its expanded introduction and single-colon, balanced speech. Colon 2 repeats μου, a unifying sound in the preceding period. The repeated μου makes it Thomas' personal confession.[51]

Thomas' response to Jesus' command is often taken by commentators as the Gospel's climax. But from the point of view of sound, this can hardly be. In period 22 both verbs occur in the aorist and the formula ἀπεκρίθη καὶ εἶπεν (*lit.*, he answered and said) is the common sign of narration in John's Gospel, occurring 79 times. This pushes Thomas' confession into the background.[52] The narrative has also consistently marked with brevity and hiatus the dramatic moments in which characters come to faith. Period 22 is not set apart as a dramatic moment. Although the period is brief, its cola are expanded beyond what is grammatically necessary. Thomas' speech is not economical but expressed in parallel form.

Period 23

1 **λέγει αὐτῷ** ὁ Ἰησοῦς,
2 Ὅτι*ἑώρακάς με πεπίστευκας;
3 μακάριοι οἱ μὴ*ἰδόντες καὶ πιστεύσαντες.

Jesus' response to Thomas' confession is introduced with λέγει, a period marker in unit 2 with Jesus' dialogue with Mary Magdalene. As in unit 2 the present aspect foregrounds the action. Again Jesus' speech is framed in parallel cola. Implicit in the question, "Have you believed?" is its tentative tone, whereas Ἑωράκαμεν (we've seen) in the perfect is the true confession that instigated the Thomas sequence (18.5). Indeed, Jesus questions the relationship between seeing and believing, as indicated by incidences of hiatus that precede ἑώρακάς in colon 2 and ἰδόντες in colon 3. Mary had seen Jesus but thought he was the gardener; it was his voice to which she responded Ἑώρακα (14.2). So too it is with the disciples; Jesus comes and stands and speaks and they see. Consistently Jesus comes and speaks and they see. Sight follows voice, sound.

The beatitude in colon 3 is cast in two aorist participles, indicating the background and divorcing seeing and believing. This is the risen Jesus' position. Truly blessed are those who believe without seeing, like the beloved disciple—and like Mary Magdalene, who hears and then says Ἑώρακα.

In the end, the narrative comes back to its first examples of faith. As Lindars has observed, "Being absent when Jesus appeared to the disciples on Easter night, Thomas was virtually in the position of the Christian who has not seen the risen Jesus, and he should not have needed a further appearance in order to come to faith" (1972, p. 616).[53] Thus the narrator suggests that faith comes from hearing the word, not seeing the risen Jesus.

Period 24

1 Πολλὰ μὲν **οὖν** καὶ*ἄλλα σημεῖα*ἐποίησεν ὁ Ἰησοῦς ἐνώπιον τῶν μαθητῶν [αὐτοῦ],
2 ἃ οὐκ ἔστιν γεγραμμένα*ἐν τῷ βιβλίῳ τούτῳ·
3 ταῦτα δὲ γέγραπται
4 ἵνα πιστεύσητε
5 ὅτι Ἰησοῦς ἐστιν ὁ Χριστὸς ὁ υἱὸς τοῦ θεοῦ,
6 καὶ ἵνα πιστεύοντες ζωὴν ἔχητε*ἐν τῷ ὀνόματι αὐτοῦ.

Period 24 concludes the unit, both sections, and probably originally the gospel. The construction of its cola signals a shift in voice. The cola are longer than those in any period in this unit. Like previous intrusions of the narrator, these cola are elongated and set in parallel. Colon 1 mentions many signs and thus expands the scene to a encompass a broader scope that now includes the gospel's audience. The doubled occurrence of γράφειν (to write) in cola 2 and 3 and paired ἵνα clauses in cola 4 and 6 frame the closing in parallel cola, connected with the repeated concluding ου sound in cola 5 and 6. Thus the narrator's voice mimics the voice of Jesus in the elaborated parts of his speeches, set in parallel. The voice of Jesus has become conflated with the narrator's voice, and both are meant to bring the audience to faith.

The use of the perfect rather than the aorist to describe the writing of the "book" indicates the book's continuing validity. The perfect of γράφειν has frequently been used by the fourth gospel and the other gospels to indicate the fulfillment of scripture. The book is at the apron of the stage, impinging on the audience, making a claim that its writing has enduring value. Furthermore, writing in the ancient world is strongly connected with auditory activity. One writes so that others may hear.

Cola 4 and 6 are built around πιστευ-.[54] The purpose of writing/hearing is that of bringing to faith. In between cola 3 and 5 is the confession of faith, ὁ Χριστὸς ὁ υἱὸς τοῦ θεοῦ. Thus cola 4 and 6 form an inclusio around the confession of faith.

This final period argues that faith now comes through hearing—and therefore, by implication, not through seeing. The audience of the book confronts in its sound the Christ, the son of God. The conclusion is an apologetic for the book itself. The community needs nothing else. It has been written (γέγραπται), and they know ποῦ ἔθηκαν αὐτόν (where they've put him): Jesus still stands in the midst of the community. Their hearing of the book enables them to say Ἑωράκαμεν τὸν κύριον (we've seen the master).

CONCLUSION

Sound mapping is not a substitute for exegesis but it lays a foundation. Exegesis that ignores sounds, ignores clues to interpretation. The sound map of John 20 makes several important contributions.

Again, sound emerges as the primary clue to unit definition and narrative structure. The episode's first section employs strong auditory signals to unify its two units. Unit 1, the tomb's discovery, repeats τὸ μνηεῖον throughout at the ends of cola, like a slow pulse on a kettledrum. Interplay between Peter and the beloved disciple employs sound signals to imply shifts in the men's relative status. Chief among these is the transformation of the thematic phrase that names the beloved disciple. Unit 2 is punctuated with λέγει, stressing the immediacy of its dialogue. Unit 3 marks its periods with καὶ τοῦτο εἰπών, shifting from unit 2's sole emphasis on speech to the actions that follow speech. The closing units 4 and 5 are organized around the naming and identify of Thomas and expanded speeches set in parallel. In John 20, elaboration is anticlimactic, while climactic moments are expressed in single-cola speeches.

Finally, we have seen that the author's dramatic use of verbal aspect, combined with other sound cues, suggests how each scene should be viewed and interpreted. In John's gospel, verbal aspect serves as a primary clue to a character's progress in the journey of faith, and the resurrection appearances provide the key to the author's dramatic use of verbal aspect throughout the gospel.

The sound map shows that Thomas' confession is not the climax but one in a series of examples of coming to faith. All come to faith, yet in different ways. The beloved disciple and Mary Magdalene are held up as the prime examples because they, like the gospel's auditors, come to faith by hearing Jesus' words. Mary comes to believe not when she sees Jesus' face, but when she hears his voice. Thomas does not believe when he places his hands in Jesus' wounds, but when he hears Jesus' invitation to see and touch him. His story is framed as denouement, following the climactic moments of silence and emptiness at the tomb. His speech style is conflated with the elaborated style of speech that has become typical of both Jesus and the narrator, not with Jesus' brief and dramatic announcements to Mary and the disciples.

As these differences unfold, verbal aspect signals the dynamics of each character's journey of faith and suggests how the gospel's audience should come to faith as well. The present and perfect aspects depict living, active faith that does not depend on seeing proof. The narrator's voice approves a way of coming to faith that depends only on hearing the gospel. Thomas' story makes explicit what the narrative's climax implies: that hearing, not seeing, is believing.

Appendix

Sound Map on The Resurrection

John 20

SECTION 1: τὸ μνημεῖον

UNIT 1

Period 1

1 Τῇ δὲ μιᾷ τῶν σαββάτων
Μαρία ἡ Μαγδαληνὴ ἔρχεται πρωῒ σκοτίας ἔτι οὔσης
εἰς τὸ μνημεῖον,
2 καὶ βλέπει τὸν λίθον ἠρμένον
ἐκ τοῦ μνημείου.

Period 2

1 τρέχει **οὖν**
2 καὶ ἔρχεται πρὸς Σίμωνα Πέτρον
καὶ πρὸς τὸν ἄλλον μαθητὴν ὃν ἐφίλει ὁ Ἰησοῦς,
3 καὶ λέγει αὐτοῖς,
4 Ἦραν τὸν κύριον
ἐκ τοῦ μνημείου,
5 καὶ* οὐκ οἴδαμεν ποῦ*ἔθηκαν αὐτόν.

Period 3

1 Ἐξῆλθεν **οὖν** ὁ Πέτρος καὶ ὁ ἄλλος μαθητής,
2 καὶ ἤρχοντο εἰς τὸ μνημεῖον.
3 ἔτρεχον δὲ οἱ δύο ὁμοῦ·
4 καὶ ὁ ἄλλος μαθητὴς προέδραμεν τάχιον τοῦ Πέτρου
5 καὶ ἦλθεν πρῶτος εἰς τὸ μνημεῖον,
6 καὶ παρακύψας βλέπει κείμενα τὰ*ὀθόνια,*
7 οὐ μέντοι*εἰσῆλθεν.

Period 4

1 ἔρχεται **οὖν** καὶ Σίμων Πέτρος ἀκολουθῶν αὐτῷ,
2 καὶ εἰσῆλθεν εἰς τὸ μνημεῖον·
3 καὶ θεωρεῖ τὰ*ὀθόνια κείμενα,
4 καὶ τὸ σουδάριον, ὃ*ἦν ἐπὶ τῆς κεφαλῆς αὐτοῦ,*
5 οὐ μετὰ τῶν ὀθονίων κείμενον
6 ἀλλὰ χωρὶς ἐντετυλιγμένον εἰς ἕνα τόπον.

Period 5

1 τότε***οὖν** εἰσῆλθεν καὶ ὁ ἄλλος μαθητὴς ὁ ἐλθὼν πρῶτος
εἰς τὸ μνημεῖον,
2 καὶ εἶδεν
3 καὶ ἐπίστευσεν·
4 οὐδέπω γὰρ ᾔδεισαν τὴν γραφὴν ὅτι δεῖ αὐτὸν ἐκ νεκρῶν
ἀναστῆναι.

Period 6

1 ἀπῆλθον **οὖν** πάλιν πρὸς αὐτοὺς οἱ μαθηταί.

UNIT 2

Period 7

1 Μαρία δὲ εἱστήκει **πρὸς τῷ μνημείῳ** ἔξω κλαίουσα.
2 ὡς **οὖν** ἔκλαιεν παρέκυψεν **εἰς τὸ μνημεῖον,**
3 καὶ θεωρεῖ δύο ἀγγέλους ἐν λευκοῖς καθεζομένους,
ἕνα πρὸς τῇ κεφαλῇ
καὶ ἕνα πρὸς τοῖς ποσίν,
4 ὅπου ἔκειτο τὸ σῶμα τοῦ Ἰησοῦ.
5 καὶ λέγουσιν αὐτῇ ἐκεῖνοι,
6 Γύναι, τί κλαίεις;

Period 8

1 **λέγει*αὐτοῖς**
2 ὅτι*Ἦραν τὸν κύριόν μου,
3 καὶ*οὐκ οἶδα ποῦ*ἔθηκαν αὐτόν.
4 ταῦτα εἰποῦσα ἐστράφη εἰς τὰ ὀπίσω,
5 καὶ θεωρεῖ τὸν Ἰησοῦν ἑστῶτα,
6 καὶ οὐκ ᾔδει ὅτι Ἰησοῦς ἐστιν.

Period 9

1 **λέγει*αὐτῇ** Ἰησοῦς,
2 Γύναι, τί κλαίεις;
3 τίνα ζητεῖς;

Period 10

1 ἐκείνη δοκοῦσα ὅτι*ὁ κηπουρός ἐστιν **λέγει*αὐτῷ,**
2 Κύριε,*
3 εἰ σὺ*ἐβάστασας **αὐτόν,**
4 εἰπέ μοι ποῦ*ἔθηκας **αὐτόν,**
5 κἀγὼ* **αὐτὸν** ἀρῶ.

Period 11
1 **λέγει*αὐτῇ** Ἰησοῦς,
2 Μαρία.

Period 12
1 στραφεῖσα*ἐκείνη **λέγει*αὐτῷ** Ἑβραϊστί,
2 Ραββουνι ὃ λέγεται Διδάσκαλε.

Period 13
1 **λέγει*αὐτῇ** Ἰησοῦς,
2 Μή μου ἅπτου,*
3 οὔπω γὰρ ἀναβέβηκα πρὸς τὸν πατέρα·
4 πορεύου δὲ πρὸς τοὺς ἀδελφούς μου
5 καὶ εἰπὲ*αὐτοῖς,
6 Ἀναβαίνω πρὸς τὸν πατέρα μου καὶ πατέρα ὑμῶν
καὶ θεόν μου καὶ θεὸν ὑμῶν

Period 14
1 ἔρχεται Μαρία ἡ Μαγδαληνὴ ἀγγέλλουσα τοῖς μαθηταῖς
2 ὅτι Ἑώρακα τὸν κύριον,
3 καὶ ταῦτα εἶπεν αὐτῇ.

SECTION 2: Εἰρήνη ὑμῖν

UNIT 3

Period 15
1 Οὔσης οὖν ὀψίας τῇ ἡμέρᾳ ἐκείνῃ τῇ μιᾷ σαββάτων,
καὶ τῶν θυρῶν κεκλεισμένων
ὅπου ἦσαν οἱ μαθηταὶ διὰ τὸν φόβον τῶν Ἰουδαίων,
ἦλθεν ὁ Ἰησοῦς
2 καὶ ἔστη εἰς τὸ μέσον
3 καὶ λέγει αὐτοῖς,
4 **Εἰρήνη ὑμῖν.**

Period 16
1 **καὶ τοῦτο εἰπὼν** ἔδειξεν τὰς χεῖρας καὶ τὴν πλευρὰν αὐτοῖς.
2 ἐχάρησαν οὖν οἱ μαθηταὶ ἰδόντες τὸν κύριον.
3 εἶπεν οὖν αὐτοῖς πάλιν,
4 Εἰρήνη ὑμῖν·
5 καθὼς ἀπέσταλκέν με ὁ πατήρ,
6 κἀγὼ πέμπω ὑμᾶς.

Period 17
1 **καὶ τοῦτο εἰπὼν** ἐνεφύσησεν
2 καὶ λέγει αὐτοῖς,

3 Λάβετε πνεῦμα ἅγιον·
4 ἄν τινων ἀφῆτε τὰς ἁμαρτίας
ἀφέωνται αὐτοῖς,
5 ἄν τινων κρατῆτε
κεκράτηνται.

UNIT 4

Period 18

1 Θωμᾶς δὲ εἷς ἐκ τῶν δώδεκα,
2 ὁ λεγόμενος Δίδυμος,
3 οὐκ ἦν μετ' αὐτῶν ὅτε ἦλθεν Ἰησοῦς.
4 ἔλεγον **οὖν** αὐτῷ οἱ ἄλλοι μαθηταί,
5 Ἑωράκαμεν τὸν κύριον.

Period 19

1 ὁ δὲ εἶπεν αὐτοῖς,
2 Ἐὰν μὴ ἴδω ἐν ταῖς χερσὶν αὐτοῦ τὸν τύπον τῶν ἥλων
3 καὶ βάλω τὸν δάκτυλόν μου εἰς τὸν τύπον τῶν ἥλων
4 καὶ βάλω μου τὴν χεῖρα εἰς τὴν πλευρὰν αὐτοῦ,
5 οὐ μὴ πιστεύσω.

UNIT 5

Period 20

1 Καὶ μεθ' ἡμέρας ὀκτὼ πάλιν ἦσαν ἔσω οἱ μαθηταὶ αὐτοῦ
καὶ Θωμᾶς μετ' αὐτῶν.
2 ἔρχεται ὁ Ἰησοῦς τῶν θυρῶν κεκλεισμένων,
3 καὶ ἔστη εἰς τὸ μέσον
4 καὶ εἶπεν,
5 **Εἰρήνη ὑμῖν**.

Period 21

1 εἶτα λέγει τῷ Θωμᾷ,
2 Φέρε τὸν δάκτυλόν **σου** ὧδε
3 καὶ ἴδε τὰς χεῖράς **μου**
4 καὶ φέρε τὴν χεῖρά **σου**
5 καὶ βάλε εἰς τὴν πλευράν **μου**
6 καὶ μὴ γίν**ου** ἄπιστος
7 ἀλλὰ πιστός.

Period 22

1 ἀπεκρίθη Θωμᾶς καὶ εἶπεν αὐτῷ,
2 Ὁ κύριός **μου** καὶ ὁ θεός **μου**.

Period 23

1 **λέγει αὐτῷ** ὁ Ἰησοῦς,
2 Ὅτι ἑώρακάς με πεπίστευκας;
3 μακάριοι οἱ μὴ ἰδόντες καὶ πιστεύσαντες.

Period 24

1 Πολλὰ μὲν **οὖν** καὶ ἄλλα σημεῖα ἐποίησεν ὁ Ἰησοῦς ἐνώπιον
τῶν μαθητῶν [αὐτοῦ],

2 ἃ οὐκ ἔστιν γεγραμμένα ἐν τῷ βιβλίῳ τούτῳ·

3 ταῦτα δὲ γέγραπται

4 ἵνα πιστεύσητε

5 ὅτι Ἰησοῦς ἐστιν ὁ Χριστὸς ὁ υἱὸς τοῦ θεοῦ,

6 καὶ ἵνα πιστεύοντες ζωὴν ἔχητε ἐν τῷ ὀνόματι αὐτοῦ.

English Translation

SECTION 1: THE TOMB

UNIT 1

Period 1

1 On Sunday,
by the half-light of the early morning, Mary of Magdala comes to the tomb

2 and sees that the stone has been moved away from the tomb.

Period 2

1 So she runs

2 and comes to Simon Peter
and the other disciple, the one that Jesus loved most,

3 and tells them,

4 "They've taken the Master from the tomb,

5 and we don't know where they've put him."

Period 3

1 So Peter and the other disciple went out,

2 and they make their way to the tomb.

3 The two of them were running along together,

4 but the other disciple ran faster than Peter

5 and was the first to reach the tomb.

6 Stooping down, he could see the strips of burial cloth lying there;

7 but he didn't go in.

Period 4

1 Then Simon Peter comes along behind him

2 and went in.

3 He too sees the strips of burial cloth there,

4 and also the cloth they had used to cover his head,

5 lying not with the strips of burial cloth

6 but rolled up by itself.

Period 5

1 Then the other disciple, who had been the first to reach the tomb, came in.

2 He saw all this,
3 and he believed.
4 But neither of them yet understood the prophecy that he was destined to rise from the dead.

Period 6

1 So these disciples went back home.

UNIT 2

Period 7

1 Mary, however, stood crying outside,
2 and in her tears she stooped to look into the tomb,
3 and she sees two heavenly messengers in white seated,
    one at the head
    and the other at the feet,
4 where Jesus' body had lain.
5 "Woman, why are you crying?"
6 they ask her.

Period 8

1 She tells them,
2 "They've taken my Master away,
3 and I don't know where they've put him."
4 No sooner had she said this than she turned around
5 and sees Jesus standing there,
6 but she didn't know that it was Jesus.

Period 9

1 Jesus says to her,
2 "Woman, why are you crying?
3 Who is it you're looking for?"

Period 10

1 She could only suppose that it was the gardener, and so she says to him,
2 "Please, mister,
3 if you've moved him,
4 tell me where you've put him
5 so I can take him away."

Period 11

1 Jesus says,
2 "Mary."

Period 12

1 She turns around and exclaims in Hebrew,
2 "Rabbi!" (which means "Teacher").

Period 13

1 Jesus tells her,
2 "Don't touch me,"
3 because I have not yet gone back to the Father.
4 But go to my brothers
5 and tell them this:
6 'I'm going back to my Father and your Father—
to my God and your God.'"

Period 14

1 Mary of Magdala goes and reports to the disciples,
2 "I have seen the Master,"
3 and relates everything he had told her.

SECTION 2: PEACE TO YOU

UNIT 3

Period 15

1 That Sunday evening,
the disciples had locked the doors
for fear of the Judeans,
but Jesus came
2 and stood in front of them
3 and he greets them:
4 "Peace."

Period 16

1 Then he showed them his hands and his side.
2 The disciples were delighted to see the Master.
3 Jesus greets them again:
4 "Peace,
5 Just as the Father sent me,
6 so now I'm sending you."

Period 17

1 And at this he breathed over them
2 and says,
3 "Here's some holy spirit. Take it.
4 If you forgive anyone their sins,
they are forgiven;
5 if you do not release them from their sins,
they are not released."

UNIT 4

Period 18

1 Now Thomas, one of the twelve,
2 the one known as "the Twin,"

3 hadn't been with them when Jesus put in his appearance.
4 So the other disciples tried to tell him,
5 "We've seen the Master."

Period 19
1 But he responded,
2 "Unless I see the holes the nails made,
3 and put my finger in them
4 and my hand in his side,
5 I'll never believe."

UNIT 5

Period 20
1 A week later the disciples were again indoors, and Thomas was with them.
2 The doors were locked, but Jesus comes
3 and stood in front of them,
4 and said, "Peace."

Period 21
1 Then he says to Thomas,
2 "Put your finger here,
3 and look at my hands;
4 take your hand
5 and put it in my side.
6 Don't be skeptical
7 but be a believer."

Period 22
1 Thomas responded,
2 "My Master! My God!"

Period 23
1 Jesus asks,
2 "Do you believe because you have seen me?"
3 Those who can believe without having to see are the ones to be congratulated."

Period 24
1 Although Jesus performed many more miracles for his disciples to see
2 than could be written down in this book,
3 these are written down
4 so you will come to believe
5 that Jesus is the anointed, God's son—
6 and by believing this have life in his name

ENDNOTES

1. Porter (1994, p. 21) defines verbal aspect as "a semantic (meaning) category by which a speaker or writer grammaticalizes . . . a perspective on a an action by the selection of a particular tense-form in the verbal system."
2. OED, s.v. aorist; LSJ, s.v. ὁριζω.
3. This difference is one reason many commentators see Jn 21 as an addition to the Gospel.
4. For English translation, see the appendix.
5. See Mark 16:2 and parallels. See BDF 247 for a discussion of this idiomatic usage based on Hebrew usage; also Zerwick, (1979, p. 154). The verbal agreement between the Marcan parallels and John is so close that one must consider dependency. Mark 16:9 deviates from this idom and employs an ordinal numeral.
6. πρὸς (towards) τῷ μνημείῳ occurs in the the opening of the second unit, not in final but medial position. It is part of the sound pattern connected with τὸ μνημείον, but not part of the pattern connected with the ἐκ/εἰς prepositional phrases. εἰς τὸ μνημεῖον also occurs at the end of the second colon of unit 2 and functions there as a reverberation of the first unit's structural device, easing the transition to a new unit.
7. John often uses οὖν in this fashion. See for example, both chapters 19 and 21. Οὖν occurs 200 times in the fourth gospel, 20 times in John 19, 11 in John 20, and 9 in John 21. By way of comparison, it occurs 6 times in Mark, 56 in Matthew, and 33 in Luke.
8. For translation of all of John 20, see the appendix.
9. *Lit.*, On the first day of the week; while it was still dark.
10. Καὶ τὸ φῶς ἐν τῇ σκοτίᾳ φαίνει, καὶ ἡ σκοτία αὐτὸ οὐ κατέλαβεν (John 1:5, Light was shining in darkness, and darkness did not master it). See also John 6:17, 8:12, 12:35, 36; 1 John 1:5, 2:8, 11.
11. While the point goes beyond our discussion, if the audience of the Fourth Gospel knows Mark's narrative, and Τῇ δὲ μιᾷ τῶν σαββάτων and ἔρχεται πρωῒ suggest this possibility, then they would be expecting σκοτία to lead to fear. But as we shall see, it will be otherwise.
12. Some think he may also be the ἄλλος μαθητής (the other disciple) who accompanies Peter to the court of the high priest.
13. The disciple whom Jesus loved.
14. See Chapter 10 for a discussion of thematic phrases. The examples illustrated there come from Matthew, but they describe a

virtually universal literary phenomenon in Hellenistic Greek. Such phrases function like epithets in Greek poetry in terms of their verbal economy and metonymic implication as described in Foley (1995, pp. 5–7). But unlike epithets, thematic phrases in literary prose do not respond to metrical requirements or other unique characteristics of oral composition. Although Hellenistic literary compositions are published primarily through speech and received by listening, they are not orally composed like the Homeric epics but instead are composed and stored in memory with written support, as we have shown in Chapter 2, The Woven Composition.

15. Brown represents an interesting case in that he has changed his position from his Anchor Bible Commentary, where he identified the beloved disciple with John, son of Zebedee (1966, v, 1, pp. XCII--XCVIII). In *The Community of the Beloved Disciple*, he argues that the character is mysterious and not one of the twelve (1979, pp. 31–34).
16. Most commentators opt for the relative clause (ὃν ἐφίλει ὁ Ἰησοῦς) being a parenthetical edition by an editor (Brown, 1970, v. 2, p. 983), while Bultman understands it to mean, "and to that other one who . . ." (p. 684, n1) and so not a parenthetical, editorial addition. Sound alone cannot solve the question of sources, but instead attends to the phrase's impact in oral performance.
17. The vocative is frequent, but the titular κύριος had only occurred previously twice (6:23; 11:2). Here it probably only means "sir," as the reference to the gardner makes clear.
18. Among us, and we have seen.
19. Later in this same scene, Jesus says, ἀμὴν ἀμὴν λέγω σοι ὅτι ὃ οἴδαμεν λαλοῦμεν καὶ ὃ ἑωράκαμεν μαρτυροῦμεν (... we tell what we know, and we give evidence about what we've seen, John 3:11).
20. The difference in sound between θεωρεῖ and βλέπει serves to distinguish the two characters, even though here there is no apparent semantic difference.
21. *Lit.*, the one coming first.
22. This is the only place in chapter 20 where "rise from the dead" (ἐκ νεκρῶν ἀναστῆναι) occurs.
23. Comes (1.1) ... sees (1.2) ... runs (2.1) ... comes (2.2) ... and says (2.3)
24. *Lit.*, he entered, he saw, he believed.
25. As Ashton has so forcibly argued: "He [John] is able to record the response the beloved disciple makes, not to the voice of an intermediary, but to a vision of emptiness" (1991, p. 506).

26. One might even add "knowing" to the list since the narrator concludes that they as yet did not know about Jesus' resurrection from the dead.
27. John frequently employs the so-called "historic present." (see BDF #321). Λέγει occurs 123 times in this gospel, while εἶπεν occurs 115 times. By comparison in Mark λέγει=62, εἶπεν= 59; in Matthew λέγει=54, εἶπεν= 119; in Luke λέγει=14, εἶπεν= 231 (similar proportions in Acts). This usage is also common in Hellenistic authors. The frequent use of the present in some authors has been explained as once the present is used, its frequency becomes mechanical. Fanning thinks this might be the case at times in John: "It seems that the choice of tenses in some of these cases is due to a combination of a kind of 'linguistic momentum' (use of one historical present prompts several in series) and an idiomatic predilection to use the historical present more comonly with some verbs" (Fanning 1990, p. 235).
28. Where Jesus' body had lain.
29. They ask her.
30. Since weeping is an expected activity of a woman (Osiek 1993, p. 103), its association with Mary in this period in not surprising.
31. This would indicate the previous uses of ὁ κύϱιος should in the absence of contraindications be similarily understood.
32. Her response is the same as that of two unnamed disciples in 1:38.
33. Jesus' response to Mary in 2.10 has often been mistranslated. BDAG, 126, collects the evidence to show that the sense is not "don't touch me" as though Jesus were forbidding Mary to touch him. Given the Thomas story which follows, such a position would involve either an awful contradiction (over which exegetes have strained) or a terrible sexism. As Bauer shows, the sense is "Don't cling to me!" or "Let me go!".
34. I have not yet gone back to the Father.
35. "As God is my witness before you all: You'll see the sky split open and God's messengers traveling to and from the son of Adam."
36. No one has gone up to heaven except the one who came down from there—the son of Adam. In the wilderness Moses elevated the snake; in the same way the son of Adam is destined to be elevated, so everyone who believes in him can have real life.
37. *Lit.*, when it was evening.
38. Cola 5 and 6 echo the farewel discourse by repeating peace, joy, mission and the Spirit.

John 17:18.

καθὼς ἐμὲ	ἀπέστειλας	εἰς τὸν κόσμον,
κἀγὼ	ἀπέστειλα αὐτοὺς	εἰς τὸν κόσμον·

39. Ἐνεφύσησεν alludes to Gen 2:7, where God "formed man of dust from the ground, and breathed (ἐνεφύσησεν) into his nostrils the breath of life." Thus the commissioning is a creation story.
40. Who does away with the sin of the world.
41. The one known as "the Twin."
42. Brown worries about why it is not the "eleven" here since the death of Judas, but this gospel does not report Judas' death. Ἰούδας ὁ παραδιδοὺς αὐτὸν functions as a thematic phrase in this gospel.
43. "Lord, is there anyone else we can turn to? You have the words of real life! We have become believers and are certain that you are God's holy one."
44. "Isn't this why I chose you twelve? Even so, one of you is a devil." (He was of course referring to Judas, son of Simon Iscariot, one of the twelve, who was going to turn him in.)
45. "Master, we don't know where you're going. How can we possibly know the way?"
46. The Gospel of Thomas may well provide a possible explanation about extra-textual references triggered by the metonymic title "Thomas the Twin." In that Gospel, Thomas is redundantly referred to as "Didymos Judas Thomas." But by contrast to the Fourth Gospel, Thomas is the mystic seer (see GThom 13). In the Gospel of Thomas, Thomas is the hero while the other disciples play the role of buffoons. But in John, Thomas does not seem to understand. It is not hard to imagine that among the community of the beloved disciple the claims of Thomas' followers as represented in the tradition of the Gospel of Thomas are viewed with a certain irony and scorn (Pagels 2003, pp. 58–9).
47. *Lit.,* hands / finger / hand.
48. Zerwick (1963, 444) notes its frequent use in the New Testament in comparison to Greek papyri where it is infrequent. He also notes that it appears to have a strong emotional emphasis. BDF #364 (3).
49. Μή in the present tense forbids continuing an act (Zerwick, #246).
50. *Lit.,* unbelieving but believing.
51. As Schnackenburg (1982, v. 3, p. 329) shrewdly notes, it is "The concluding words which normally reveal the real intention," referring to Jesus' final response.

52. It certainly echoes the prologue (θεὸς ἦν ὁ λόγος). (Schnackenburg, v. 3, p. 332).
53. Ashton (442) remarks, "Where faith is concerned, physical vision is a handicap rather than an advantage, since there is always a risk of confusing vision with faith and even of preferring it. Thomas is rebuked for insisting on touching as well." Schnackenburg (3:329) makes a similar point; Brown (2:1050) strongly rejects this position.
54. The textual evidence concerning the aspect of the verb in colon 3 is inconclusive (Metzger 1971, p. 256). From the point of view of a sound analysis, the argument could go either way. The present aspect would match colon 6 and the present aspect indicates the center stage, viewing coming to faith as a process of hearing this book. The aorist would correspond to the shift in aspect in other cola, from present to aorist. It would view believing as the background accomplished by the reading, hearing, and accepting of the book.

WORKS CONSULTED

Ashton, John, 1991. *Understanding the Fourth Gospel*. Oxford: Clarendon.

Brown, Raymond. 1979. *The Community of the Beloved Disciple: The Life, Loves, and Hates of an Individual Church in New Testament Times*. New York: Paulist Press.

Brown, Raymond E. 1966. *The Gospel according to John (i-xii)*. 2 vols. Vol. 1, *Anchor Bible*. Garden City: Doubleday.

———. 1970. *The Gospel according to John (xiii-xxi)*. 2 vols. Vol. 2, *Anchor Bible*. Garden City: Doubleday.

Bultmann, Rudolf. 1971. *The Gospel of John: A Commentary*. Translated by G. R. Beasley-Murray, R. W. N. Hoare and J. K. Riches. Philadelphia: Westminster.

Fanning, B. M. 1990. *Verbal Aspect in New Testament Greek*. Oxford: Clarendon Press.

Foley, John Miles. 1995. *The Singer of Tales in Performance*. Bloomington: Indiana University Press.

Lindars, Barnabas. 1972. *The Gospel of John, New Century Bible*. London: Oliphants.

Metzger, Bruce M. 1971. *A Textual Commentary on the Greek New Testament*. New York: United Bible Societies.

Osiek, Carolyn. 1993. The Women at the Tomb: What Are They Doing There? *Ex Auditu* 9:97–107.

Pagels, Elaine. 2003. *Beyond Belief.* New York: Random House.

Porter, Stanley E. 1989. *Verbal Aspect in the Greek of the New Testament, with Reference to Tense and Mood.* New York: Peter Lang.

——. 1994. *Idioms of the Greek New Testament.* 2nd ed, *Biblical Languages: Greek.* Sheffield: JSOT Press.

Schnackenburg, Rudolf. 1982. *The Gospel According to St. John.* Translated by D. Smith and G. A. Kon. 3 vols. Vol. 3. New York: Crossroad.

Zerwick, Max, and Mary Grosvenor. 1979. *A Grammatical Analysis of the Greek New Testament.* Rome: Biblical Institute Press.

Zerwick, Maximilian. 1963. *Biblical Greek Illustrated by Examples, Scripta Pontificii Instituti Biblici 114.* Rome: Pontifical Biblical Press.

Chapter 9

Sound and Narrative
Luke's Nativity

LUKE: THE MUSICAL

Many have noted the sophisticated prose of Luke/Acts, its large vocabulary, and its rich literary style. Amid such verbal artistry, we should expect elaborate sound effects that support a polished performance. We need look no further than the gospel's beginning to hear the strains of Luke's elaborate soundtrack. Like a musical's overture, the opening sounds of the Gospel of Luke suggest its narrative trajectory and theological themes. Sound mapping shows that Luke's literary skill serves a deeper purpose than mere ornament or embellishment; indeed, his soundtrack presents a birth narrative that transforms the theme of promise and fulfillment into an epic drama with a universal conclusion.

THE NATIVITY IN CONTEXT

Luke's nativity scene in 2:1–20 is a single episode in the larger narrative of Mary, Joseph, and Jesus in chapter 2—a story that exhibits many parallels to his first chapter's narrative of Zechariah, Elizabeth, and John. As in every Greek composition, sound is employed to signal unit boundaries and implement narrative parallels, thereby supporting a narrative's progress and guiding an audience's interpretation.

Luke's gospel begins with a prologue (see Alexander 1993, for secular parallels)[1]. The narrative proper begins in 1:5 with a cluster of narrative markers, including ἐγένετο at the beginning of a colon, a time reference marked in days, an allusion to the Roman empire, and a reference to its Israelite inhabitants.

1:5[2]
Ἐγένετο ἐν ταῖς ἡμέραις Ἡρῴδου βασιλέως τῆς Ἰουδαίας
ἱερεύς τις ὀνόματι Ζαχαρίας ἐξ ἐφημερίας Ἀβιά,
καὶ γυνὴ αὐτῷ ἐκ τῶν θυγατέρων Ἀαρών,
καὶ τὸ ὄνομα αὐτῆς Ἐλισάβετ.

Then in 1:8, ἐγένετο is repeated in initial position with the connector δέ, and an echo of the time marker in days occurs with τῆς ἐφημερίας.

1:8[3]
Ἐγένετο δὲ ἐν τῷ ἱερατεύειν αὐτὸν
ἐν τῇ τάξει τῆς ἐφημερίας αὐτοῦ ἔναντι τοῦ θεοῦ,

These narrative markers in 1:8, repeated from 1:5, narrow the story's focus from an imperial context to a local story. Taken together, this cluster of narrative markers occurring in 1:5 and reinforced in 1:8 marks the beginning of a major narrative unit in Luke's gospel.

This same cluster of markers denotes the gospel's next major narrative unit in 2:1–5, including ἐγένετο,[4] time expressed in days, an imperial reference that sets the context and several specific citations indicating an Israelite nexus that focuses the local story. As in 1:5–8, the markers in 2:1–6 are repeated and therefore reinforced. See chart 9.1.

Chart 9.1[5]

Markers	**Chapter 1**	**Chapter 2**
ἐγένετο	**Ἐγένετο**	**Ἐγένετο δὲ**
days	**ἐν ταῖς ἡμέραις**	**ἐν ταῖς ἡμέραις ἐκείναις**
Imperial reference	Ἡρῴδου βασιλέως τῆς Ἰουδαίας	ἐξῆλθεν δόγμα παρὰ Καίσαρος Αὐγούστου ἀπογράφεσθαι πᾶσαν τὴν οἰκουμένην. (2:1)
Israelite reference	ἱερεύς τις ὀνόματι **Ζαχαρίας** ἐξ ἐφημερίας Ἀβιά, καὶ γυνὴ αὐτῷ ἐκ τῶν θυγατέρων Ἀαρών, καὶ τὸ ὄνομα αὐτῆς **Ἐλισάβετ** (1:5)	Ἀνέβη δὲ καὶ **Ἰωσὴφ** ἀπὸ τῆς Γαλιλαίας ἐκ πόλεως Ναζαρὲθ εἰς τὴν Ἰουδαίαν εἰς πόλιν Δαυὶδ ἥτις καλεῖται Βηθλέεμ, διὰ τὸ εἶναι αὐτὸν ἐξ οἴκου καὶ πατριᾶς Δαυίδ, ἀπογράψασθαι σὺν **Μαριὰμ** τῇ ἐμνηστευμένῃ αὐτῷ, οὔσῃ ἐγκύῳ. (2:4–5)
ἐγένετο δέ	**Ἐγένετο δὲ ἐν** τῷ ἱερατεύειν αὐτὸν	**ἐγένετο δὲ** ἐν τῷ εἶναι αὐτοὺς ἐκεῖ
days	ἐν τῇ τάξει τῆς **ἐφημερίας** αὐτοῦ ἔναντι τοῦ θεοῦ (1·8)	ἐπλήσθησαν **αἱ ἡμέραι** τοῦ τεκεῖν αὐτήν, (2:6)

That no major division of the narrative occurs between 1:5 and 2:1 is confirmed by the fact that between 1:8 and 2:1 internal episodes are always marked with καί or δέ, and ἐγένετο never occurs in initial position in a colon but only after καί (1:23, 41, 59, 65) or ὡς (1:44).

1:23 **καὶ ἐγένετο** ὡς ἐπλήσθησαν αἱ ἡμέραι τῆς λειτουργίας αὐτοῦ
ἀπῆλθεν εἰς τὸν οἶκον αὐτοῦ[6]
1:41 **καὶ ἐγένετο** ὡς ἤκουσεν τὸν ἀσπασμὸν τῆς Μαρίας ἡ Ἐλισάβετ[7]
1:59 **καὶ ἐγένετο** ἐν τῇ ἡμέρᾳ τῇ ὀγδόῃ ἦλθον περιτεμεῖν τὸ παιδίον[8]
1:65 **καὶ ἐγένετο** ἐπὶ πάντας φόβος τοὺς περιοικοῦντας αὐτούς[9]

1:44 ἰδοὺ γὰρ **ὡς ἐγένετο** ἡ φωνὴ τοῦ ἀσπασμοῦ σου εἰς τὰ ὦτά μου,
ἐσκίρτησεν ἐν ἀγαλλιάσει τὸ βρέφος ἐν τῇ κοιλίᾳ μου[10]

Similarly, once chapter 2 repeats the major narrative markers in 2:1 and 2:6, internal episodes are always marked with καί or δέ, and ἐγένετο occurs only with καί, connecting the episode with the larger narrative.

2:13 **καὶ** ἐξαίφνης **ἐγένετο** σὺν τῷ ἀγγέλῳ
πλῆθος στρατιᾶς οὐρανίου αἰνούντων τὸν θεὸν καὶ λεγόντων[11]
2:15 **Καὶ ἐγένετο** ὡς ἀπῆλθον ἀπ᾽ αὐτῶν εἰς τὸν οὐρανὸν οἱ
ἄγγελοι[12]
2:42 **καὶ** ὅτε **ἐγένετο** ἐτῶν δώδεκα, ἀναβαινόντων αὐτῶν
κατὰ τὸ ἔθος τῆς ἑορτῆς[13]
2:46 **καὶ ἐγένετο** μετὰ ἡμέρας τρεῖς εὗρον αὐτὸν ἐν τῷ ἱερῷ
καθεζόμενον ἐν μέσῳ τῶν διδασκάλων[14]

Thus chapters 1 and 2 each comprise complete major narrative units. Chapter 3 begins the next major narrative unit with a new imperial reference (to Tiberius) and a new reference to Israel. It reprises ἐγένετο in a new configuration.

3:1 Ἐν ἔτει δὲ πεντεκαιδεκάτῳ τῆς ἡγεμονίας Τιβερίου Καίσαρος,
ἡγεμονεύοντος Ποντίου Πιλάτου τῆς Ἰουδαίας,
καὶ τετρααρχοῦντος τῆς Γαλιλαίας Ἡρῴδου,
Φιλίππου δὲ τοῦ ἀδελφοῦ αὐτοῦ τετρααρχοῦντος τῆς
Ἰτουραίας
καὶ Τραχωνίτιδος χώρας,
καὶ Λυσανίου τῆς Ἀβιληνῆς τετρααρχοῦντος,
3:2 ἐπὶ ἀρχιερέως Ἅννα καὶ Καϊάφα,
ἐγένετο ῥῆμα θεοῦ ἐπὶ Ἰωάννην τὸν Ζαχαρίου υἱὸν ἐν τῇ
ἐρήμῳ.[15]

All three instances of major narrative divisions are framed in mixed style, using both grammatical subordination and parataxis to join cola. This consistent set of aural clues organizes the gospel's opening narratives.

THE NATIVITY[16]

PART 1: IMPERIAL CONTEXT (2:1–5)

Period 1

1 **Ἐγένετο δὲ** ἐν ταῖς ἡμέραις ἐκείναις
2 ἐξῆλθεν δόγμα παρὰ Καίσαρος Αὐγούστου
3 ἀπογράφεσθαι πᾶσαν τὴν *οἰκουμένην*.
4 αὕτη ἀπογραφὴ πρώτη **ἐγένετο ἡ**γεμονεύοντος τῆς Συρίας Κυρηνίου.

Period 2

1 καὶ ἐπορεύοντο πάντες ἀπογράφεσθαι, ἕκαστος εἰς τὴν ἑαυτοῦ πόλιν.
2 Ἀνέβη δὲ καὶ Ἰωσὴφ ἀπὸ τῆς Γαλιλαίας
ἐκ πόλεως Ναζαρὲθ
εἰς τὴν Ἰουδαίαν
εἰς πόλιν Δαυὶδ ἥτις καλεῖται Βηθλέεμ,
διὰ τὸ εἶναι αὐτὸν ἐξ *οἴκου* καὶ πατριᾶς Δαυίδ,
3 ἀπογράψασθαι σὺν Μαριὰμ τῇ ἐμνηστευμένῃ αὐτῷ, οὔσῃ ἐγκύῳ.

The nativity episode begins with two well rounded periods whose cola are connected by grammatical subordination. Period 1 opens a new narrative episode that parallels the gospel's first episode, which begins in 1:5. Period 1, colon 1 repeats distinctive sounds from 1:5 and elongates them by adding ἐκείναις (those) with its rhyming inflectional ending:

1:5 Ἐγένετο ἐν ταῖς ἡμέραις
2:1 Ἐγένετο δὲ ἐν ταῖς ἡμέραις ἐκείναις

Continuing the parallel, colon 2 refers to Caesar Augustus, placing his name and title at the end of a colon for emphasis, just as 1:5 referred to Ἡρῴδου βασιλέως τῆς Ἰουδαίας (Herod King of the Jews). Cola 3–4 repeat the ου phoneme from Caesar's title in colon 2, reinforcing this sound. Colon 4 repeats ἀπογραφ- from colon 3. Cola 2–4 each contain a prominent π sound in the middle of the colon. Colon 4 both reprises sounds from the period's opening ἐγένετο, rounding the period, and is elongated by repetitions of the ου phoneme and the similar sounds ευ and υ, recalling Caesar's name. Elongation signals closure.

The sound effects of period 1 unify the period and establish an imperial context for the episode by lending emphasis to Καίσαρος Αὐγούστου (Caesar Augustus) and the scope of his power, conceived of as πᾶσαν τὴν οἰκουμένην (the whole civilized world). The sending out of an imperial δόγμα (decree) serves as a narrative vehicle to convey the empire's hierarchical structure. The construction of colon 2 imitates the hierarchical structure it describes. Ἐξ and παρά stress motion, δόγμα underlines imperial power, and the placement of Καίσαρος Αὐγούστου at the colon's end, a naturally emphatic location, points to the source of this hierarchy.

The γραφ lexeme had appeared in the prologue and is connected with κράτιστε Θεόφιλε.

1:3

ἔδοξε **κ**ἀμοὶ παρη**κ**ολουθη**κ**ότι ἄνωθεν πᾶσιν ἀ**κ**ριβῶς **κ**αθε**ξ**ῆς σοι
γράψαι, **κ**ράτιστε Θεόφιλε[17]

In period 2, γραφ is connected with Καίσαρος Αὐγούστου. Ἀπογράψασθαι reinforces the emphasis on imperial power established in period 1. Both names contain a divine reference and employ a κ/ξ sound. The parallel references to writing set up a contrast between imperial edicts and the gospel.[18]

Period 2 opens with sounds that indicate its connection with period 1. It repeats the ου/ευ sounds associated with the emperor's title, the medial π sound, and ἀπογράφεσθαι. Similarly, the final colon in period 2 repeats ἀπογράφεσθαι and ου/ευ/υ sounds, rounding the period by reprising sounds that occurred at its beginning. Beginning and ending the period with these echoes of empire serves to bracket the period's narrative action within the emperor's order for a written record of the empire's inhabitants. The middle colon 2 repeats both the π phoneme and ἀπο, recalling ἀπογράφεσθαι. It narrates Joseph's movement out of Galilean Nazareth to Judea and Bethlehem with a series of parallel prepositional phrases. The prepositions emphasize directional movement and repeat πόλιν/πόλεως (city) from colon 1. They also reverse the directional movement of the geographical elements in the angel's announcement to Mary in 1:26–27 and repeat Joseph's and Mary's names, indicating their compliance with the emperor's δόγμα. See chart 9.2.

The narrative motion gradually narrows focus from the whole empire, πᾶσαν τὴν οἰκουμένην, to the town of Bethlehem, emphasizing the scope of imperial reach and its hierarchical organization. The last two prepositional phrases expand the established parallel arrangement:

Period 2, colon 2 (conclusion)

	εἰς πόλιν **Δαυὶδ** ἥτις καλεῖται Βηθλέεμ,
διὰ τὸ εἶναι αὐτὸν	ἐξ οἴκου καὶ πατριᾶς **Δαυίδ**

Chart 9.2[19]

1:26–27	**Period 2 (2:3–5)**
Ἐν δὲ τῷ μηνὶ τῷ ἕκτῳ ἀπεστάλη ὁ ἄγγελος Γαβριὴλ ἀπὸ τοῦ θεοῦ	Ἀνέβη δὲ καὶ **Ἰωσὴφ**
εἰς πόλιν τῆς Γαλιλαίας ᾗ ὄνομα Ναζαρὲθ πρὸς παρθένον ἐμνηστευμένην	**ἀπὸ τῆς Γαλιλαίας ἐκ πόλεως Ναζαρὲθ** εἰς τὴν Ἰουδαίαν εἰς πόλιν Δαυὶδ ἥτις καλεῖται Βηθλέεμ,
ἀνδρὶ ᾧ ὄνομα Ἰωσὴφ **ἐξ οἴκου Δαυίδ,** καὶ τὸ ὄνομα τῆς παρθένου **Μαριάμ.**	διὰ τὸ εἶναι αὐτὸν **ἐξ οἴκου καὶ πατριᾶς Δαυίδ,** ἀπογράψασθαι σὺν **Μαριὰμ** τῇ ἐμνηστευμένῃ αὐτῷ, οὔσῃ ἐγκύῳ.

Added word groups occur after the first and before the second prepositional phrase. This structural complication suggests a complication in the narrative plot. Joseph's movement out of Nazareth in obedience to Caesar is oriented toward Bethlehem, the home of David, Israel's great king. Joseph is identified not only as a resident of the οἰκουμένη of Caesar Augustus, but also as part of David's οἶκος (house). Thus the narrative action that takes place in an imperial context also associates the actors with a different οἶκος than Caesar's and suggests an alternative allegiance. As soon as colon 3 reprises ἀπογράψασθαι from colon 1 and from the previous period, it adds pressure to the plot's complicating element by stating that Joseph's journey will result not only in recording Joseph's name, but also the names of those with him, Mary and her child. Mary's pregnancy adds urgency to the burgeoning list of traveling inhabitants of the empire

PART 2: BIRTH (2:6–7)

Period 3

1	**ἐγένετο δὲ** ἐν τῷ εἶναι	αὐτοὺς ἐκεῖ
2	ἐπλήσθησαν αἱ ἡμέραι τοῦ τεκεῖν	αὐτήν,
3	καὶ ἔτεκεν τὸν υἱὸν	αὐτῆς τὸν πρωτότοκον·
4	καὶ ἐσπαργάνωσεν	αὐτὸν
5	καὶ ἀνέκλινεν	αὐτὸν ἐν φάτνῃ,
6	διότι οὐκ ἦν	αὐτοῖς τόπος ἐν τῷ καταλύματι.

Period 3 signals structural changes by re-introducing ἐγένετο. We have seen that ἐγένετο functions as a narrative marker at the beginning of Luke's gospel. In period 3, ἐγένετο echoes its recent occurrence in period 1 and invokes the structural role of this marker. The recurrence of ἐγένετο in periods 1 and 3 parallels its occurrences in 1:5 and 1:8. The marker's doubled occurrence establishes the beginning of an episode and sets the scene, both in chapter 1 and here in chapter 2.

In addition to repeating ἐγένετο from period 1, period 3 also rehearses sounds similar to those in 1:8, which repeats ἐγένετο from 1:5.

1:8	**Ἐγένετο δὲ**	**ἐν τῷ** ἱερατεύειν	αὐτὸν	ἐν τῇ τάξει
2:6	**ἐγένετο δὲ**	**ἐν τῷ** εἶναι	αὐτοὺς	ἐκεῖ

Consistent with the gospel's structural signals thus far, these similarities between 1:8 and 2:6 signal larger narrative parallels; note, for instance, that both introduce episodes narrating an angel's appearance that instills fear. See chart 9.3.

The episode introduced by ἐγένετο δέ in 1:8 featured negative consequences for Zechariah because of his incorrect response to the angel's announcement, building narrative tension. The episode introduced in period 3 (2:6) recalls its structural analog, the angel's visit to Zechariah, and presents the possibility that this time the angel's announcement might meet with the correct response.

Chart 9.3[20]

1:8–13	**2:6–10**
Ἐγένετο δὲ ἐν τῷ ἱερατεύειν αὐτὸν ἐν τῇ τάξει τῆς ἐφημερίας αὐτοῦ ἔναντι τοῦ θεοῦ,	**ἐγένετο δὲ ἐν τῷ εἶναι αὐτοὺς ἐκεῖ** ἐπλήσθησαν αἱ ἡμέραι τοῦ τεκεῖν αὐτήν,
κατὰ τὸ ἔθος τῆς ἱερατείας ἔλαχε τοῦ θυμιᾶσαι εἰσελθὼν εἰς τὸν ναὸν τοῦ κυρίου, καὶ πᾶν τὸ πλῆθος ἦν τοῦ λαοῦ προσευχόμενον ἔξω τῇ ὥρᾳ τοῦ θυμιάματος·	καὶ ἔτεκεν τὸν υἱὸν αὐτῆς τὸν πρωτότοκον· καὶ ἐσπαργάνωσεν αὐτὸν καὶ ἀνέκλινεν αὐτὸν ἐν φάτνῃ, διότι οὐκ ἦν αὐτοῖς τόπος ἐν τῷ καταλύματι. Καὶ ποιμένες ἦσαν ἐν τῇ χώρᾳ τῇ αὐτῇ ἀγραυλοῦντες καὶ φυλάσσοντες φυλακὰς τῆς νυκτὸς ἐπὶ τὴν ποίμνην αὐτῶν.
ὤφθη δὲ αὐτῷ **ἄγγελος κυρίου** ἑστὼς ἐκ δεξιῶν τοῦ θυσιαστηρίου τοῦ θυμιάματος. καὶ ἐταράχθη Ζαχαρίας ἰδών, καὶ **φόβος** ἐπέπεσεν ἐπ' αὐτόν.	καὶ **ἄγγελος κυρίου** ἐπέστη αὐτοῖς καὶ δόξα κυρίου περιέλαμψεν αὐτούς, καὶ **ἐφοβήθησαν φόβον μέγαν.**
εἶπεν δὲ πρὸς αὐτὸν ὁ ἄγγελος,	**καὶ εἶπεν αὐτοῖς ὁ ἄγγελος,**

Cola are blended differently in period 3 than in the previous episode. Whereas periods 1 and 2 comprised long cola combined through grammatical subordination, cola in period 3 are brief and combined paratactically. This structural shift quickens the narrative pace, imitating the tension and rhythm of childbirth. All six cola in period 3 iterate the third person pronoun, drawing attention to the actors. In the first and last cola, the pronoun occurs in plural form, referring to the family. Cola 2–5 shift to the singular, focusing attention first on Mary (cola 2 and 3), then on the infant (cola 4 and 5). Like the previous period that used the first and last cola to frame the journey of Mary and Joseph in the context of the Roman Empire, period 3 places the birth of Jesus (cola 2–5) in the context of the family (cola 1–6). Cola 2 and 6 are longer than the other cola in the period. Colon 2 introduces the onset of a new narrative development. Colon 6 is elongated by διότι (because), which interrupts the parataxis, and by ούκ…τόπος ἐν τῷ καταλύματι (*lit.*, no place in the inn). The elongation shifts the narrative context and signals closure.[21]

PART 3: SHEPHERDS AND ANGELS (2:8–14)

Period 4

1 Καὶ ποιμένες ἦσαν ἐν τῇ χώρᾳ τῇ αὐτῇ ἀγραυλοῦντες
2 καὶ φυλάσσοντες φυλακὰς τῆς νυκτὸς ἐπὶ τὴν ποίμνην αὐτῶν.
3 καὶ ἄγγελος κυρίου ἐπέστη αὐτοῖς
4 καὶ δόξα κυρίου περιέλαμψεν αὐτούς,
5 καὶ ἐφοβήθησαν φόβον μέγαν.
6 καὶ εἶπεν αὐτοῖς ὁ ἄγγελος,

Period 5

1 Μὴ φοβεῖσθε,
2 ἰδοὺ γὰρ εὐαγγελίζομαι ὑμῖν χαρὰν μεγάλην ἥτις ἔσται παντὶ τῷ λαῷ,
3 ὅτι ἐτέχθη ὑμῖν σήμερον σωτὴρ ὅς ἐστιν Χριστὸς κύριος ἐν πόλει Δαυίδ·
4 καὶ τοῦτο ὑμῖν τὸ σημεῖον,
5 εὑρήσετε βρέφος ἐσπαργανωμένον καὶ κείμενον ἐν φάτνῃ.

Period 6

1 καὶ ἐξαίφνης **ἐγένετο** σὺν τῷ ἀγγέλῳ πλῆθος στρατιᾶς οὐρανίου
2 αἰνούντων τὸν θεὸν καὶ λεγόντων,
3 Δόξα ἐν ὑψίστοις θεῷ
4 καὶ ἐπὶ γῆς εἰρήνη ἐν ἀνθρώποις εὐδοκίας.

Period 4 begins a new narrative episode, marked by longer cola that break the previous period's pattern of brief cola that repeat the third person pronoun. The structural shift in period 4 accompanies a focus on a new location, fields in that region, and new actors, shepherds. New narrative elements introduce new sounds that are repeated at the period's beginning: ποιμένες (shepherds) in colon 1, ποίμην (sheep) in colon 2; φυλάσσοντες φυλακάς (keeping watch) in colon 2; α and η sounds predominate in cola 1 and 2. Cola 3 and 4 are arranged in parallel. Some parallel elements are repeated: καί, κυρίου (lord), and the third person pronoun. The parallelism slows the pace and focuses attention on the angel. Colon 5 emphasizes fear by repeating –φοβ- and qualifying the noun with μέγαν (great). The great fear the shepherds experienced exceeds that of Zechariah in 1:12, which was simply depicted: καὶ φόβος ἐπέπεσεν ἐπ' αὐτόν.[22] All six cola are joined by καί, continuing the paratactic style of period 3, but with a different rhythm created by the internal parallelism of cola 3–4. The strong paratactic structure of this period leads to the inclusion of colon 6 in this period, whereas logically it would belong to the next period. This periodic division indicates the breathing (or breath-spacing) of the composition and sets the angel's speech apart.

Period 5 comprises the angel's speech. Cola are joined by subordination and not parataxis, with the exception of colon 4, which begins with καί. Colon 1 begins with a prohibition of fear, repeating -φοβ- from period 4, colon 5 and reprising the fear trope from the angel's visits to Zechariah (1:12–13) and Mary (1:30).[23] Colon 2 repeats μεγα- from colon 5 in the previous period, but now it modifies χαράν (joy) instead of φόβος.[24]

By means of repeated sounds, the relative clause at the end of colon 3 reprises ἐν πόλει Δαυίδ (in the city of David) from the episode that set the imperial context (period 2, colon 2). The colon includes σωτήρ (savior), an imperial title, and Χριστὸς representing the alternative empire of Israel. The promised one is also described as κυρίος (lord), an imperial title as well as a euphemism for God. Its occurrence here exploits the growing ambiguity over which reign will have supremacy. Compared to those in the previous period, cola 2 and 3 are long and employ little hiatus. Σημεῖον (sign) in colon 4 reprises the similar sounding σήμερον (today) in colon 3, emphasizing the sign's immediacy. In colon 5, two participles with the same inflectional ending describe the infant as did the narrator at Jesus' birth in period 3, cola 5–6. This sets up a contrast between the imperial titles and a βρέφος (baby).

Period 6 repeats ἐγένετο in its first colon, but since ἐγένετο does not occur initially in the colon it does not mark a new narrative episode. The first and last cola in period 6 begin with καί, but the middle two cola are not joined paratactically.[25] In colon 2 paired participles elongate the introduction to the angels' speech. The promised outcomes named in cola 3 and 4 affect both the heavenly realm inhabited by God and the earthly realm inhabited by humans.

PART 4: SHEPHERDS AND FAMILY (2:15–20)

Period 7

1 Καὶ **ἐγένετο** ὡς ἀπῆλθον ἀπ' αὐτῶν εἰς τὸν οὐρανὸν οἱ ἄγγελοι,
2 οἱ ποιμένες ἐλάλουν πρὸς ἀλλήλους,
3 Διέλθωμεν δὴ ἕως Βηθλέεμ
4 καὶ ἴδωμεν τὸ *ῥῆμα* τοῦτο τὸ **γεγον**ὸς ὃ ὁ κύριος ἐ**γνώ**ρισεν ἡμῖν.

Like the previous period, period 7's four cola are arranged so that the first and last cola are introduced by καί. Like the first colon in period 6, colon 1 repeats ἐγένετο initially, signalling the beginning of a new narrative episode, and concludes with οἱ ἄγγελοι (*lit.*, the angels) and οὐρανός (heaven). Placement at the colon's end draws attention to the angels and the link to the previous period. Colon 2 opens with the other actors from the previous episode, οἱ ποιμένες (the shepherds). The juxtaposition of these actors emphasizes their narrative relationship. Colon 2 reports the shepherds' speech to each other. Unlike Zechariah and Mary when they were visited by an angel in chapter 1, the shepherds do not speak to the angel but to each other. Colon 3 repeats Βηθλέεμ (Bethlehem), not from the angel's speech to them in periods 5 and 6, but from the imperial setting reported in period 2. The intensifying particle δή adds urgency to their exortation.[26] Fragments of the narrative marker ἐγένετο are sounded in colon 4 with γεγονός (what has happened) and ἐγνώρισεν (made known). These sounds round the period by repeating sounds from the first colon. They emphasize the shepherd's expectation that the angel's announcement would be shown to be true. The elongated final colon signals closure.

Period 8

1 καὶ ἦλθον σπεύσαντες
2 καὶ ἀνεῦρον τήν τε Μαριὰμ
καὶ τὸν Ἰωσὴφ
καὶ τὸ βρέφος κείμενον ἐν τῇ φάτνῃ·

As the focus shifts in period 8 back to the family in Bethlehem, parataxis returns and verifies in simple form the shepherds' expectations. The period's continuous style is reminiscent of period 3, which reported the infant's birth. The second colon repeats τὸ βρέφος as a marker for Jesus, accentuating his lowliness *vis-à-vis* the exaltation of both Augustus and the angel's message. This description of Jesus places him at the bottom of the Roman imperial hierarchy The narrative implies a clear contrast in the hierarchies of heaven and earth.

Period 9

1 ἰδόντες δὲ ἐγνώρισαν περὶ τοῦ *ῥήματος* τοῦ λαληθέντος αὐτοῖς
περὶ τοῦ παιδίου τούτου.
2 καὶ πάντες οἱ ἀκούσαντες ἐθαύμασαν
περὶ τῶν λαληθέντων ὑπὸ τῶν ποιμένων
πρὸς αὐτούς·

Period 9 makes explicit the shepherds' verification of the angels' promise. Colon 1 repeats ῥῆμα (saying) from period 7, colon 4, referring to the substance of the promise. The shepherds acknowledge what they have seen by speaking to each other, just as they had done when they agreed to go to Bethlehem. Period 9's two cola are arranged in parallel with initial participles followed by finite verbs having implied plural subjects and then by prepositional phrases beginning with περὶ (concerning). Both cola of period 9 repeat medial π sounds and the phoneme ου(ς), reminiscent of sounds that occurred in periods 1 and 2, which set the imperial context. This echo of the story's beginning contrasts Αὐγυστου and τοῦ παιδίου (child) and suggests that the episode is drawing to a close.

Period 10

1 ἡ δὲ Μαριὰμ πάντα συνετήρει τὰ *ῥήματα* ταῦτα συμβάλλουσα
ἐν τῇ καρδίᾳ αὐτῆς.
2 καὶ ὑπέστρεψαν οἱ ποιμένες δοξάζοντες καὶ αἰνοῦντες τὸν θεὸν
ἐπὶ πᾶσιν οἷς ἤκουσαν καὶ εἶδον
3 καθὼς ἐλαλήθη πρὸς αὐτούς.

Period 10 opens with a shift of subject, signaled by δέ, to the singular Mary. Colon 1 repeats the medial π phoneme in πάντα (all). It also repeats ῥημα, the third reference to the story's events (the others occurred in 7.4 and 9.1). Cola 2 and 3 also contain the medial π phoneme. Colon 3 opens with καθώς (just as), drawing a conclusion and reinforcing the theme of promise and fulfillment.

CONCLUSIONS

SOUND STRUCTURES THE NARRATIVE

Sound organizes the gospel's beginning and shapes the upcoming narrative. Following the prologue, which has its own sound structure, sound markers with parallel construction divide the first part of this gospel into three major units.

Unit 1
1:5 Ἐγένετο ἐν ταῖς ἡμέραις[27]

Unit 2
2:1 Ἐγένετο δὲ ἐν ταῖς ἡμέραις ἐκείναις[28]

Unit 3
3.1 Ἐν ἔτει δὲ πεντεκαιδεκάτῳ τῆς ἡγεμονίας Τιβερίου Καίσαρος[29]

Unit two has three narrative episodes, the first one of which we have examined above. A new narrative episode begins in 2:21 and 2:22, marked by καὶ ὅτε. Repetition of ὅτε with καί at the beginning of their cola indicates the role of ὅτε as a narrative marker. These signals divide the narrative in progress but do not cue the beginning of a new major narrative unit, since καί connects the narrative and the division is not reinforced by supporting signals. Subsequent minor divisions occur through chapter two. In every case, the divisions are introduced by καί, followed either by a change of subject or by a verb, adverb, or particle that has functioned as a narrative marker in the preceding narrative. The formal similarity of these narrative markers indicates that they introduce new episodes in a continuing narrative. See chart 9.4.

The episode following the narrative marker in 2:46 concludes with sustained parataxis, consistent with the previous use of καί as a narrative marker.

Luke 2:50–52[31]

1 καὶ αὐτοὶ οὐ συνῆκαν τὸ ῥῆμα ὃ ἐλάλησεν αὐτοῖς.
2 καὶ κατέβη μετ᾽ αὐτῶν
3 καὶ ἦλθεν εἰς Ναζαρέθ,
4 καὶ ἦν ὑποτασσόμενος αὐτοῖς.
5 καὶ ἡ μήτηρ αὐτοῦ διετήρει πάντα τὰ ῥήματα ἐν τῇ καρδίᾳ αὐτῆς.

6 Καὶ Ἰησοῦς προέκοπτεν [ἐν τῇ]	σοφίᾳ	
καὶ	ἡλικίᾳ	
καὶ	χάριτι	παρὰ θεῷ
καὶ		ἀνθρώποις.

Colon 6, elongated with phrases joined by καί, draws this major narrative unit to a close. This closing is confirmed by the opening period of chapter 3 (see above).

SOUND ADVANCES NARRATIVE THEMES

By employing parallelism in the construction of the angel's visits to Zechariah, Mary, and the shepherds, Luke's birth narrative focuses

Chart 9.4[30]

Verse	Narrative Marker	Chapter 2	Marker Type
21	Καὶ ὅτε	ἐπλήσθησαν ἡμέραι ὀκτὼ τοῦ περιτεμεῖν αὐτόν,	(new marker)
22	Καὶ ὅτε	ἐπλήσθησαν αἱ ἡμέραι τοῦ καθαρισμοῦ αὐτῶν κατὰ τὸν νόμον Μωϋσέως,	2:21
25	Καὶ ἰδοὺ ἄνθρωπος ἦν	ἐν Ἰερουσαλὴμ ᾧ ὄνομα Συμεών,	(change of subject)
33	καὶ ἦν ὁ πατὴρ αὐτοῦ καὶ ἡ μήτηρ	θαυμάζοντες ἐπὶ τοῖς λαλουμένοις περὶ αὐτοῦ.	(change of subject)
36	Καὶ ἦν Ἅννα προφῆτις,		(change of subject)
39	Καὶ ὡς	ἐτέλεσαν πάντα τὰ κατὰ τὸν νόμον κυρίου,	2:15
42	καὶ ὅτε ἐγένετο	ἐτῶν δώδεκα,	2:21, 22
46	καὶ ἐγένετο	μετὰ ἡμέρας τρεῖς εὗρον αὐτὸν ἐν τῷ ἱερῷ καθεζόμενον ἐν μέσῳ τῶν διδασκάλων	1:24, 59, 65

and draws attention to the promises the angels articulate. Many have noticed these parallels (see Brown 1979), but sound mapping adds a new dimension by showing how effectively these parallels advance Luke's drama—for they are not merely simple alignments suggesting the fulfillment of promises, but rather by building on each other they evolve into new dramatic possibilities.

Zechariah (1:13–17)[32]

1 **εἶπεν δὲ πρὸς αὐτὸν ὁ ἄγγελος,**
2 **Μὴ φοβοῦ**, Ζαχαρία,
3 διότι εἰσηκούσθη ἡ δέησίς σου,
4 καὶ ἡ γυνή σου Ἐλισάβετ γεννήσει υἱόν σοι,
5 **καὶ καλέσεις τὸ ὄνομα αὐτοῦ Ἰωάννην**.
6 καὶ ἔσται ***χαρά*** σοι καὶ ἀγαλλίασις,
7 καὶ πολλοὶ ἐπὶ τῇ γενέσει αὐτοῦ ***χαρήσονται***·
8 ἔσται γὰρ **μέγας** ἐνώπιον [τοῦ] **κυρίου**,
9 καὶ οἶνον καὶ σίκερα οὐ μὴ πίῃ,
10 καὶ πνεύματος ἁγίου πλησθήσεται ἔτι ἐκ κοιλίας μητρὸς αὐτοῦ,
11 καὶ ***πολλοὺς τῶν υἱῶν Ἰσραὴλ ἐπιστρέψει*** ἐπὶ **κύριον τὸν θεὸν** αὐτῶν.

12 καὶ αὐτὸς προελεύσεται ἐνώπιον αὐτοῦ
ἐν πνεύματι καὶ δυνάμει Ἠλίου,
13 ***ἐπιστρέψαι*** καρδίας πατέρων ἐπὶ τέκνα
14 καὶ ἀπειθεῖς ἐν φρονήσει δικαίων,
15 ἑτοιμάσαι κυρίῳ λαὸν κατεσκευασμένον.

Mary (1:30–33)[33]

1 **καὶ εἶπεν ὁ ἄγγελος αὐτῇ,**
2 **Μὴ φοβοῦ**, Μαριάμ,
3 εὗρες γὰρ χάριν παρὰ τῷ θεῷ·
4 καὶ ἰδοὺ συλλήμψῃ ἐν γαστρὶ
5 καὶ τέξῃ υἱόν,
6 **καὶ καλέσεις τὸ ὄνομα αὐτοῦ** Ἰ**ησοῦν**.
7 οὗτος ἔσται **μέγας** καὶ **υἱὸς ὑψίστου** κληθήσεται,
8 καὶ δώσει αὐτῷ **κύριος ὁ θεὸς τὸν θρόνον Δαυὶδ τοῦ πατρὸς αὐτοῦ,**
9 καὶ ***βασιλεύσει ἐπὶ τὸν οἶκον Ἰακὼβ*** εἰς τοὺς αἰῶνας,
10 καὶ ***τῆς βασιλείας*** αὐτοῦ οὐκ ἔσται τέλος.

Shepherds (2:10–14)[34]

1 **καὶ εἶπεν αὐτοῖς ὁ ἄγγελος,**
2 **Μὴ φοβεῖσθε,**
3 ἰδοὺ γὰρ ***εὐαγγελίζομαι*** ὑμῖν **χαρὰν μεγάλην**
ἥτις ἔσται παντὶ τῷ λαῷ,
4 ὅτι ἐτέχθη ὑμῖν σήμερον ***σωτὴρ***
ὅς ἐστιν Χριστὸς κύριος **ἐν πόλει Δαυίδ·**
5 καὶ τοῦτο ὑμῖν τὸ σημεῖον,
6 εὑρήσετε ***βρέφος*** ἐσπαργανωμένον καὶ κείμενον ἐν φάτνῃ.
7 καὶ ἐξαίφνης ἐγένετο σὺν τῷ ἀγγέλῳ πλῆθος ***στρατιᾶς*** οὐρανίου
8 αἰνούντων τὸν θεὸν καὶ λεγόντων,
9 Δόξα ἐν **ὑψίστοις θεῷ**
10 καὶ ἐπὶ γῆς εἰρήνη ἐν ἀνθρώποις εὐδοκίας.

The speeches of the angels in chapters 1 and 2 exhibit formal parallels. All three speeches have formulaic and parallel introductions (the speech to Mary places the pronoun referring to her at the end of the colon, whereas the other two have the angel in terminal position). In all three cases the angel tells the one visited not to be afraid. All three speeches promise imperial power for the child they prophesy. The speeches to Zechariah and Mary specify the child's name while the speech to the shepherds confers titles on the promised child.

The three speeches also exhibit significant differences. They differ in length, make different promises and predictions, and employ different vocabulary. The speeches also engage different literary styles.

Two employ paratactic style, while one is elegant. The sound differences lead to interpretation. The paratactic style of the angel's speech to Mary might be explained by Mary's lowly state, dictated by her social class and gender. But similar paratactic style is employed in the speech to Zechariah, a priest of Israel, while the speech to the shepherds, whose status in the empire's hierarchy is nearly as low as Mary's, exhibits a much more elegant style than the other two. Clearly, the recipient's status does not determine style; rather, a more complex dynamic is at work.

After their formulaic beginnings, the speeches do not follow a predictable pattern. Similarities and differences among the speeches highlight their distinctiveness. The speeches are therefore framed not so much to exhibit parallels as to show progression along a trajectory. The speeches become progressively shorter and their message becomes clearer and more explicit. In the speech to Zechariah John is hailed as a bringer of joy (χαρά) and is called great (μέγας) before the lord. His status is made comparable to Elijah's, for the angel promises that John will turn many of the sons of Israel toward the lord God. The angel promises Mary that her son, too, will be great (μέγας). But in contrast with John, Jesus is designated as the one to be called υἱὸς ὑψίστου (son of the most high). In addition to his achieving of greatness, the angel promises, the lord God will give Jesus the throne of David, and he will reign (βασιλεύσει) over Jacob's house in perpetuity, and his dominion (τῆς βασιλείας αὐτοῦ) will not end. The announcement suggests an expansion of dominion beyond Israel, drawing the audience into the sense of anticipation depicted on the part of the narrative's characters.

The angel's speech to the shepherds confirms the expectation of expanded dominion beyond the house of Jacob. The angel claims to bring good news (εὐαγγελίζομαι) framed in terms of an imperial edict. To the shepherds, the angel promises great joy (χαρὰν μεγάλην) in contrast to their previous great fear (ἐφοβήθησαν φόβον μέγαν). Note that whereas fear had fallen on Zechariah (φόβος ἐπέπεσεν ἐπ' αὐτόν) at the approach of the angel and Mary was deeply troubled (διεταράχθη), the shepherds experienced a great fear (ἐφοβήθησαν φόβον μέγαν). The greater intensity of their fear is appropriate for those who receive the εὐαγγελία of a σωτήρ ὅς ἐστιν Χριστὸς κύριος.[35] After all, the angel is soon equipped with the imperial accoutrements of a στρατιᾶς οὐρανίου (heavenly army), and his message concludes with Δόξα ἐν ὑψίστοις θεῷ (glory to God in the highest). In keeping with the angel's imperial message, the speech's literary style employs less parataxis and longer cola joined by grammatical subordination.

As the speeches become progressively more explicit about Jesus' imperial dominion, they also create sustained tension between the grandeur of imperial rule and the lowliness of those who receive the angel's messages. Not only will John become great before the lord and filled with a holy spirit, but he is destined for an eminence equal to that of Elijah, a prophet who prepares the way—though not to that of a ruler. In the speech to Mary, Jesus is also destined to become great and son of the most high and to sit on the throne of David. The angel announces to the shepherds that Jesus will be a savior, messiah, and lord. Yet in both speeches to them (2:12 and 2:16) he is called a βρέφος (baby), a newborn infant, emphasizing his fragile state. Thus the speeches emphasize the theme of Mary's hymn, praising God for exalting the lowly (ὕψωσεν ταπεινούς).

Luke's nativity sets the stage for large narrative themes of promise and fulfillment, competing empires, and the dominion of the lowly.

Appendix

The Nativity

Luke 2:1–20

PART 1: IMPERIAL CONTEXT (2:1–5)

Period 1

1 **Ἐγένετο δὲ** ἐν ταῖς ἡμέραις ἐκείναις
2 ἐξῆλθεν δόγμα παρὰ Καίσαρος Αὐγούστου
3 ἀπογράφεσθαι πᾶσαν τὴν *οἰκουμένην*.
4 αὕτη ἀπογραφὴ πρώτη **ἐγένετο ἡγεμ**ονεύοντος τῆς Συρίας Κυρηνίου.

Period 2

1 καὶ ἐπορεύοντο πάντες ἀπογράφεσθαι, ἕκαστος εἰς τὴν ἑαυτοῦ πόλιν.
2 Ἀνέβη δὲ καὶ Ἰωσὴφ ἀπὸ τῆς Γαλιλαίας
ἐκ πόλεως Ναζαρὲθ
εἰς τὴν Ἰουδαίαν
εἰς πόλιν Δαυὶδ ἥτις καλεῖται Βηθλέεμ,
διὰ τὸ εἶναι αὐτὸν ἐξ *οἴκου* καὶ πατριᾶς Δαυίδ,
3 ἀπογράψασθαι σὺν Μαριὰμ τῇ ἐμνηστευμένῃ αὐτῷ, οὔσῃ ἐγκύῳ.

PART 2: BIRTH (2:6–7)

Period 3

1 **ἐγένετο δὲ** ἐν τῷ εἶναι αὐτοὺς ἐκεῖ
2 ἐπλήσθησαν αἱ ἡμέραι τοῦ τεκεῖν αὐτήν,
3 καὶ ἔτεκεν τὸν υἱὸν αὐτῆς τὸν πρωτότοκον·
4 καὶ ἐσπαργάνωσεν αὐτὸν
5 καὶ ἀνέκλινεν αὐτὸν ἐν φάτνῃ,
6 διότι οὐκ ἦν αὐτοῖς τόπος ἐν τῷ καταλύματι.

PART 3: SHEPHERDS AND ANGELS (2:8–14)

Period 4

1 Καὶ ποιμένες ἦσαν ἐν τῇ χώρᾳ τῇ αὐτῇ ἀγραυλοῦντες
2 καὶ φυλάσσοντες φυλακὰς τῆς νυκτὸς ἐπὶ τὴν ποίμνην αὐτῶν.
3 καὶ ἄγγελος κυρίου ἐπέστη αὐτοῖς
4 καὶ δόξα κυρίου περιέλαμψεν αὐτούς,
5 καὶ ἐφοβήθησαν φόβον μέγαν.
6 καὶ εἶπεν αὐτοῖς ὁ ἄγγελος,

Period 5

1 Μὴ φοβεῖσθε,

2 ἰδοὺ γὰρ εὐαγγελίζομαι ὑμῖν χαρὰν μεγάλην ἥτις ἔσται παντὶ τῷ λαῷ,
3 ὅτι ἐτέχθη ὑμῖν σήμερον σωτὴρ ὅς ἐστιν Χριστὸς κύριος ἐν πόλει Δαυίδ·
4 καὶ τοῦτο ὑμῖν τὸ σημεῖον,
5 εὑρήσετε βρέφος ἐσπαργανωμένον καὶ κείμενον ἐν φάτνῃ.

Period 6

1 καὶ ἐξαίφνης **ἐγένετο** σὺν τῷ ἀγγέλῳ πλῆθος στρατιᾶς οὐρανίου
2 αἰνούντων τὸν θεὸν καὶ λεγόντων,
3 Δόξα ἐν ὑψίστοις θεῷ
4 καὶ ἐπὶ γῆς εἰρήνη ἐν ἀνθρώποις εὐδοκίας.

PART 4: SHEPHERDS AND FAMILY (2:15–20)

Period 7

1 Καὶ **ἐγένετο** ὡς ἀπῆλθον ἀπ' αὐτῶν εἰς τὸν οὐρανὸν οἱ ἄγγελοι,
2 οἱ ποιμένες ἐλάλουν πρὸς ἀλλήλους,
3 Διέλθωμεν δὴ ἕως Βηθλέεμ
4 καὶ ἴδωμεν τὸ *ῥῆμα* τοῦτο τὸ **γεγον**ὸς ὃ ὁ κύριος ἐγνώρισεν ἡμῖν.

Period 8

1 καὶ ἦλθον σπεύσαντες
2 καὶ ἀνεῦρον τήν τε Μαριὰμ
καὶ τὸν Ἰωσὴφ
καὶ τὸ βρέφος κείμενον ἐν τῇ φάτνῃ·

Period 9

1 ἰδόντες δὲ ἐγνώρισαν περὶ τοῦ *ῥήμα*τος τοῦ λαληθέντος αὐτοῖς
περὶ τοῦ παιδίου τούτου.
2 καὶ πάντες οἱ ἀκούσαντες ἐθαύμασαν
περὶ τῶν λαληθέντων ὑπὸ τῶν ποιμένων πρὸς αὐτούς·

Period 10

1 ἡ δὲ Μαριὰμ πάντα συνετήρει τὰ *ῥήματα* ταῦτα συμβάλλουσα ἐν τῇ καρδίᾳ αὐτῆς.
2 καὶ ὑπέστρεψαν οἱ ποιμένες δοξάζοντες καὶ αἰνοῦντες τὸν θεὸν
ἐπὶ πᾶσιν οἷς ἤκουσαν καὶ εἶδον
3 καθὼς ἐλαλήθη πρὸς αὐτούς.

English Transation

PART 1: IMPERIAL CONTEXT (2:1–5)

Period 1

1 In those days it so happened
2 that a decree was issued by Emperor Augustus
3 that a census be taken of the whole civilized world.

4 This first census was taken while Quirinius was governor of Syria.

Period 2

1 Everybody had to travel to their ancestral city to be counted in the census.
2 So Joseph too went up from Galilee,
    from the town of Nazareth,
    to Judea,
    to the town of David called Bethlehem,
  because he was a descendant of David
3 to be counted in the census with Mary, to whom he was engaged; Mary was pregnant.

PART 2: BIRTH (2:6–7)

Period 3

1 It so happened while they were there
2 that the time came for her to give birth
3 and she gave birth to a son, her firstborn.
4 She wrapped him in strips of cloth
5 and laid him in a feeding trough,
6 because the travelers' shelter was no place for those things.

PART 3: SHEPHERDS AND ANGELS (2:8–14)

Period 4

1 Now in the same area there were shepherds living outdoors.
2 They were keeping watch over their sheep at night
3 when a messenger of the Lord stood near them
4 and the glory of the Lord shone around them.
5 They became terrified.
6 But the messenger said to them,

Period 5

1 "Don't be afraid:
2 I bring you good news of a great joy, which is to benefit the whole nation:
3 today in the city of David, the Savior was born to you—he is the Anointed, the Lord.
4 And this will be a sign for you:
5 you will find a baby wrapped in strips of cloth and lying in a feeding trough."

Period 6

1 And suddenly there appeared with the messenger a whole troop of the heavenly army
2 praising God and saying:
3 Glory to God in the highest,
4 and on earth peace to people whom he has favored!

PART 4: SHEPHERDS AND FAMILY (2:15–20)

Period 7

1 It so happened when the messengers left and returned to heaven
2 that the shepherds said to one another,
3 "Come on! Let's go over to Bethlehem
4 and see what has happened, the event the Lord has told us about."

Period 8

1 And they hurried away,
2 and found Mary
        and Joseph,
        and the baby lying in a feeding trough.

Period 9

1 And when they saw it they reported what they had been told about this child.
2 Everyone who listened was astonished at what the shepherds told them.

Period 10

1 But Mary took all this in and reflected on it.
2 And the shepherds returned, glorifying and praising God
                                        for all they had heard and seen;
3 everything turned out just as they had been told.

CHARTS IN ENGLISH

Chart 9.1

Markers	**Chapter 1**	**Chapter 2**
ἐγένετο	There happened	There happened
days	In the days	in those days
Imperial reference	of Herod, king of Judea	that a decree was issued by Emperor Augustus that a census be taken of the whole civilized world. (2:1)
Israelite reference	to be this priest named Zechariah, who belonged to the priestly clan of Abijah. His wife, a descendant of Aaron, was named Elizabeth. (1:5)	So Joseph too went up from Galilee, from the town of Nazareth, to Judea, to the town of David called Bethlehem, because he was a descendant of David, to be counted in the census with Mary, to whom he was engaged; Mary was pregnant.. (2:4–5)
ἐγένετο δέ	And it happened while he was serving as a priest	It so happened while they were there
days	in his priestly order before God (1:8)	that the time came for her to give birth, (2:6)

Chart 9.2

1:26–27	**Period 2 (2:3–5)**
In the sixth month the heavenly messenger Gabriel was sent from God to a town in Galilee called Nazareth, to a virgin engaged to a man named Joseph, of the house of David. The virgin's name was Mary.	Everybody had to travel to their ancestral city to be counted in the census. So Joseph too went up from Galilee, from the town of Nazareth, to Judea, to the town of David called Bethlehem, because he was a descendant of David, to be counted in the census with Mary, to whom he was engaged; Mary was pregnant.

Chart 9.3

1:8–13	2:6–10
While he was serving as priest before God when his priestly clan was on temple duty, it so hap-pened	It so happened while they were there that the time came for her to give birth;
that he was chosen by lot, according to the custom of the priesthood, to enter the sanctuary of the Lord and burn incense. At the hour of incense, while a huge crowd was praying outside,	and she gave birth to a son, her firstborn. She wrapped him in strips of cloth and laid him in a feeding trough, because the travelers' shelter was no place for those things. Now in the same area there were shepherds living outdoors. They were keeping watch over their sheep at night,
there appeared to him a messenger of the Lord standing to the right of the altar of incense. When he saw him, Zechariah was shaken and overcome by fear.	when a messenger of the Lord stood near them and the glory of the Lord shone around them. They became terrified
But the heavenly messenger said to him,	But the messenger said to them,

Chart 9.4

Verse	Narrative Marker		Marker Type
21	And when	eight days were finished for circumcising hi,	(new marker)
22	And when	the time came for their purification according to the Law of Moses,	2:21
25	And behold there was a man	in Jerusalem, named Simeon,	(change of subject)
33	And his father and mother were	astonished at what was being said about him.	(change of subject)
36	And there was a prophetess Anna,		(change of subject)
39	And when	they had carried out everything required by the Law of the Lord,	2:15
42	And when he was	twelve years old,	2:21, 22
46	And it happened	after three days that they found him in the temple area, sitting among the teachers	1:24, 59, 65

ENDNOTES

1. Bovon (2002, p. 16) remarks that the author "attempts to elevate Christian traditions, until that time conveyed in vernacular style, to this higher plane."
2. In the days of Herod, king of Judea, there happened to be this priest named Zechariah, who belonged to the priestly clan of Abijah. His wife, a descendant of Aaron, was named Elizabeth.
3. While he was serving as priest before God when his priestly clan was on temple duty.
4. While ἐγένετο with δέ indicates a connection to the previous story, it still marks the beginning of a major narrative unit because the days, imperial reference, and Israel reference occur with it, and καί does not occur.
5. Translation for Chart 1 is in Appendix at end of chapter.
6. And it so happened, when his time of official service was completed, that he went back home.
7. And it so happened that when Elizabeth heard Mary's greeting, the baby jumped in her womb.
8. And so on the eighth day they came to circumcise the child.
9. All their neighbors became fearful.
10. You see, when the sound of your greeting reached my ears, the baby jumped for joy in my womb.
11. And suddenly there appeared with the messenger a whole troop of the heavenly army praising God and saying.
12. It so happened when the messengers left and returned to heaven.
13. And when he was twelve years old, they went up for the festival as usual.
14. And after three days it so happened that they found him in the temple area, sitting among the teachers, listening to them and asking them questions.
15. In the fifteenth year of the rule of Emperor Tiberius, when Pontius Pilate was governor of Judea, Herod tetrarch of Galilee, his brother Philip tetrarch of the district of Iturea and Trachonitis, and Lysanias tetrarch of Abilene, during the high-priesthood of Annas and Caiaphas, the word of God came to John, son of Zechariah, in the wilderness.
16. See Appendix for translation.
17. It seemed good that I, too, after thoroughly researching everything from the beginning, should set them systematically in writing for you, Theophilus.
18. The historicity of the worldwide census has long been debated. Fitzmyer concludes "that the census is a purely literary device

use by him to associate Mary and Joseph, residents of Nazareth, with Bethlehem (1981, p. 393). This may well be true, but the sound map also suggests that the ἀπογραφὴ underlines and contrasts the imperial power of Augustus and that of heaven and contrasts imperial ἀπο**γραφὴ** and the gospel as **γραφὴ**.

19. Translation for Chart 2 is in Appendix at end of chapter.
20. Translation for Chart 3 is in Appendix at end of chapter.
21. καταλύμα normally means lodging or guest room, see BDAG[3], 521; so used in 22:11 for the upper room, which probably comes from Mark 14:14. Luke 10:34 employs πανδοχεῖον, the specific term for an inn.
22. Was overcome by fear.
23. Fitzmyer (1981, p. 325) among many others sees this trope coming from the Hebrew Bible.
24. Luke does not use the noun εὐαγγελίον (although it occurs twice in Acts, 15:7 and 20:24), but the verb εὐαγγελίζομαι occurs ten times (15 times in Acts). Given the density of imperial references and terms in this section, the sound map suggests that this word is meant to draw yet another contrast between Jesus and the emperor. Koester (1990, p. 3–4) has shown how Christian usage of the term must relate to the Augustan religio-political propaganda.
25. Unlike Zachariah's and Mary's encounters with Gabriel, the shepherds do not respond to the angel; the angels nevertheless have a second speech here as they do in 1:19–29, 33–35.
26. BDF 451 (4) and BDAG[3], 222.
27. *Lit.,* It happened in the days.
28. *Lit.,* It happened in those days.
29. In the fifteenth year of the rule of Emperor Tiberius
30. For translation see Chart 4 in Appendix at the end of the chapter.
31. Luke 2:50–52

    1 And they did not understand what he was talking about.
    2 And he went down with them
    3 and came to Nazareth,
    4 and was obedient to them.
    5 And his mother took note of all these saying in her heart.
    6 And Jesus, precocious as he was,
    continued to excel in learning
    and gain respect in the eyes of God
    and others.

32. Zechariah (1:13–17)

    1 But the heavenly messenger said to him,
    2 "Don't be afraid, Zechariah,

3 for your prayer has been heard,
4 and your wife Elizabeth will bear you a son,
5 and you are to name him John.
6 And you will be joyful and elated,
7 and many will rejoice at his birth,
8 because he will be great in the sight of the Lord;
9 he will drink no wine or beer,
10 and he will be filled with holy spirit from the very day of his birth.
11 And he will cause many of the children of Israel to turn to the Lord their God.
12 He will precede him in the spirit
and power of Elijah:
13 he will turn the hearts of the parents back towards their children,
14 and the disobedient back towards the ways of righteousness,
15 and will make people ready for their Lord."

33. Mary (1:30–33)
1 The heavenly messenger said to her,
2 "Don't be afraid, Mary.
3 You see, you have found favor with God.
4 Listen to me: you will conceive in your womb
5 and give birth to a son,
6 and you will name him Jesus.
7 He will be great, and will be called son of the Most High.
8 xAnd the Lord God will give him the throne of David, his father.
9 He will rule over the house of Jacob forever;
10 and his dominion will have no end."

34. Shepherds (2:10–14)
1 But the messenger said to them,
2 "Don't be afraid:
3 I bring you good news of a great joy,
which is to benefit the whole nation;
4 today a Savior was born to you
he is the Anointed, the Lord in the city of David,.
5 And this will be a sign for you:
6 you will find a baby wrapped in strips of cloth and lying in a feeding trough."
7 And suddenly there appeared with the messenger a whole troop of the heavenly army
8 praising God and saying:

9 Glory to God in the highest,
10 and on earth peace to people whom he has favored!

35. *Lit.*, a savior, who is a Messiah, the lord.

WORKS CONSULTED

Alexander, Loveday. 1993. *The Preface to Luke's Gospel, Literary Convention and Social Context in Luke 1.1–4 and Acts 1.1.* Cambridge: Cambridge University Press.

Bovon, François. 2002. *Luke 1: A Commentary on the Gospel of Luke 1:1–9:50.* Translated by C. M. Thomas, *Hermeneia.* Minneapolis: Fortress.

Brown, Raymond E. 1979. *The Birth of the Messiah, A Commentary on the Infancy Narratives in Matthew and Luke.* Garden City, NY: Doubleday.

Fitzmyer, Joseph. 1981. *The Gospel According to Luke (I-IX).* Vol. 28, *Anchor Bible Series.* Garden City, NY: Doubleday & Co.

Koester, Helmut. 1990. *Ancient Christian Gospels.* Philadelphia: Trinity Press International.

Chapter 10

Sound and Structure

The Sermon on the Mount

Literature perceived by ear and stored in the mind needs elaborate structuring devices if it is to be comprehensible and memorable. Sound defines small narrative units, as Mark's crucifixion story and the resurrection appearances in John's gospel illustrate. Sound lets us listen in on an overture for Luke's gospel in the nativity story. A sound map of Matthew's Sermon on the Mount illustrates how sound organizes non-narrative material and forges structural devices employed later in the gospel.

A sound map of the Sermon on the Mount is displayed at the end of this chapter, but because of the Sermon's length, a full description of the map will not be attempted in this chapter.[1] Instead, this chapter analyzes the Sermon's sound structure and suggests some of its impacts on other portions of Matthew's gospel.

STRUCTURAL COMPARISONS
THE GOLDEN RULE (7:12)

While many commentators agree on the Sermon's major sectional divisions through Mt 6:18, they disagree about the Sermon's organization from that point forward, precisely because they do not take account of the Sermon's aural clues and are therefore not susceptible to the effects of its ear training.

Many commentators propose that the phrases τὸν νόμον ἢ τοὺς προφήτας (the law and the prophets) in 5:17 and ὁ νόμος καὶ οἱ προφῆται in 7:12 establish the boundaries of the Sermon's main section, bracketing Matthew's treatment of Jesus' approach to the Jewish scriptures.[2] Betz, Davies and Allison, and Luz represent major examples of this position.[3] All three find sectional boundaries after 5:12, 5:16, 5:20, 5:48 and 6:18 as does the outline proposed in the sound map, but each argues for different sectional divisions after 6:18.

HANS DIETER BETZ

Betz interprets the Sermon on the Mount as an *epitome* of sayings in the "transcultural" genre of "teachings," including analogs in the Hebrew scriptures, Egyptian and Jewish wisdom literature, and the

Hellenistic philosophical tradition (1995, pp. 74–75).[4] Betz (1995, p. 62) contends that the main body of the Sermon includes 5:17–7:12 because the Sermon is "constructed as a ring composition, as indicated by the expression "the law and the prophets" in 5:17 and 7:12. "This large portion of the Sermon consists of three parts, one section "dealing with the interpretation of the Torah (5:17–48), a second section dealing with cultic rituals (6:1–18), and a third section devoted to the affairs of daily life (6:19–7:12)." Betz (1995, pp. 63 -64) notes that both secular literature and the literature of Judaism in the first century CE follow the convention of dividing the formal principles of a religion into three groups. He cites his debt to Davies for showing the importance of triadic organization and of the Sermon on the Mount as a philosophical counterproposal; nonetheless, he argues, "the adversary was not Jamnia but Greek philosophy."

Betz (1995, p. 423) contends that the section of the Sermon on the Mount beginning at 6:19 ends at 7:12 with the golden rule. He comments on the difficulty of discerning the Sermon's organization in this section. Betz labels 6:19–7:12, "The Conduct of Daily Life." He admits that his title for the section "is not mentioned anywhere in the text itself," but is suitable because it "is descriptive of the content of the section with its sayings compositions, and for other literary reasons." Ultimately, Betz's section division at 7:12 rests on his interpretation of that section's conceptual unity, his understanding of how its expressed ideas cohere. His organizational scheme derives from the composition's signifieds, not its signifiers; it is based on abstract semantic meaning, not the Sermon's performed quality as spoken sound.

The same principle guides Betz's remaining sectional divisions. His next section (7:13–23) contains "three sections of eschatological warnings," and the final section (7:24–27) contains "the peroration, using the parable of the two builders," the importance of which is indicated by its emphasis on "hearing and doing" the sayings of Jesus, a significant theme in the Sermon and the gospel, according to Betz (1995, pp. 65–66,82–84).

Although Betz's organizational scheme demonstrates certain similarities to the structural requirements of an *epitome*, his scheme relies on an abstract notion of the Sermon's meaning, a notion that depends upon careful rereading and sustained reflection on the Sermon as a whole.[5] But the organizing power of such abstract concepts, with their heavy emphasis on the signified rather than the signifier, is not consistent with the dynamics of auditory reception, the primary mode of meaning-making in the Greco-Roman world, where compositions primarily were published in the form of speech.[6]

Moreover, Betz's scheme relies on the single repetition of "the law and the prophets" in 7:12 to establish the boundaries of the Sermon's main body. Although the law and the prophets is an important theme in the Sermon and in Matthew's gospel, its infrequent expression in the Sermon and the lack of corroboration from other aural devices argue against any role for this phrase as a major structuring device in the Sermon. In short, the phrase does not occur often enough to qualify as a thematic element. Other phrases, beginning with the predictive structural signal μακάριοι οἱ in the beatitudes, exhibit more structural importance. The frequent repetition of μακάριοι οἱ (congratulations to) establishes an expectation for repeated beginning sounds in the Sermon. Other repeated phrases with clear thematic significance are ἡ βασιλεία τῶν οὐρανῶν (Heaven's domain) and the related phrases ὁ οὐρανὸς καὶ ἡ γῆ (heaven and earth) and πάτερ ἡμῶν ὁ ἐν τοῖς οὐρανοῖς (our father in the heavens) (Lee 2005, pp. 264–66).

While Betz's scheme acknowledges the importance of repetition, it does not take account of the several fundamental functions of repetition as a structuring device in compositions received as speech. These dynamics, outlined in chapter 4, depend upon reprisal of speech sounds with sufficient frequency to store sound patterns in memory. A single repetition, especially when disconnected from its original iteration by the passage of time and many intervening aural patterns, does not exert the sort of organizational influence posited in schemes such as Betz's ring composition. The phrase ὁ νόμος καὶ οἱ προφῆται (the law and the prophets) may well be thematically significant in the Sermon and in the gospel on other grounds, but its single repetition (two occurrences) in the Sermon are not sufficient to supply the Sermon's primary organizational signal. In fact, no single auditory signal can organize such a large body of material. An audience needs multiple sound clues to establish a large organizational scheme.

W. D. DAVIES AND DALE ALLISON

Davies and Allison's *International Critical Commentary* adduces a related but somewhat different structural arrangement, based upon their analysis of the Sermon's structure as a collection of triads that provide a Christian response to the religious teaching of Jamnia. Davies and Allison mark sectional boundaries at 6:19–34, 7:1–12, and 7:13–29. They argue that 6:19–34 is followed by 7:1–12, its "structural twin," since both sections deliver an instruction, including an exhortation (6:19–21 and 7:1–2), a parable about the eye (6:22–23 and 7:3–5), another parable (6:24 and 7:6), and an encouraging passage referring to the Father's care (6:25–34 and 7:7–11). The golden rule (7:12) provides their conclusion.[7] Davies and Allison's analysis of the instruction portion of these passages (6:19–24 and 7:1–6) also observes that these portions of the Sermon share an argument *a minori ad maius*, as well as repeated key words and "major illustrations" such as the birds of the air and lilies of the field in 6:19–24 and the son's requests to the father in 7:9–10 (1988, p. 626).[8]

The final section of the Sermon, according to Davies and Allison, consists of 7:13–27 because its content pertains to false prophets. They find corroboration for this organizational scheme in its division into three component parts, the two ways (7:13–14), false prophets (7:15–23), and two builders (7:24–27) (1988, p. 694).

The structure proposed by Davies and Allison presents several problems. First, as Betz (1995, p. 423) observes, the triadic arrangement of 6:19–34 is not clear, since it appears that the golden rule (7:12) provides the third and concluding component for both 6:19–34 and 7:1–12. The structural analysis based on the Sermon's sound map actually provides a more satisfactory parallel triadic arrangement with twin structures than that proposed by Davies and Allison: section 6 (6:19–7:6) includes three prohibitions—μὴ θησαυρίζετε, 6:16; μὴ κρίνετε, 7:1; and μὴ δῶτε, 7:6 (don't acquire possessions, don't pass judgment, don't offer sacred things)—followed in section 7 (7:7–20) by three imperatives—αἰτεῖτε, 7:7; εἰσέλθατε, 7:13, προσέξετε, 7:15 (ask, seek, knock). The Sermon's sound map also accounts for the repeated key words (μεριμνάω and αἰτέω) (worry and ask) that Davies and Allison note as similar features of the parallel sections 6:19–34 and 7:1–12.[9] Finally, Davies and Allison's organizational scheme, like that of Betz, fundamentally depends upon an abstract, conceptual unity available only to silent readers whose meaning-making strategies depend almost exclusively on semantic meaning derived during silent reading.

ULRICH LUZ

Luz posits still another organizational scheme, a chiastic, symmetrical arrangement. He finds concentric rings around the Πάτηρ ἡμῶν (our father) prayer (6:7–15), which he views as the Sermon's centerpiece, with corresponding sections before and after it.[10] Like Davies and Allison, Luz sees parallel structural components in the passage under discussion, but his structural parallels extend throughout the Sermon, based on inclusios, section lengths and formal correspondences. Luz contends that the Sermon's narrative introduction (5:1–2) corresponds to its conclusion (7:28–8:1a); the beatitudes (5:3–16) to the Sermon's final section (7:13–27); the "introit" of the main body (5:17–20) to its conclusion (7:12); and the antitheses (5:21–48) to the section on possessions, judging, and prayer (6:19–7:11). He also argues that the sections before (6:1–6) and after (6:16–18) the Πάτηρ ἡμῶν prayer correspond to each other and deal with the subject of righteousness (1989, pp. 211–13).

Luz's proposal contains elements of the schemes outlined by both Betz and Davies and Allison. Like the latter, Luz's scheme assigns singular status to 7:12 as a verse that stands alone in the Sermon's structure.[11] Like Betz, he associates 7:12 with 5:17–20, which contains the previous mention of the law and the prophets. Both Luz and Davies and Allison identify 7:13–27 as the Sermon's final section.

Luz's structural arrangement presents some of the same difficulties as the schemes proposed by Betz and by Davies and Allison. It relies on a conceptual unity not available to listeners who must process spoken compositions in real time and store them in memory. Indeed, Luz admits that the Sermon's "architectonic symmetry" emerges "only when the Sermon on the Mount is read in context, and even then it does not reveal itself in the first reading but only to repeated perusal and, in a manner of speaking, in an 'optical' view" (1989, p. 213). For Luz, the Sermon's structure indicates that "the Gospel of Matthew was intended in the first place for reading and not for hearing" (1989, p. 213, n.2). This is a highly problematic claim, because the Sermon on the Mount is presented in Matthew's gospel as a speech. Even more important, as we have seen, is the undeniable fact that Matthew's gospel, like all ancient Greek compositions, was crafted in a rhetorical culture for largely illiterate audiences who came to know the Sermon only by hearing it spoken aloud.

The symmetrical structure Luz adduces is available only through private, silent reading. A listener would have to hold the entire Sermon in memory all at once, perceiving only at the end and after sustained reflection that the Πάτηρ ἡμῶν prayer provides its structural nucleus. Luz's organizational scheme does not explain the function of the strong auditory signals that occur in the Sermon before the Πάτηρ ἡμῶν prayer. Some of these signals, such as the anaphoric character of the beatitudes and the repetitive parallelism of the antitheses, are evident even in English translation. According to Luz's scheme, these organizational signals are secondary to the centrality of the Πάτηρ ἡμῶν prayer, but in order to perceive the prayer as the Sermon's center, ancient listeners would have had to ignore the Sermon's many strong structural signals and somehow hold its entire content in memory without structural support until its conceptual unity centered on the prayer emerged at the end of the final ring. But as Luz himself admits, this is possible only for a silent reader.

AN ALTERNATIVE BASED ON SOUND ANALYSIS

All three outlines analyzed above posit a major structural division after 7:12. This hypothesis can be tested against the Sermon's sound map. If 7:12 concludes a main portion of the Sermon, it should exhibit clear signals for unit closure.

7:12[12]

1	Πάντα οὖν	ὅσα ἐὰν θέλητε ἵνα	ποιῶσιν ὑμῖν οἱ ἄνθρωποι,
2		οὕτως καὶ ὑμεῖς	ποιεῖτε αὐτοῖς·
3		οὗτος γάρ ἐστιν ὁ νόμος καὶ οἱ προφῆται.	

Contrary to expectation for the end of a structural unit, this passage shows only weak structural signals based upon sound, including repetition of the rough breathing associated with o/ου vowel sounds at or near the beginning of each colon and the repetition of a form of ποιεῖν (to do) in the middle of the first and second cola. The passage does not show indications of rounding or balance, which are conventional signals for closure in periodic structure.

But in fairness to the outlines advanced by Betz, Davies and Allison, and Luz, section beginnings frequently show clearer indications of structure than section endings, so perhaps 7:12 does not furnish the most important clue to its structural importance. Even while presenting only weak auditory signals for closure, 7:12 might still be understood as a conclusion to a major section of the Sermon if clear indications of a structural shift to a new major section could be found in 7:13.

7:13[13]

Εἰσέλθατε διὰ τῆς στενῆς πύλης·
ὅτι πλατεῖα ἡ πύλη καὶ εὐρύχωρος ἡ ὁδὸς ἡ ἀπάγουσα εἰς τὴν ἀπώλειαν,
καὶ πολλοί εἰσιν οἱ εἰσερχόμενοι δι' αὐτῆς·

In fact, 7:13 offers no such signal of a major structural shift. Its opening sounds, Εἰσέλθατε, evoke previous imperative verbs with similar inflectional endings in 7:7 (Αἰτεῖτε, ζητεῖτε, κρούετε) (ask, seek, knock). Thus 7:12 not only fails to signal section closure, but 7:13 clearly signals its connection to previous sounds. The Sermon offers no significant auditory evidence of an organizational shift, let alone a major structural cleavage, after 7:12.

All three outlines examined above by Betz, Davies and Allison, and Luz ignore a crucial structural clue in 7:7, a signal that is available only at the level of sound. This clue signals the beginning of the Sermon's section 7.

The Opening Period of Section 7 (7:7):[14]

1	Αἰτεῖτε,	καὶ	δοθήσεται	ὑμῖν·
2	ζητεῖτε,	καὶ	εὑρήσετε·	
3	κρούετε,	καὶ	ἀνοιγήσεται	ὑμῖν.

The repeated opening sounds of the imperative verbs, reinforced by their rhyming inflectional endings and the close parallelism of the period's component cola, conform to the listening convention established in the Sermon's first section (μακάριοι; congratulations), and sustained throughout the Sermon.

From the Sermon's beginning, repetition of initial sounds trains the ear to listen for subsequent repetitions and thus organizes the Sermon into its major sections. Chapter 4 demonstrated how the eightfold repetition of μακάριοι (congratulations) in the beatitudes establishes an expectation of repeated beginning sounds to mark unit boundaries. Chapter 4 also showed that, having established an expectation of repeated beginnings, sound patterns can be modified to effect a transition from one section to the next. The transition from the beatitudes to the sayings about salt of the earth and light of the world is accomplished through a sophisticated aural device: the repeated beginning sounds μακάριοι οἱ are modified in the final beatitude to μακάριοί ἐστε (congratulations to you) (5:11). In 5:13 ὑμεῖς ἐστε (you are) introduces the salt saying and is repeated in 5:14 with the light saying. Thus the modified form of the initial beatitude pattern, μακάριοί ἐστε, supplies common beginning sounds for both the beatitudes (μακάριοι οἱ) (congratulations to you) and the salt and light section (ὑμεῖς ἐστε) (you are). By employing opening sounds to orient an audience, the Sermon draws sustained attention to initial sounds and thereby trains an audience to depend upon those repeated beginnings for organizational clues.

The Sermon subsequently confirms the organizational clue of repeated opening sounds and reinforces the expectation that beginning sounds will orient a listener to what follows. For example, the use of antitheses in the section 5:21–48 intensifies an audience's ear training and rigidly reinforces the organizational devices of repeated beginnings and similarly structured component units. The antitheses open with Ἠκούσατε ὅτι ἐρρέθη τοῖς ἀρχαίοις (as you know, our ancestors were told) (5:21). This phrase or a variation recurs in 5:27, 33, 38, and 43, and each repetition introduces a component unit that exhibits the same organizational structure. This pattern includes a statement of the law (you have heard it said . . .), counterstatement (but I say to you . . .), illustrations from case law set in parallel (e. g., offense from the eye and the hand, 5:29–30), and a conclusion (e. g., be perfect, as your heavenly father is perfect 5:48). The aural devices that establish this section's structure are evident even in translation.

The Sermon's sound map shows that repeated opening sounds organize all its parts into a hierarchical structure. Repeated beginnings establish the boundaries for the Sermon's eight major sections, composed of smaller units with similar sound signatures. Chart 10.1 summarizes the organization according to repeated beginnings.

Chart 10.1 Sectional divisions of the Sermon on the Mount[15]

Section boundary:	Repeated beginning sounds	Occurrences of repeated beginnings
5:3–12	Μακάριοι οἱ . . . ὅτι αὐτοί (αὐτῶν)	5:3, 4, 5, 6, 7, 8, 9, 10, 11
5:13–16	Ὑμεῖς ἐστε	5:13, 14
5:17–20	Μὴ νομίσητε	5:17
5:21–48	Ἠκούσατε ὅτι ἐρρέθη τοῖς .αρχαίοις	5:21, 27, 33, 38, 43
6:1–18	Προσ- . . . Ὅταν	6:1, 2, 5, 7, 16
6:19–7:6	Μή + [imperative verb]	6:19, 7:1, 6
7:7–20	[Imperative Verb]	7:7, 13, 15
7:21–28	Οὐ πᾶς	7:21, 24

The beatitudes and the antitheses present the clearest examples of the Sermon's use of repeated opening sounds to create structure. The success of this acoustic device is evident in the agreement we find among various commentators' outlines of the Sermon's structure from 5:3–6:18.

As Chapter 4 has shown, established sound patterns can be varied and modified in many ways without losing their organizational function or communicative power. In fact, pattern variation engages an audience by rewarding close attention and lending variety—a strategy we can discern and appreciate as the Sermon on the Mount applies the technique of repeated beginnings in varied and progressively more sophisticated ways.

For example, the section that follows the antitheses (6:1–6:18, section 5 on the sound map) alternates two repeating patterns within a section. The section begins with Προσέχετε (take care) (6:1), and the unit containing the Lord's prayer opens with Προσευχόμενοι (when you pray) (6:7). By way of effective contrast to this use of προσ- as its repeated opening sound the intervening units all open with ὅταν (when) (6:2, 5, and 16) and follow a common structure.

In a different variation of repeated beginnings, Section 6 of the Sermon's sound map (6:19–7:6), employs prohibitions as repeated beginnings. Each unit opens with the negative particle μή, with a different prohibition each time (6:19, 7:1, and 7:6). This section's structure is the most widely varied in the Sermon.

After the extended, complex, and widely varied structure of section 6, the Sermon furnishes at the beginning of section 7 the same kind of clear auditory clue that was forged at the Sermon's beginning.

7:7

1	Αἰτεῖτε,	καὶ	δοθήσεται	ὑμῖν·
2	ζητεῖτε,	καὶ	εὑρήσετε·	
3	κρούετε,	καὶ	ἀνοιγήσεται	ὑμῖν.

As in the beatitudes, short, parallel cola are repeated in rapid succession, including the repetition of καί in each colon, rhyming inflectional endings for the verbs in cola 1 and 3, and the repetition of ὑμῖν in cola 1 and 3. by means of the striking similarities of these opening cola, the Sermon's primary organizational signal is invoked and a new structural boundary is established.

As Davies and Allison observe, this section parallels some of the structural features of the preceding section; but the parallel is different and clearer than they recognize. In 7:7, three imperatives open section 7 and are echoed at the beginning of each of its units: αἰτεῖτε (ask), unit 1 (7:7–12); εἰσέλθατε (try to get in), unit 2 (7:13–14); and προσέχετε (be on the lookout), unit 3 (7:15–20). These three imperatives reprise the three prohibitions that organize the preceding section 6 (6:19–7:6).

Section 6 Component Units

Unit 1: **Μὴ θησαυρίζετε** ὑμῖν θησαυροὺς ἐπὶ τῆς γῆς[16] (6:19–34)

Unit 2: **Μὴ κρίνετε**[17] (7:1–5)

Unit 3: **Μὴ δῶτε** τὸ ἅγιον τοῖς κυσίν[18] (7:6)

Section 7 (7:7–12) derives its unity and coherence from its organization around three imperative statements. This pattern is forecast in 7:7 and developed throughout the section. This structural configuration echoes, reinforces, and is reinforced by that of the three prohibitions in the previous section. Section 7 ends with 7:20, the conclusion of its third structural unit:

Unit 7.3 (7:15–20) [19]

1.1 **Προσέχετε** ἀπὸ τῶν ψευδοπροφητῶν,
1.2 οἵτινες ἔρχονται πρὸς ὑμᾶς ἐν ἐνδύμασιν προβάτων,
1.3 ἔσωθεν δέ εἰσιν λύκοι ἅρπαγες.
1.4 ἀπὸ τῶν καρπῶν αὐτῶν ἐπιγνώσεσθε αὐτούς·

2.1 μήτι συλλέγουσιν ἀπὸ ἀκανθῶν σταφυλὰς
2.2 ἢ ἀπὸ τριβόλων σῦκα;
2.3 οὕτως πᾶν δένδρον ἀγαθὸν καρποὺς καλοὺς ποιεῖ,
2.4 τὸ δὲ σαπρὸν δένδρον καρποὺς πονηροὺς ποιεῖ·

3.1 οὐ δύναται δένδρον ἀγαθὸν καρποὺς πονηροὺς ποιεῖν,
3.2 οὐδὲ δένδρον σαπρὸν καρποὺς καλοὺς ποιεῖν.

4.1 πᾶν δένδρον μὴ ποιοῦν καρπὸν καλὸν ἐκκόπτεται
4.2 καὶ εἰς πῦρ βάλλεται.
4.3 ἄρα γε ἀπὸ τῶν καρπῶν αὐτῶν ἐπιγνώσεσθε αὐτούς.

This structural unit follows a now predictable pattern, with an introductory period elaborating the opening imperative, Προσέχετε (be on the lookout). Middle periods 2 and 3 run in close parallel, including repetitions of δένδρον (tree), ἀγαθόν (healthy, sound), σαπρόν (diseased, rotten), καρπούς (fruit), καλούς (choice), and ποιεῖ/ποεῖν (produce). Period 4 closes the section by echoing these parallels with ποιοῦν (produce), καρπόν (fruit), and καλόν (choice) in its opening colon, by the implications of these repeated terms in ellipsis in colon 2, and by an elongated colon 3 that rounds out the structure and signals closure. These concluding signals are confirmed in the subsequent period.

7:21

Οὐ πᾶς ὁ λέγων μοι, Κύριε κύριε,
εἰσελεύσεται εἰς τὴν βασιλείαν τῶν οὐρανῶν
ἀλλ' ὁ ποιῶν τὸ θέλημα τοῦ πατρός μου τοῦ ἐν τοῖς οὐρανοῖς[20]

This period confirms the concluding signals of the previous colon by signaling a structural shift that is here accomplished by introducing a new set of sound signals, many of which have already been designated as thematic in the Sermon, including τὴν βασιλείαν τῶν οὐρανῶν (heaven's domain), τοῦ πατρός μου (my father), and the repetition of οὐρανῶν/ οὐρανοῖς (heaven, skies). The colon's opening sounds, Οὐ πᾶς (not everyone), also signal a structural break, and will become designated as a new repeated beginning sound group when they are repeated in 7:24. This collection of structural clues confirms that 7:7–20 coheres as a structural unit and that a new unit, the Sermon's final section, begins with 7:21.

The Sermon's final section, section 8 on the sound map (7:21–27), employs the structuring technique established in the beatitudes and used throughout the Sermon, the repetition of beginning sounds. Section 8 (οὐ πᾶς, not everyone) applies this technique more simply than in some previous sections, and thus in a manner consistent with expectations for the end of a speech. The beginning sounds of section 8, οὐ πᾶς (not everyone), are repeated only once in 7:24 πᾶς οὖν (everyone), organizing the section into two brief units with similar structures. The Sermon's aural demands decrease as the speech reaches its end and the gospel resumes its narrative.

Kennedy (1984, pp. 48–63), whose outline of the Sermon on the Mount is based upon his rhetorical analysis, presents an outline compatible with the sectional divisions suggested by the Sermon's sound map. Kennedy finds a development from simple structure at the beginning to increasingly complex structure until just past the midpoint, where a climax generally occurs in Greek compositions, and a denouement at the end. See chart 10.2.

Chart 10.2 Comparison of rhetorical and sound structures

Kennedy's outline	Versification	Sound Analysis
Proem	5:3–16	Section 1 (μακάριοι, congratulations) Section 2 (ὑμεῖς ἐστε, you are)
Proposition	5:17–20	Section 3 (μὴ νομίσητε, don't imagine)
Headings: Group 1	5:21–48	Section 4 (ἠκούσατε, you have heard [*lit.*])
Group 2	6:1–18	Section 5 (προσ- . . . ὅταν, from . . . whenever)
Group 3	6:19–7:20	Section 6 (μή [don't] + imperative verb) Section 7 (imperative verb)
Epilogue	7:21–27	Section 8 (οὐ πᾶς, not everyone)

Kennedy (1984, pp. 59–62) argues that 7:12 is embedded in a third group of rhetorical headings in the Sermon, comprising 6:19–7:20, which correspond to sections 6 and 7 on the sound map. He ascribes particular importance to 5:17–20 as the proposition of the Sermon, the explication of which is the Sermon's purpose. Nevertheless, Kennedy does not assign correlative importance to the phrase "the law and the prophets" when it is repeated in 7:12. And besides failing to argue that 7:12 marks a sectional break in the Sermon, he delineates no break whatsoever between sections 6 and 7 in the sound outline. Still, this presents no conflict between Kennedy's outline and the outline that emerges from sound analysis, inasmuch as sections 6 and 7 are linked because they both begin their units with imperative verbs and thus similar sound signals. Rhetorically, the third group of headings in Kennedy's outline, 6:19–7:20, consists of a series of imperative statements: three negative imperatives are followed by three positive imperatives. The sections are aurally distinguished in their repeated beginning sounds only by the opening negative particles in the component units of section 6. The support Kennedy's analysis lends to a sound analysis of the Sermon is notable because Kennedy's outline is informed by his expertise in classical rhetoric, which was supported by grammar, the Hellenistic Greek science of sound.[21] It therefore ascribes central importance to the dynamics of speech and, implicitly, to the impact of sound.

Sound mapping and analysis identifies an organizational scheme that accounts for the Sermon's most notable structural features: repetition of initial sounds established in the beatitudes; repetition of structural units in parallel elaborated first in the beatitudes and notably in the antitheses; and clear signals for closure at the ends of structural units. These structural signals operate at the level of the signifier and are therefore empirically verifiable, unlike structural proposals that rely on a silent reader's reflective interpretation of the Sermon's abstract meaning on a semantic level.

SUBSEQUENT USE OF THE SERMON'S SOUND CLUES

Listeners become oriented to a composition through the patterned repetition of sounds that train the ear to comprehend a composition's λόγος or *res*. The Sermon and all successful spoken compositions craft aural devices that function as economical codes that become available for subsequent use to achieve certain effects. It is reasonable to expect such devices in the Sermon to recur elsewhere in the gospel as organizational and semantic clues. The following three examples suggest ways that structural devices forged in the Sermon on the Mount subsequently serve to shape the gospel's reception.[22]

HEAVEN AND EARTH

Matthew characteristically substitutes ἡ βασιλεία τῶν οὐρανῶν (heaven's domain) for the more typical synoptic gospel term ἡ βασιλεία τοῦ Θεοῦ (God's imperial rule). Matthew's favorite name for God is Πάτερ ἡμῶν ὁ ἐν τοῖς οὐρανοῖς (our father in the heavens), and variations of this phrase. Matthew develops the term οὐρανός (heaven) as a keyword that he frequently pairs with γῆ (earth). The terms occur together in significant places throughout the Sermon, including the beatitudes (5:3–5), the Πάτηρ ἡμῶν (our father) prayer (6:10), the aphorism about the treasure (6:19–20), and On anxiety (6:26, 28; here ἀγρός [wild] substitutes for γῆ). These distinctively Matthean additions to Q material represent Matthew's compositional voice. The paired terms also occur prominently in Matthew's own material, such as the antitheses (5:34–35), the conclusion of the fourth sermon (18:18–20), and the gospel's climactic, concluding scene (28:18). Matthew exploits the aural signal of repeated, paired terms to single them out for emphasis.

Employing the paired terms heaven and earth in strategic locations throughout the Sermon both provides verbal economy and allows Matthew to associate various topics with God the father and the coming kingdom without elaborating a logical connection. Matthew does not normally speak of the kingdom of God, but the kingdom of heaven, enacted and apprehended on earth and defined in terms of its earthly effects.[23] Thus an aural device, the repetition of ὁ οὐρανός and ἡ γῆ, plays a significant role in advancing Matthew's theological project, the depiction of an immanent God, Emmanuel,[24] and a final judgment based upon heavenly affirmation of what one has done to "the least of these" on earth (25:31–46).

THE SOUND OF AUTHORITY

The Sermon's sections 3 (5:17–20) and 4 (5:21–48) on the sound map introduce the phrase ἀμὴν γὰρ λέγω ὑμῖν (let me tell you) which, along with several variations, claims authority for Jesus' speech. The narrative section that concludes the Sermon attests to the importance of this theme, for it states that Jesus taught as one having authority, and thus unlike their scribes (ὡς ἐξουσίαν ἔχων καὶ οὐχ ὡς γραμματεῖς αὐτῶν, 7:29). Section 3 employs elegant style ironically to uphold the law on the basis of Jesus' authority rather than its inherent legitimacy. Section 4, the antitheses, incorporates the λέγω (I tell) phrase into its legal diction that elevates Jesus' authority over that of the law.[25]

The same phrase re-emerges as a primary organizational feature in the gospel's fourth sermon (Mt 18:3–20), where it highlights thematic terms and marks the boundaries of this passage's component units. Λέγω introduces Jesus' speech in 18:3 as well as the final periods in each of the passage's component units (18:6–10, 12–14, 15–20), and is doubled at the Sermon's end (18:18–19).[26]

In the fourth sermon, the λέγω phrase consistently occurs with some of the gospel's thematic terms, especially οὐρανός and γῆ (heaven and earth). Here the term οὐρανός is doubled after the first occurrence of the λέγω phrase (18:3): εἰς τὴν βασιλείαν τῶν οὐρανῶν, 18:3; ἐν τῇ βαλισεία τῶν οὐρανῶν, 18:4 (in Heaven's domain). After the second occurrence of the λέγω phrase in 18:10, οὐρανός is doubled again, in its second occurrence merging with the πατήρ (father) phrase: οἱ ἄγγελοι αὐτῶν ἐν οὐρανοῖς διὰ παντὸς βλέπουσι τὸ πρόσωπον τοῦ πατρός μου τοῦ ἐν οὐρανοῖς (their guardian angels constantly gaze on the face of my Father in heaven). After the third occurrence of the λέγω phrase (18:13), the πατήρ phrase recurs, containing the thematic term οὐρανός (heaven) (18:14). At the conclusion of the speech, the λέγω (I tell) phrase occurs twice, in 18:18 and 19.

Mt 18:18–19[27]

Ἀμὴν λέγω ὑμῖν,
ὅσα ἐὰν δήσητε ἐπὶ τῆς γῆς ἔσται δεδεμένα ἐν οὐρανῷ
καὶ ὅσα ἐὰν λύσητε ἐπὶ τῆς γῆς ἔσται λελυμένα ἐν οὐρανῷ.
Πάλιν [ἀμὴν] [28]**λέγω ὑμῖν** ὅτι
ἐὰν δύο συμφωνήσωσιν ἐξ ὑμῶν
ἐπὶ τῆς γῆς
περὶ παντὸς πράγματος οὗ ἐὰν αἰτήσωνται,
γενήσεται αὐτοῖς παρὰ τοῦ πατρός μου τοῦ ἐν οὐρανοῖς.

The terms οὐρανός and γῆ (heaven and earth) occur together twice after the λέγω phrase in 18:18, and after its final occurrence in 18:19, we find ἐπὶ τῆς γῆς (on earth), balanced by the πατήρ phrase. The λέγω phrase functions as a strong structural signal in the gospel's fourth sermon, marking the sermon's beginning and end, delineating its component units, and announcing both the thematic terms οὐρανός and γῆ (heaven and earth), and the related phrases τὴν βασιλείαν τῶν οὐρανῶν (heaven's domain) and τοῦ πατρὸς ὑμῶν τοῦ ἐν οὐρανοῖς (our father in heaven).

The gospel's narrative section 26:1–35 employs λέγω in yet another way to reinforce the sound of Jesus' authority. This section's structure transforms the markers that organize the birth narrative (Mt 1:18–2:23). Here each scene begins with a temporal marker, usually a genitive absolute construction or the adverb τότε, and ends with a quotation from scripture.

Matthew's birth narrative (1:18–2:23)[29]

Scene 1:	**Joseph's dream (1:18–25)**
Temporal marker:	δὲ Ἰησοῦ Χριστοῦ ἡ γένεσις οὕτως ἦν. (1:18)
Closing quotation:	Ἰδοὺ ἡ παρθένος ἐν γαστρὶ ἕξει καὶ τέξεται υἱόν, καὶ καλέσουσιν τὸ ὄνομα αὐτοῦ Ἐμμανουήλ (1:23)
Scene 2:	**Herod hears of the Magi's visit to Jerusalem (2:1–6)**
Temporal marker:	Τοῦ δὲ Ἰησοῦ γεννηθέντος ἐν Βηθλέεμ τῆς Ἰουδαίας ἐν ἡμέραις Ἡρῴδου τοῦ βασιλέως (2:1)
Closing quotation:	Καὶ σύ, Βηθλέεμ γῆ Ἰούδα, οὐδαμῶς ἐλαχίστη εἶ ἐν τοῖς ἡγεμόσιν Ἰούδα· ἐκ σοῦ γὰρ ἐξελεύσεται ἡγούμενος, ὅστις ποιμανεῖ τὸν λαόν μου τὸν Ἰσραήλ. (2:6)
Scene 3:	**The magi's journey (2:7–15)**
Temporal marker:	Τότε Ἡρῴδης λάθρᾳ καλέσας τοὺς μάγους ἠκρίβωσεν παρ' αὐτῶν τὸν χρόνον τοῦ φαινομένου ἀστέρος (2:7)
Closing quotation:	Ἐξ Αἰγύπτου ἐκάλεσα τὸν υἱόν μου (2:15)
Scene 4:	**Scene 4: Herod's slaughter of the infants (2:16–18)**
Temporal marker:	Τότε Ἡρῴδης ἰδὼν ὅτι ἐνεπαίχθη ὑπὸ τῶν μάγων ἐθυμώθη λίαν (2:16)
Closing quotation:	Φωνὴ ἐν Ῥαμὰ ἠκούσθη, κλαυθμὸς καὶ ὀδυρμὸς πολύς· Ῥαχὴλ κλαίουσα τὰ τέκνα αὐτῆς, καὶ οὐκ ἤθελεν παρακληθῆναι, ὅτι οὐκ εἰσίν. (2:18)
Scene 5:	**Joseph's dream (2:19–23)**
Temporal marker:	Τελευτήσαντος δὲ τοῦ Ἡρῴδου (2:19)
Closing quotation:	Ναζωραῖος κληθήσεται. (2:23)

This arrangement divides the narrative into a series of tableaux in which a scriptural quotation closes and interprets each episode.

By contrast, the gospel's final narrative section features episodes that begin with temporal markers similar to those in the birth narrative, but instead of closing with a quotation from scripture, they close with Jesus' speech, introduced by a λέγω statement (26:13, 21, 29, and 34). In the second scene, two λέγω statements occur:

Mt 26:6–34[30]

Scene 1:	**The anointing at Bethany (26:6–13)**
Temporal marker:	Τοῦ δὲ Ἰησοῦ γενομένου ἐν Βηθανίᾳ ἐν οἰκίᾳ Σίμωνος τοῦ λεπροῦ, (26:6)
Closing λέγω statement:	**ἀμὴν λέγω ὑμῖν,** ὅπου ἐὰν κηρυχθῇ τὸ εὐαγγέλιον τοῦτο ἐν ὅλῳ τῷ κόσμῳ, λαληθήσεται καὶ ὃ ἐποίησεν αὕτη εἰς μνημόσυνον αὐτῆς. (26:13)
Scene 2:	**The betrayal and last supper (26:14–30)**
Temporal marker:	Τότε πορευθεὶς εἷς τῶν δώδεκα (26·14)
Closing λέγω statement:	καὶ ἐσθιόντων αὐτῶν εἶπεν, **Ἀμὴν λέγω ὑμῖν** ὅτι εἷς ἐξ ὑμῶν παραδώσει με. (26:21) **λέγω δὲ ὑμῖν,** οὐ μὴ πίω ἀπ' ἄρτι ἐκ τούτου τοῦ γενήματος τῆς ἀμπέλου ἕως τῆς ἡμέρας ἐκείνης ὅταν αὐτὸ πίνω μεθ' ὑμῶν καινὸν ἐν τῇ βασιλείᾳ τοῦ πατρός μου. (26:29)
Scene 3:	**Jesus predicts Peter's denial (26:31–35)**
Temporal marker:	Τότε λέγει αὐτοῖς ὁ Ἰησοῦς (26·31)
Closing λέγω statement:	ἔφη αὐτῷ ὁ Ἰησοῦς, **Ἀμὴν λέγω σοι** ὅτι ἐν ταύτῃ τῇ νυκτὶ πρὶν ἀλέκτορα φωνῆσαι τρὶς ἀπαρνήσῃ με. (26:34)

Surely Jesus' pronouncements in these episodes serve a similar function to that of the scripture quotations in Matthew's birth narrative, for the similarity of aural organization at the gospel's beginning and end invites its audience to hear in Jesus' pronouncements the authoritative ring of scripture. In the gospel's closing episode Jesus begins his commissioning speech, Ἐδόθη μοι πᾶσα ἐξουσία ἐν οὐρανῷ καὶ ἐπὶ [τῆς] γῆς (all authority has been given to me in heaven and on earth). (28:18). Here his jurisdiction over heaven and earth coincides with that of the Father and his kingdom as described in the beatitudes in the Sermon's section 1 and the Πάτηρ ἡμῶν prayer in the Sermon's section 5. The λέγω statement as an aural device serves one of the gospel's fundamental themes, the establishment of Jesus' teaching as authoritative. With Jesus' concluding speech, the realm of the kingdom is established in the present place and time: καὶ ἰδοὺ ἐγὼ μεθ' ὑμῶν εἰμι πάσας τὰς ἡμέρας ἕως τῆς συντελείας τοῦ αἰῶνος (I'll be with you day in and day out as long as this world continues its course) (28:20).

MERCY, NOT SACRIFICE

The stylistic sophistication of the Sermon's section 3 (5:17–20) and the ironic tone of the antitheses (5:21–48) make it possible for Jesus' speech to critique the Law's demands while still paying respect to them (Lee 2005, pp. 151–97). The first antithesis places priority on reconciliation over ritual sacrifice. Not only does Matthew's Jesus twice quote Hosea 6:6, "I want mercy, not sacrifice" (9:13, 12:7), but this message reverberates throughout the gospel and reaches its climax in Jesus' final sermon, when he declares that the Law's weightier concerns (τὰ βαρύτερα τοῦ νόμου) are justice, mercy, and trust (τὴν κρίσιν καὶ τὸ ἔλεος καὶ τὴν πίστιν, 23:23). These passages depict the Law as an incomplete vehicle, for although its aim is justice, the Law alone neither reliably recognizes nor promotes righteousness.[31] It is noteworthy, for example, that in the Πάτηρ ἡμῶν prayer in the Sermon's section 5, Jesus elevates private, practical works of goodness above public ritual practices, a teaching that is consistent with the gospel's theme of hidden righteousness.[32] And in the judgment scene narrated in the gospel's final sermon, Jesus employs an authoritative λέγω statement to declare that judgment will be based on the treatment of "the least of these" (25:40, 45). Thus Jesus' speech in the Sermon on the Mount and throughout Matthew's gospel creates an image of the heavenly realm as those moments on earth when God is present in human acts of mercy toward those who are suffering and in need.

This holds true even in the midst of scholarly debate over the identity of "the least" between particularist (Christian disciples) and universalist (all who are in need) interpretations of 25:40.[33] Sound alone cannot resolve this debate, but Kingsbury's perspective on audience identification is helpful here. He explains:

> Because [in Matthew's depiction of them] the disciples possess conflicting traits, the reader is invited, depending on the attitude Matthew as narrator or Jesus takes toward them on any given occasion, to identify with them or to distance himself or herself from them. It is through such granting or withholding of approval on cue, therefore, that the reader becomes schooled in the values that govern the life of discipleship in Matthew's story (1988, p. 14).

The Sermon blurs the boundary between the brother and the opponent in the first antithesis (5:21–26), between God's beloved and those of little faith in the prohibition of anxiety in section 6 (6:28–30), and even between the evil and the good in the last antithesis (5:43–48). Ultimately, Matthew's gospel argues that τὰ ἔθνη (all peoples) should be included in the Christian community.

CONSISTENCY OF AURAL DEVICES

The subsequent prominent use in Matthew's gospel of aural devices coined in the Sermon on the Mount argues strongly against interpretative approaches to the Sermon that view it as one of the author's pre-existing sources. This theory, articulated most extensively by Betz, claims that the Sermon's literary and theological integrity indicates a distinct author and manuscript tradition.[34] Betz writes:

> I assume that the Gospels of Matthew and Luke incorporated separate versions of Q, which, even before their incorporation, had undergone a process during which they had also been subjected to modifications (Q^{Matt} and Q^{Luke}). That Q^{Matt} and Q^{Luke} share a great deal of material and roughly the same order means that at some earlier stage they must have come from a common source (Q). This hypothesis would explain why Q^{Matt} included the S[ermon on the] M[ount], while Q^{Luke} included the S[ermon on the] P[lain]. Assuming this hypothesis, one can conclude that, prior to their incorporation, the SM and the SP existed in written form as independent textual units. In other words, the SM and the SP existed first as separate compositional units before they were incorporated into Q^{Matt} and Q^{Luke}. For their material they drew on the same pool of sayings of Jesus that Q drew on, so that in some instances a double representation of sayings resulted in Q^{Matt} and Q^{Luke} on the one hand in the SM and the SP on the other hand (1995, p. 8).

The evidence derived from sound makes the opposite case. Aural devices forged in the Sermon are consistently applied throughout the gospel, suggesting that the author of the first gospel consistently employed a distinctive set of compositional strategies with respect to both sources and original material.[35] The foregoing sound analysis of the Sermon on the Mount offers an empirical method for demonstrating both the Sermon's integrity as a unit and the overall coherence of the gospel—and it avoids the dubious strategy of positing separate authorship of the Sermon.

Appendix

The Sermon on the Mount

Matt 5–7

INTRODUCTION (5:1–2)

1 Ἰδὼν δὲ τοὺς ὄχλους ἀνέβη εἰς τὸ ὄρος·
2 καὶ καθίσαντος αὐτοῦ προσῆλθαν αὐτῷ οἱ μαθηταὶ αὐτοῦ·
3 καὶ ἀνοίξας τὸ στόμα αὐτοῦ ἐδίδασκεν αὐτοὺς λέγων,

SECTION 1 μακάριοι (5:3–12)

1.1 **Μακάριοι** οἱ πτωχοὶ τῷ πνεύματι,
1.2 ὅτι αὐτῶν ἐστιν *ἡ βασιλεία τῶν οὐρανῶν.*

2.1 **μακάριοι** οἱ πενθοῦντες,
2.2 ὅτι αὐτοὶ παρακληθήσονται.

3.1 **μακάριοι** οἱ πραεῖς,
3.2 ὅτι αὐτοὶ κληρονομήσουσιν *τὴν γῆν.*

4.1 **μακάριοι** οἱ πεινῶντες καὶ διψῶντες *τὴν δικαιοσύνην,*
4.2 ὅτι αὐτοὶ χορτασθήσονται.

5.1 **μακάριοι** οἱ ἐλεήμονες,
5.2 ὅτι αὐτοὶ ἐλεηθήσονται.

6.1 **μακάριοι** οἱ καθαροὶ τῇ καρδίᾳ,
6.2 ὅτι αὐτοὶ τὸν θεὸν ὄψονται.

7.1 **μακάριοι** οἱ εἰρηνοποιοί,
7.2 ὅτι [αὐτοὶ] υἱοὶ θεοῦ κληθήσονται.

8.1 **μακάριοι** οἱ δεδιωγμένοι ἕνεκεν *δικαιοσύνης,*
8.2 ὅτι αὐτῶν ἐστιν *ἡ βασιλεία τῶν οὐρανῶν.*

9.1 **μακάριοί ἐστε**
9.2 ὅταν ὀνειδίσωσιν ὑμᾶς
9.3 καὶ διώξωσιν
9.4 καὶ εἴπωσιν πᾶν πονηρὸν καθ' ὑμῶν [ψευδόμενοι] ἕνεκεν ἐμοῦ·

10.1 χαίρ**ετε** καὶ ἀγαλλι**ᾶσθε,**
10.2 ὅτι ὁ μισθὸς ὑμῶν πολὺς *ἐν τοῖς οὐρανοῖς·*
10.3 οὕτως γὰρ ἐδίωξαν τοὺς προφήτας τοὺς πρὸ ὑμῶν.

SECTION 2 Ὑμεῖς ἐστε (5:13–16)

Unit 2.1 (5:13)

1.1 **Ὑμεῖς ἐστε** τὸ ἅλας τῆς γῆς·
1.2 ἐὰν δὲ τὸ ἅλας μωρανθῇ,

1.3 ἐν τίνι ἁλισθήσεται;
1.4 εἰς οὐδὲν ἰσχύει ἔτι εἰ μὴ βληθῆναι ἔξω καὶ καταπατεῖσθαι ὑπὸ τῶν ἀνθρώπων.

Unit 2.2 (5:14–16)

2.1 **Ὑμεῖς ἐστε** τὸ φῶς τοῦ κόσμου.
2.2 οὐ δύναται πόλις κρυβῆναι ἐπάνω ὄρους κειμένη·
2.3 οὐδὲ καίουσιν λύχνον καὶ τιθέασιν αὐτὸν ὑπὸ τὸν μόδιον
2.4 ἀλλ' ἐπὶ τὴν λυχνίαν,
2.5 καὶ λάμπει πᾶσιν τοῖς ἐν τῇ οἰκίᾳ.

3.1 οὕτως λαμψάτω τὸ φῶς ὑμῶν ἔμπροσθεν τῶν ἀνθρώπων,
3.2 ὅπως ἴδωσιν ὑμῶν τὰ καλὰ ἔργα
3.3 καὶ δοξάσωσιν *τὸν πατέρα ὑμῶν τὸν ἐν τοῖς οὐρανοῖς.*

SECTION 3 Μὴ νομίσητε (5:17–20)

1.1 **Μὴ νομίσητε**
1.2 ὅτι ἦλθον καταλῦσαι *τὸν νόμον ἢ τοὺς προφήτας·*
1.3 οὐκ ἦλθον καταλῦσαι
1.4 ἀλλὰ πληρῶσαι.

2.1 *ἀμὴν γὰρ λέγω ὑμῖν,*
2.2 ἕως ἂν παρέλθῃ *ὁ οὐρανὸς καὶ ἡ γῆ,*
2.3 ἰῶτα ἓν ἢ μία κεραία οὐ μὴ παρέλθῃ ἀπὸ τοῦ νόμου
2.4 ἕως ἂν *πάντα γένηται.*

3.1 ὃς ἐὰν οὖν λύσῃ μίαν τῶν ἐντολῶν τούτων τῶν ἐλαχίστων
3.2 καὶ διδάξῃ οὕτως τοὺς ἀνθρώπους,
3.3 ἐλάχιστος κληθήσεται ἐν τῇ *βασιλείᾳ τῶν οὐρανῶν·*

4.1 ὃς δ' ἂν ποιήσῃ
4.2 καὶ διδάξῃ,
4.3 οὗτος μέγας κληθήσεται ἐν τῇ *βασιλείᾳ τῶν οὐρανῶν.*

5.1 *λέγω γὰρ ὑμῖν* ὅτι
5.2 ἐὰν μὴ περισσεύσῃ ὑμῶν *ἡ δικαιοσύνη* πλεῖον τῶν γραμματέων καὶ Φαρισαίων,
5.3 οὐ μὴ εἰσέλθητε εἰς *τὴν βασιλείαν τῶν οὐρανῶν.*

SECTION 4 Ἠκούσατε (5:21–48)

Unit 4.1 (5:21–26)

1.1 **Ἠκούσατε ὅτι ἐρρέθη τοῖς ἀρχαίοις,**
1.2 Οὐ φονεύσεις·
1.3 ὃς δ' ἂν φονεύσῃ, ἔνοχος ἔσται τῇ κρίσει.

2.1 *ἐγὼ δὲ λέγω ὑμῖν*
2.2 ὅτι πᾶς ὁ ὀργιζόμενος τῷ ἀδελφῷ αὐτοῦ ἔνοχος ἔσται τῇ κρίσει·
2.3 ὃς δ' ἂν εἴπῃ τῷ ἀδελφῷ αὐτοῦ, Ῥακά, ἔνοχος ἔσται τῷ συνεδρίῳ·

2.4 ὃς δ' ἂν εἴπῃ, Μωρέ, ἔνοχος ἔσται εἰς τὴν γέενναν τοῦ πυρός.

3.1 ἐὰν οὖν προσφέρῃς τὸ δῶρόν σου ἐπὶ τὸ θυσιαστήριον
3.2 κἀκεῖ μνησθῇς ὅτι ὁ ἀδελφός σου ἔχει τι κατὰ σοῦ,
3.3 ἄφες ἐκεῖ τὸ δῶρόν σου ἔμπροσθεν τοῦ θυσιαστηρίου
3.4 καὶ ὕπαγε
3.5 πρῶτον διαλλάγηθι τῷ ἀδελφῷ σου,
3.6 καὶ τότε ἐλθὼν πρόσφερε τὸ δῶρόν σου.

4.1 ἴσθι εὐνοῶν τῷ ἀντιδίκῳ σου ταχὺ
4.2 ἕως ὅτου εἶ μετ' αὐτοῦ ἐν τῇ ὁδῷ,
4.3 μήποτέ σε παραδῷ ὁ ἀντίδικος τῷ κριτῇ,
4.4 καὶ ὁ κριτὴς τῷ ὑπηρέτῃ,
4.5 καὶ εἰς φυλακὴν βληθήσῃ·

5.1 *ἀμὴν λέγω σοι,*
5.2 οὐ μὴ ἐξέλθῃς ἐκεῖθεν
5.2 ἕως ἂν ἀποδῷς τὸν ἔσχατον κοδράντην.

UNIT 4.2 (5:27–32)

1.1 **Ἠκούσατε ὅτι ἐρρέθη,**
1.2 Οὐ μοιχεύσεις.

2.1 *ἐγὼ δὲ λέγω ὑμῖν*
2.2 ὅτι πᾶς ὁ βλέπων γυναῖκα πρὸς τὸ ἐπιθυμῆσαι αὐτὴν
2.3 ἤδη ἐμοίχευσεν αὐτὴν ἐν τῇ καρδίᾳ αὐτοῦ.

3.1 εἰ δὲ ὁ ὀφθαλμός σου ὁ δεξιὸς σκανδαλίζει σε,
3.2 ἔξελε αὐτὸν καὶ βάλε ἀπὸ σοῦ·
3.3 συμφέρει γάρ σοι ἵνα ἀπόληται ἓν τῶν μελῶν σου
3.4 καὶ μὴ ὅλον τὸ σῶμά σου βληθῇ εἰς γέενναν.

4.1 καὶ εἰ ἡ δεξιά σου χεὶρ σκανδαλίζει σε,
4.2 ἔκκοψον αὐτὴν καὶ βάλε ἀπὸ σοῦ·
4.3 συμφέρει γάρ σοι ἵνα ἀπόληται ἓν τῶν μελῶν σου
4.4 καὶ μὴ ὅλον τὸ σῶμά σου εἰς γέενναν ἀπέλθῃ.
5.1 Ἐρρέθη δέ,
5.2 Ὃς ἂν ἀπολύσῃ τὴν γυναῖκα αὐτοῦ, δότω αὐτῇ ἀποστάσιον.

6.1 *ἐγὼ δὲ λέγω ὑμῖν*
6.2 ὅτι πᾶς ὁ ἀπολύων τὴν γυναῖκα αὐτοῦ παρεκτὸς λόγου πορνείας ποιεῖ
6.3 αὐτὴν μοιχευθῆναι,
6.4 καὶ ὃς ἐὰν ἀπολελυμένην γαμήσῃ μοιχᾶται.

Unit 4.3 (5:33–37)

1.1 Πάλιν **ἠκούσατε ὅτι ἐρρέθη τοῖς ἀρχαίοις,**
1.2 Οὐκ ἐπιορκήσεις, ἀποδώσεις δὲ τῷ κυρίῳ τοὺς ὅρκους σου.

2.1 *ἐγὼ δὲ λέγω ὑμῖν*
2.2 μὴ ὀμόσαι ὅλως·
2.3 μήτε ἐν τῷ οὐρανῷ, ὅτι θρόνος ἐστὶν τοῦ θεοῦ·
2.4 μήτε ἐν τῇ γῇ, ὅτι ὑποπόδιόν ἐστιν τῶν ποδῶν αὐτοῦ·
2.5 μήτε εἰς Ἱεροσόλυμα, ὅτι πόλις ἐστὶν τοῦ μεγάλου βασιλέως·
2.6 μήτε ἐν τῇ κεφαλῇ σου ὀμόσῃς,
ὅτι οὐ δύνασαι μίαν τρίχα λευκὴν ποιῆσαι ἢ μέλαιναν

3.1 ἔστω δὲ ὁ λόγος ὑμῶν ναὶ ναί, οὒ οὔ·
3.2 τὸ δὲ περισσὸν τούτων ἐκ τοῦ πονηροῦ ἐστιν.

Unit 4.4 (5:38–42)
1.1 **Ἠκούσατε ὅτι ἐρρέθη,**
1.2 Ὀφθαλμὸν ἀντὶ ὀφθαλμοῦ καὶ ὀδόντα ἀντὶ ὀδόντος.

2.1 *ἐγὼ δὲ λέγω ὑμῖν*
2.2 μὴ ἀντιστῆναι τῷ πονηρῷ·

3.1 ἀλλ' ὅστις σε ῥαπίζει εἰς τὴν δεξιὰν σιαγόνα [σου],
3.2 στρέψον αὐτῷ καὶ τὴν ἄλλην·

4.1 καὶ τῷ θέλοντί σοι κριθῆναι καὶ τὸν χιτῶνά σου λαβεῖν,
4.2 ἄφες αὐτῷ καὶ τὸ ἱμάτιον·

5.2 καὶ ὅστις σε ἀγγαρεύσει μίλιον ἕν,
5.2 ὕπαγε μετ' αὐτοῦ δύο.

6.1 τῷ αἰτοῦντί σε δός,
6.2 καὶ τὸν θέλοντα ἀπὸ σοῦ δανίσασθαι μὴ ἀποστραφῇς.

Unit 4.5 (5:43–48)
1.1 **Ἠκούσατε ὅτι ἐρρέθη,**
1.2 Ἀγαπήσεις τὸν πλησίον σου καὶ μισήσεις τὸν ἐχθρόν σου.

2.1 *ἐγὼ δὲ λέγω ὑμῖν,*
2.2 ἀγαπᾶτε τοὺς ἐχθροὺς ὑμῶν
2.3 καὶ προσεύχεσθε ὑπὲρ τῶν διωκόντων ὑμᾶς,
2.4 ὅπως γένησθε υἱοὶ *τοῦ πατρὸς ὑμῶν τοῦ ἐν οὐρανοῖς,*
2.5 ὅτι τὸν ἥλιον αὐτοῦ ἀνατέλλει ἐπὶ πονηροὺς καὶ ἀγαθοὺς
2.6 καὶ βρέχει ἐπὶ δικαίους καὶ ἀδίκους

3.1 ἐὰν γὰρ ἀγαπήσητε τοὺς ἀγαπῶντας ὑμᾶς,
3.2 τίνα μισθὸν ἔχετε;
3.3 οὐχὶ καὶ οἱ τελῶναι τὸ αὐτὸ ποιοῦσιν;

4.1 καὶ ἐὰν ἀσπάσησθε τοὺς ἀδελφοὺς ὑμῶν μόνον,
4.2 τί περισσὸν ποιεῖτε;
4.3 οὐχὶ καὶ οἱ ἐθνικοὶ τὸ αὐτὸ ποιοῦσιν;

5.1 Ἔσεσθε οὖν ὑμεῖς τέλειοι
5.2 ὡς ὁ πατὴρ ὑμῶν ὁ οὐράνιος τέλειός ἐστιν.

SECTION 5 Προσ- . . . ὅταν (6:1–18)

Unit 5.1 (6:1)

1.1 **Προσ**έχετε [δὲ] *τὴν δικαιοσύνην* ὑμῶν
1.2 μὴ ποιεῖν ἔμ**προσ**θεν τῶν ἀνθρώπων **πρὸς** τὸ θεαθῆναι αὐτοῖς
1.3 εἰ δὲ μήγε,
1.4 μισθὸν οὐκ ἔχετε παρὰ *τῷ πατρὶ ὑμῶν τῷ ἐν τοῖς οὐρανοῖς*

Unit 5.2 (6:2–4)

1.1 **Ὅταν** οὖν ποιῇς ἐλεημοσύνην,
1.2 μὴ σαλπίσῃς ἔμπροσθέν σου,
1.3 ὥσπερ οἱ ὑποκριταὶ ποιοῦσιν ἐν ταῖς συναγωγαῖς καὶ ἐν ταῖς ῥύμαις,
1.4 ὅπως δοξασθῶσιν ὑπὸ τῶν ἀνθρώπων·

2.1 *ἀμὴν λέγω ὑμῖν,*
2.2 ἀπέχουσιν τὸν μισθὸν αὐτῶν.

3.1 σοῦ δὲ ποιοῦντος ἐλεημοσύνην
3.2 μὴ γνώτω ἡ ἀριστερά σου τί ποιεῖ ἡ δεξιά σου,
3.3 ὅπως ᾖ σου ἡ ἐλεημοσύνη ἐν τῷ κρυπτῷ·
3.4 καὶ *ὁ πατήρ σου* ὁ βλέπων ἐν τῷ κρυπτῷ [αὐτὸς] ἀποδώσει σοι.

Unit 5.3 (6:5–6)

1.1 Καὶ **ὅταν προσ**εύχησθε,
1.2 οὐκ ἔσεσθε ὡς οἱ ὑποκριταί·
1.3 ὅτι φιλοῦσιν ἐν ταῖς συναγωγαῖς
καὶ ἐν ταῖς γωνίαις τῶν πλατειῶν ἑστῶτες προσεύχεσθαι,
1.4 ὅπως φανῶσιν τοῖς ἀνθρώποις·

2.1 *ἀμὴν λέγω ὑμῖν,*
2.2 ἀπέχουσιν τὸν μισθὸν αὐτῶν.

3.1 σὺ δὲ ὅταν **προσ**εύχῃ,
3.2 εἴσελθε εἰς τὸ ταμεῖόν σου
3.3 καὶ κλείσας τὴν θύραν σου πρόσευξαι
τῷ πατρί σου τῷ ἐν τῷ κρυπτῷ·
3.4 καὶ *ὁ πατήρ σου* ὁ βλέπων ἐν τῷ κρυπτῷ ἀποδώσει σοι.

Unit 5.4 (6:7–15)

1.1 **Προσ**ευχόμενοι δὲ μὴ βατταλογήσητε ὥσπερ οἱ ἐθνικοί,
1.2 δοκοῦσιν γὰρ ὅτι ἐν τῇ πολυλογίᾳ αὐτῶν εἰσακουσθήσονται.
1.3 μὴ οὖν ὁμοιωθῆτε αὐτοῖς,

1.4 οἶδεν γὰρ *ὁ πατὴρ ὑμῶν* ὧν χρείαν ἔχετε πρὸ τοῦ ὑμᾶς αἰτῆσαι αὐτόν.

1.5 Οὕτως οὖν **προσ**εύχεσθε ὑμεῖς·

2.1 *Πάτερ ἡμῶν ὁ ἐν τοῖς οὐρανοῖς,*
2.2 ἁγιασθήτω τὸ ὄνομά σου,
2.3 ἐλθέτω *ἡ βασιλεία σου,*
2.4 γενηθήτω τὸ θέλημά σου,
2.5 ὡς ἐν *οὐρανῷ καὶ ἐπὶ γῆς.*

3.1 Τὸν ἄρτον ἡμῶν τὸν ἐπιούσιον δὸς ἡμῖν σήμερον·
3.2 καὶ ἄφες ἡμῖν τὰ ὀφειλήματα ἡμῶν,
3.3 ὡς καὶ ἡμεῖς ἀφήκαμεν τοῖς ὀφειλέταις ἡμῶν·
3.4 καὶ μὴ εἰσενέγκῃς ἡμᾶς εἰς πειρασμόν,
3.5 ἀλλὰ ῥῦσαι ἡμᾶς ἀπὸ τοῦ πονηροῦ.

4.1 Ἐὰν γὰρ ἀφῆτε τοῖς ἀνθρώποις τὰ παραπτώματα αὐτῶν,
4.2 ἀφήσει καὶ ὑμῖν *ὁ πατὴρ ὑμῶν ὁ οὐράνιος·*
4.3 ἐὰν δὲ μὴ ἀφῆτε τοῖς ἀνθρώποις,
4.4 οὐδὲ *ὁ πατὴρ ὑμῶν* ἀφήσει τὰ παραπτώματα ὑμῶν.

Unit 5.5 (6:16–18)

1.1 **Ὅταν** δὲ νηστεύητε,
1.2 μὴ γίνεσθε ὡς οἱ ὑποκριταὶ σκυθρωποί,
1.3 ἀφανίζουσιν γὰρ τὰ πρόσωπα αὐτῶν
1.4 ὅπως φανῶσιν τοῖς ἀνθρώποις νηστεύοντες·

2.2 ἀμὴν λέγω ὑμῖν,
2.3 ἀπέχουσιν τὸν μισθὸν αὐτῶν.

3.1 σὺ δὲ νηστεύων ἄλειψαί σου τὴν κεφαλὴν καὶ τὸ πρόσωπόν σου νίψαι,
3.2 ὅπως μὴ φανῇς τοῖς ἀνθρώποις νηστεύων
3.3 ἀλλὰ *τῷ πατρί σου* τῷ ἐν τῷ κρυφαίῳ·
3.4 καὶ *ὁ πατήρ σου* ὁ βλέπων ἐν τῷ κρυφαίῳ ἀποδώσει σοι.

SECTION 6 μή+[imperative verb] (6:19–7:6)

Unit 6.1 (6:19–34)

1.1 **Μὴ θησαυρίζετε** ὑμῖν θησαυροὺς ἐπὶ τῆς *γῆς,*
1.2 ὅπου σὴς καὶ βρῶσις ἀφανίζει,
1.3 καὶ ὅπου κλέπται διορύσσουσιν καὶ κλέπτουσιν·

2.1 θησαυρίζετε δὲ ὑμῖν θησαυροὺς *ἐν οὐρανῷ,*
2.2 ὅπου οὔτε σὴς οὔτε βρῶσις ἀφανίζει,
2.3 καὶ ὅπου κλέπται οὐ διορύσσουσιν οὐδὲ κλέπτουσιν·

3.1 ὅπου γάρ ἐστιν ὁ θησαυρός σου,
3.2 ἐκεῖ ἔσται καὶ ἡ καρδία σου.

4.1 Ὁ λύχνος τοῦ σώματός ἐστιν ὁ ὀφθαλμός.

5.1 ἐὰν οὖν ᾖ ὁ ὀφθαλμός σου ἁπλοῦς,
5.2 ὅλον τὸ σῶμά σου φωτεινὸν ἔσται·

6.1 ἐὰν δὲ ὁ ὀφθαλμός σου πονηρὸς ᾖ,
6.2 ὅλον τὸ σῶμά σου σκοτεινὸν ἔσται.

7.1 εἰ οὖν τὸ φῶς τὸ ἐν σοὶ σκότος ἐστίν,
7.2 τὸ σκότος πόσον.

8.1 Οὐδεὶς δύναται δυσὶ κυρίοις δουλεύειν·
8.2 ἢ γὰρ τὸν ἕνα μισήσει καὶ τὸν ἕτερον ἀγαπήσει,
8.3 ἢ ἑνὸς ἀνθέξεται καὶ τοῦ ἑτέρου καταφρονήσει·
8.4 οὐ δύνασθε θεῷ δουλεύειν καὶ μαμωνᾷ.

9.1 Διὰ τοῦτο *λέγω ὑμῖν*,
9.2 **μὴ μεριμνᾶτε** τῇ ψυχῇ ὑμῶν τί φάγητε [ἢ τί πίητε],
9.3 μηδὲ τῷ σώματι ὑμῶν τί ἐνδύσησθε·
9.4 οὐχὶ ἡ ψυχὴ πλεῖόν ἐστιν τῆς τροφῆς
9.5 καὶ τὸ σῶμα τοῦ ἐνδύματος;

10.1 ἐμβλέψατε εἰς τὰ πετεινὰ *τοῦ οὐρανοῦ*
10.2 ὅτι οὐ σπείρουσιν
10.3 οὐδὲ θερίζουσιν
10.4 οὐδὲ συνάγουσιν εἰς ἀποθήκας,
10.5 καὶ *ὁ πατὴρ ὑμῶν ὁ οὐράνιος* τρέφει αὐτά·
10.6 οὐχ ὑμεῖς μᾶλλον διαφέρετε αὐτῶν;
10.7 τίς δὲ ἐξ ὑμῶν **μεριμνῶν** δύναται προσθεῖναι ἐπὶ τὴν ἡλικίαν αὐτοῦ πῆχυν ἕνα;

11.1 καὶ περὶ ἐνδύματος **τί μεριμνᾶτε**;
11.2 καταμάθετε τὰ κρίνα *τοῦ ἀγροῦ* πῶς αὐξάνουσιν·
11.3 οὐ κοπιῶσιν
11.4 οὐδὲ νήθουσιν·
11.5 *λέγω δὲ ὑμῖν*
11.6 ὅτι οὐδὲ Σολομὼν ἐν πάσῃ τῇ δόξῃ αὐτοῦ περιεβάλετο ὡς ἓν τούτων.

12.1 εἰ δὲ τὸν χόρτον *τοῦ ἀγροῦ* σήμερον ὄντα
12.2 καὶ αὔριον εἰς κλίβανον βαλλόμενον
12.3 ὁ θεὸς οὕτως ἀμφιέννυσιν,
12.4 οὐ πολλῷ μᾶλλον ὑμᾶς,
12.5 ὀλιγόπιστοι;

13.1 **μὴ οὖν μεριμνήσητε**
13.2 λέγοντες, Τί φάγωμεν;

13.3 ἤ, Τί πίωμεν;
13.4 ἤ, Τί περιβαλώμεθα;
13.5 πάντα γὰρ ταῦτα τὰ ἔθνη ἐπιζητοῦσιν·
13.6 οἶδεν γὰρ *ὁ πατὴρ ὑμῶν ὁ οὐράνιος* ὅτι χρῄζετε τούτων ἁπάντων.
13.7 ζητεῖτε δὲ πρῶτον *τὴν βασιλείαν* καὶ *τὴν δικαιοσύνην* αὐτοῦ,
13.8 καὶ ταῦτα πάντα προστεθήσεται ὑμῖν.

14.1 **μὴ οὖν μεριμνήσητε** εἰς τὴν αὔριον,
14.2 ἡ γὰρ αὔριον μεριμνήσει αὑτῆς·
14.3 ἀρκετὸν τῇ ἡμέρᾳ ἡ κακία αὐτῆς.

Unit 6.2 (7:1–5)

1.1 Μὴ κρίνετε,
1.2 ἵνα μὴ κριθῆτε·
1.3 ἐν ᾧ γὰρ κρίματι κρίνετε κριθήσεσθε,
1.4 καὶ ἐν ᾧ μέτρῳ μετρεῖτε μετρηθήσεται ὑμῖν.

2.1 τί δὲ βλέπεις τὸ κάρφος τὸ ἐν τῷ ὀφθαλμῷ τοῦ ἀδελφοῦ σου,
2.2 τὴν δὲ ἐν τῷ σῷ ὀφθαλμῷ δοκὸν οὐ κατανοεῖς;

3.1 ἢ πῶς ἐρεῖς τῷ ἀδελφῷ σου,
3.2 Ἄφες ἐκβάλω τὸ κάρφος ἐκ τοῦ ὀφθαλμοῦ σου,
3.3 καὶ ἰδοὺ ἡ δοκὸς ἐν τῷ ὀφθαλμῷ σοῦ;

4.1 ὑποκριτά,
4.2 ἔκβαλε πρῶτον τὴν δοκὸν ἐκ τοῦ ὀφθαλμοῦ σοῦ,
4.3 καὶ τότε διαβλέψεις ἐκβαλεῖν τὸ κάρφος ἐκ τοῦ ὀφθαλμοῦ τοῦ ἀδελφοῦ σου.

Unit 6.3 (7:6)

1.1 **Μὴ δῶτε** τὸ ἅγιον τοῖς κυσίν,
1.2 μηδὲ βάλητε τοὺς μαργαρίτας ὑμῶν ἔμπροσθεν τῶν χοίρων,
1.3 μήποτε καταπατήσουσιν αὐτοὺς ἐν τοῖς ποσὶν αὐτῶν
1.4 καὶ στραφέντες ῥήξωσιν ὑμᾶς.

SECTION 7 [imperative verb] (7:7–20)

Unit 7.1 (7:7–12)

1.1 **Αἰτεῖτε,** καὶ δοθήσεται ὑμῖν·
1.2 **ζητεῖτε,** καὶ εὑρήσετε·
1.3 **κρούετε,** καὶ ἀνοιγήσεται ὑμῖν.

2.1 πᾶς γὰρ ὁ αἰτῶν λαμβάνει
2.2 καὶ ὁ ζητῶν εὑρίσκει
2.3 καὶ τῷ κρούοντι ἀνοιγήσεται.

3.1 ἢ τίς ἐστιν ἐξ ὑμῶν ἄνθρωπος,
3.2 ὃν αἰτήσει ὁ υἱὸς αὐτοῦ ἄρτον— μὴ λίθον ἐπιδώσει αὐτῷ;
3.3 ἢ καὶ ἰχθὺν αἰτήσει— μὴ ὄφιν ἐπιδώσει αὐτῷ;

4.1 εἰ οὖν ὑμεῖς πονηροὶ ὄντες
οἴδατε δόματα ἀγαθὰ διδόναι τοῖς τέκνοις ὑμῶν,
4.2 πόσῳ μᾶλλον *ὁ πατὴρ ὑμῶν ὁ ἐν τοῖς οὐρανοῖς*
δώσει ἀγαθὰ τοῖς αἰτοῦσιν αὐτόν.

5.1 Πάντα οὖν ὅσα ἐὰν θέλητε ἵνα ποιῶσιν ὑμῖν οἱ ἄνθρωποι,
5.2 οὕτως καὶ ὑμεῖς ποιεῖτε αὐτοῖς·
5.3 οὗτος γάρ ἐστιν *ὁ νόμος καὶ οἱ προφῆται.*

Unit 7.2 (7:13–14)

1.1 Εἰσέλθατε διὰ τῆς στενῆς πύλης·

2.1 ὅτι πλατεῖα ἡ πύλη
2.2 καὶ εὐρύχωρος ἡ ὁδὸς ἡ ἀπάγουσα εἰς τὴν ἀπώλειαν,
2.3 καὶ πολλοί εἰσιν οἱ εἰσερχόμενοι δι᾽ αὐτῆς·

3.1 τί στενὴ ἡ πύλη
3.2 καὶ τεθλιμμένη ἡ ὁδὸς ἡ ἀπάγουσα εἰς τὴν ζωήν,
3.3 καὶ ὀλίγοι εἰσὶν οἱ εὑρίσκοντες αὐτήν.

Unit 7.3 (7:15–20)

1.1 **Προσέχετε** ἀπὸ τῶν ψευδοπροφητῶν,
1.2 οἵτινες ἔρχονται πρὸς ὑμᾶς ἐν ἐνδύμασιν προβάτων,
1.3 ἔσωθεν δέ εἰσιν λύκοι ἅρπαγες.
1.4 ἀπὸ τῶν καρπῶν αὐτῶν ἐπιγνώσεσθε αὐτούς·

2.1 μήτι συλλέγουσιν ἀπὸ ἀκανθῶν σταφυλὰς
2.2 ἢ ἀπὸ τριβόλων σῦκα;
2.3 οὕτως πᾶν δένδρον ἀγαθὸν καρποὺς καλοὺς ποιεῖ,
2.4 τὸ δὲ σαπρὸν δένδρον καρποὺς πονηροὺς ποιεῖ·

3.1 οὐ δύναται δένδρον ἀγαθὸν καρποὺς πονηροὺς ποιεῖν,
3.2 οὐδὲ δένδρον σαπρὸν καρποὺς καλοὺς ποιεῖν.

4.1 πᾶν δένδρον μὴ ποιοῦν καρπὸν καλὸν ἐκκόπτεται
4.2 καὶ εἰς πῦρ βάλλεται.
4.3 ἄρα γε ἀπὸ τῶν καρπῶν αὐτῶν ἐπιγνώσεσθε αὐτούς.

SECTION 8 Οὐ πᾶς (7:21–27)

Unit 8.1 (7:21–23)

1.1 **Οὐ πᾶς** ὁ λέγων μοι,
1.2 Κύριε κύριε,
1.3 εἰσελεύσεται εἰς *τὴν βασιλείαν τῶν οὐρανῶν,*
1.4 ἀλλ᾽ ὁ ποιῶν τὸ θέλημα *τοῦ πατρός μου τοῦ ἐν τοῖς οὐρανοῖς.*

2.1	πολλοὶ ἐροῦσίν μοι ἐν ἐκείνῃ τῇ ἡμέρᾳ,			
2.2	Κύριε κύριε,			
2.3	οὐ	τῷ σῷ ὀνόματι		ἐπροφητεύσαμεν,
2.4	καὶ	τῷ σῷ ὀνόματι	δαιμόνια	ἐξεβάλομεν,
2.5	καὶ	τῷ σῷ ὀνόματι	δυνάμεις πολλὰς	ἐποιήσαμεν;

3.1 καὶ τότε ὁμολογήσω αὐτοῖς ὅτι
3.2 Οὐδέποτε ἔγνων ὑμᾶς·
3.3 ἀποχωρεῖτε ἀπ᾽ ἐμοῦ οἱ ἐργαζόμενοι τὴν ἀνομίαν.

Unit 8.2 (7:24–27)
1.1 **Πᾶς οὖν** ὅστις ἀκούει μου τοὺς λόγους τούτους
1.2 καὶ ποιεῖ αὐτοὺς
1.3 ὁμοιωθήσεται ἀνδρὶ φρονίμῳ,
1.4 ὅστις ᾠκοδόμησεν αὐτοῦ τὴν οἰκίαν ἐπὶ τὴν πέτραν.
1.5 καὶ κατέβη ἡ βροχὴ
1.6 καὶ ἦλθον οἱ ποταμοὶ
1.7 καὶ ἔπνευσαν οἱ ἄνεμοι
1.8 καὶ προσέπεσαν τῇ οἰκίᾳ ἐκείνῃ,
1.9 καὶ οὐκ ἔπεσεν,
1.10 τεθεμελίωτο γὰρ ἐπὶ τὴν πέτραν.

2.1 καὶ πᾶς ὁ ἀκούων μου τοὺς λόγους τούτους
2.2 καὶ μὴ ποιῶν αὐτοὺς
2.3 ὁμοιωθήσεται ἀνδρὶ μωρῷ,
2.4 ὅστις ᾠκοδόμησεν αὐτοῦ τὴν οἰκίαν ἐπὶ τὴν ἄμμον.
2.5 καὶ κατέβη ἡ βροχὴ
2.6 καὶ ἦλθον οἱ ποταμοὶ
2.7 καὶ ἔπνευσαν οἱ ἄνεμοι
2.8 καὶ προσέκοψαν τῇ οἰκίᾳ ἐκείνῃ,
2.9 καὶ ἔπεσεν,
2.10 καὶ ἦν ἡ πτῶσις αὐτῆς μεγάλη.

CLOSING TRANSITION (7:28–29)

1	Καὶ ἐγένετο ὅτε ἐτέλεσεν ὁ Ἰησοῦς τοὺς λόγους τούτους		
2	ἐξεπλήσσοντο οἱ ὄχλοι ἐπὶ τῇ διδαχῇ αὐτοῦ·		
3	ἦν γὰρ διδάσκων αὐτοὺς	ὡς ἐξουσίαν	ἔχων
4	καὶ οὐχ	ὡς οἱ γραμματεῖς	αὐτῶν

English Transation

INTRODUCTION (5:1–2)

1 Taking note of the crowds, he climbed up the mountain,
2 and when he had sat down, his disciples came to him.
3 He then began to speak, and this is what he would teach them:

SECTION 1 (5:3–12)

1.1 Congratulations to the poor in spirit!
1.2 Heaven's domain belongs to them.

2.1 Congratulations to those who grieve!
2.2 They will be consoled.

3.1 Congratulations to the gentle!
3.2 They will inherit the earth.

4.1 Congratulations to those who hunger and thirst for justice!
4.2 They will have a feast.

5.1 Congratulations to the merciful!
5.2 They will receive mercy.

6.1 Congratulations to those with undefiled hearts!
6.2 They will see God.

7.1 Congratulations to those who work for peace!
7.2 They will be known as God's children.

8.1 Congratulations to those who have suffered persecution for the sake of justice!
8.2 Heaven's domain belongs to them.

9.1 Congratulations to you
9.2 when they denounce you
9.3 and persecute you
9.4 and spread malicious gossip about you because of me.

10.1 Rejoice and be glad!
10.2 In heaven you will be more than compensated.
10.3 Remember, this is how they persecuted the prophets who preceded you.

SECTION 2 (5:13–16)

Unit 2.1 (5:13)

1.1 You are the salt of the earth.
1.2 But if salt loses its zing,
1.3 how will it be made salty?
1.4 It then has no further use than to be thrown out and stomped on.

Unit 2.2 (5:14–16)

2.1 You are the light of the world.
2.2 A city sitting on top of a mountain can't be concealed.
2.3 Nor do people light a lamp and put it under a bushel basket
2.4 but rather on a lampstand,
2.5 where it sheds light for everyone in the house.

3.1 That's how your light is to shine in the presence of others,
3.2 so they can see your good deeds
3.3 and acclaim your Father in the heavens.

SECTION 3 (5:17–20)
1.1 Don't imagine
1.2 that I have come to annul the Law or the Prophets.
1.3 I have come not to annul
1.4 but to fulfill.

2.1 I swear to you,
2.2 before the world disappears,
2.3 not one iota, not one serif, will disappear from the Law,
2.4 until that happens.

3.1 Whoever ignores one of the most trivial of these regulations,
3.2 and teaches others to do so,
3.3 will be called trivial in Heaven's domain.

4.1 But whoever acts on <these regulations>
4.2 and teaches <others to do so>,
4.3 will be called great in Heaven's domain.

5.1 Let me tell you:
5.2 unless your religion goes beyond that of the scholars and Pharisees,
5.3 you won't set foot in Heaven's domain.

SECTION 4 (5:21–48)
Unit 4.1 (5:21–26)
1.1 As you know, our ancestors were told,
1.2 "You must not kill"
1.3 and "Whoever kills will be subject to judgment."

2.1 But I tell you:
2.2 those who are angry with a companion will be brought before a tribunal.
2.3 And those who say to a companion, 'You moron,' will be subject to the sentence of the court.
2.4 And whoever says, 'You idiot,' deserves the fires of Gehenna.

3.1 So, even if you happen to be offering your gift at the altar
3.2 and recall that your friend has some claim against you,
3.3 leave your gift there at the altar.
3.4 First go
3.5 and be reconciled with your friend,
3.6 and only then return and offer your gift.

4.1 You should come to terms quickly with your opponent while you are both

4.2 on the way <to court>,
4.3 or else your opponent will hand you over to the judge,
4.4 and the judge <will turn you over> to the bailiff,
4.5 and you are thrown in jail.

5.1 I swear to you,
5.2 you'll never get out of there
5.3 until you've paid the last dime.

Unit 4.2 (5:27–32)
1.1 As you know, we once were told,
1.2 "You are not to commit adultery."

2.1 But I tell you:
2.2 Those who leer at a woman and desire her
2.3 have already committed adultery with her in their hearts.

3.1 And if your right eye gets you into trouble,
3.2 rip it out and throw it away!
3.3 You would be better off to lose a part of your body,
3.4 than to have your whole body thrown into Gehenna.
4.1 And if your right hand gets you into trouble,
4.2 cut it off and throw it away!
4.2 You would be better off to lose a part of your body,
4.4 than to have your whole body wind up in Gehenna.

5.1 We once were told,
5.2 "Whoever divorces his wife should give her a bill of divorce."

6.1 But I tell you:
6.2 Everyone who divorces his wife (except in the case of infidelity)
6.3 makes her the victim of adultery;
6.4 and whoever marries a divorced woman commits adultery.

Unit 4.3 (5:33–37)
1.1 Again, as you know, our ancestors were told,
1.2 "You must not break an oath," and "Oaths sworn in the name of God must be kept."

2.1 But I tell you:
2.2 Don't swear at all.
2.3 Don't invoke heaven, because it is the throne of God,
2.4 and don't invoke earth, because it is God's footstool,
2.5 and don't invoke Jerusalem, because it is the city of the great king.
2.6 You shouldn't swear by your head either, since you aren't able to turn a single hair either white or black.

3.1 Rather, your responses should be simply "Yes" and "No."
3.2 Anything that goes beyond this is inspired by the evil one.

Unit 4.4 (5:38–42)

1.1 As you know, we once were told,
1.2 "An eye for an eye" and "A tooth for a tooth."

2.1 But I tell you:
2.2 Don't react violently against the one who is evil:

3.1 when someone slaps you on the right cheek,
3.2 turn the other as well.

4.1 If someone is determined to sue you for your shirt,
4.2 let that person have your coat along with it.

5.1 Further, when anyone conscripts you for one mile,
5.2 go along an extra mile.

6.1 Give to the one who begs from you;
6.2 and don't turn away the one who tries to borrow from you.

Unit 4.5 (5:43–48)

1.1 As you know, we once were told,
1.2 "You are to love your neighbor" and "You are to hate your enemy."

2.1 But I tell you:
2.2 Love your enemies
2.3 and pray for your persecutors.
2.4 You'll then become children of your Father in the heavens.
2.5 <God> causes the sun to rise on both the bad and the good,
2.6 and sends rain on both the just and the unjust.

3.1 Tell me, if you love those who love you,
3.2 why should you be commended for that?
3.3 Even the toll collectors do as much, don't they?

4.1 And if you greet only your friends,
4.2 what have you done that is exceptional?
4.3 Even the pagans do as much, don't they?

5.1 To sum up, you are to be as liberal in your love
5.2 as your heavenly Father is.

SECTION 5 (6:1–18)

Unit 5.1 (6:1)

1.1 Take care that
1.2 you don't flaunt your religion in public to be noticed by others.
1.3 Otherwise,
1.4 you will have no recognition from your Father in the heavens.

Unit 5.2 (6:2–4)

1.1 For example, when you give to charity,
1.2 don't bother to toot your own horn

1.3 as some phony pietists do in houses of worship and on the street.
1.4 They are seeking human recognition.

2.1 I swear to you,
2.2 their grandstanding is its own reward.

3.1 Instead, when you give to charity,
3.2 don't let your left hand in on what your right hand is up to,
3.3 so your acts of charity may remain hidden.
3.4 And your Father, who has an eye for the hidden, will applaud you.

Unit 5.3 (6:5–6)

1.1 And when you pray,
1.2 don't act like phonies.
1.3 They love to stand up and pray in houses of worship
1.4 and on street corners,
1.5 so they can show off in public.

2.1 I swear to you,
2.2 their prayers have been answered!

3.1 When you pray,
3.2 go into a room by yourself
3.3 and shut the door behind you. Then pray to your Father, the hidden one.
3.4 And your Father, with his eye for the hidden, will applaud you.

Unit 5.4 (6:7–15)

1.1 And when you pray, you should not babble on as the pagans do.
1.2 They imagine that the length of their prayers will command attention.
1.3 So don't imitate them.
1.4 After all, your Father knows what you need before you ask.
1.5 Instead, you should pray like this:

2.1. Our Father in the heavens,
2.2 your name be revered.
2.3 Impose your imperial rule,
2.4 enact your will on earth as you have in heaven.

3.1 Provide us with the bread we need for the day.
3.2 Forgive our debts
3.3 to the extent that we have forgiven those in debt to us.
3.4 And please don't subject us to test after test,
3.5 but rescue us from the evil one.

4.1 For if you forgive others their failures and offenses,
4.2 your heavenly Father will also forgive yours.
4.3 And if you don't forgive the failures and mistakes of others,
4.4 your Father won't forgive yours.

Unit 5.5 (6:16–18)

1.1 When you fast,
1.2 don't make a spectacle of your remorse as the pretenders do.
1.3 As you know, they make their faces unrecognizable
1.4 so their fasting may be publicly recognized.

2.1 I swear to you,
2.2 they have been paid in full.

3.1 When you fast, comb your hair and wash your face,
3.2 so your fasting may go unrecognized in public.
3.3 But it will be recognized by your Father, the hidden one,
3.4 and your Father, who has an eye for the hidden, will applaud you.

SECTION 6 (6:19–34)

Unit 6.1 (6:19–34)

1.1 Don't acquire possessions here on earth,
1.2 where moths and insects eat away
1.3 and where robbers break in and steal.

2.1 Instead, gather your nest egg in heaven,
2.2 where neither moths nor insects eat away
2.3 and where no robbers break in or steal.

3.1 As you know, what you treasure
3.2 is your heart's true measure.

4.1 The eye is the body's lamp.

5.1 It follows that if your eye is clear,
5.2 your whole body will be flooded with light.

6.1 If your eye is clouded,
6.2 your whole body will be shrouded in darkness.

7.1 If, then, the light within you is darkness,
7.2 how dark that can be!

8.1 No one can be a slave to two masters.
8.2 No doubt that slave will either hate one and love the other,
8.3 or be devoted to one and disdain the other.
8.4 You can't be enslaved to both God and a bank account!

9.1 That's why I tell you:
9.2 Don't fret about your life—what you're going to eat and drink—
9.3 or about your body—what you're going to wear.
9.4 There is more to living than food
9.5 and clothing, isn't there?

10.1 Take a look at the birds of the sky:
10.2 they don't plant

10.3 or harvest,
10.4 or gather into barns.
10.5 Yet your heavenly Father feeds them.
10.6 You're worth more than they, aren't you?
10.7 Can any of you add one hour to life by fretting about it?

11.1 Why worry about clothes?
11.2 Notice how the wild lilies grow:
11.3 they don't slave
11.4 and they never spin.
11.5 Yet let me tell you,
11.6 even Solomon at the height of his glory was never decked out like one of them.

12.1 If God dresses up the grass in the field,
12.2 which is here today and tomorrow is thrown into an oven,
12.3 won't <God
12.4 care for> you even more,
12.5 you who don't take anything for granted?

13.1 So don't fret.
13.2 Don't say, 'What am I going to eat?'
13.3 or 'What am I going to drink?'
13.4 or 'What am I going to wear?'
13.5 These are all things pagans seek.
13.6 After all, your heavenly Father is aware that you need them.
13.7 You are to seek <God's> domain, and his justice first,
13.8 and all these things will come to you as a bonus.

14.1 So don't fret about tomorrow.
14.2 Let tomorrow fret about itself.
14.3 The troubles that the day brings are enough.

Unit 6.2 (7:1–5)

1.1 Don't pass judgment,
1.2 so you won't be judged.
1.3 Don't forget, the judgment you hand out will be the judgment you get back.
1.4 And the standard you apply will be the standard applied to you.

2.1 Why do you notice the sliver in your friend's eye,
2.2 but overlook the timber in your own?

3.1 How can you say to your friend,
3.2 'Let me get the sliver out of your eye,'
3.3 when there is that timber in your own?

4.1 You phony,
4.2 first take the timber out of your own eye

4.3 and then you'll see well enough to remove the sliver from your friend's eye.

Unit 6.3 (7:6)

1.1 Don't offer to dogs what is sacred,
1.2 and don't throw your pearls to pigs,
1.3 or they'll trample them underfoot
1.4 and turn and tear you to shreds.

SECTION 7 (7:7–20)

Unit 7.1 (7:7–12)

1.1 Ask—it'll be given to you;
1.2 seek—you'll find;
1.3 knock—it'll be opened for you.

2.1 Rest assured: everyone who asks receives;
2.2 everyone who seeks finds;
2.3 and for the one who knocks it is opened.

3.1 Who among you
3.2 would hand a son a stone when it's bread he's asking for?
3.3 Again, who would hand him a snake when it's fish he's asking for? Of course no one would!

4.1 So if you, worthless as you are, know how to give your children good gifts,
4.2 isn't it much more likely that your Father in the heavens will give good things to those who ask him?

5.1 Consider this: Treat people in ways
5.2 you want them to treat you.
5.3 This sums up the whole of the Law and the Prophets.

Unit 7.2 (7:13–14)

1.1 Try to get in through the narrow gate.

2.1 Wide
2.2 and smooth is the road that leads to destruction.
2.3 The majority are taking that route.

3.1 Narrow
3.1 and rough is the road that leads to life.
3.3 Only a minority discover it.

Unit 7.3 (7:15–20)

1.1 Be on the lookout for phony prophets,
1.2 who make their pitch disguised as sheep;
1.3 inside they are really voracious wolves.
1.4 You'll know who they are by what they produce.

2.1 Since when do people pick grapes from thorns
2.2 or figs from thistles?
2.3 Every healthy tree produces choice fruit,
2.4 but the rotten tree produces spoiled fruit.

3.1 A healthy tree cannot produce spoiled fruit,
3.2 any more than a rotten tree can produce choice fruit.

4.1 Every tree that does not produce choice fruit gets cut down
4.2 and tossed on the fire.
4.3 Remember, you'll know who they are by what they produce.

SECTION 8 (7:21–27)

Unit 8.1 (7:21–23)

1.1 Not everyone who addresses me
1.2 as 'Master, master,'
1.3 will get into Heaven's domain—
1.4 only those who carry out the will of my Father in heaven.

2.1 On that day many will address me:
2.2 'Master, master,
2.3 didn't we use your name when we prophesied?
2.4 Didn't we use your name when we exorcised demons?
2.5 Didn't we use your name when we performed all those miracles?'

3.1 Then I will tell them honestly:
3.2 'I never knew you;
3.3 get away from me, you subverters of the Law!'

Unit 8.2 (7:24–27)

1.1 Everyone who pays attention to these words of mine
1.2 and acts on them
1.3 will be like a shrewd builder
1.4 who erected a house on bedrock.
1.5 Later the rain fell,
1.6 and the torrents came,
1.7 and the winds blew
1.8 and pounded that house,
1.9 yet it did not collapse,
1.10 since its foundation rested on bedrock.

2.1 Everyone who listens to these words of mine
2.2 and doesn't act on them
2.3 will be like a careless builder,
2.4 who erected a house on the sand.
2.5 When the rain fell,
2.6 and the torrents came,

2.7 and the winds blew
2.8 and pounded that house,
2.9 it collapsed.
2.10 Its collapse was colossal.

CLOSING TRANSITION (7:28–29)
1 And so, when Jesus had finished this discourse,
2 the crowds were astonished at his teaching,
3 since he had been teaching them on his own authority,
4 unlike their <own> scholars.

Charts in English

Chart 10.2

Matthew's birth narrative (1:18–2:23)

Scene 1:	**Joseph's dream (1:18–25)**
Temporal marker:	The birth of Jesus the Anointed took place as follows (1:18).
Closing quotation:	Behold, a virgin will conceive a child and she will give birth to a son, and they will name him Emmanuel (which means "God with us") (1:23).
Scene 2:	**Herod hears of the Magi's visit to Jerusalem (2:1–6)**
Temporal marker:	Jesus was born at Bethlehem, Judea, when Herod was king (2:1).
Closing quotation:	And you, Bethlehem, in the province of Judah, you are by no means least among the leaders of Judah. Out of you will come a leader who will shepherd my people, Israel (2:6).
Scene 3:	**The magi's journey (2:7–15)**
Temporal marker:	Then Herod called the astrologers together secretly and ascertained from them the precise time the star became visible (2:7).
Closing quotation:	Out of Egypt I have called my son (2:15).
Scene 4:	**Scene 4: Herod's slaughter of the infants (2:16–18)**
Temporal marker:	When Herod realized he had been duped by the astrologers, he was outraged (2:16).
Closing quotation:	In Ramah the sound of mourning and bitter grieving was heard: Rachel weeping for her children. She refused to be consoled: They were no more (2:18).

Scene 5:	**Joseph's dream (2:19–23)**
Temporal marker:	After Herod's death . . . (2:19).
Closing quotation:	He will be called a Nazorean (2:23).

Chart 10.3

Mt 26:6–34

Scene 1:	**The anointing at Bethany (26:6–13)**
Temporal marker:	While Jesus was in Bethany at the house of Simon the leper . . . (26:6).
Closing λέγω statement:	So help me, wherever this good news is announced in all the world, what she has done will be told in memory of her (26:13).
Scene 2:	**The betrayal and last supper (26:14–30)**
Temporal marker:	Then one of the twelve . . . (26·14).
Closing λέγω statement:	And as they were eating, he said, "So help me, one of you is going to turn me in" (26:21). Now I tell you, I certainly won't drink any of this fruit of the vine from now on, until that day when I drink it for the first time with you in my Father's domain! (26:29)
Scene 3:	**Jesus predicts Peter's denial (26:31–35)**
Temporal marker:	Then Jesus says to them . . . (26·31)
Closing λέγω statement:	Jesus said to him, "So help me, tonight before the rooster crows you will disown me three times!" (26:34)

ENDNOTES

1. For a full description of the Sermon's sound map, see Lee (2005, pp. 125–266).
2. See, for example, Betz (1995, p. 427): ". . . 5:17–20 and 7:12 play the role of the hermeneutical frame around the body of the SM." See also Gundry (1994, p. 78) and Stanton (1992, p. 297). Kingsbury (1988, p. 64) explains. "'the law and the prophets' denotes quite simply the whole of the OT as it is known to Matthew, the implied author, and functions as scripture."
3. See Scott (1995, pp. 361–70) for an earlier comparison of the outline presented here with that of other commentators, including Strecker, Bornkamm, Davies and Allison, and Luz.
4. Betz (1985, p. 15) elaborates his description of the Sermon's literary genre as "an *epitome* presenting the theology of Jesus in a systematic fashion. The *epitome* is a composition carefully

designed out of sayings of Jesus grouped according to thematic points of doctrine considered to be of primary importance. Correspondingly, its function is to provide the disciple of Jesus with the necessary tool for becoming a Jesus theologian." But see Carlston (1988, pp. 50–51) who notes that Betz fails to show that this genre had gained currency in Jewish literature in the first century CE, and questions whether the Sermon on the Mount actually functions as an *epitome,* since that genre assumes the teacher is correctible, whereas the Sermon on the Mount implies that Jesus' authority as a teacher is absolute. Stanton (1992, pp. 310–11) further critiques Betz's identification of the Sermon's genre as an *epitome* on the grounds that the Sermon is only a partial presentation of Jesus' teachings and it is by no means brief.

5. This is the case despite Betz's recognition (1995, p. 5) that, "at the time, most people continued to 'hear' the books as they were read aloud to them in gatherings of Christians. Thus these texts [the Sermon on the Mount and the Sermon on the Plain] function primarily as oral and only secondarily as written texts."
6. Moreover, Carlston (1988, p. 54) notes that the four guiding hermeneutical principles Betz finds in the Sermon (5:17–20) are not logically consistent.
7. Allison (1999, p. 35) interprets the golden rule in 7:12 as the passage that "brings to a climax the central section [5:17–7:12] of the Sermon on the Mount." This interpretation is consistent with that of others, such as Bornkamm (1978, pp. 419–32) and Luz (1989, p. 212).
8. Allison (1999, pp. 36–40) also notes the importance of the Sermon's triadic organization, but he places additional emphasis on its chiastic arrangement around the Lord's prayer, as articulated by Dumais (1995, pp. 88–89).
9. See below for a discussion of the structural importance of αἰτέω (ask) in 7:7. See chapter 11, "Manuscript and Memory: Q on Anxiety," for a discussion of μεριμνάω (worry).
10. Kennedy (1984, pp. 58–59) also argues that the Lord's prayer function as the Sermon's "centerpiece," but not because of its central structural placement. From a rhetorical standpoint, the Lord's prayer relates to the thesis articulated in 6:1 at the beginning of its section. It exhibits artful composition and it occurs just past the Sermon's midpoint, the typical place for the climax of a speech.
11. Davies and Allison (1988, pp. 625–28) see 7:12 as the conclusion to the twin structures of the two sections 6:19–34 and 7:1–12.
12. "Consider this: Treat people in ways you want them to treat you. This sums up the whole of the Law and the Prophets."

13. "Try to get in through the narrow gate. Wide and smooth is the road that leads to destruction. The majority are taking that route. Narrow and rough is the road that leads to life. Only a minority discover it."
14. "Ask—it'll be given to you; seek—you'll find; knock—it'll be opened for you."
15. Chart 10.1 is not included in the Appendix.
16. "Don't acquire possessions here on earth. . . ."
17. "Don't pass judgment. . . ."
18. "Don't offer to dogs what is sacred. . . ."
19. "Be on the lookout for phony prophets, who make their pitch disguised as sheep; inside they are really voracious wolves. You'll know who they are by what they produce. Since when do people pick grapes from thorns or figs from thistles? Every healthy tree produces choice fruit, but the rotten tree produces spoiled fruit. A healthy tree cannot produce spoiled fruit, any more than a rotten tree can produce choice fruit. Every tree that does not produce choice fruit gets cut down and tossed on the fire. Remember, you'll know who they are by what they produce."
20. "Not everyone who addresses me as 'Master, master,' will get into Heaven's domain—only those who carry out the will of my Father in heaven."
21. See chapter 3, "The Grammar of Sound."
22. Carlston (1988, p. 56) elucidates five examples illustrating the coherence of the Sermon on the Mount with the rest of Matthew's gospel. His examples overlap in several ways with those elaborated here. They include the themes of true discipleship, the kingdom of heaven, the father in heaven, evil and the evil one, and the phrase "scribes and Pharisees."
23. "The Kingdom of Heaven is a reality that can only be described in terms of both the present and the future" (Kingsbury 1975, p. 140). Nevertheless, as Kingsbury's nuanced description of the kingdom of heaven in Matthew indicates the reality of the kingdom in the present is essential for Matthew (1975, p. 137–46).
24. Note among other sources the treatment of Matthew's theology in van Aarde (1994).
25. So Luz (1989, p. 271): "Thus it becomes clear that . . . the Old Testament law has its authority not from itself but through Jesus. The antitheses make this completely clear."
26. Schweizer (1975, pp. 358–60) also notices the structural implications of this recurring phrase in Matthew 18. He analyzes its impact redactionally, interpreting the phrase's authoritative impact as evidence of Matthew's community's effort to set their

own requirements for certain internal affairs, apart from the conventions of Jewish law.

27. I swear to you, whatever you bind on earth will be considered bound in heaven, and whatever you release on earth will be considered released in heaven. Again I assure you, if two of you on earth agree on anything you ask for, it will be done for you by my Father in heaven.
28. Textual evidence for the inclusion of ἀμὴν is mixed. Codex Vaticanus includes it, for example, while Sinaiticus omits it. N and W have δέ instead of ἀμὴν. It is easy to imagine that the scribal tradition differed concerning the basis upon which the repetition of the λέγω statement is preserved, with witnesses such as Vaticanus echoing the previous iteration and preserving all of its sounds, and other witnesses achieving a consistent logic, more in tune with the conceptual coherence of the written text.
29. See Chart 10.2 in the Appendix.
30. See Chart 10.3 in the Appendix.
31. Snodgrass elaborates the importance of the mercy code in Matthew's understanding of the law. Snodgrass states unequivocally that, "Matthew's view of the law is that it is unquestionably enduring in validity," but he explains that for Matthew the law "was not a monolithic entity. It was diverse with various laws pointing in different directions. In Matthew's presentation of Jesus' teaching those diverse laws are organized by and subsumed under the love commands and the mercy code. Whereas his contemporaries had organized the law under ideas of holiness and ritual purity, Jesus reorganized it in keeping with God's love. The law is not to be treated as the focus of the canon. Rather, one must read the law and the prophets and interpret all the scriptures in accordance with the love commands, the 'golden' rule, and God's desire for mercy instead of sacrifice" (1988, p. 554).
32. This notion is discussed from different perspectives in Scott (1990, pp. 83–102), who claims that Matthew defines righteousness in terms of apparent unrighteousness, with Joseph as the gospel's first example, and in Betz (1995, p. 343), who observes that the Sermon's prohibition of conspicuous piety in 6:4, 6, and 18, implies that righteousness should imitate "the invisibility of God's work."
33. See Stanton (1992, pp. 207–31) for a summary of the argument.
34. Betz (1978, pp. 3–19), reprinted as (Betz 1979, pp. 285–97), articulates this theory, and has held to this view (1991, pp. 74–80) despite criticism such as that articulated by Carlston (1988, pp. 56–57), who argues that Betz fails to account for the "sheer

improbability" of a source for Q, especially one dated before 50 CE, and that Betz does not deal adequately with the "Matthean use of the material" available in Q and its consistency throughout the gospel. Betz (1995, p. 88) states, "the two *epitomai* of the SM and the SP were created by the early Jesus movement, the one (the SM) to instruct converts from Judaism, the other (the SP) to instruct those coming from a Greek background." This proposal has not gained wide acceptance.

35. Others have also argued that the Sermon's formal, stylistic, and theological features are consistent with the rest of Matthew's gospel. Stanton (1992, pp. 318–25), for example, argues that Matthew's five sermons presume the same *Sitz im Leben* for the evangelist's audience. Luz (1989, pp. 37–39) notes that Matthew creates a "seamless course of narrative" incorporating consistent themes signaled by key words.

WORKS CONSULTED

Allison, D. C. 1999. *The Sermon on the Mount: Inspiring the Moral Imagination, Companions to the New Testament*. New York: Crossroad.

Betz, Hans Deiter. 1978. Die Makarismen der Bergpredigt (Matthäus 5, 3–12). *ZTK* 75:3–19.

———. 1979. The Sermon on the Mount (Matt 5:3–7:27): Its Literary Genre and Function. *JR* 59:285–97.

———. 1985. The Sermon on the Mount (Matt 5:3–7:27): Its Literary Genre and Function. In *Essays on the Sermon on the Mount*, edited by H. D. Betz. Philadelphia: Fortress.

———. 1991. The Sermon on the Mount: In Defense of a Hypothesis. *BR* 36:74–80.

———. 1995. *The Sermon on the Mount, Hermeneia*. Minneapolis: Fortress.

Bornkamm, Günther. 1978. Der Aufbau Der Bergpredigt. *NTS* 24:419–32.

Carlston, Charles E. 1988. Betz on the Sermon on the Mount: A Critique. *CBQ* 50:47–57.

Davies, W.D., and D.C. Allison. 1988. *A Critical and Exegetical Commentary on the Gospel According to Matthew*. 3 vols. Vol. 1, *International Critical Commentary*. Edinburgh: T & T Clark.

Dumais, Marcel. 1995. *Le sermon sur la montagne: État de la recherche interpretation bibliographie*. Paris: Letouzey et Ané.

Gundry, Robert H. 1994. *Matthew: A Commentary on His Handbook for a Mixed Church under Persecution*. 2d ed. Grand Rapids, MI: Eerdmans.

Kennedy, George A. 1984. *New Testament Interpretation through Rhetorical Criticism*. Edited by C. H. Long, *Studies in Religion*. Chapel Hill, NC: The University of North Carolina Press.

Kingsbury, Jack Dean. 1975. *Matthew: Structure, Christology, Kingdom.* Philadelphia: Fortress.

———. 1988. *Matthew as Story*. 2d ed. Philadelphia: Fortress.

Lee, Margaret E. 2005. A Method for Sound Analysis in Hellenistic Greek: The Sermon on the Mount as a Test Case. D.Theol., Melbourne College of Divinity, Melbourne.

Luz, Ulrich. 1989. *Matthew 1–7: A Commentary*. Translated by W. C. Linss, *EKKNT*. Minneapolis: Augsburg.

Schweizer, Eduard. 1975. *The Good News According to Matthew.* Translated by D. E. Green. Atlanta: John Knox.

Scott, Bernard Brandon. 1990. The Birth of the Reader. *Semeia* 52:83–102.

Scott, Bernard Brandon, and Margaret E. Dean. 1995. A Sound Map of the Sermon on the Mount. In *Treasures Old and New: Recent Contributions to Matthean Studies*, edited by D. Bauer and M. A. Powell. Atlanta: Scholars.

Snodgrass, Klyne R. 1988. Matthew and the Law. In *SBLSP*, edited by D. J. Lull. Atlanta: Scholars.

Stanton, Graham N. 1992. *A Gospel for a New People: Studies in Matthew.* Edinburgh: T.&T. Clark.

van Aarde, Andries. 1994. *God-With-Us: The Dominant Perspective in Matthew's Story, and Other Essays*. Edited by A. v. Aarde. Vol. Supplementum 5, *Hervormde Teologiese Studies*. Pretoria: University of Pretoria.

Chapter 11

Manuscript and Memory
Q on Anxiety

INTRODUCTION

On Anxiety as performed in Matthew (6:25–35) and Luke (12:22b–32) presents a unique opportunity to test our claims about the roles of sound and memory in Greek literary composition. On Anxiety provides two peformances of a relatively long passage from a single source—in this case, Q.[1] In most reconstructions of Q, On Anxiety forms the longest section of Q's earliest and formative stratum (Robinson, Hoffmann, and Kloppenborg 2000, p. lxiii; Verbin 2000, p. 146). The passage is unique in that no larger set of Q sayings has been preserved in the same order,[2] and few Q sayings as performed by Matthew and Luke show such extensive verbatim agreement.

If literature was known primarily through public performance and if it was stored most often and most reliably on the wax tablets of the mind, then literary evidence for multiple performances of the same material can help to trace the dynamics of oral transmission and memorial preservation, as well as the sound structure of each composition. On Anxiety in Matthew and Luke gives access both to performed and literary dimensions of the same material. Sound analysis of these different performances can also offer clues for a reconstruction of Q.

The Lord's Prayer and the Beatitudes illustrate the contrast. Both entail verbatim agreements but the passages are briefer than On Anxiety, and the agreements between Luke's and Matthew's performances are less extensive.

THE LORD'S PRAYER & THE BEATITUDES

Unlike On Anxiety, the Lord's Prayer is brief. Most discrepancies between Luke's and Matthew's performances entail words that occur in Matthew but not in Luke. See chart 11.1. Though briefer by far than On Anxiety, the Beatitudes are longer than those of the Lord's Prayer, exhibit less verbatim agreement between Luke's and Matthew's performances, and contain a greater number of words that occur in Matthew but not in Luke. See chart 11.2.

Chart 11.1 The Lord's Prayer

Luke 11:2b-4[3]	Matthew 6:9b-15
Πάτερ,	**Πάτερ** ἡμῶν ὁ ἐν τοῖς οὐρανοῖς,
ἁγιασθήτω τὸ ὄνομά σου·	**ἁγιασθήτω τὸ ὄνομά σου,**
ἐλθέτω ἡ βασιλεία σου	**ἐλθέτω ἡ βασιλεία σου,** γενηθήτω τὸ θέλημά σου, ὡς ἐν οὐρανῷ καὶ ἐπὶ γῆς.
τὸν ἄρτον ἡμῶν τὸν ἐπιούσιον δίδου **ἡμῖν** τὸ καθ' ἡμέραν	**Τὸν ἄρτον ἡμῶν τὸν ἐπιούσιον** δὸς **ἡμῖν σήμερον·**
καὶ ἄφες ἡμῖν τὰς ἁμαρτίας **ἡμῶν,** **καὶ** γὰρ αὐτοὶ ἀφίομεν παντὶ **ὀφείλοντι ἡμῖν**	**καὶ ἄφες ἡμῖν** τὰ ὀφειλήματα **ἡμῶν,** ὡς **καὶ** ἡμεῖς ἀφήκαμεν τοῖς **ὀφειλέταις ἡμῶν·**
καὶ μὴ εἰσενέγκῃς ἡμᾶς εἰς πειρασμόν.	**καὶ μὴ εἰσενέγκῃς ἡμᾶς εἰς πειρασμόν,**
	ἀλλὰ ῥῦσαι ἡμᾶς ἀπὸ τοῦ πονηροῦ. Ἐὰν γὰρ ἀφῆτε τοῖς ἀνθρώποις τὰ παραπτώματα αὐτῶν, ἀφήσει καὶ ὑμῖν ὁ πατὴρ ὑμῶν ὁ οὐράνιος· ἐὰν δὲ μὴ ἀφῆτε τοῖς ἀνθρώποις, οὐδὲ ὁ πατὴρ ὑμῶν ἀφήσει τὰ παραπτώματα ὑμῶν.

Because sound mapping facilitates discovery of a composition's structure and meaning, sound analysis can point out the compositional strategies employed by the authors of Matthew and Luke as they incorporated Q into their narratives, and at the same time add a new dimension to comparative analyses of the Sayings Source, even though that document is hypothetical and reconstructed.

COMMON ELEMENTS OF PERFORMANCES IN MATTHEW AND LUKE

The occurrences of Q sayings in the gospels of Matthew and Luke typically exhibit a fragmentary quality, because the two authors frequently place Q sayings in different narrative settings. For example, Matthew pairs the Q sayings about salt (5:13) and light (5:14–16) and situates them in the Sermon on the Mount after the beatitudes (5:3–12), while Luke employs the sayings separately, placing the salt saying

Chart 11.2 The Beatitudes

Luke 6:20-23[4]	**Matthew 5:3-12**
Μακάριοι οἱ πτωχοί, **ὅτι** ὑμετέρα ἐστὶν **ἡ βασιλεία** τοῦ θεοῦ.	**Μακάριοι οἱ πτωχοὶ** τῷ πνεύματι, **ὅτι** αὐτῶν ἐστιν **ἡ βασιλεία** τῶν οὐρανῶν.
	μακάριοι οἱ πενθοῦντες, ὅτι αὐτοὶ παρακληθήσονται.
	μακάριοι οἱ πραεῖς, ὅτι αὐτοὶ κληρονομήσουσιν τὴν γῆν.
μακάριοι οἱ πεινῶντες νῦν, **ὅτι χορτασθήσεσθε.**	**μακάριοι οἱ πεινῶντες** καὶ διψῶντες τὴν δικαιοσύνην, **ὅτι** αὐτοὶ **χορτασθήσονται.**
μακάριοι οἱ κλαίοντες νῦν, ὅτι γελάσετε.	
	μακάριοι οἱ ἐλεήμονες, ὅτι αὐτοὶ ἐλεηθήσονται.
	μακάριοι οἱ καθαροὶ τῇ καρδίᾳ, ὅτι αὐτοὶ τὸν θεὸν ὄψονται.
	μακάριοι οἱ εἰρηνοποιοί, ὅτι [αὐτοὶ] υἱοὶ θεοῦ κληθήσονται.
	μακάριοι οἱ δεδιωγμένοι ἕνεκεν δικαιοσύνης, ὅτι αὐτῶν ἐστιν ἡ βασιλεία τῶν οὐρανῶν.
μακάριοί ἐστε ὅταν μισήσωσιν **ὑμᾶς** οἱ ἄνθρωποι, καὶ **ὅταν** ἀφορίσωσιν ὑμᾶς καὶ ὀνειδίσωσιν καὶ ἐκβάλωσιν τὸ ὄνομα ὑμῶν ὡς πονηρὸν **ἕνεκα** τοῦ υἱοῦ τοῦ ἀνθρώπου· **χάρητε** ἐν ἐκείνῃ τῇ ἡμέρᾳ καὶ σκιρτήσατε, ἰδοὺ γὰρ **ὁ μισθὸς ὑμῶν πολὺς ἐν τῷ οὐρανῷ·** κατὰ τὰ αὐτὰ γὰρ ἐποίουν **τοῖς προφήταις** οἱ πατέρες αὐτῶν.	**μακάριοί ἐστε** **ὅταν** ὀνειδίσωσιν **ὑμᾶς** καὶ διώξωσιν καὶ εἴπωσιν πᾶν πονηρὸν καθ' ὑμῶν [ψευδόμενοι] **ἕνεκεν** ἐμοῦ· **χαίρετε** καὶ ἀγαλλιᾶσθε, ὅτι **ὁ μισθὸς ὑμῶν πολὺς ἐν τοῖς οὐρανοῖς·** οὕτως γὰρ ἐδίωξαν **τοὺς προφήτας** τοὺς πρὸ ὑμῶν.

(14:34–35) after Jesus' speech on the cost of discipleship (14:25–33), and the saying about hiding one's light (8:16) between the parable of the Sower (8:4–15) and Jesus' encounter with his mother and brothers (8:19–20). The continuity and verbal similarity of the long cluster of sayings that comprise On Anxiety in Matthew and Luke is therefore notable and encourages the use of sound mapping to enhance analytic insight.

The following tables display the performances of On Anxiety in Matthew and Luke in parallel columns, divided colometrically. Differences between the Matthean and Lukan versions appear in boldface type and shared words that occur in different order appear in italics. Following the display of each section, the similarities between the two evangelists' performances of this Q passage are described. See chart 11.3.

Both performances begin with διὰ τοῦτο λέγω ὑμῖν,[7] a rhetorical introduction. The referent implied by τοῦτο is unclear, especially since in Matthew and Luke different material precedes the discourse On Anxiety. The introduction thus indicates the unit's previous connection to a larger, unknown issue. Both performances open with a prohibition of anxiety concerning σῶμα (body) and ψύχη (life) framed as a neither/nor statement followed by a two-part explanatory statement. The initial prohibition is thus presented as two sets of paired statements in which full statement occurs with the ψύχη phrase, while the σῶμα phrase implies its verb in an ellipsis. In both

Chart 11.3 Initial Prohibition[5]

Luke 12:22b-23	Matt 6:25
Διὰ τοῦτο λέγω ὑμῖν,	Διὰ τοῦτο λέγω ὑμῖν,
First Pair	
μὴ μεριμνᾶτε τῇ ψυχῇ τί φάγητε, μηδὲ τῷ σώματι τί ἐνδύσησθε.	μὴ μεριμνᾶτε τῇ ψυχῇ **ὑμῶν** τί φάγητε **[ἢ τί πίητε]**[6], μηδὲ τῷ σώματι **ὑμῶν** τί ἐνδύσησθε· ος;
Second Pair	
ἡ **γὰρ** ψυχὴ πλεῖόν ἐστιν τῆς τροφῆς καὶ τὸ σῶμα τοῦ ἐνδύματος.	**οὐχὶ** ἡ ψυχὴ πλεῖόν ἐστιν τῆς τροφῆς καὶ τὸ σῶμα τοῦ ἐνδύματος;

performances the first elided term is μεριμνᾶτε (fret) and the second is πλεῖον ἐστιν (there is more). See chart 11.4.

In both performances the first example or proof is drawn from birds. It contains an introduction, a ὅτι clause framed as a neither/nor statement, an explanatory statement, and a rhetorical question arguing, "If this is true, is not that even more true?" Next occurs a minor, corroborating illustration about the inability to control one's life span, followed by another rhetorical question, τί μεριμνᾶτε (why worry). See chart 11.5.

A second proof from flowers comes next. Both performances of the second example include an introduction, a neither/nor statement, an

Chart 11.4 First example

Luke 12:24-26	Matt 6:26-28a
Introduction	
κατανοήσατε τοὺς κόρακας	**ἐμβλέψατε εἰς τὰ πετεινὰ τοῦ οὐρανοῦ**
Neither/Nor Statement	
ὅτι οὐ σπείρουσιν οὐδὲ θερίζουσιν,	ὅτι οὐ σπείρουσιν οὐδὲ θερίζουσιν
Explanatory Statement	
οἷς οὐκ ἔστιν ταμεῖον οὐδὲ ἀποθή**κη**, καὶ **ὁ θεὸς** τρέφει αὐ**τούς**·	**οὐδὲ συνάγουσιν** εἰς ἀποθή**κας**,
Rhetorical Question	
πόσῳ *μᾶλλον ὑμεῖς* διαφέρετε **τῶν πετεινῶν**.	καὶ **ὁ πατὴρ ὑμῶν ὁ οὐράνιος** τρέφει αὐ**τά**· **οὐχ** *ὑμεῖς μᾶλλον* διαφέρετε **αὐτῶν**;
Minor Illustration	
τίς δὲ ἐξ ὑμῶν μεριμνῶν δύναται ἐπὶ τὴν ἡλικίαν αὐτοῦ *προσθεῖναι* πῆχυν;	τίς δὲ ἐξ ὑμῶν μεριμνῶν δύναται *προσθεῖναι* ἐπὶ τὴν ἡλικίαν αὐτοῦ πῆχυν **ἕνα**;
Rhetorical Question	
εἰ οὖν οὐδὲ ἐλάχιστον δύνασθε, *τί* **περὶ τῶν λοιπῶν** μεριμνᾶτε;	καὶ περὶ **ἐνδύματος** *τί* μεριμνᾶτε;

Chart 11.5 Second example

Luke 12:27-28	**Matt 6:28b-30**
Introduction	
κατανο**ήσατε** τὰ κρίνα πῶς αὐξάν**ει**·	κατα**μάθετε** τὰ κρίνα **τοῦ ἀγροῦ** πῶς αὐξάν**ουσιν**·
Neither/Nor Statement	
οὐ κοπι**ᾷ** οὐδὲ νήθ**ει**·	οὐ κοπι**ῶσιν** οὐδὲ νήθ**ουσιν**·
Explanatory Statement	
λέγω δὲ ὑμῖν, οὐδὲ Σολομὼν ἐν πάσῃ τῇ δόξῃ αὐτοῦ περιεβάλετο ὡς ἓν τούτων.	λέγω δὲ ὑμῖν **ὅτι** οὐδὲ Σολομὼν ἐν πάσῃ τῇ δόξῃ αὐτοῦ περιεβάλετο ὡς ἓν τούτων.
Minor Illustration	
εἰ δὲ **ἐν ἀγρῷ** τὸν χόρτον *ὄντα* *σήμερον* καὶ αὔριον εἰς κλίβανον βαλλόμενον ὁ θεὸς οὕτως ἀμφι**άζει**,	εἰ δὲ τὸν χόρτον **τοῦ ἀγροῦ** *σήμερον ὄντα* καὶ αὔριον εἰς κλίβανον βαλλόμενον ὁ θεὸς οὕτως ἀμφι**έννυσιν**,
Rhetorical Question	
πόσῳ μᾶλλον ὑμᾶς, ὀλιγόπιστοι.	**οὐ** πολλῷ μᾶλλον ὑμᾶς, ὀλιγόπιστοι;

explanatory saying about Solomon that is identical in Matthew and Luke and is introduced by λέγω δὲ ὑμῖν, a corroborating illustration framed in terms of the "how much more" argument, and an address to the listener as ὀλιγόπιστοι (*lit.*, little faith).

In both cases the second proof is presented in a format similar to that of the first: an introduction, a neither/nor illustration from the natural world, a minor corroborating illustration, and a "how much more" rhetorical question. See chart 11.6.

In their conclusions, both Matthew and Luke reiterate the opening general prohibition, followed by a paired reference to eating and drinking, a negative comparison to τὰ ἔθνη (pagans) concerning ταῦτα πάντα (all these things), a statement about the father, a kingdom saying (τὴν βασιλείαν αὐτοῦ), and assurance that God will provide those things (ταῦτα) that are needed. Then Matthew and Luke append their own unique final sayings.

Chart 11.6 Conclusion

Luke 12:29-31	Matt 6:31-34
Prohibition	
καὶ **ὑμεῖς** μὴ ζητεῖτε τί φάγη**τε** καὶ τί πίη**τε**, **καὶ μὴ μετεωρίζεσθε·**	μὴ **οὖν μεριμνήσητε λέγοντες,** Τί φάγ**ωμεν**; ἤ, Τί πί**ωμεν**; **ἤ, Τί περιβαλώμεθα;**
Comparison	
ταῦτα γὰρ πάντα τὰ ἔθνη **τοῦ κόσμου** ἐπιζητοῦσιν·	*πάντα γὰρ ταῦτα* τὰ ἔθνη ἐπιζητοῦσιν·
Father	
ὑμῶν **δὲ** ὁ πατὴρ *οἶδεν*	*οἶδεν* **γὰρ** ὁ πατὴρ *ὑμῶν* **ὁ οὐράνιος** ὅτι χρῄζετε τούτων **ἁπάντων**.
Kingdom	
ὅτι χρῄζετε τούτων. **πλὴν** ζητεῖτε τὴν βασιλείαν αὐτοῦ,	ζητεῖτε **δὲ πρῶτον** τὴν βασιλείαν **καὶ τὴν δικαιοσύνην** αὐτοῦ,
Promise	
καὶ ταῦτα προστεθήσεται ὑμῖν.	καὶ ταῦτα **πάντα** προστεθήσεται ὑμῖν.
Luke's ending	**Matthew's ending**
Μὴ φοβοῦ, τὸ μικρὸν ποίμνιον, ὅτι εὐδόκησεν ὁ πατὴρ ὑμῶν δοῦναι ὑμῖν τὴν βασιλείαν.	**μὴ οὖν μεριμνήσητε εἰς τὴν αὔριον, ἡ γὰρ αὔριον μεριμνήσει αὑτῆς· ἀρκετὸν τῇ ἡμέρᾳ ἡ κακία αὐτῆς.**

Q IN MEMORY

On Anxiety's component parts cohere as vivid images organized by a simple, three-part scheme: an initial prohibition, two parallel examples, and a conclusion. This simple structure encompasses multiple components whose details can be easily recalled both accurately and in order because they are connected through pairing and parallel arrangement. The initial prohibition is framed as a paired imperative followed by a pair of explanatory statements. The examples from the birds and flowers are arranged in parallel. Both proofs are elaborated by minor examples—the span of human life and that of grass. The proofs are framed by introductory statements and concluding rhetorical questions. The conclusion to On Anxiety in both Matthew and Luke reiterates the initial prohibition, elaborated by a pair of statements about eating and drinking. Both conclusions compare anxiety over eating and drinking with the concerns of τὰ ἔθνη (the pagans), affirm the father's acknowledgement of the legitimacy of such needs, an instruction to seek the kingdom, and a promise that what is needed will be provided.

The structural signals of pairing and parallelism that organize On Anxiety are implemented through sound. The sound and structure of the initial prohibition shapes the entire passage. The double prohibition of anxiety over ψύχη (life) and σῶμα (body) predicts the doubled examples from birds and flowers. Each example multiplies the use of paired arrangement by presenting with its main illustration (birds, flowers) a minor, corroborating illustration (life span, grass), creating nested pairs of statements, or pairs within pairs. The syllables οὐ, οὐδέ, and μή recur throughout the passage. The initial prohibition, μὴ μεριμνᾶτε (don't fret), is subsequently recast as a rhetorical question, τί μεριμνᾶτε (why worry), that marks the end of the first illustration. The conclusion reiterates the initial prohibition and elongates the ending, signaling closure.

This remarkable verbatim agreement and agreement in structure and sound deployment require and also suggest an explanation. For successful storage in memory and accurate recall, multiple elements must be linked together in an ordered sequence so that once the first element is retrieved from memory, all successive elements will follow (see above, chapter 2, Woven Text). As Quintilian notes, ease of recollection is enhanced when details are "linked to one another like dancers hand in hand."[8] The three-part structure derived from verbatim agreements between these two performances of On Anxiety exhibits such links. Its opening sounds, μὴ μεριμνᾶτε, are repeated at the end of the first example as τί μεριμνᾶτε. The first proof draws an example from the sky and the second proof from the earth, metonymically encompassing everything in between. The vivid contrast between natural beauty and Solomon's glory engages a powerful trope in second temple Judaism. Two striking features—the verbatim agreement of the long colon referring to Solomon in the second example (see 3.6 below), and the occurrence of the introductory λέγω δὲ ὑμῖν (*lit.*, I say to you) in both versions—attest to the passage's mnemonic impact. It is further noteworthy that this memorable saying forges the connection between the examples and the conclusion, which is organized around summary statements (ταῦτα πάντα, all these) and the paired elements of the father and the kingdom, and thus forms the response to the dilemma posed by earthly cares.

Small reminds us that the ancients composed in memory, drawing complete units of remembered material from τόποι (places) in a mental θησαύρος (treasury). "Wholes are not dissected" when new compositions are created by combining remembered sources (1997, p. 186). Both performances preserve the introductory διὰ τοῦτο λέγω ὑμῖν, even though it has no necessary logical connection with the passage's content in either gospel (see, for example, Jacobson 1992, p. 190). Moreover, beginnings are consistently stronger than endings in ancient literature. Storage in memory would account for both the preservation of the logically unnecessary διὰ τοῦτο and the greater variation between Matthew and Luke at the passage's end.

To be sure, sound alone cannot substantiate a proposal about the form of a Q saying or its tradition history, but sound evidence from On Anxiety in Matthew and Luke suggests two postulates about Q. First, the extent of verbatim agreement indicates that the authors of Matthew and Luke had access to a manuscript of Q, because verbatim preservation was not valued or generally practiced in antiquity. Admittedly, the ancient *ars memoria* could be and sometimes were applied to verbatim memorization of literature, making it possible that On Anxiety could have been stored accurately in memory verbatim, even in the absence of the vivid imagery and memorable structure of this sayings cluster.[9] But the process of committing a passage to memory word for word required a written copy—either on a roll, wax tablets, or some other material. Surely the achievement of such extensive verbal correspondence in two separate performances of this passage would have required a manuscript, if only as a tool to commit the passage to memory. In any event, writing support was typically employed even to commit to memory only the gist of a passage, its λόγος (see chapters 1 and 2). The existence of a manuscript containing this sayings cluster therefore appears necessary.[10]

Second, On Anxiety's simple, memorable structure based on paired sayings suggests that the cluster of sayings comprising this passage was stored in Q intact and in the order represented by both Matthew and Luke, both in manuscript and in memorial τόποi. The theoretical possibility that the authors of Matthew and Luke consulted a manuscript of Q containing this passage while composing their gospels cannot be absolutely eliminated, but it is more likely that they did not copy this passage from a papyrus roll, but rather drew it from the wax tablets of the mind. This probability accounts for both the passage's remarkable stability and its patterns of variation that comport with normal compositional practice. Such literary protocols explain the scarcity of variation between the two versions at the beginning of the passage, the more extensive variations at the end, and the stability of the compelling Solomon saying in the middle, with its introductory phrase λέγω δὲ ὑμῖν that rehearses the introduction to the initial prohibition, διὰ τοῦτο λέγω ὑμῖν.

ON ANXIETY IN MATTHEW

Matthew's performance exhibits characteristics of his distinctive style in the context of broad verbatim agreement with On Anxiety in Luke.

On Anxiety in Matthew[11]
Initial Prohibition

1.1 Διὰ τοῦτο λέγω ὑμῖν,
1.2 **μὴ μεριμνᾶτε** τῇ ψυχῇ ὑμῶν τί φάγητε [ἢ τί πίητε],
1.3 μηδὲ τῷ σώματι ὑμῶν τί ἐνδύσησθε·
1.4 οὐχὶ ἡ ψυχὴ πλεῖόν ἐστιν τῆς τροφῆς
1.5 καὶ τὸ σῶμα τοῦ ἐνδύματος;

First example

2.1 ἐμβλέψατε εἰς τὰ πετεινὰ *τοῦ οὐρανοῦ*
2.2 ὅτι οὐ σπείρουσιν
2.3 οὐδὲ θερίζουσιν
2.4 οὐδὲ συνάγουσιν εἰς ἀποθήκας,
2.5 καὶ *ὁ πατὴρ ὑμῶν ὁ οὐράνιος* τρέφει αὐτά·
2.6 οὐχ ὑμεῖς μᾶλλον διαφέρετε αὐτῶν;
2.7 τίς δὲ ἐξ ὑμῶν **μεριμνῶν** δύναται προσθεῖναι ἐπὶ τὴν ἡλικίαν αὐτοῦ πῆχυν ἕνα;

Second example

3.1 καὶ περὶ ἐνδύματος **τί μεριμνᾶτε**;
3.2 καταμάθετε τὰ κρίνα *τοῦ ἀγροῦ* πῶς αὐξάνουσιν·
3.3 οὐ κοπιῶσιν
3.4 οὐδὲ νήθουσιν·
3.5 λέγω δὲ ὑμῖν
3.6 ὅτι οὐδὲ Σολομὼν ἐν *πάσῃ* τῇ δόξῃ αὐτοῦ περιεβάλετο ὡς ἓν τούτων.

4.1 εἰ δὲ τὸν χόρτον *τοῦ ἀγροῦ* σήμερον ὄντα
4.2 καὶ αὔριον εἰς κλίβανον βαλλόμενον
4.3 ὁ θεὸς οὕτως ἀμφιέννυσιν,

4.4 οὐ πολλῷ μᾶλλον ὑμᾶς,
4.5 ὀλιγόπιστοι;

Conclusion
5.1 **μὴ οὖν μεριμνήσητε** λέγοντες,
5.2 Τί φάγωμεν;
5.3 ἤ, Τί πίωμεν;
5.4 ἤ, Τί περιβαλώμεθα;
5.5 *πάντα* γὰρ ταῦτα τὰ ἔθνη ἐπιζητοῦσιν·
5.6 οἶδεν γὰρ *ὁ πατὴρ ὑμῶν ὁ οὐράνιος* ὅτι χρῄζετε τούτων ἁπάντων.
5.7 ζητεῖτε δὲ πρῶτον *τὴν βασιλείαν* καὶ *τὴν δικαιοσύνην* αὐτοῦ,
5.8 καὶ ταῦτα πάντα προστεθήσεται ὑμῖν.

6.1 **μὴ οὖν μεριμνήσητε** εἰς τὴν αὔριον,
6.2 ἡ γὰρ αὔριον μεριμνήσει αὑτῆς·
6.3 ἀρκετὸν τῇ ἡμέρᾳ ἡ κακία αὐτῆς.

Given Matthew's compositional style—his distinctive vocabulary, structural conventions, and theological project[12]—the extensive verbatim agreement between Matt 6:25–34 and Luke 12:22b–32 is remarkable. The scarcity of distinctively Matthean elements in his performance of On Anxiety is uncharacteristic. The initial prohibition exhibits only three divergences from Luke. The absence or presence of ἢ τί πίητε in Matthew's version is uncertain. If present, then Q's initial doublet becomes a doublet with a nested doublet in the initial phrase. The occurrence of ὑμῶν (τῇ ψυχῇ ὑμῶν / τῷ σώματι ὑμῶν) in Matthew's version is consistent with his evident concern throughout this gospel with the shifting boundary between "you" and "them" in an effort to persuade the audience to include τὰ ἑθνή in their mission (Matt 28:19). The difference between οὐχί in Matthew's version and *γάρ* in Luke's is slight at the semantic level, but Matthew's performance places relatively greater emphasis on negation (οὐχί) whereas Luke's performance employs grammatical subordination (γάρ) and a less contentious diction.

Matthew's first example employs the triplet ὅτι **οὐ** σπείρουσιν **οὐδὲ** θερίζουσιν **οὐδὲ** συνάγουσιν εἰς ἀποθήκας,[13] which is expressed as two doublets in Luke: ὅτι **οὐ** σπείρουσιν **οὐδὲ** θερίζουσιν and ὅτι . . . οἷς. . . . The appellative for God and the use of οὐκ instead of *πόσῳ* in the rhetorical question also distinguish Matthew's performance. Referring to God as ὁ πατὴρ ὑμῶν ὁ οὐρανοις[14] is certainly Matthean because it functions thematically in that gospel (among many others Luz 1989, p. 401). This thematic phrase for God probably influenced the occurrence of τοῦ οὐρανοῦ in the opening colon, which should also be seen as Matthean, making it doubtful that ἐμβλέψατε εἰς τὰ πετεινά[15] was in the Q saying. Matthew's performance employs τὰ πετεινά instead of τοὺς κόρακας, perhaps engaging the term used in Q's "how much more" argument in this example (so Luz 1989, p. 401). Expression of the ὅτι clause as a triplet with **οὐδὲ** συνάγουσιν introduces a Matthean concern. It also deviates from the passage's strong preference for pairs, by expressing the neither/nor illustration as a list of three instead of as nested doublets. Use of οὐχ in the "how much more" argument emphasizes the three-element series of οὐ/ὀὐδέ/οὐδέ in the illustration, and echoes the use of οὐχί in the rhetorical question of the initial prohibition. In the minor illustration, life span, Matthew's differential placement of προσθεῖναι (*lit.*, to add) accommodates the occurrence of ἕνα (one) at the colon's end. The closing rhetorical question emphasizes τί μεριμνᾶτε at its end, whereas Luke's example employs another paired statement that emphasizes the contrast between the assonant ἐλάχιστον (*lit.*, least) and λοιπῶν (*lit.*, rest), both holding penultimate position in their cola.

In the second example's introduction, καταμάθετε (notice) is consistent with Matthew's distinctive vocabulary.[16] The occurrence of τοῦ ἀγροῦ (*lit.*, of the field) in both the introduction and the minor illustration correlates with the double occurrence of ὁ οὐρανός (*lit.*, heaven) in Matthew's performance of the first example. This modification again suggests Matthew's distinctive voice. In his performance of Q material, Matthew frequently supplies the contrasting terms οὐρανός and either γῆ (earth) or a word such as ἀγρός (field) that refers to the earthly realm.[17] Similarly, introducing the Solomon saying with ὅτι clearly parallels the occurrence of ὅτι to introduce the first example. As in the first example as performed by Matthew, the "how much more" argument is introduced with a negative particle (οὐ) instead of πόσῳ.

Consistent with appropriate expectations for memorial processes, the passage's conclusion admits of relatively more variation between Matthew's and Luke's performances than in the initial prohibition or the parallel examples. Matthew's version includes μεριμνήσητε (don't fret), a variation of μεριμνᾶτε in the initial prohibition. Echoing the structure of the first example in Matthew, the conclusion presents a triplet (**Τί** φάγωμεν; **ἤ, Τί** πίωμεν; **ἤ, Τί** περιβαλώμεθα;)[18] rather than a nested pair of questions (τί φάγητε **καὶ** τί πίητε / **καὶ** μὴ μετεωρίζεσθε)[19]. In another echo of the first example, ὁ πατὴρ ὑμῶν ὁ οὐρανιος recurs. The Father statement in Matthew is connected to the ἔθνη (pagans) statement by γάρ, emphasizing the separate premise and conclusion, whereas in Luke's version, ὑμῶν δέ in the parallel colon emphasizes the contrast between τὰ ἔθνη and ὑμῶν.

In the final cola, τὴν δικαιοσύνην (rigtheousness) rehearses one of Matthew's thematic phrases (Luz 1989, 401; Gundry 1994, 118). Like the first example's concluding colon, Matthew's conclusion to the passage emphasizes the singularity of the goal over the paired elements articulated in Luke's version. Thus the occurrences of πρῶτον (first) and πάντα (all) emphasize the search for the kingdom, whereas Luke's ending balances seeking for the kingdom with receiving everything else.

The distinctive elements of Q's prohibition of anxiety as performed by Matthew have relatively little impact at the level of semantic meaning but their effect is dramatic at the level of structure. Analysis of the passage's periodic structure in Matthew and Luke makes this impact evident. While the literary style of On Anxiety is more continuous than highly periodic, the boundaries of periods can be discerned in both Matthew and Luke. Phonetically fluid cola are linked by paratactic or logical connectives in a style appropriate for philosophical discourse. Highlighted features below indicate distinctive aspects of Matthew's performance.

The Sermon on the Mount's sound structure employs repeated beginning sounds as a primary structural device (See chapter 10, Sermon on the Mount). These repetitions lend coherence to the Sermon's eight sections. On Anxiety, embedded in section 6 of the Sermon, is organized around prohibitions. The three units that comprise section 6 all begin with prohibitions: μὴ θησαυρίζετε (6:19, Don't acquire), μὴ κρίνετε (7:1, Don't pass judgment), and μὴ δῶτε (7:6, Don't offer). Thus the format and sound signature of On Anxiety, μὴ μεριμνᾶτε, is consistent with this section's organizing sounds.

In Matthew's first period, the use of οὐχι instead of γάρ to connect the initial prohibition with its correlative pair of statements concerning ἡ ψυχή (life) and τὸ σῶμα (body) emphasizes the negative particle, whereas Luke's version emphasizes a balanced set of two paired statements. Similarly in period 3, Matthew has one colon (καὶ περὶ ἐνδύματος τί μεριμνᾶτε;)[20] where Luke's performance has two (εἰ οὖν οὐδὲ ἐλάχιστον δύνασθε / τί περὶ τῶν λοιπῶν μεριμνᾶτε;).[21] Thus Luke's paired cola conclude the first proof, while Matthew's single colon 3.1 begins a new period that introduces the second proof.

3.1
καὶ περὶ ἐνδύματος **τί μεριμνᾶτε;**

Repetition of μεριμνᾶτε serves a structural purpose because it echoes Matthew's use throughout the Sermon on the Mount of repeated sounds at unit beginnings. In this case, the repeated sounds mark the beginning of a period rather than a unit of a major compositional section.

5.1
μὴ οὖν μεριμνήσητε

Μεριμνήσητε occurs at the beginning of period 5, but is absent in the parallel colon in Luke. Again, the rehearsal of the initial prohibition at the beginning of a period reinforces the primary feature of the Sermon on the Mount's sound signature, the repetition of sounds heard at the beginning of a unit.

With period 6, Matthew adds his conclusion to On Anxiety.

Period 6
1 **μὴ** οὖν **μεριμνήσητε** εἰς τὴν αὔριον,
2 ἡ γὰρ αὔριον **μεριμνήσει** αὐτῆς·
3 ἀρκετὸν τῇ ἡμέρᾳ ἡ κακία αὐτῆς.

These two occurrences of (μὴ) μεριμνάω in Matthew's conclusion reinforce his unique structural device in this section of the Sermon: repeated prohibitions.

Thus, while Matthew's performance of Q's On Anxiety contains cola arranged in the same order as in Luke's performance, periodic boundaries and hence each period's highlighted elements differ from those in Luke's performance.

ON ANXIETY IN LUKE

Luke's periodic structure shows notable differences from Matthew's.

On Anxiety in Luke[22]
Initial prohibition
1.1 Διὰ τοῦτο λέγω ὑμῖν,
1.2 μὴ μεριμνᾶτε τῇ ψυχῇ τί φάγητε,
1.3 μηδὲ τῷ σώματι τί ἐνδύσησθε.
1.4 ἡ γὰρ ψυχὴ πλεῖόν ἐστιν τῆς τροφῆς
1.5 καὶ τὸ σῶμα τοῦ ἐνδύματος.

First example
2.1 **κατανοήσατε** τοὺς κόρακας
2.2 ὅτι οὐ σπείρουσιν οὐδὲ θερίζουσιν,
2.3 οἷς οὐκ ἔστιν ταμεῖον οὐδὲ ἀποθήκη,
2.4 καὶ ὁ θεὸς τρέφει αὐτούς·
2.5 πόσῳ μᾶλλον ὑμεῖς διαφέρετε τῶν πετεινῶν.

3.1 τίς δὲ ἐξ ὑμῶν μεριμνῶν δύναται ἐπὶ τὴν ἡλικίαν αὐτοῦ προσθεῖναι πῆχυν;

3.2 εἰ οὖν οὐδὲ ἐλάχιστον δύνασθε,
3.3 τί περὶ τῶν λοιπῶν μεριμνᾶτε;

Second example
4.1 **κατανοήσατε** τὰ κρίνα πῶς αὐξάνει·
4.2 οὐ κοπιᾷ οὐδὲ νήθει·
4.3 λέγω δὲ ὑμῖν,
4.4 οὐδὲ Σολομὼν ἐν πάσῃ τῇ δόξῃ αὐτοῦ περιεβάλετο ὡς ἓν τούτων.

5.1 εἰ δὲ ἐν ἀγρῷ τὸν χόρτον ὄντα σήμερον
5.2 καὶ αὔριον εἰς κλίβανον βαλλόμενον ὁ θεὸς οὕτως ἀμφιάζει,
5.3 πόσῳ μᾶλλον ὑμᾶς,
5.4 ὀλιγόπιστοι.

Conclusion
6.1 καὶ ὑμεῖς μὴ ζητεῖτε
6.2 τί φάγητε
6.3 καὶ τί πίητε,
6.4 καὶ μὴ μετεωρίζεσθε·

7.1 ταῦτα γὰρ πάντα τὰ ἔθνη τοῦ κόσμου ἐπιζητοῦσιν·
7.2 ὑμῶν δὲ ὁ πατὴρ οἶδεν
7.3 ὅτι χρῄζετε τούτων.
7.4 πλὴν ζητεῖτε τὴν βασιλείαν αὐτοῦ,
7.5 καὶ ταῦτα προστεθήσεται ὑμῖν.

Again, even though the continuous style in which this passage was crafted calls for periodic boundaries that are relatively weak, they can be discerned. Whereas Matthew supplies repeated beginning sounds to organize On Anxiety into periods and units, Luke's performance of the passage relies on parallelism and balanced cola for its primary organizational signals. The initial prohibition is structured around two sets of paired statements, and the two subsequent examples mirror the two-part structure of the initial prohibition. Both begin with κατανοήσατε and they are set in parallel, with one period each dedicated to a major and minor example. The conclusion likewise consists of two periods balanced by paired statements.

Luke's performance further differs from Matthew's in its use of nested pairs. The neither/nor statement in Luke's first example, **οὐ** σπείρουσιν **οὐδὲ** θερίζουσιν (2.2),[23] forms a pair with the two elements opposed in the following colon, οἷς **οὐκ** ἔστιν ταμεῖον **οὐδὲ** ἀποθήκη (2.3).[24] Similarly in the conclusion, the pair **τί** φάγητε **καὶ τί** πίητε (6.2–3),[25] forms a pair with the following colon, **καὶ** μὴ μετεωρίζεσθε·(6.4).[26] At precisely these points, Matthew's version contains triplets rather than nested pairs.

Finally, the matter of contextual setting must be considered. On Anxiety is situated differently in Luke's gospel than in Matthew's. Luke, following his unique ending of On Anxiety (12:32), appends the Q saying about heavenly treasure (12:33–34). In this amended form, On Anxiety is situated between two parables, the rich fool (12:13–21) and the watchful servants (12:35–48). While a thematic connection can be construed in this material, the surrounding compositional units do not impose structural considerations on the internal periodic structure of Luke's On Anxiety in the same way that the Sermon on the Mount's hierarchical organization imposes structural demands on Matthew's performance. Because Luke situates this section between two parables, each having its own internal organization, less pressure is exerted on the Q structure of On Anxiety to conform to the surrounding material.[27]

CRITIQUE OF THE Q PROJECT

The International Q Project has published a reconstruction of Q, making possible various comparisons between particular performances of On Anxiety and a hypothetical version of Q. The proposed reconstruction raises questions to which the foregoing sound analysis can offer enlightening responses. Since the Q Project has not yet published its rationale for judgments about Q's original form for On Anxiety, the content of these offerings cannot be known, but in any case the results of the Project's decisions will be amenable to evaluation at the level of sound. See chart 11.7.

DECISIONS ABOUT BALANCE AND PARALLELISM

The Q Project judges Matthew's version of the initial prohibition (period 1 in both Matthew and Luke) to represent the more original form of Q, suggesting that Luke eliminated two occurrences of ὑμῶν while Matthew preserved them. Matthew's preference here for the more specific reference would reflect a departure from other usages of Q in Matthew, such as the beatitudes, in which Luke names the (literally) poor (6:20), whereas Matthew blesses the poor in spirit (5:3).

More significantly, Matthew's version of the second pair of statements in the initial prohibition emphasizes the negative particle over the connection between the two statement pairs. The Q Project's preference for Matthew's triplet (οὐ/οὐδέ/οὐδέ) over Luke's doublet (οὐ/οὐδέ) in period 2 is consistent with their finding that οὐχι rather than γάρ represents the more original reading in period 1.[31] The Q Project judges that Luke also added πόσῳ in his period 5. If this is the case,

Chart 11.7. Luke and Matthew in Periods—International Q

Luke 12:22b-	Matt 6:25-35	Q
Period 1	**Period 1**	
Διὰ τοῦτο λέγω ὑμῖν, μὴ μεριμνᾶτε τῇ ψυχῇ τί φάγητε, μηδὲ τῷ σώματι τί ἐνδύσησθε. ἡ **γὰρ** ψυχὴ πλεῖόν ἐστιν τῆς τροφῆς καὶ τὸ σῶμα τοῦ ἐνδύματος.	Διὰ τοῦτο λέγω ὑμῖν, μὴ μεριμνᾶτε τῇ ψυχῇ **ὑμῶν** τί φάγητε **[ἢ τί πίητε]**, μηδὲ τῷ σώματι **ὑμῶν** τί ἐνδύσησθε· **οὐχὶ** ἡ ψυχὴ πλεῖόν ἐστιν τῆς τροφῆς καὶ τὸ σῶμα τοῦ ἐνδύματος;	Διὰ τοῦτο λέγω ὑμῖν, μὴ μεριμνᾶτε τῇ ψυχῇ ὑμῶν τί φάγητε μηδὲ τῷ σώματι ὑμῶν τί ἐνδύσησθε οὐχὶ ἡ ψυχὴ πλεῖόν ἐστιν τῆς τροφῆς καὶ τὸ σῶμα τοῦ ἐνδύματος;
Period 2	**Period 2**	
κατανοήσατε τοὺς κόρακας ὅτι οὐ σπείρουσιν οὐδὲ θερίζουσιν, οἷς οὐκ ἔστιν ταμεῖον οὐδὲ ἀποθή**κη**, καὶ **ὁ θεὸς** τρέφει αὐ**τούς**· **πόσῳ** μᾶλλον ὑμεῖς διαφέρετε **τῶν πετεινῶν**.	**ἐμβλέψατε εἰς τὰ πετεινὰ τοῦ οὐρανοῦ** ὅτι οὐ σπείρουσιν οὐδὲ θερίζουσιν **οὐδὲ συνάγουσιν εἰς** ἀποθή**κας**, καὶ **ὁ πατὴρ ὑμῶν ὁ οὐράνιος** τρέφει αὐτά· **οὐχ** ὑμεῖς μᾶλλον διαφέρετε **αὐτῶν**;	κατανοήσατε τοὺς κόρακας ὅτι οὐ σπείρουσιν οὐδὲ θερίζουσιν, οὐδὲ συνάγουσιν εἰς ἀποθήκας καὶ ὁ θεὸς τρέφει αὐτούς · οὐχ ὑμεῖς μᾶλλον διαφέρετε τῶν πετεινῶν.
Period 3		
τίς δὲ ἐξ ὑμῶν μεριμνῶν δύναται ἐπὶ τὴν ἡλικίαν αὐτοῦ *προσθεῖναι* πῆχυν;	τίς δὲ ἐξ ὑμῶν μεριμνῶν δύναται *προσθεῖναι* ἐπὶ τὴν ἡλικίαν αὐτοῦ πῆχυν **ἕνα**;	τίς δὲ ἐξ ὑμῶν μεριμνῶν δύναται προσθεῖναι ἐπὶ τὴν ἡλικίαν αὐτοῦ πῆχυν
	Period 3	
εἰ οὖν οὐδὲ ἐλάχιστον δύνασθε, *τί* **περὶ τῶν λοιπῶν** μεριμνᾶτε;	καὶ περὶ ἐνδύματος *τί* μεριμνᾶτε;	καὶ περὶ ἐνδύματος τί μεριμνᾶτε;

Period 4		
κατα**νοήσατε** τὰ κρίνα πῶς αὐξάν**ει**· οὐ κοπι**ᾷ** οὐδὲ νήθ**ει**· λέγω δὲ ὑμῖν, οὐδὲ Σολομὼν ἐν πάσῃ τῇ δόξῃ αὐτοῦ περιεβάλετο ὡς ἓν τούτων.	κατα**μάθετε** τὰ κρίνα **τοῦ ἀγροῦ** πῶς αὐξάν**ουσιν**· οὐ κοπι**ῶσιν** οὐδὲ νήθ**ουσιν**· λέγω δὲ ὑμῖν **ὅτι** οὐδὲ Σολομὼν ἐν πάσῃ τῇ δόξῃ αὐτοῦ περιεβάλετο ὡς ἓν τούτων.	κατα[[μάθε]]τε τὰ κρίνα πῶς αὐξάν[[ει]] οὐ κοπι[[ᾷ]] οὐδὲ νήθ[[ει]] λέγω δὲ ὑμῖν, οὐδὲ Σολομὼν ἐν πάσῃ τῇ δόξῃ αὐτοῦ περιεβάλετο ὡς ἓν τούτων.
Period 5	**Period 4**	
εἰ δὲ **ἐν ἀγρῷ** τὸν χόρτον *ὄντα σήμερον* καὶ αὔριον εἰς κλίβανον βαλλόμενον ὁ θεὸς οὕτως ἀμφι**άζει**, **πόσῳ** μᾶλλον ὑμᾶς, ὀλιγόπιστοι.	εἰ δὲ τὸν χόρτον **τοῦ** **ἀγροῦ** *σήμερον ὄντα* καὶ αὔριον εἰς κλίβανον βαλλόμενον ὁ θεὸς οὕτως ἀμφι**έννυσιν**, **οὐ** πολλῷ μᾶλλον ὑμᾶς, ὀλιγόπιστοι;	εἰ δὲ ἐν ἀγρῷ τὸν χόρτον ὄντα σήμερον καὶ αὔριον εἰς κλίβανον βαλλόμενον ὁ θεὸς οὕτως ἀμφιέ[[ννυσιν]], οὐ πολλῷ μᾶλλον ὑμᾶς, ὀλιγόπιστοι;
Period 6	**Period 5**	
καὶ **ὑμεῖς** μὴ ζητεῖτε τί φάγ**ητε** καὶ τί πί**ητε**, **καὶ μὴ μετεωρίζεσθε**·	μὴ **οὖν μεριμνήσητε** **λέγοντες**, Τί φάγ**ωμεν**; ἤ, Τί πί**ωμεν**; **ἤ, Τί περιβαλώμεθα**;	μὴ [[οὖν]] μεριμνήσητε λέγοντες, Τί φάγωμεν [[ἤ,]] Τί πίωμεν; [[ἤ,]] Τί περιβαλώμεθα;
Period 7		
ταῦτα γὰρ *πάντα* τὰ ἔθνη **τοῦ κόσμου** ἐπιζητοῦσιν· *ὑμῶν* **δὲ** ὁ πατὴρ *οἶδεν* ὅτι χρῄζετε τούτων. **πλὴν** ζητεῖτε τὴν βασιλείαν αὐτοῦ, καὶ ταῦτα προστεθήσεται ὑμῖν.	*πάντα* γὰρ *ταῦτα* τὰ ἔθνη ἐπιζητοῦσιν· *οἶδεν* **γὰρ** ὁ πατὴρ *ὑμῶν* **ὁ οὐράνιος** ὅτι χρῄζετε τούτων **ἁπάντων.** ζητεῖτε **δὲ πρῶτον** τὴν βασιλείαν **καὶ τὴν** **δικαιοσύνην** αὐτοῦ, καὶ ταῦτα **πάντα** προστεθήσεται ὑμῖν.	πάντα γὰρ ταῦτα τὰ ἔθνη ἐπιζητοῦσιν· οἶδεν [[γὰρ]] ὁ πατὴρ ὑμῶν ὅτι χρῄζετε τούτων [[ἁπάντων]] ζητεῖτε δὲ τὴν βασιλείαν αὐτοῦ καὶ ταῦτα [[πάντα]] προστεθήσεται ὑμῖν
Luke's ending	**Period 6**	
Μὴ φοβοῦ, τὸ μικρὸν ποίμνιον, ὅτι εὐδόκησεν ὁ πατὴρ ὑμῶν δοῦναι ὑμῖν τὴν βασιλείαν.	**μὴ οὖν μεριμνήσητε** **εἰς τὴν αὔριον,** ἡ γὰρ αὔριον μεριμνήσει αὑτῆς· ἀρκετὸν τῇ ἡμέρᾳ ἡ κακία αὐτῆς.	

then Luke's performance of Q would have strengthened Q's primary organizational feature of paired statements and Matthew would have weakened it. Thus Luke's concluding cola in the prohibition and the conclusion to the minor illustrations in both examples would have emphasized the balance between two elements.

The Q Project prefers Luke's introduction to the first proof over Matthew's, presumably because Matthew's version includes τοῦ οὐρανοῦ (*lit.*, of heaven), a thematic term for Matthew. Yet the Q Project finds Matthew's opening to the second proof to be the more original reading, preferring καταμάθετε (notice) to κατανοήσατε (think about) as the more original reading.[32] If Q contained καταμάθετε, then Luke altered his source to intensify the parallelism of the proofs, introducing both with κατανοήσατε.

DECISIONS ABOUT DOUBLETS AND TRIPLETS

The Q Project judges Matthew's version of the ὅτι clause in the first example to reflect Q. If this is the case, then Q contained a triplet and a singlet, which Luke has converted to two doublets, one of which contains an internal doublet. See chart 11.8.

If the Q Project has accurately reconstructed Q, then in this instance Matthew has found in his source precisely at this point a passage that comports with his preference for sets of three,[34] while Luke has subtly altered Q to construct from a triplet various configurations of pairs. This is highly unlikely.

Chart 11.8

Luke[33]	**Matthew**
First doublet: οὐ/οὐδέ: ὅτι οὐ σπείρουσιν οὐδὲ θερίζουσιν,	**Triplet: οὐ/ οὐδέ/ οὐδέ:** ὅτι οὐ σπείρουσιν οὐδὲ θερίζουσιν **οὐδὲ συνάγουσιν εἰς** ἀποθήκας, καὶ **ὁ πατὴρ** ὑμῶν **ὁ οὐράνιος** τρέφει αὐτά·
Second doublet: **κόρακας/ ὑμεῖς:** **(Internal doublet: οὐκ/ οὐδὲ:** οἷς οὐκ ἔστιν ταμεῖον οὐδὲ ἀποθή**κη**, καὶ **ὁ θεὸς** τρέφει αὐ**τούς**· **πόσῳ** μᾶλλον ὑμεῖς διαφέρετε **τῶν πετεινῶν**.	**Singlet:** **οὐχ** ὑμεῖς μᾶλλον διαφέρετε **αὐτῶν**;

Similarly, at the end of the first illustration, the Q Project proposes that Luke, having simplified Q in the initial prohibition by eliminating ὑμεῖς, here has added εἰ οὖν οὐδὲ ἐλάχιστον δύνασθε[35] in the middle of his period 3. Such an addition would have created in Luke's version another doublet that concludes the first proof and balances the protasis with the apodosis:

εἰ οὖν οὐδὲ ἐλάχιστον δύνασθε,
τί περὶ τῶν λοιπῶν μεριμνᾶτε;

The parallel colon in Matthew's version functions as the beginning of period 3 and the introduction to the second example. See chart 11.9

Thus Matthew and Luke both frame the minor illustration as a singlet at the end of the first example but Matthew has another singlet at the beginning of his second example, whereas Luke concludes the first example with a doublet.

Finally, the Q Project has preferred as original Matthew's triplet at the beginning of the conclusion over Luke's two doublets. See chart 11.10.

If the Q Project's reconstruction is correct, then Luke has again altered his source to form nested pairs—as in the ὅτι clause of the first example –while Matthew has retained a triplet in Q. Again, this is an unlikely hypothesis given Matthew's preference elsewhere for triplets and Luke's for doublets.

Chart 11.9

Luke	**Matthew**
	Period 3
Doublet: **εἰ οὖν οὐδὲ ἐλάχιστον** δύνασθε, τί **περὶ τῶν λοιπῶν** μεριμνᾶτε;	**Singlet:** καὶ περὶ ἐνδύματος τί μεριμνᾶτε;
Period 4	
κατανο**ήσατε** τὰ κρίνα πῶς αὐξάν**ει**· οὐ κοπι**ᾷ** οὐδὲ νήθ**ει**· λέγω δὲ ὑμῖν, οὐδὲ Σολομὼν ἐν πάσῃ τῇ δόξῃ αὐτοῦ περιεβάλετο ὡς ἓν τούτων.	κατα**μάθετε** τὰ κρίνα **τοῦ ἀγροῦ** πῶς αὐξάν**ουσιν**· οὐ κοπι**ῶσιν** οὐδὲ νήθ**ουσιν**· λέγω δὲ ὑμῖν **ὅτι** οὐδὲ Σολομὼν ἐν πάσῃ τῇ δόξῃ αὐτοῦ περιεβάλετο ὡς ἓν τούτων.

Chart 11.10

Luke	**Matthew**
καὶ ὑμεῖς μὴ ζητεῖτε	μὴ **οὖν μεριμνήσητε λέγοντες,**
Doublet: τί . . . καὶ τί/ μὴ· (Internal doublet: τί/τί·) τί φάγητε καὶ τί πίητε, **καὶ μὴ μετεωρίζεσθε·**	**Triplet: τί/τί/τί:** Τί φάγωμεν; ἤ, Τί πίωμεν; **ἤ, Τί περιβαλώμεθα;**

IMPLICATIONS OF SOUND FOR A RECONSTRUCTION OF Q

To be sure, sound alone provides an insufficient basis for determining how Matthew and Luke used their sayings source, nor is the reconstruction of Q's On Anxiety within the scope of our project. Nevertheless, careful attention to sound can help frame questions for analysis and suggest directions for interpretation. The reconstruction proposed by the International Q Project decides in favor of Matthew's performance of On Anxiety at critical structural points. Their reconstruction consistently, though tentatively, prefers readings that downplay the organization of the Q passage in sets of balanced pairs. For example, the preference for οὐχι over γάρ in the initial prohibition is insignificant at a semantic level but important structurally, since orally performed compositions exploit the ear training potential of opening cola to orient an audience. Opening sounds guide an audience and shape comprehension of subsequent sounds that will be processed in real time. Matthew's οὐχι emphasizes negation whereas Luke's γάρ emphasizes the connection between two sets of statements. Based upon Matthew's placement of this Q passage in a section of the Sermon on the Mount that is organized around prohibitions, it seems more likely that the emphatic negative comes from Matthew than Q.

In both the first example and the conclusion, the Q Project has preferred Matthew's triplet structure to an organization of Q based on doublets. This stands in contrast to the doublets expressed elsewhere in Q and proposed in the reconstruction: the two examples (birds and flowers); the double occurrence of the logically unnecessary λέγω ὑμῖν, a formula found frequently in Q in several variations[36] (and here used to introduce the initial prohibition and the forceful Solomon saying); the format of the initial prohibition (ψυχή and σῶμα); and the format of the second example (neither toil nor spin).

Even more, textual evidence indicates that the doublet κατανοήσατε τὰ κρίνα πῶς αὐξάνει· οὐ κοπιᾷ οὐδὲ νήθει[37] has an early and persistent history as a doublet. Before Q existed in manuscript form, the second example was, οὐ ξαίνει οὐδὲ νήθει ("neither card nor spin").[38] The Q saying became πῶς αὐξάνει· οὐ κοπιᾷ οὐδὲ νήθει, supplying οὐ κοπιᾷ when οὐ ξαίνει became αὐξάνει, presumably to retain the doublet.

The demands of Q's ongoing preservation in memory, even when a manuscript presumably existed, suggest strong advantages for balanced pairs in the Q version of On Anxiety. Admittedly, memory prefers triads under certain circumstances—and especially in oral storytelling, as the well-known rule of three attests. But Q is not a narrative. Furthermore, the rule of three typically applies to the overarching structure of a story or composition, since it aids in preserving the integrity of the whole. Indeed, On Anxiety itself employs a memorable three-part structure: (1) its initial prohibition, (2) its examples from the natural world, and (3) its conclusion. The preservation of items within a governing structure may be accomplished through a variety of devices. The sound structure of the initial prohibition encourages an audience to listen for chained pairs rather than than sets of threes or combined pairs and triads like those in Matthew's performance. Although a three-part structure organizes On Anxiety as a whole, a scheme of chained pairs and nested doublets accounts well for the mnemonic stability of a passage that is organized around a pair of vivid examples from the birds and flowers.

More likely original, then, *pace* the Q Project's proposed reconstruction, are Luke's γάρ, his πόσῳ, his doublet in the first example, and his doublet in the conclusion. This is especially true since Matthew's renditions of these passages accommodates both his preference for threes within a compositional unit as well as the structural demands of situating On Anxiety in a part of the Sermon on the Mount organized by prohibitions. No such external structural needs or redactional tendencies appear as compelling for Luke.

ON ANXIETY AND THE SERMON ON THE MOUNT

If the structural differences between Matthew's and Luke's performances of On Anxiety are attributable to Matthew as the sound maps above suggest, then this remarkable passage from Q has exerted a profound influence on the structure of the Sermon on the Mount. To situate this early instructional speech in its entirety in the Sermon, Matthew has exploited its prohibitionary format and adapted that format to his structural convention of using repeated beginning sounds to organize major structural units (see above Chapter 10, "Sound and

Structure: The Sermon on the Mount"). Matthew's performance shifts periodic boundaries in period 3, placing the prohibition at the beginning of a period instead of at its end. Matthew has also added a repetition of the prohibition in periods 5 and 6, and doubled the occurrence of μεριμνάω in the appended conclusion to the Q speech. Recast in this way as a long prohibition with repeated beginning sounds, On Anxiety elaborates the opening prohibition of the first unit of the Sermon's section 6, μὴ θησαυρίζετε (6:19–21, Don't acquire), also from Q (Q 12:33–34). Two more units framed as prohibitions follow: μὴ κρίνετε (7:1–5/Q 6:36–38, Don't pass judgment); and μὴ δῶτε (7:6, Don't offer). The Sermon's next section (section 6) mirrors the triadic arrangement of prohibitions, and section 7 (7:7–20) is organized around three imperatives, beginning with and forecast by the initial threefold imperative in 7:7, also from Q (11:9). The two imperatives that complete the triad are εἰσέλθατε (7:13–14/Q 13:23–24, Try to get in) and προσέχετε (7:15–20, Be on the lookout). The arrangement of Q material in triads is notable throughout these long sections of the Sermon on the Mount because it signals a Matthean structural preference for threes that is not evident in the parallel material as performed by Luke.

If our sound-based proposal is correct, then Matthew has modified Q's prohibition of anxiety in a manner similar to his modification of Q's beatitudes (5:3–12/Q 6:20b–23). Where Q has three beatitudes beginning with μακάριοι οἱ and a concluding beatitude that begins μακάριοί ἐστε, Matthew multiplies the repeated beginnings and presents eight beatitudes beginning with μακάριοι οἱ before his transitional beatitude beginning μακάριοί ἐστε. Even more, our proposal concerning the impact of On Anxiety on the Sermon's structure explains both the uncharacteristically subtle Matthean redaction of On Anxiety as well as the structural impact of Matthew's editorial hand. The Matthean redaction remained subtle because he included in the Sermon a Q instructional speech that was stored intact both in manuscript and in memory. His redaction had significant structural impact because its format as a prohibition shaped two series of triads, a set of three prohibitions (the Sermon's section 6, 6:19–21) and a matching set of three imperatives (the Sermon's section 7, 7:7–20).

CONCLUSION

Sound mapping a hypothetical manuscript would appear to be a daunting task, but this exercise has shown that sound mapping can contribute to the reconstruction and understanding of Q. By paying close attention to the demands of sound and how Q might function as a remembered composition, sound mapping can illuminate its structure and organization. It cannot accomplish a reconstruction or definitively decide interpretative issues, but it can provide useful insights and point to fruitful avenues for further research.

Appendix
Charts in English

Chart 11.1 The Lord's Prayer

Luke 11:2b–4	**Matthew 6:9b–15**
Father	Our Father in the heavens,
your name be revered. Impose your imperial rule.	your name be revered. Impose your imperial rule, enact your will on earth as you have in heaven.
Provide us with the bread we need day by day.	Provide us with the bread we need for the day.
Forgive our sins, since we too forgive everyone in debt to us.	Forgive our debts to the extent that we have forgiven those in debt to us
And please don't subject us to test after test.	And please don't subject us to test after test, but rescue us from the evil one. For if you forgive others their failures and offenses, your heavenly Father will also forgive yours. And if you don't forgive the failures and mistakes of others, your Father won't forgive yours.

Chart 11.2 The Beatitudes

Luke 6:20–23	Matthew 5:3–12
Congratulations, you poor! God's domain belongs to you.	Congratulations to the poor in spirit! Heaven's domain belongs to them.
	Congratulations to those who grieve! They will be consoled.
	Congratulations to the gentle! They will inherit the earth.
Congratulations, you hungry! You will have a feast.	Congratulations to those who hunger and thirst for justice! They will have a feast.
Congratulations, you who weep now! You will laugh.	
	Congratulations to the merciful! They will receive mercy.
	Congratulations to those with undefiled hearts! They will see God.
	Congratulations to those who work for peace! They will be known as God's children.
	Congratulations to those who have suffered persecution for the sake of justice! Heaven's domain belongs to them.
Congratulations to you when people hate you, and when they ostracize you and denounce you and scorn your name as evil, because of the son of Adam! Rejoice on that day, and jump for joy! Just remember, your compensation is great in heaven. Recall that their ancestors treated the prophets the same way.	Congratulations to you when they denounce you and persecute you and spread malicious gossip about you because of me. Rejoice and be glad! In heaven you will be more than compensated. Remember, this is how they persecuted the prophets who preceded you.

Chart 11.3 Initial Prohibition

Luke 12:22b–23	Matt 6:25
That's why I tell you:	That's why I tell you:
First Pair	
Don't fret about life—what you're going to eat— or about your body—what you're going to wear.	Don't fret about your life—what you're going to eat and drink— or about your body—what you're going to wear.
Second Pair	
Remember, there is more to living than food and clothing.	There is more to living than food and clothing, isn't there?

Chart 11.4 First example

Luke 12:24–26	Matt 6:26–28a
Introduction	
Think about the crows:	Take a look at the birds of the sky:
Neither/Nor Statement	
they don't plant or harvest,	they don't plant or harvest,
Explanatory Statement	
they don't have storerooms or barns. Yet God feeds them.	or gather into barns.
Rhetorical Question	
You're worth a lot more than the birds!	Yet your heavenly Father feeds them. You're worth more than they, aren't you?
Minor Illustration	
Can any of you add an hour to life by fretting about it?	Can any of you add one hour to life by fretting about it?
Rhetorical Question	
So if you can't do a little thing like that, why worry about the rest?	Why worry about clothes?

Chart 11.5 Second example

Luke 12:27–28	Matt 6:28b–30
Introduction	
Think about how the lilies grow:	Notice how the wild lilies grow:
Neither/Nor Statement	
they don't slave and they never spin.	they don't slave and they never spin.
Explanatory Statement	
Yet let me tell you, even Solomon at the height of his glory was never decked out like one of them.	Yet let me tell you, even Solomon at the height of his glory was never decked out like one of them.
Minor Illustration	
If God dresses up the grass in the field, which is here today and tomorrow is tossed into an oven,	If God dresses up the grass in the field, which is here today and tomorrow is thrown into an oven,
Rhetorical Question	
it is surely more likely <that God cares for> you, you who don't take anything for granted!	won't <God care for> you even more, you who don't take anything for granted?

Chart 11.6 Conclusion

Luke 12:29–31	Matt 6:31–34
Prohibition	
And don't be constantly on the lookout for what you're going to eat and what you're going to drink. Don't give it a thought.	So don't fret. Don't say, 'What am I going to eat?' or 'What am I going to drink?' or 'What am I going to wear?'
Comparison	
These are all things the world's pagans seek,	These are all things pagans seek.
Father	
and your Father is aware that you need them.	After all, your heavenly Father is aware that you need them.

Kingdom	
Instead, you are to seek <God's> domain,	You are to seek <God's> domain, and his justice first,
Promise	
and these things will come to you as a bonus.	and all these things will come to you as a bonus.
Luke's ending	**Matthew's ending**
Don't be afraid, little flock, for it has delighted your Father to give you his domain.	So don't fret about tomorrow. Let tomorrow fret about itself. The troubles that the day brings are enough.

Chart 11.7 International Q

That's why I tell you:
Don't fret about your life—what you're going to eat—
or about your body—what you're going to wear.
There is more to living than food and clothing, isn't there?
Think about the crows:
they don't plant
or harvest,
or gather into barns.
Yet God feeds them.
You're worth a lot more than the birds!
Can any of you add one hour to life by fretting about it?
Why worry about clothes?
[[Notice]] how the wild lilies grow:
they don't slave
and they never spin.
Yet let me tell you,
even Solomon at the height of his glory was never decked out like one of them.
If God dresses up the grass in the field, which is here today and tomorrow is thrown into an oven,
won't <God care for> you even more,
you who don't take anything for granted?
[[So]] don't fret.
Don't say,
'What am I going to eat?'
[[or]] 'What am I going to drink?'

[[or]] 'What am I going to wear?'
These are all things pagans seek.
[[For]], your heavenly Father sees that you need them [[all]].
Seek <God's> domain
and [[all]] these things
will come to you as a bonus.

ENDNOTES

1. We accept the Q hypothesis as well established, while acknowledging that some reject it. We are assuming no solution to the issue of strata in Q, nor are we making any assumptions about how an early original saying was elaborated into this Q section. See Tuckett (1996, pp. 149–55) and Jacobson (1992, pp. 191–2).
2. But note Robinson's proposal that in the Q archetype available to Matthew and Luke the sayings about ψυχή (life) and σῶμα (body) (Q 12: 22b–23), the saying about extending the life span (Q 12:25), and the anticlimactic kingdom saying (Q 12:29b–30) were secondary. *Critical Edition*, pp. lxv-lxvi.
3. For a translation see Appendix, Chart 11.1, Lord's Prayer.
4. For a translation see Appendix 2, Chart 11.2, The Beatitudes.
5. For a translation of the Matthean and Lucan passages see Appendix, Chart 11.3-6.
6. Whether this phrase should be included or excluded is difficult to determine. See summary in Metzger (1971, p. 17).
7. *Lit.*, I say to you.
8. He insists that "there can be no mistake" in recall. *Inst.* 11.2.20.
9. But if this were the case, the lesser frequency of verbatim agreement in briefer Q passages, such as the Beatitudes and the Lord's Prayer, would require explanation.
10. Robinson has shown that a scribal error existed in Q: "the presence of αὐξάν- in both Matthew and Luke leads to the unavoidable conclusion that αὐξάν- is a scribal error already in the archetype of Q presupposed in Matthew and Luke. Hence an emendation of the text prior to Q is in place. The original text must have read οὐ ξαιν-, lilies 'do not card,' which is corrupted to read αὐξάν-, they 'grow'" (Robinson, Hoffmann, and Kloppenborg 2000, p. c).
11. For a translation, see Appendix, Charts 3–6.
12. See Gundry (1994, pp. 2–3 and 674–82), Luz (1989, pp. 49–70) and chapter 10 of this book for summaries of distinctive aspects of Matthew's vocabulary and style.
13. They don't plant or harvest, or gather into barns.

14. Your heavenly Father.
15. Look at the birds.
16. While Mt. 6:28 attests the only occurrence of καταμανθάνειν in the New Testament, his use of the same lexical stem is distinctive among the synoptics, with μαθητέυω occurring 3 times in Matthew but nowhere in Mark or Luke, and μαθητής occurring 72 times in Matthew but only 46 times in Mark and 37 times in Luke. Luz (1989, p. 62) includes these words among those that are formulaic and redactional in Matthew.
17. Notable examples include the beatitudes (Mt 5:3–6 // Lk 6:20) and the Lord's Prayer (Mt 6:9–10 // Lk 11:2).
18. This suggests that ἢ τί πίητε was absent in the Matthean performance and added by scribe attuned to the Matthean performance. 'What am I going to eat' or 'What and I going to drink?' or 'What am I going to wear?'
19. What you're going to eat and what you're going to drink. Don't give it a thought.
20. Why worry about clothes?
21. So if you can't do a little thing like that, / why worry about the rest?
22. For a translation, see Appendix, Charts 11.3–6.
23. They don't plant or harvest.
24. They don't have storerooms or barns.
25. What you're going to eat and what you're going to drink.
26. Don't give it a thought.
27. Talbert sees Luke 12:1–48 and chapter 16 as parallel and organized around three themes: "(1) the threat of hell, (2) riches and (3) faithful or unfaithful stewardship" (1974, p. 55).
28. For a translation, see Appendix 3, On Anxiety.
29. For a translation, see Appendix 3, On Anxiety.
30. For a translation, see Appendix 4, Q
31. The Q Project also judges that Luke both removed οὐχ in period 2 and in the same colon shifted ὑμεῖς from its postpositive position. This possibility is consistent with the Q Project's decision that ὑμῶν occurred in the initial prohibition.
32. But the Q Project prefers Luke's αὐξάνει to Matthew's αὐξάνουσιν.
33. For a translation, see Appendix, Charts 11.3–6.
34. The Lord's prayer provides an instructive parallel. Luke's (11:2b) performance contains a pair of entreaties (ἁγιασθήτω τὸ ὄνομά σου· ἐλθέτω ἡ βασιλεία σου), whereas Matthew's performance

contains three (ἁγιασθήτω τὸ ὄνομά σου, ἐλθέτω ἡ βασιλεία σου, γενηθήτω τὸ θέλημά σου, ὡς ἐν οὐρανῷ καὶ ἐπὶ γῆς). Most commentators see Matthew's third entreaty as redactional and Luke's version as closely resembling Q. The Q Project (206–207) reconstructs Q at this point as identical to Luke's performance. Similarly, Matthew's beatitudes are arranged in three sets of three, whereas Luke has two sets of two. Again the Q Project (46–53), in concert with the prevailing scholarly consensus, reconstructs Q as nearly identical with Luke's performance.

35. So if you can't do a little thing like that.
36. 3:8 (λέγω γὰρ ὑμῖν); 7:9 (λέγω ὑμῖν; ἀμὴν λέγω ὑμῖν in Mt 8:10), 7:26 (λέγω ὑμῖν); 7:28 (λέγω ὑμῖν; ἀμὴν λέγω ὑμῖν in Mt 11:11); 10:12 (λέγω ὑμῖν; ἀμὴν λέγω ὑμῖν in Mt 10:15); 10:24 (λέγω γὰρ ὑμῖν; γὰρ λέγω ὑμῖν in Mt 13:17); 11:51 (λέγω ὑμῖν; ἀμὴν λέγω ὑμῖν in Mt 23:36); 12:22(διὰ τοῦτο λέγω ὑμῖν); 12:44 λέγω ὑμῖν; ἀμὴν λέγω ὑμῖν in Mt 24:47); 13:35 (λέγω [δὲ] ὑμῖν; λέγω γὰρ ὑμῖν in Mt 23:39); 15:7 (ἀμὴν λέγω ὑμῖν in Mt 18:13).
37. Think about how the lilies grow: they don't slave and they never spin.
38. See Gospel of Thomas 36 (P. Oxy. 655) in Robinson (2000, p. c).

WORKS CONSULTED

Gundry, Robert H. 1994. *Matthew: A Commentary on His Handbook for a Mixed Church under Persecution*. 2d ed. Grand Rapids, MI: Eerdmans.

Jacobson, Arland D. 1992. *The First Gospel, An Introduction to Q, Foundations & Facets*. Sonoma, CA: Polebridge.

Luz, Ulrich. 1989. *Matthew 1–7: A Commentary*. Translated by W. C. Linss, *Evangelisch-Katholischer Kommentar zum Neuen Testament*. Minneapolis: Augsburg.

Metzger, Bruce M. 1971. *A Textual Commentary on the Greek New Testament*. New York: United Bible Societies.

Robinson, James M., Paul Hoffmann, and John S. Kloppenborg, eds. 2000. *The Critical Edition of Q, Hermeneia*. Minneapolis: Fortress Press.

Small, Jocelen Penny. 1997. *Wax Tablets of the Mind. Cognitive Studies of Memory and Literacy in Classical Anitiquity*. London and New York: Routledge.

Talbert, Charles H. 1974. *Literary Patterns, Theological Themes, and the Genre of Luke-Acts*. Vol. 20, *SBLMonSer*. Missoula: Scholars Press.

Tuckett, Christopher M. 1996. *Q and the History of Early Christianity*. Peabody, MA: Hendrickson.

Verbin, John S. Kloppenborg. 2000. *Excavating Q: The History and Setting of the Sayings Gospel*. Minneapolis: Fortress.

Conclusion

Next Steps

Our exploration of sound mapping and analysis has sought to recapture dimensions of the New Testament as speech and thus restore crucial elements of the ancient compositions that do not appear in printed books, and especially not in translations. Our books have fallen silent. Sound mapping depends on a renewed understanding of ancient Greek literature as composed, publicly performed, and published through speech—and only then received through hearing and for the most part stored in memory. The ancients wrote to be heard. We predicate sound analysis on a conviction that essential sound features of Greek compositions are encoded in their grammar and remain available, even to a silent interpreter. These convictions derive from ancient reflections on the Greek language by experts in listening, the ancient authors themselves, who understood sound's power and exploited auditory dynamics to convey meaning. If our convictions hold true, then sound mapping can claim for this analytical tool an empirical dimension, the aural quality of a composition's sounds.

A primary benefit of sound analysis is its power to illuminate a composition's structure. Because New Testament compositions were spoken aloud and processed in real time through listening, sound necessarily served as their primary organizing device. Recapturing this dimension of sound makes it possible to discern a structure that often differs from the organization imposed by editors of printed Bibles both in Greek and translation, schemes that too frequently depend on abstract, logical concepts external to the compositions themselves. Listening to New Testament compositions manifests their organic structure and opens new avenues to interpretation.

Sound mapping is an analytical tool, not an interpretative method or exegetical approach. Sound mapping should precede exegesis and sound analysis should indicate the features that demand attention. Every tool serves a specific purpose and implies practical considerations. As newly proposed analytical tools for New Testament study, sound mapping and analysis derive from the unique dynamics of speech and auditory reception. It is appropriate to enumerate the characteristics and associated practical considerations of these analytical tools.

SOUNDS ARE MEANT TO BE HEARD

Consistent with the insights of modern reception theory, meaning arises in reception. For compositions published through the spoken word, reception takes place in the course of listening. Hearers process sounds one at a time in linear sequence, guided by repeated sounds that organize sound patterns in memory. The linear character of auditory reception profoundly influences the dynamics of a spoken composition's performance and its auditory reception.

Attention to linear, spoken sounds requires a modern interpreter to begin with a systematic examination of the composition. Because contemporary readers access the Greek New Testament almost exclusively through silent reading—and often have a particular translation implanted in their memory—those who would practice sound analysis must adopt a fairly labor-intensive discipline of close reading and analysis, even down to the level of syllable, to compensate for the disadvantage of not actually hearing a composition's sounds. We can learn to hear a composition, but we can never achieve anything like native listening skill in a language now dead.[1] Contemporary readers achieve only with effort what ancient listeners apprehended with ease, a feeling for the rhythms and melodies of the New Testament.

Visually mapping a composition's sounds disciplines a silent reader to attend not only to things signified but also to signifiers in linear sequence. The addition of visual cues such as boldfaced type, underscoring, and spatial alignment to create a sound map admittedly provides a poor substitute for actual listening activity; yet failing to approach a composition with such graphic aids denies an interpreter access to the New Testament's foundational basis for making meaning, its sounds.

The demands of aural reception entail at least two important considerations. First, this style of close reading can be slow and tedious. The labor required to recapture in silence a composition's musical genius is inefficient at best. Moreover, it is impossible to annotate all of a composition's aural features. Each visual delineation of a sound pattern necessarily obscures other patterns. As an interpreter chooses what to depict on a sound map, the choice necessarily suppresses other sound patterns and risks losing them in silence. And because compositions employ distinctive sound features integral to their rhetorical purposes, our graphic schemes necessarily vary and cannot be applied in a rigidly uniform way. Perhaps it is better to create multiple sound maps for any composition, but this remedy is only partial.

Some sounds remain obscure because they remain unspoken and our ears are not trained to hear them.

A second major consideration in attending to the sounds of a New Testament composition is that it must be read in Greek. A composition's organizing sounds are available only in its original language. While translation of the Greek New Testament into various vernaculars and its resultant general availability have yielded important benefits that should be neither abridged nor undervalued, a reading knowledge of Greek is prerequisite to creating a useful sound analysis of any New Testament composition.

SOUND BUILDS STRUCTURE

In public performance, a chorus of remembered sounds requires organization for meaning. To be sure, repetition serves as sound's primary structuring tool, but as we have seen, repetition functions differently in auditory reception that depends more heavily on the signifier than it does in silent reading, which places a relatively higher value on the signified and on semantics. Sound analysis requires interpreters to discern a kind of repetition that entails more than mere reiteration of phrases or even words. Rather, the duplication of sounds that creates structure and semantic nuance originates at the level of the phoneme and the syllable. Therefore, discerning a composition's sound structure requires mapping repetitions that have no apparent logical or semantic connection. But in so doing an interpreter eventually discovers repeated sound sequences and syntactic patterns that connect words, phrases, and cola in ways that remain invisible to abstract logic and so may not otherwise be recognized.

One difficulty sometimes resulting from a sound map that plots repeated phonemes, syllables, and other auditory patterns is the sheer profusion of data it produces. Comprehending and interpreting an abundance of evidence is made even more difficult by a silent reader's lack of aural fluency. A visual chart of repeated sounds and sound patterns presents to the eye testimony originally designed for the ear. A contemporary interpreter, far more skilled at discerning the conceptual coherence of related ideas, must strain to apprehend the connections implied by a spoken composition and its aural signifiers.

The primary benefit of analyzing sounds encoded in grammar is the emergence of structural devices integral to a composition's organization. The discipline of charting a composition's elements phoneme by phoneme guards against the natural tendency of interpreters to import pre-existing ideas about a composition's structure and meaning into a composition.

SOUND TRAINS THE EAR

Sound schemes vary by composition, and each composition carries its own interpretive key. A composition's sounds train the ear by shaping an audience's comprehension of previous sounds in light of subsequent sounds. This ear training effect also characterizes other listening processes, such as listening to music and advertising. Musical compositions establish primary themes that are repeated through reprisal and variation. Secondary melodic motifs add texture to a composition's development, and rhythmic motifs regulate its pace. Similarly, spoken compositions establish their own rules for guiding the listening process toward comprehension.

Submitting to a spoken composition's ear training entails discernment of larger, more comprehensive sound patterns than those charted at grammatical and phonetic levels. Sound analysis charts these larger patterns that comprise sometimes extensive collections of auditory evidence. An interpreter must identify characteristic features of these more comprehensive patterns and annotate them graphically, perhaps even spatially by separating them from the surrounding sounds.

Ear training effects of spoken compositions also entail attention to literary style. In the Greco-Roman world, competent listeners attended to a composition's periodic style as a primary clue to its message. Style and meaning were expected to cohere, so that a composition's sounds suited its purpose. Sound analysis requires some knowledge of literary genre and style in Hellenistic Greek. Better yet, it requires a community of scholars, sharing their various perspectives on the vast expanse of extant Hellenistic literature. While we have studied the New Testament in this book, it is part of the larger world of Hellenistic Greek, all of which employs the sound dynamics we have described.

Learning to detect a composition's ear training effects requires practice. While silent readers of ancient compositions can learn to apprehend a composition's distinctive aural characteristics, perceiving how the data are connected frequently entails intuition, even for experienced native listeners. Perceiving comprehensive sound patterns can be like getting a joke, or smiling amid the flood of memory in response to a familiar tune. Frequently, patterns and remembered images emerge in an intuitive flash, as a vast body of aural evidence suddenly snaps together. Intuition is not willy-nilly, but is built up from experience and practice. One can discipline the eye and train the ear, but one cannot compel the associative activities of the mind. Its insights may not come, or they may lead an interpreter to hypotheses that in retrospect are not fully justified by the evidence and must subsequently be revised. Yet even the ears of a silent reader can be trained by a wealth of aural evidence preserved in a literary composition. An interpreter can engage and prompt the intuition through disciplined analysis, verifying insights at the phonetic, grammatical and syntactic levels.

The primary benefit of attending to a composition's ear training effects is that doing so enables an interpreter to apprehend a composition on its own terms, based on signals that inhere in the composition. Attention to a composition's ear training may be the only access an interpreter can gain to a composition's structural organization, a feature that is fundamental to its meaning.

SOUND INFLUENCES MEANING

Meaning-making with sound imposes time constraints. Unlike silent reading, which allows rereading at will, listening occurs in real time with no opportunity for review on demand. Experienced listeners to Hellenistic Greek placed a high value on euphony and they associated certain speech sounds with specific emotions and natural phenomena because they acknowledged that sound made a contribution to meaning apart from semantics. Moreover, because sound builds structure, certain sound groups are singled out for emphasis in spoken compositions because hearers cannot process all of a composition's sounds in real time. Auditory triggers invoke associations between sounds whether or not these associations conform to logic. Connections of this sort that function at the level of the signifier add a dimension to meaning not available to silent readers, whose primary dependence for meaning is on each word's semantic load.

A search for meaning should rest on a spoken composition's various and complex aural dynamics. It must be disciplined and guided by sound, attending to a composition's sound structure, its ear training effects, its system of selected sounds and their implied referential connections—for these features direct an interpreter's search for the meaning of a composition. Again, nothing less than a community of scholars is required to plumb the depths of these referential connections that evoke mythic structures, broad linguistic competencies, and aspects of a social world that for a contemporary exegete remain at best remote.

Attending to sound necessarily delays the creation of meaning until the meticulous work of sound analysis is accomplished. More fundamentally, postponement of the search for meaning and consistent engagement with a composition's sounds places an interpreter's pre-existing expectations, hopes, and convictions at risk. A cumulative effort to recapture the New Testament's spoken character is a necessary prerequisite to interpretation. As an interpreter follows the clues embedded in a composition's signifiers, the journey may lead to unexpected destinations. It may also enlighten thorny hermeneutical problems. But the ultimate benefit of attending to aural dynamics is the access it provides to the listening experience of a composition's original audiences.

CONCLUSION

Sound analysis can uncover the structure and clues to meaning encoded in a composition's sounds. We have claimed an empirical basis for sound mapping and analysis, but this empirical dimension does not locate meaning back in the composition itself, nor does it mitigate an audience's meaning-making project. Sound analysis can neither supplant nor replace other critical approaches to the New Testament, nor would such an outcome be desirable. Rather, sound analysis provides the interpretative endeavor with an additional tool: an analytical process that serves as a basis for other critical approaches. The foundational character of sound analysis means that it does not replace other methods, but rather should become the first step and direct other methods. Our work will have accomplished its goal if other practitioners can replicate its results using the strategies outlined here, and productively apply tools for sound analysis to other compositions.

Possible directions for sound mapping and analysis might include collaborative development of a sound-mapped edition of the New Testament or at least a Greek New Testament displayed in cola. Sound maps of selected compositions from secular Hellenistic Greek literature would further expand and enrich sound analysis, as well as provide possibly instructive parallels to parts of the New Testament. Sound mapping and analysis could profitably be used to influence the layout of printed translations in order that their typography reflect not chapter and verse divisions imposed by later editors, but each composition's organic structure. Establishing connections between sound mapping and performance criticism should likewise prove beneficial, since it would help us understand the performance context of ancient publication. And finally, just as live performance can test interpretative hypotheses prompted by sound analysis, sound maps can also inform live performances of New Testament compositions in translation by providing performance clues in matters of gesture, tone of voice, and emphasis.

Sound analysis breathes life into New Testament interpretation by straining to hear the melodies lying dormant in our manuscripts. It reinvigorates our silent texts by restoring their breath, their embodied dimension. When allowed to live and breathe again, the New Testament's sounds weave a web that furnishes a new nexus for meaning and invites new creativity in interpretation.

ENDNOTE

1. This is a primary reason why sound recordings of the Greek would not compensate for sound mapping. Our lack of native fluency would mitigate any value of a recording. Furthermore, a sound map would be needed in the first place to guide the performance.

Index of Ancient Authors

HEBREW BIBLE

NEW TESTAMENT

Index of Modern Authors

LaVergne, TN USA
14 February 2010
173057LV00004B/7/P